Eavan Boland's Evolution as an Irish Woman Poet

EAVAN BOLAND'S EVOLUTION AS AN IRISH WOMAN POET
An Outsider Within an Outsider's Culture

Pilar Villar-Argáiz

With a Preface by
Eibhear Walshe

The Edwin Mellen Press
Lewiston•Queenston•Lampeter

Library of Congress Cataloging-in-Publication Data

Villar-Argaiz, Pilar.
  Eavan Boland's evolution as an Irish woman poet : an outsider within an outsider's culture / Pilar Villar-Argaiz ; with a preface by Eibhear Walshe.
      p. cm.
  Includes bibliographical references and index.
  ISBN-13: 978-0-7734-5383-8
  ISBN-10: 0-7734-5383-0
  1. Boland, Eavan--Criticism and interpretation. 2. Women and literature--Ireland--History--20th century. 3. English poetry--Women authors--History and criticism. 4. English poetry--Irish authors--History and criticism. 5. Feminism--Ireland. I. Title.
  PR6052.O35Z94 2007
  821'.914--dc22

                                                         2007017117
hors série.

A CIP catalog record for this book is available from the British Library.

Front cover photograph of Eavan Boland taken by her husband Kevin Casey.
Used with permission.

        The Edwin Mellen Press   The Edwin Mellen Press
              Box 450   Box 67
         Lewiston, New York   Queenston, Ontario
         USA 14092-0450   CANADA L0S 1L0

                        The Edwin Mellen Press, Ltd.
                        Lampeter, Ceredigion, Wales
                        UNITED KINGDOM SA48 8LT

                    Printed in the United States of America

"[W]e were outsiders using someone else's language, fighting our way through someone else's history, finding ourselves in the space between exclusion and possession, [...] women have been outsiders within an outsider's culture." (Interview with Allen-Randolph 1999b: 304)

For Jose

Table of contents

Preface by Dr. Eibhear Walshe

In reality, Irish history is a hard and relentless account of suffering. It is about failure, defeat, and the harshness of the most brutal kinds of survival. It is not about heroism. The fact that Irish history chose to be about heroism opened a fault line for me. It made me question what the real Irish story was, and where I fitted into it as an Irish poet. Inevitably, all this served to gender my sense of Irishness. The history and the heroism seemed male: the past, with all its silences, seemed female. Interview with Eavan Boland.

Eavan Boland's poetry has always negotiated, in a clear sighted and compelling way, the legacy of Irish history for the contemporary writer and she has used her poems to test questions of linguistic, racial and sexual identity in the light of this past. In this impressive examination of the poetry of Eavan Boland, Pilar Villar Argáiz provides a valuable study of one of the most influential of Ireland's contemporary writers. This wide ranging and exhaustively researched study is clear and accessible, and deals with Boland within the context of postcolonial and feminist reading. As Boland herself put it "*I was aware that some of my themes, my interests were right at the edges of Irish poetry, at the very margins. That became an additional spur for me*". Although Boland's writings have attracted a great deal of scholarly attention in Irish studies, this book is important in that Dr Pilar Villar Argáiz has linked her feminist readings of Boland's poetry within a context of postcolonial theory and modern Irish writing. This book considers the whole corpus of Boland's poetry and situates her poetry within discourses of Irish nationalism, colonialism and feminism, thus providing a thorough and most convincing reading of the particular nature of Boland's poetical imagination.

The critical approach used throughout this book is one where cultural history and contemporary feminist literary criticism inform the reading of each poem, and she uses history, culture and private imagination to illuminate the writings of Eavan Boland. Her approach is clear, direct, eloquent and to the point, and provides a backdrop of imaginative and poetic development for each poem. The most original point of the study is the exploration of a feminist postcolonial approach to interpret Boland's poetry, supported by the inclusion of an extensive interview with the poet herself. Throughout, the relationship between theory and poetic expression within Boland's work is always lucidly delineated, presenting a coherent account of one Irish woman's developing and fluid poetic imagination. By considering feminism and postcolonialism, the writer places Boland at the intersections between the two ideologies within modern Irish writing and culture. Most crucially, Boland's reckoning with her 'Irishness' as a poet is a key consideration. Boland comments that, for an Irish writer, *"Irish nationalism, the physical intensity of its songs, images, traditions, is not something an Irish poet could easily walk away from. There's no way to simply and intellectually disown where you come from, because it would mean disowning who you are"*.

The structure of the book allows for an exploration of crucial themes in Boland's writings and useful chapter headings, like 'The poet as pilgrim', 'Commemorating lost heroes,' 'Acceptance and servitude: uncritical representations of women' and most usefully, 'A dispossessed and submissive female voice'; all give a thematic framework from which to read Boland. In addition, Boland's own critical writings, impressive as they are, were used skilfully and aptly. Dr Villar Argáiz has provided all of the relevant materials connected with the poems, the interviews and reviews and other secondary sources on Boland. In addition, she draws on some of the important writers on feminism, postcolonialism and on Ireland. In her bibliography, the range of her research is apparent and she traces all of the important writings by Eavan Boland, as well as other critical essays and relevant critical studies. The sheer thoroughness and professionalism of the bibliography indicates the serious nature of this large scale research project and marks this book as an original and an authoritative study of Eavan Boland's poetry. In this book Pilar Villar Argáiz has produced a major piece of critical writing where her knowledge of Irish studies and of feminist criticism is apparent. This full length book on a contemporary Irish woman writer is something of a rarity in Irish studies and most welcome.

Eibhear Walshe
English department
University College Cork
Ireland

Acknowledgements

Over the five years of my work on this book, I have been blessed with personal and institutional encouragements of many kinds. For their generous support in the form of fellowships and grants from 2001 to 2005, I thank the University of Granada and the Spanish Ministry of Education. Special thanks are due to the English Department at the University of Granada, for a subvention in direct aid of the publication of this book. My thanks also to Carcanet for their kind permission to reproduce the writings of Eavan Boland.

I would like to express special gratitude to Eavan Boland, for our continuous exchanges and for her generosity with her time when granting me an interview on the 14th of June 2004, during my attendance at the 19th International James Joyce Symposium celebrated in the National College of Ireland, Dublin. What was initially conceived as a rather informal coffee-time meeting turned out to be a captivating and exciting two-hour conversation. Her compelling charisma, as well as her essential comments, have not only strengthened my relationship with her poetry, but infused me with the necessary courage and energy to believe in what I was doing. I am also deeply grateful to Eavan Boland for grating me permission to use her photograph in the front cover and include the original interview as an appendix to my book.

This book could not have been written without the unconditional dedication, patience and constructive criticism of Dr Encarnación Hidalgo Tenorio. I thank her for having read this manuscript and for once again helping me to discover what I was trying to say. Her friendship and wise counsel over more than six years have shaped my work and I hope my life as well.

Special thanks are due to Prof. Andrew Blake, from King Alfred's College, Winchester; whose invaluable supervision from February to June, 2003, redirected the course of my investigation, and confirmed my decision to approach Boland's work from a postcolonial, and not merely feminist, perspective. Gratitude is also due to Dr Mick Jardine, for his amazing master's course "Postcolonial Fiction and Theory", conducted at this very same university. I am also indebted to Dr Carolina Amador, for welcoming me so generously to the Department of Languages and Cultural Studies at the University of Limerick, during the summer of 2004, where I finished compiling the biographical material necessary for my work. In addition, I owe a great debt of gratitude to the Women's Education, Research and Resource Centre, at University College Dublin, for their warm hospitality during my stay in Dublin as a visiting scholar during June 2006 and February 2007. In particular, special thanks to Ailbhe Smyth, Katherine O'Donnell, Paula Murphy, and Noreen Giffney for their support and interest in my research.

This manuscript also benefited from the invaluable proofreading assistance of Dr Graeme Porte (from the English Department, University of Granada) and Kate Antosik Parsons (from the Women's Education, Research and Resource Centre, UCD). Their hard work, passionate involvement in the project, and accuracy to detail have been admirable, and I thank them for that.

I also want to thank Prof. Luis Quereda Rodríguez-Navarro (from the English Department at the University of Granada), who guided my beginning research in Boland's poetry. It is a privilege for me to count on the support of colleagues of such professional and personal quality.

Others to whom I am much obliged for shared insights, encouragement, hospitality, and friendship are Dr Eibhear Walshe, Prof. Inés Praga Terente, Dr Ríona NíFhrigil, Prof. William Pratt, Theo Dorgan, Gerry Murphy, Dr Luz Mar González Arias, Pablo Fernández García, and Emer Small.

On a personal level, my family have kept me going in more ways than they know. Writing this book has helped me to appreciate the support of my parents, grandmother and brothers. I have dedicated this work with much love and admiration to my husband Jose Manuel Castellano Ubago. Whatever its failings, this is a better book for having been written with Jose's daily support, encouragement and understanding through my entire project.

1

Introduction

1.1. Introductory remarks

Writing a book on the Irish woman poet Eavan Boland from a non-native perspective seems at first to be a handicap.[1] I am an outsider dealing with a subject which is still very controversial. The conflict for women writers in establishing their own literary tradition, and their exclusion from the literary history, seem to have been more problematic in Ireland than in other countries. The country's particular cultural and political conditions have reinforced the hostility of Irish society towards women writers even as late as in the last decades of the twentieth century. In his preface to *Heathcliff and the Great Hunger*, Eagleton (1995: ix) claims: "For an Irish writer to intervene these days in debates over Irish culture and history is always a risky business; for an outsider it is well-nigh suicidal".

Accepting the risk, I intend in the present study to deal with some issues which have not been treated as they deserved, probably because the Irish literary tradition has been regarded as the 'untouchable' foundation on which this nation is built. I will focus my study on the work of Eavan Boland, who is considered one of the most important contemporary women poets in Ireland (Gelpi 1999: 210). Boland has influenced a whole generation of women writers who recognise women as active authors of their own texts, and not merely decorative emblems or passive objects, as some traditional national canons have advocated.

Boland's work has received the critical attention that, by virtue of both its scope and achievements, it certainly demands. Much stimulating research has focused on Boland's subversion of inherited literary standards, her revision of nationalist and mythological iconographies, her interest in domesticity, and her deconstruction of history as a 'master' and 'masculine' narrative.[2] Nevertheless, whereas all these issues have been explored in depth, less attention has been directed to Boland's struggle as an Irish woman poet in "a troubled land" of conflicting "evolving selves and identities" (Haberstroh 2001: 9). The legacy of imperialism, colonialism and nationalism, and the power relations of gender, race and sexuality at the heart of these ideologies are central concerns in her poetry.

This new study revaluates Boland's work in the light of postcolonialism, an approach which is certainly controversial, not only within the Irish academic field, but also among international scholarship.[3] I am particularly disposed towards a reading of Boland's poetry as determined by Ireland's status as a postcolonial country. The assumption upon which this study is based is similar to that which underlines Gerry Smyth's *Decolonisation and Criticism* (1998: 9): due to the colonial relationship between Ireland and England, much of contemporary Irish literature can be usefully read as a strategic cultural activity of decolonisation. It is difficult to postulate when Ireland became postcolonial. What is clear is that there are three landmark moments when the country enters a new stage of political independence: the Anglo-Irish Treaty accepted by the Dáil in January 1922, which created an Irish Free State of twenty-six counties; Eamon de Valera's constitution of 1937, which more explicitly declared Ireland's sovereignty; and the declaration of the Republic of Ireland and its disaffiliation from the British Commonwealth in April 1949 (Smyth 1998: 91). Maybe Irish writers such as Eavan Boland are still concerned with the colonial legacy due to the recent history of these events. The general belief held by postcolonial critics is that colonialism does not finish with the withdrawal of the foreign rulers from

Ireland. For many Irish men and women, the post-independence period did not bring liberation, but reinforced encoded forms of imperialism (Lloyd 1987: x; Lloyd 1993: 113; Deane 1994: 84; Kiberd 1996: 32; Smyth 1998: 92-93). The reasons put forward to justify this are the following: (1) the national bourgeoisie has perpetuated many power structures of the former colonial government; (2) Irish women have been profoundly affected by an overwhelming sexual conservatism in the aftermath of independence; (3) the postcolonial subject has found difficulty in escaping the systems of thought which structured the dominant discourses of imperialism and nationalism; (4) the persistence of British rule over six counties of Northern Ireland makes the decolonising programme even more difficult, mostly for those writers of Northern descent. In this sense, some Irish postcolonial critics widely believe that the effects of cultural dependency are still palpable long after the departure of the British military power from the Republic of Ireland, and that this is observed in contemporary Irish literature. As Smyth (1998: 94) argues, Irish identity in the "'postcolonial' epoch still depend[s] on its colonial history for a sense of its own reality"; or as Kiberd (1996: 6) puts it, it is "less easy to decolonise the mind than the territory".

The postcolonial debate has awoken the interest of more than one literary critic in Ireland. With their reading of Frantz Fanon, Edward Said, Homi Bhabha, Gayatri Spivak, and other postcolonial voices, they have attempted to arrive at an understanding of Irish literature as a postcolonial cultural production.[4] In this study, I intend to follow this trend in the Irish academia, embracing postcolonial theories and critiques, inside and outside the Irish academic debate. A reading of such texts is clearly helpful for a comprehensive approach to Eavan Boland's poetry, as her work is infused with an awareness of the historic impact of her own specific kind of colonial – and hence postcolonial – inheritance.

Nevertheless, the postcolonial approach is not sufficient for a thorough analysis of a poetry that is certainly shaped by gender issues. As Wilson (1990a: xii) has noted, women in Ireland represent a special complexity, a complexity which is "twofold", for it encompasses both "their female and national identities".

In fact, women in Ireland have been doubly colonised, both by imperialism and also by a restrictive nationalism which has been fused to Catholicism. This colonialism becomes more apparent if we bear in mind the fusion of the feminine and the national in the Irish literary tradition. Irish women's simplification by colonialist and nationalist texts is a constant preoccupation for Boland. In one of her interviews, the woman poet addresses this issue: "[w]e are a postcolonial country. We now have a further postcolonial problem in the way women are perceived" (Consalvo 1992: 98). In a later interview, Eavan Boland defines the reality of Irish women as follows:

> we were outsiders using someone else's language, fighting our way through someone else's history, finding ourselves in the space between exclusion and possession, […] women have been outsiders within an outsider's culture (Allen-Randolph 1999b: 304).

Boland's poetry clearly exposes the consequences of the dual colonialism she sharply criticises. By virtue of determinant factors such as gender, nationality, and ethnicity, Boland finds that she has been excluded, both as an Irish citizen and also as a woman, from the subject position available in the dominant culture. In this sense, the construction and reconstruction of categories such as 'Irishness' and 'womanhood' become a pressing issue throughout a career as prolific as hers. That is why a postcolonial reading of Boland's poetry necessarily needs to be complemented by a feminist approach.

In adopting such a joint perspective, it is important to bear in mind that Boland perceives both forms of colonialism (imperialist and patriarchal) as analogous movements. The woman poet has explained her belief that the oppression of women under the powerful impact of nationalism and Catholicism in Ireland is very similar to the oppression the Irish themselves experienced under British rule: "Womanhood and Irishness are metaphors for one another. There are resonances of humiliations, oppression, and silence in both of them and I think you can understand one better by experiencing the other" (interview with Wilson

1990b: 84). This quotation serves to illustrate how Boland unites under the same descriptive procedures both sorts of colonialisms, patriarchal victimisation and colonial subordination. In fact, her poetry shows how colonialism is, and can only be, one. The union Boland establishes between women's and Irish people's oppression is better understood if one bears in mind her definition of colonialism. Boland views colonialism as a cultural movement whose damaging effects can be clearly traced through art: firstly, Irish culture has been negatively affected and reshaped by British imperialism; and secondly, Irish poetry has functioned, in its reliance on feminine iconography, as another form of colonialism for women. In an interview with Allen-Randolph (1993b: 125), Boland has argued that "power has just as much to do with a poetic sphere of operation as any other [...], power has operated in the making of canons, the making of taste, the nominating of what poems should represent the age and so on". In this sense, and as Atfield (1997: 173) notes, colonialism for Boland is defined as "the establishment of ruling power systems by imposition" and how this is reflected in the cultural terrain. Consequently, Boland's concern with colonialism is with how it has affected artistic representation. By the same token, decolonisation for Boland is going to be carried out through the artistic medium: to find freedom as a speaking voice in poetry is the ultimate decolonisation she looks for.

With the exception of Meaney (1993), Atfield (1997), and Fulford (2002a), there are no studies which focus on Boland's poetry from a feminist postcolonial approach. Here and there we find comments such as Reizbaum's, who notes "the attempts to marginalise Boland's poetry within an arguably marginalised literature" (1989: 472). Apart from these brief remarks, Boland's work is rarely considered within a dual feminist and postcolonial framework. Her work, in this sense, still needs to be regarded as a result of the different amalgams of colonialisms (patriarchal, imperialist, and nationalist) that have affected and still affect contemporary Irish women. In her essay "Daughters of Colony", Boland (1997a: 18) calls for a "gender-conscious postcolonial critique", a critique that takes into account how Irish women have been colonised in two different ways, by distorting and simplifying images in imperialist and nationalist discourses. Furthermore, Boland explicitly declares the need to study Irish women's writing from a perspective that not only attends to these two forms of colonisation, but also to women's marginalisation by the Irish literary canon (with their manifold simplifications) and by later postcolonial literary scholars (such as the Field Day's, with their 1991 anthology). It is this form of gender-oriented postcolonial critique that I intend to adopt in my study of Boland's poetry.

In order to do so, I will use jointly feminist and postcolonial approaches in my analysis of how Boland tries to overcome marginalisation as a postcolonial gendered subject. Their focus on gender and colonial oppression, and their theories of resistance to conventional patriarchal and imperial discourses can be very helpful in deciphering Boland's aesthetic concerns in her poetry. My approach is very similar to the one adopted by feminist postcolonial critics such as Donaldson (1992: 138-139), Mohanty (1991b: 74) and Spivak (1993: 17). All these scholars stress the need to negotiate the meaning of female identity in relation to categories such as race, class, nationality, culture, and religion. They defend a form of politics that draws upon all these elements, because, faithful to deconstructive beliefs, they argue that there is no such a thing as a "transparently universal ground of being" (Donaldson 1992: 137).

1.2. Aims and methodological approach

The main objective of this book is to investigate, from the dual framework of feminist and postcolonial studies, Eavan Boland's evolution as an Irish woman poet. Boland's poetic career is an exemplary illustration of the hesitations and difficulties that haunt and have haunted women poets in Ireland. In her long journey as a writer, we come across an Irish woman striving to overcome the internal trauma of her colonised nation, and a woman gradually searching for her own place as a female poet in a mainly andocentric literary tradition. That is why Boland gradually undermines the (presumably authentic) representations of 'woman' and 'nation' she has inherited.

At the beginning, Boland produces a 'masculine' poetry, hiding her womanhood out of fear of being rejected by Ireland's poetic community. Her initial work takes for granted notions such as 'Irishness' and 'Irish poet'. Boland writes within well-defined parameters that dictate what and how the Irish poem has to communicate. In her intermediate phase, Boland becomes a radical feminist. The main focus at this stage of her literary career is to protest with energy against her own oppression as a woman in a patriarchal and sexist culture, and to defend her own distinctive reality as a gendered subject, previously ignored in her initial poems. Now, Boland takes for granted notions such as 'womanhood', and engages in a revolutionary project according to which this category is defended as a whole and unitary concept. It is not until her mature phase where 'Irishness' and 'womanhood' will be understood as social constructs and not as transcendental and universal notions. By moving beyond 'gender' and 'race' impositions, Boland achieves her own (artistic) decolonisation as a gendered postcolonial subject. In this sense, the woman poet will scrutinise the foundations upon which imperialist, nationalist, and feminist ideologies have been based in order to justify their claims. Her mature poetry dismantles the belief that the poet has to become a public political figure, a spokesperson who speaks on behalf of an oppressed community. Therefore, and in contrast to her previous two phases, Boland subjects all forms of knowledge and privilege to a process of unravelling: notions such as 'place', 'nation', 'home', and 'womanhood' cannot be defended in essentialist terms, for these are changeable, relative, and heterogeneous categories.

In this sense, Boland's poetic career follows a certain evolution, from an initial imitation of the main tenets that have shaped the (Irish) literary tradition, to a gradual rejection and subversion of them. Accordingly, I will try to see the extent to which the critical mode developed by Elaine Showalter as regards women writers can be applied to Boland's poetry. Showalter (1999: 11-13) defends the existence of three phases in the literary work of a woman artist whose aim is to achieve self-assertion. These three phases, she explains, are applicable to all kinds of subcultures: the 'Feminine' phase, the 'Feminist' phase, and the

'Female' phase. Surprisingly enough, the evolution Showalter traces in the feminine literary tradition is almost identical to that analysed by Frantz Fanon (1990: 31-149) and Albert Memmi (1990: 168-205) in their study of the colonial subject affected by race. Both anti-colonial intellectuals coincide in identifying three phases in the colonial subject's journey towards a satisfactory (cultural) decolonisation: a phase of unconditional 'Assimilation', a phase of a constraining 'Cultural Nationalism', and a final phase of 'Liberation'. I will show that the similarities of these theoretical models indicate that the gendered subject and the colonial subject share in many ways not only the nature of their oppression but also the methods employed to overcome their marginalised status.

In order to trace more accurately this evolution I make use of more recent theorisations of identity-formation in the fields of postcolonial and feminist studies. I apply, on the one hand, the postcolonial postulates by prominent voices such as Edward Said (1994, 1995), Homi Bhabha (1995), Gayatri Spivak (1988a, 1988b, 1990a, 1990b, 1993, 1994, 1996, 1999), and Stuart Hall (1990, 1996a, 1996b, 1997). On the other hand, I use the theories proposed by Hélène Cixous (1981, 1994), Luce Irigaray (1985, 1991), and Julia Kristeva (1981, 1986a, 1986b, 1986c, 1986d), whose work is representative of the main trend in French feminism. There are strong parallels between both fields of criticism, mainly because they are interested in looking at the different ways in which subjects have been marginalised and relegated to the position of subordinated 'Others' by colonialism and/or patriarchy.

The most important point of contact between contemporary postcolonial theory and French feminism is mainly their project for deconstructing Western thought. Postcolonial theory and criticism, as Walder (1998: 58-59) explains, were part of the decentring movement of post-1960s thought in the West, marked by a general scepticism of familiar liberal humanist conceptions of the individual and society. In this sense, one of the most important features of postcolonial studies is its critique of the Western dominant ideology of humanism and its consequent deconstruction of core concepts like 'subject' and 'identity' (Moore-

Gilbert 2000: 172, Hall 1996b: 248). This deconstruction is prompted by an initial questioning of the pattern of binaries (West/East; Europe/Third World; coloniser/colonised) that has been identified as fundamental to Western thought.

In its critique of essentialism, postcolonial studies intersects with French feminism. De Beauvoir's (1997: 295) famous statement in *The Second Sex* that "[o]ne is not born, but rather becomes a woman" epitomises the mid-twentieth-century idea that femininity is a social construction, an assertion that became central to the subsequent feminist postulates of Cixous's, Irigaray's, and Kristeva's. In different ways, as we will see, these feminist critics have striven to avoid perpetuating a patriarchal logic which defines woman as man's 'Other'. Although they will find problems when ultimately undermining the very oppositional polarity between masculinity and femininity, their critique of the paradigm of binary thought links their theories with the deconstructive moves of postcolonial theory. Like Said, Bhabha, and Spivak, these French feminist critics are deeply influenced by postmodernism and poststructuralism.[5] Jacques Derrida has a particular repercussion in their work. Derrida defies a system of binary oppositions which positions the male as the legitimate and standard principle, the norm "against which truth and value are measured", a process he defines as "phallogocentric" (Gamble 2001: 215). His theories become a starting point from which Cixous, Irigaray, and Kristeva attempt to displace the subject – the individual (bourgeois white male) subject – of Western humanism (Mohanty 1991b: 73).

Secondly, French feminism resembles postcolonial theory in its concern with the idea of agency and resistance, how the gendered and/or post(colonial) subject resists patriarchal and/or imperial power. Postcolonial critics such as Said (1994: 277), Bhabha (1995: 13) and Spivak (1988a: 253-254) argue that the freeing of the colonised subject from his/her disabling position is found in the construction of new liberating narratives, narratives which surpass national and race boundaries. These theorists can be defined as "syncreticist", using Ashcroft, Griffiths and Tiffin's coinage (2002: 29). They locate decolonisation in the fusion or reconciliation of the different elements, colonial and postcolonial, and stress the plurality of identity through various versions of the concept of 'hybridity'. 'Hybridity' involves cultural syncretism, and the possibility of occupying a non-essentialist liminal stance that disrupts coloniser and colonised binaries. Like Said, Bhabha, and Spivak, the three French feminist critics under discussion agree on the fact that, in order to achieve liberation, women must move beyond the patriarchal binary opposition of the 'self' and the 'Other'. Their idea of 'decolonisation', in this sense, is achieved by means of concepts almost identical to the ones developed by postcolonial theory. As we will see, Cixous (1994: 44) and Irigaray (1985: 244-245) develop an image of a new woman in terms of fluidity, ambivalence, and instability, as a category which is able to surpass masculine representations. Their strategies of "bisexuality" and "amorous exchange" are very similar to the cultural syncreticism Said, Bhabha and Spivak advocate. On the other hand, in Julia Kristeva's "Woman's Time" (1986c: 189), we come across a powerful critique and redefinition of the concept of the 'nation' very similar to the one carried out by Bhabha in "Dissemination" (1994: 291-322). Her call for a "third attitude" as the most efficient mode of resistance is almost identical to Bhabha's advocacy of a "Third Space", a liminal position from which to counteract authoritarian ideologies. The similarity of their approaches stems from the fact that both feminist and postcolonial schools attempt to move beyond essentialist identity-claims that base their premises on fixed definitions of 'man'/'woman' and 'coloniser'/'colonised'. In different ways, all of them advocate hybridity, boundary crossing, and fluidity as the best option to adopt for the postcolonial/gendered subject.

Finally, French feminism interacts with postcolonialism in its concern with the specific problems raised by women's relation to language and writing. Therefore, like Said, Bhabha, and Spivak, French feminists focus on discourse and how it can be used as a vehicle for subverting patriarchal and imperial power. Luce Irigaray's (1991: 124) concept of "mimesis", for instance, is very similar to Bhabha's (1995: 87) employment of the term "mimicry". Both theorists advocate the 'appropriation' of the discourses of power in order to subvert and undermine them. What unites Cixous, Irigaray, and Kristeva is their belief that there is an area of textual production that can be labelled 'feminine', which is located below the surface of patriarchal discourse, and which at times comes to the fore in the form of disruptions of this 'masculine' language. Although they draw on essentialist concepts in their postulation of a distinctive female mode of discourse, their usage of references to the female body and identity are highly allegorical and ironic, and, as Gamble (2001: 225) explains, does "not necessarily denote [their] belief in the existence of a fundamental female identity".

By bringing together Showalter, Memmi, and Fanon's premises with other postcolonial and feminist theorisations of identity, I will demonstrate how gendered and national identities are represented in Boland's mature poetry in terms of fluidity and hybridity. Boland achieves ultimate artistic liberation by crossing gendered and national boundaries.

1.3. Boland's work seen against Showalter's, Memmi's, and Fanon's critical models

In *A Literature of Their Own* (originally published in 1977), Elaine Showalter studies the work of women writers since the nineteenth century under the premise that, as a minority group, it has always had to fight against its exclusion from a male-dominated literary canon. Showalter (1999: 13) argues that, in relation to the literary mainstream, women's writing has moved through the phases of subordination, protest, and self-discovery, phases which bear witness to the advent of a more confident and independent female literature. Her main focus is the evolution of a female literary tradition in the English novel. In order to study this evolution, this critic looks at English women novelists collectively, establishing a parallelism between women's writing and what she has termed "literary subcultures" (pp. 11-13). Like all literary subcultures, Showalter (1999: 13) argues, women's writing goes through three major phases:

First, there is a prolonged phase of *imitation* of the prevailing modes of the dominant tradition, and *internalisation* of its standards of art and its views on social roles. Second, there is a phase of *protest* against these standards and values, and *advocacy* of minority rights and values, including a demand for autonomy. Finally, there is a phase of *self-discovery*, a turning inward free from some of the dependency of opposition, a search of identity.

These stages are identified respectively as "Feminine", "Feminist", and "Female". Showalter proceeds to explain that these phases are "obviously not rigid categories", clearly "separable in time" (p. 13). Much to the contrary, the three stages may be present in the career of a single writer and they may overlap.

A clarification of concepts such as 'feminine', 'feminist', and 'female' may be useful here. Moi (1997: 104-116) offers a very illuminating distinction between these often confused concepts within feminist literary criticism. 'Femininity' is a social construct, and the 'feminine' stands for those "patterns of sexuality and behaviour imposed by cultural and social norms" (p. 108). According to this definition, Showalter's 'Feminine' phase would be understood as that stage when women writers remain uncritical of socio-cultural constructs. On the other hand, the words 'feminist' and 'feminism' are political categories: they involve a political commitment to the fight against all forms of patriarchy and sexism (pp. 104-106). This definition coincides with what Showalter defines as the 'Feminist' phase, a stage where the woman writer both protests and advocates minority rights. Finally, 'femaleness' is "a matter of biology": it relates to the biological aspects of sexual difference. By using terms such as 'femaleness' and 'masculinity' in her discussion of women's literature in their final stage of evolution, Showalter may run dangerously close to suggesting that there are 'natural' and 'innate' patterns in the way women write. Although I will denominate Boland's mature work 'Female', I do not intend to suggest that her poetry is biologically and sexually determined. Much to the contrary, I will show how in her final evolutionary stage Boland attempts to find artistic decolonisation by moving beyond essentialist definitions of categories such as 'Irishness' and 'womanhood'. In fact, Showalter's categorisation of women writers in their final evolutionary period moves towards a possibility of deconstructing stable identity-formations.

Showalter's tripartite structure of artistic development evinces important similarities with Memmi's and Fanon's model of (artistic) decolonisation. Frantz Fanon offers a very interesting analysis of the colonised writer, this time oppressed by race and not gender. In *The Wretched of the Earth*, Fanon (1990: 31-149) distinguishes between three different phases in the process of decolonisation. Memmi's *The Colonizer and the Colonized* (1990) proposes a tripartite structure of decolonisation very similar, if not identical, to Fanon's. Memmi's book was published in 1957, four years before *The Wretched of the Earth* came into print. This makes anyone think that it would probably be this anti-colonial intellectual, and not Fanon, who inaugurated this influential evolutionary model, something ignored by postcolonial theorists and critics such as Said (1994: 331) and Amuta (2002: 158). For the purposes of this study, I will summarise Memmi's and Fanon's pattern of evolution for the colonised both during and after the colonial era.

First, Memmi (1990: 168) argues that there is an initial phase of "assimilation" or "petrifaction", in which the colonised accepts colonisation. Before passing on to the stage of revolt, any colonised subject attempts to be like the coloniser: he or she adopts the coloniser's language and ideology. According to Memmi (1990: 190), this attempt is proven unsuccessful, for the colonised can never entirely resemble the coloniser: "In order to be assimilated, it is not enough to leave one's group, but one must enter another; now he meets with the coloniser's rejection". This phase corresponds to Fanon's (1990: 31-32) initial stage of "oppression". As he explains in *The Wretched of the Earth*, it is not enough for the settler to circumscribe physically the place of the native with the help of the army and police force (pp. 31-32). The colonised is being dehumanised, he or she becomes "a sort of quintessence of evil", and all native traditions and myths become "the very sign of that poverty of spirit and of their constitutional depravity" (p. 32).

Both Memmi (1990: 195) and Fanon (1990: 74) agree on the fact that, in order to move away from the colonial situation, the colonised engages in a second (bloody) phase of protest. This violent phase is based on a vigorous attempt to recover and assert the self, the autonomous entity. Now the colonised entirely rejects the coloniser, and defends with passion his/her own distinctiveness. For Memmi (1990: 95), colonialism creates the patriotism of the oppressed, who attempt to affirm their exclusivity in national selfhood. In this phase, there is a reconstruction of old myths and neglected traditions, a return to religion and the native language, together with all those aspects which have been previously neglected by the coloniser (p. 199). Similary, Fanon (1990: 74) states that this second phase in the evolutionary process starts in the "building-up of the nation", at that very moment when the native realises he or she is not "an animal", and he or she "decides to come to terms with his own humanity" (p. 33). It is at this phase when decolonisation begins, and the native population is mainly focused on the achievement of national liberation.

But this second phase, as Memmi (1990: 201-205) and Fanon (1990: 38-39) explain, does not mean ultimate liberation, for, even after the struggle for national freedom has succeeded, there are certain features of the former colonial power which are still maintained in the national governments. The reason for this, as Memmi (1990: 202) explains, is that the colonised continues to define him/herself in the same terms imposed by the coloniser. On the other hand, nationalism can become as restrictive and exclusionist as imperialism (p. 201). Like Memmi, Fanon shows his reluctance to accept nationalism as a legitimate means of decolonisation. His argument is that the national economy of this period of independence is not set "on a new footing", and a split occurs between an incompetent native bourgeoisie in power and the peasants, who are mainly moved by the ideal of "bread and land" (Fanon 1990: 38-39). Their hostility towards the bourgeoisie becomes plainly visible: "the masses begin to sulk, they turn away from their nation in which they have being given no place, and they begin to lose interest in it" (p. 136). On the other hand, the leader of the country, refusing to break bonds with the national bourgeoisie, "asks the people to fall back into the past and to become drunk in the remembrance of the epoch which led up to independence" (pp. 135-136). Thus, Fanon implies that this period, governed by an ideal of nationalism which does not look into the present or the future, is incapable of bringing national unity and incapable of 'decolonising the mind' of the native population.

Both Memmi (1990: 198) and Fanon (1990: 148) believe that the second phase in the decolonising process is a prelude to a more "positive" and "liberating" movement. Memmi argues that, in the previous phases, the colonised depended on the figure of the coloniser, as a model to follow or as an antithesis to reject. He believes that it is only in "the decomposition of this interdependence" between coloniser and colonised that any sort of viable decolonisation is possible (p. 7). In this sense, Memmi agrees with Showalter (1999: 13), who argues that women in their final phase of decolonisation are "free from the dependency of [establishing their] opposition" towards a patriarchal literary culture. As Memmi (1990: 216) states, the colonised has to cease defining himself through the categories imposed by the colonisers, and this would certainly imply moving beyond boundaries such as East vs. West, colonised vs. coloniser. Memmi's (1990: 217) call for "revolution" and the creation of "a whole and free man" advances Fanon's (1990: 28) later advocacy in *The Wretched of the Earth* of the "veritable creation of new men". Like Memmi, Fanon describes the situation of the oppressed, the struggle for decolonisation, and how this process has to be premised on new identities. He argues that in this last stage of liberation, the national bourgeoisie, realising that in the previous period it copied its methods from those of Western political parties, finally "hears the needs" of the peasants (Fanon 1990: 148-149). It is only when "the middle class's trading sector is nationalised", and "a programme of humanism" which aims at developing "the brains of its inhabitants" begins, that the country is governed by the mass of the people, and liberation is finally brought about (ibid). Fanon's desire to move beyond ideologies such nationalism is already observed in his previous work, *Black Skin, White Masks*, where he writes against fixed and stable forms of nationalist narratives that depend on a pure and authentic race that must be preserved at all costs. Fanon (1991: 231) characterises the colonial dichotomy coloniser-colonised as the product of a "manichaeism delerium", which results in the radical division into dual oppositions such as good/evil, true/false, white/black. Fanon shows that this system of binaries is intrinsic to Western (and imperialist) thought. As he explains, 'blackness' is an artificial category created by the white man, and therefore, oppositions such as coloniser and colonised must be deconstructed in order to achieve decolonisation. Breaking race boundaries means the ultimate freedom and liberation for the individual. As Fanon (1991: 138) believes, assertion of negritude is not sufficient in itself. When quoting Sartre (1948: xl), who asserts that "negritude is the root of its own destruction, it is a transition and not a conclusion, a means and not an ultimate end" (p. 113), Fanon confesses that Sartre reminded him that his blackness was only "a minor term" (p. 138). In this sense, Fanon starts advocating a new form of politics that moves beyond national boundaries and nativist claims. By rejecting any form of exclusive patriotism and by showing the constructed nature of categories such as 'coloniser' and 'colonised' which lie at the heart of Western humanism, both Fanon and Memmi advance the claim of later theorists such as Edward Said, Homi Bhabha, Gayatri Spivak and Stuart Hall, who argue in favour of deconstructing ideologies such as imperialism and nationalism and subverting their defence of pre-established identities.

These stages of evolution applied to the political and social terrain can also be observed in (post)colonial literature.[6] Interestingly enough, Fanon, unlike Memmi, applies this evolutionary schema to the realm of culture. This might be the reason why Fanon's evolutionary schema has been more influential among postcolonial theorists and critics anxious to analyse postcolonial literary productions. Fanon (1990: 166-199) dedicates one entire chapter in *The Wretched of the Earth* to explaining the effects of this process of decolonisation on the cultured individual of the colonised race – what he calls "the native intellectual" (p. 178). He focuses on the literary evolution the colonial subject (at times symbolised by the figure of "The Negro of the Antilles") experiences in order to achieve an ultimate decolonisation, which includes the following: (1) a phase of "occupation" (in which the "Negro" wants to become white and in order to do so he or she assimilates the imperial culture); (2) a phase of a constraining "cultural nationalism" (in which this figure attempts to define him/herself by asserting his/her negritude through writing); (3) a final phase of "liberation" (in which negritude is not considered to be the final state of liberation, and the colonial subject attempts to assert him/herself within terms not imposed by the coloniser) (pp. 178-195).[7] Furthermore, Fanon asserts that these levels are more clearly observed in the work of colonised poets (p. 177).

Fanon's paradigm has become one of the most "enduring value[s]" in contemporary cultural criticism (Amuta 2002: 158). Critics of various kinds, such as Ashcroft, Griffiths and Tiffin (2002: 4-6) and Walder (1998: 77-78), have implicitly or explicitly applied Fanon's critical mode to discuss various literary productions.[8] Said (1994) has also used Fanon's tripartite structure, this time to discuss Ireland's history and Irish writers. In *Culture and Imperialism*, for instance, Said (1994: 271) relies on Fanon's theories in order to analyse the Irish people's process of decolonisation. He explains that, within the Irish Nationalist Revival, there were two distinct political moments, moments which have a correspondence with Fanon's phases: an initial moment of an anti-imperialist resistance which produced nationalist independent movements; and a more openly liberationist moment which occurred during the Western imperial mission after World War II (ibid). It is during this last phase, Said states, when the conventional nationalism of Pearse was proven to be inadequate, and it "comes the idea of liberation, a strong new post-nationalist theme that had been implicit in the works of Connolly", for instance (ibid). Furthermore, Said (1994: 282) establishes a very interesting parallelism between Yeats's poetry, "written under the shadow of imperialist domination", and "the narrative of liberation depicted so memorably in Fanon's *The Wretched of the Earth*":

> Fanon's is a discourse that anticipated triumph, liberation, that marks the second moment of decolonisation. Yeats's early work, by contrast, sounds the nationalist note and stands at a threshold it cannot cross. [...] One might at least give him credit for adumbrating the liberationist and Utopian revolutionism in his poetry that was belied and even cancelled out by his later reactionary politics. (p. 283)

Thus, Said locates Yeats within those nativist movements which resulted from the colonial encounter. His attack on Yeats is based on the poet's "outright fascism, his fantasies of old homes and families, his incoherently occult divagations" (p. 275). Yeats's nativist views prevented him from imagining a full political liberation, and therefore, he is not considered to be a "liberationist" (pp. 287-288).

Within the Irish academy, Fanon's model has also aroused great interest. Lloyd (1993: 7), for instance, recognises his indebtedness to Fanon's "critique of the identity politics of the negritude movement" and his attack on the national state. Kiberd (1996: 184) is also a self-declared follower of Fanon's dialectic of decolonisation (from occupation, through nationalism, to liberation) which he uses in order to refer to Ireland's history as a colonial and postcolonial country. He deploys Fanon's theory of the three stages of decolonisation to explain, for instance, the Literary Revival's attempt to forge a national culture that would recover a lost history and celebrate liberation from domination. As this critic (1996: 551) asserts: "The history of independent Ireland bears a remarkable similarity [...] to the phases charted by Frantz Fanon in *the Wretched of the Earth*". At the cultural level, Kiberd finds in Fanon's theoretical model a useful point of reference for an understanding of the work of Synge, Yeats, and Joyce. The tripartite structure of Synge's *The Playboy of the Western World* would correspond very systematically with Fanon's dialectic of decolonisation (p. 184). In Act One, Christy encounters a false image of himself in the broken mirror of his father's house, reflecting Irish self-disgust under colonial rule. In this sense, this would stand as an allegory of Fanon's "occupation phase". In Act Two, Christy then "discovers an over-flattering image of himself in the perfect mirror of Pegeen's shebeen". This would equate the Irish feeling of self-worth under the conditions of a self-glorifying revival, and consequently, Fanon's "nationalist phase". In Act Three, Christy, not concerned anymore with the good opinion of others, throws the mirror away and "constructs himself out of his own desire", instead of becoming the focus of the desire of others. Christy will form a conception of himself, rather than existing as a conception of others, and this would take him to Fanon's "liberationist phase". According to Kiberd (1996: 288), Synge's play, as it is structured, is indicative of the fact that the playwright clearly understood that the problem with cultural nationalism was its mimicry of the English stereotypes of the Irish. In Yeats's observations on national culture, Kiberd (1996: 325) finds another instance of Fanon's "liberationist phase", contradicting Said's assertions. According to Yeats, when the ego is released from the phase of mimic nationalism, what the poet called "a nationalism of mourning", a deeper self is freed (p. 291). In order to achieve the third phase of liberation, Yeats recurred to style, described as "a form of self-conquest", evinced in *A Vision* (p. 325). Finally, Kiberd (1996: 334) reads Joyce as an exemplary writer of Fanon's liberationist phase. Foreseeing the failure of nationalism, Joyce attempted to represent the spiritual liberation of his country by unleashing a plurality of voices. *Ulysses* records these full range of voices "which would sound together the notes that moved beyond nationalism to liberation" (p. 338). By analysing in such a way these three writers, Kiberd shows the Irish version of Fanon's (1990: 28) "veritable creation of new men".

Some critics have mentioned the difficulty of applying American, or indeed, European theories of feminist aesthetics to the Irish context (Fogarty 1994: 92). In this work, I will challenge these assumptions by demonstrating that in Boland's poetry we may observe the three phases advocated by the American feminist Elaine Showalter. As in the case of Showalter, applications of Fanon's theories to discussions on current literary productions have been looked at suspiciously. Marcey (2000: 3), for instance, has attacked current applications of Fanon out of the historical circumstances in which he wrote his work. In particular, this critic rebukes Homi Bhabha's for locating Fanon's writings as "exist[ing] outside time and space and in a purely textual dimension" (ibid). Later in his work, Marcey (2000: 26) criticises Edward Said for quoting Fanon and W.B. Yeats in a single paragraph, arguing that Fanon's theories cannot be understood as transhistorical 'facts'. Against this view, it is clear that Fanon's "insurgent and liberationist rhetoric", as Brennan (1994: 57) characterises it, can be linked to the situation of the oppressed elsewhere. As Kwadwo (2002: 30-40) notes, Fanon often identifies his ideological project "in ways that went beyond the specific Algerian situation in which he was involved". As he himself argues at the end of *The Wretched of the Earth*, "the process for liberation of mankind" is independent of the particular situation in which a person finds himself or herself, and "concerns the whole of humanity" (Fanon 1990: 253). Thus, it is not surprising to find that his writings have been approached when attempting to consider other political and theoretical uses, such as the contemporary repression of the Third World (Bewes 2002: 9), or most relevantly for the purposes of this study, the oppression of the gendered subject. Dubey (1998: 2) argues that Fanon's work can provide useful information for the projects of postcolonial feminism. Similarly, Bell (2002: 17) defends reading Fanon within a feminist theory, on the grounds that the feminist struggle is linked with Fanon's postulates in its interest in anti-colonial and anti-racist movements.

Taking into account the above mentioned, I consider Showalter's, Memmi's, and Fanon's theoretical premises crucial for an understanding of Boland's decolonising process, both as a woman poet and as an Irish citizen. Even so, I am not proposing here any notional easy fit between their models of decolonisation and Boland's poetry. Memmi and Fanon neglected important issues like feminism, and as the example of Eavan Boland's poetry immediately shows, their work needs to be viewed critically from a feminist standpoint.[9] Moreover, it is important to consider that, despite the fact that these three phases follow a coherent order in Boland's work, they are not rigid categories. Although her evolution as a poet underlies a process of initial imitation, intermediate protest and final artistic autonomy, the departure from the inherited poetic tradition is not an easy step to take, and Boland, in her process to attain self-assurance as a poet, shows backward and forward movements. Her second volume, *The War Horse* (1975), illustrates how Boland's (ideological) progression towards self-affirmation is at times delayed by the constraining tradition she has inherited. Furthermore, the three phases proposed by Showalter, Memmi, and Fanon overlap at times in Boland's career.

I do not claim to have a definite reading of Boland's poetry. For me, understanding her poetry in all its complexity is a lifelong work in progress. Nevertheless, the effort to probe deeply into its meaning is rewarding, because once we penetrate beneath the superficial level of her poems we can discover the many ways by which an Irish woman poet moves subversively among authoritarian discourses that, in their different ways, have attempted to define the two constituent aspects of Boland's identity: her 'Irishness' and her 'womanhood'.

The more I have studied, the more encouraged I have felt and the fewer limitations I have encountered as an outsider. As Boland (1997a: 10) has claimed, "[t]he attempt to define a colony and its aftermath is as much the property of those who experience it as those who analyse it". More recently, Boland has asserted in an interview the following:

> I don't accept that Irish critics are entitled to the final say on an Irish poet, or British critics on a British poet and so on. If they were, if they were the custodians of the final meaning of their own writers, then we wouldn't have Ellman's biography of Joyce, to start with. That's just one example where the outside perspective became a benchmark. There's no way that a local critic can comment definitively on anything but the Irishness or the Britishness, and that may actually obscure the work. [...] Sometimes the critic who doesn't read the local exactly is able to extract some of the essentials more quickly. (Allen-Randolph 1999b: 301-302)

In this study, it is my intention to "extract [...] the essentials" of Boland's poetry, though by no means omitting "the local" element of it.

Notes to chapter 1

---

[1] In this study, I will employ the category 'woman writer/poet' to refer to Eavan Boland. I acknowledge, nevertheless, that some Irish women, such as Katie Donovan and Ruth Hooley, have seen this nomenclature as dangerous and problematic, because it aggravates the problem of marginalisation, by concentrating on an "isolating spotlight" (Haberstroh 1996: 7, 12). Eavan Boland herself has no problem with the compound 'woman writer': "historically I knew I would have to pick up the tab as a woman writer [...], to be effective and useful as an Irish woman poet you have to be able to pick up the tab" (interview with O'Malley 1999: 255). Therefore, and relying on Boland's words, from here on I will use this label.

[2] See, for instance, Adcock (1994), Allen-Randolph (1991, 1993a, 1995), Brown (1993), Clutterbuck (1999), Collins (2000), Fogarty (1994, 1999), Foster (1999), Gelpi (1999), Haberstroh (1993, 1995), Hagen & Zelman (1991, 2004), Keen (2000), Kelly (1993), Kupillas (1999), Luftig (1993), Maguire (1999), Martin (1993), McCallum (2004), Meaney (1993), O'Donnell (1993), Riley (1997), Russell (2002), and Thurston (1999).

[3] Bery and Murray (2000: 1-4) and Innes (2000: 22) note the tendency, now in decline, to exclude Ireland (together with the other two constituent parts of the British Isles, Scotland and Wales), from the study of the postcolonial. The most outstanding theorists in the postcolonial arena have generally ignored Ireland in their discussions. Ashcroft, Griffiths and Tiffin's *The Empire Writes Back* (2002) (first published in 1989) is an illustrative example of the omission of the Irish case. The same silencing of Ireland occurs in Boehmer's *Colonial and Postcolonial Literature: Migrant Metaphors* (1995) and Walder's *Post-colonial Literatures in English* (1998). Edward Said is an important exception, as his *Culture and Imperialism* includes a long section discussing Yeats as a nationalist poet who can be understood in the same context as Aimé Césaire, Frantz Fanon, and Pablo Neruda (Said 1994: 271-283). Within the Irish academy, the so-called 'Revisionist historians' also react against postcolonial explanations of Ireland's history. Roy Foster's *Modern Ireland 1600-1972* (1989) is one of the most influential studies within this school. His work has been followed by other scholars like Bartlett (1988), Comerford (1988), Howe (2002), and Kennedy (1996).

[4] Recent exchange on Ireland's place within postcolonial studies has been carried out by Carroll (2003a, 2003b), Cleary (2003), Deane (2003), Graham (1994a, 1994b, 1995/6, 1997, 1999, 2001), Hooper and Graham (2002), Kirkland (1999), Lloyd (2003), Maley (1996, 2000), O'Dowd (1990), Smyth (1995, 1998, 1999, 2000), and Whelan (2003), to name some representative scholars. All these critics have begun to invoke Memmi, Fanon, Said, Bhabha, and Spivak as useful perspectives from which to view the relationship between Irish and British cultural history. The work of these critics has been expanded by scholars such as Bery and Murray (2000), Innes (2000), and Harte and Pettit (2000), who defend a parallel reading of Irish literature and other postcolonial literatures.

[5] Connections like these have led Ashcroft, Griffiths and Tiffin (2002: 153) to argue that the European movements of feminism, poststructuralism, and postmodernism have functioned "as the conditions of the development of postcolonial theory in its contemporary form".

[6] There are some theoretical models which bear important similarities to Memmi's and Fanon's evolutionary process of decolonisation. In "New Ethnicities", Stuart Hall (1996a) shows how Memmi's and Fanon's second and third stages can be applied to the current political context of England. Hall focuses on two different phases of England's black cultural politics. The first phase that Hall describes is dominated by a form of cultural politics which became extremely important in the British anti-racist struggles of the 1970s. It was designed to challenge and resist the

stereotypical image of blacks as "the invisible 'Other' of predominantly white [...] cultural discourses" (Hall 1996a: 441). In this phase, different communities suddenly became unified by a singular and unifying notion of "the black experience" as a counter-hegemonic form of resistance. Although Hall (1996a: 442) asserts that the notion of "the essential black subject" is necessary as a first instant of resistance, he implies that this form of cultural politics cannot take the black marginalised community very far. Negritude is not the solution, for it embraces the binary nature of the Western philosophical tradition. For Hall, there is a second form of cultural politics which is the appropriate one for the marginalised community. As he advanced in "Cultural Identity and Diaspora" (1990: 225-237), this is a politics which recognises that all individuals are made of multiple identities, and therefore seeks to negotiate and not obliterate these differences. In this phase, Black cultural politics suddenly realises "the extraordinary diversity of subject positions, social experiences, and cultural identities which compose the category 'black'", and recognise that race is "essentially a politically and culturally *constructed* category, which cannot be grounded in a set of fixed trans-cultural or transcendental racial categories" (Hall 1996a: 443).

[7] In *Culture and Imperialism*, Said (1994: 331) criticises Fanon on the grounds that he does not specify how this idea of artistic decolonisation is obtained, and that his idea of "liberation" is described more "as a process than as a goal". Indeed, Fanon's characterisation of the writer's role in liberating the colonised community is loaded with abstract and ambiguous imagery, as when he describes the liberationist phase as "a fluctuating moment" in which people dwell in "occult instability" (Fanon 1990: 182-183). This ambiguity will prompt postcolonial reformulations of Fanon's idea of liberation by Said (1994: 277) and Bhabha (1995: 38).

[8] In *The Empire Writes Back*, Ashcroft, Griffiths and Tiffin (2002: 4-6) observe that there are three main phases in the development of postcolonial literatures. These critics identify a first stage of writing produced in the colonies "by 'representatives' of the imperial power", such as Rudyard Kipling (p. 5). They go on to identify a second stage of post-colonial writing characterised by its potential for subversion. Third, there is a final stage which marks the development of independent literatures characterised by what these critics call the "abrogation" and "appropriation" of the colonial language "for new and distinctive features" (p. 6). Walder (1998: 77-78) more explicitly applies Fanon's model to writers in the newly decolonised nations of the Caribbean Islands and Africa. The first phase Fanon talks about is exemplified in the "assimilationist" poetry of Francophone Négritude writers such as Senghor. This critic observes Fanon's second stage of cultural decolonisation in the early autobiographical writings of Ngũgĩ wa Thiong'o or the Trinidadian Michael Anthony. On the other hand, Walder notes how the Jamaican poet Louise Bennet exemplifies in her production Fanon's triple paradigm.

[9] Postcolonial theory has tended to elide gender differences in constructing a single category of the colonised. Memmi's writings, for instance, mainly refer to the male colonised subject, and he employs the pronoun 'he' throughout all his formulations. Similarly, very few times, does Fanon focus on women in his theorisation of the imperial process. In *The Wretched of the Earth* and mostly in *Black Skin, White Masks*, Fanon consistently employs the term "Negro of the Antilles" in order to refer mainly to the male colonised subject. That is why he has been widely accused by critics such as Gopal (2002: 41) and Miller (1990: 122) of not engaging with how women might have experienced colonisation, or with how they might have reacted against their oppression. Except for his chapter "Algeria Unveiled", Fanon (1965: 35-67) hardly focuses on women's ability to subvert the system. This essay is one of his few statements on women's role in the liberation struggle, and how they used their veiling in order to challenge colonial rule. The veil becomes, in this sense, a symbol of resistance and not of patriarchal submission. Like Memmi's and Fanon's work, Said and Bhabha pay little attention to female agency and to postcolonial women's writers. Walder (1998: 79) notes how other influential voices, such as Abdul Jan Mohamed, with his *Manichean Aesthetics* (1983), also adopt this tendency. Gayatri Spivak has been perhaps the only

important postcolonial theorist who has articulated the relationship between feminism and the discourse of postcolonialism. Taking into account all this, it is not surprising to find that critics such as Boyce (1994: 80), Lewis and Mills (2003: 2) and Walder (1998: 79) sharply denounce the fact that there is a clear omission of women's experiences from postcolonial discussions.

2

Boland's Initial Steps as a Woman Poet

2.1. Introduction

The emergence of women's poetry at the end of the twentieth century has put and, in fact, is still putting many "definitions of Irish literature at stake" (Allen-Randolph 1999a: 205). Therefore, it is not surprising to find that this emergence has been refuted not only by the Irish audience, but also by the publishing houses.[1] Eavan Boland's work, for instance, has frequently put her in disagreement with a male-dominated literary consensus. She has, over the years, scrutinised, disturbed, and subverted assumptions over gendered identity and the role of the poet. This fact has prompted the great reluctance with which women's writing was treated by the Irish community. In order to understand the barriers Boland has found in the Irish literary panorama, it is essential to gain some insight into the extent to which women poets have often been devalued and defined in restrictive terms.

The relationship between poet and poetry has traditionally been conceived as a relation of power between a male bard and his female muse/emblem. As Gilbert and Gubar (2000: 3-5) explain in their study of nineteenth-century women writers, literature has been considered for long an exclusively male domain. Within patriarchal Western culture, it was traditionally believed that writing was a creative gift of male quality, especially marking off men from women: the author has been predominantly male; it is he who has owned the subjects of the text, those figures, usually feminine, he objectifies in his writings. On the other hand, women were made to think that they lacked creative literary power, and if they ever wrote, their work would be regarded scornfully as a hobby, a genteel accomplishment in the Victorian period like piano playing or needle-point, or as a manly task, inappropriate for women (p. 558).

Women have been denied their right to write literature in general, but poetry has been the most forbidden genre for them. The sonnet was originally a poem in praise of the poet's mistress, and the pastoral elegy was traditionally conceived to express the poet's grief over the death of a brother poet. It is not surprising to find in discourse positions a loquacious lover addressing his elevated, but absent, dead, or silent beloved. In this context, women had had no freedom to be the creative subjects of poems. In her essay "A Room of One's Own", Virginia Woolf (1974: 99) considers the fact that, although the original impulse for women in the early nineteenth century was for poetry, they were all by some strange force compelled to write novels. In this sense, no one imagined that women could find their self-fulfillment by writing poetry. On the contrary, a woman writing lyric poetry would traditionally be associated with insanity. Gilbert and Gubar (2000: 545) explain this point extensively, and summarise it by saying:

> [...] while the woman novelist may evade or exorcise her authorship anxieties by writing about madwomen and other demonic doubles, it appears that the woman poet must literally *become* a madwoman, enact the diabolical role, and lie melodramatically dead at the crossroads of tradition and genre, society and art.

Supposedly, woman's creative potential did not only lead to madness, but also to self-destruction. The well-known Celtic legend of Boann illustrates this point. According to this myth, Boann, a peasant girl, was forbidden by the mayor of her village to contemplate her reflection in the waters of the well (González Arias

2000a: 42-43). The girl, transgressing the order, looks at herself, and consequently, she causes an overflowing of the waters of the well, and she drowns. Therefore, according to this legend, any woman's attempt to define or explore herself (or give voice to her own creative potential), should be discouraged.

Even today, the woman poet in the very act of poetic assertion and self-definition inherits the alienation imposed by the patriarchal canon. Poets such as John Keats and Walt Whitman had no problem in passionately committing themselves to their art. In *Songs of Myself*, Whitman (1995: 54) declares the enormity of his bardic powers: "I celebrate myself,/ and what I assume you shall assume". In section 24 of the poem, he even proclaims himself to be "Walt Whitman, an American, one of the roughs, a kosmos" (p. 110). After a century of Whitman's poem, a woman poet has to overcome many culturally imposed barriers to make an assertion like that. She has to bridge together the words 'woman' and 'poet' in order to achieve the self-assertion and self-assurance of Whitman's lines.

In the particular case of Ireland, Irish women have had to overcome more boundaries in order to write than their female colleagues cross-culturally. This is mainly due to two reasons: (1) this country has been strongly marked by a nationalist tradition which identified the nation with a beautiful maiden or an old woman summoning her sons to maintain her wars and recover her youth; and (2) an overwhelmingly Catholic Church and a patriarchal society (the State and other political/social institutions) which have relegated women's domain to the house with scarcely any participation in the public events.[2] Many early twentieth-century poets and rebels have relied on women as motifs in their poetry, by maintaining the traditional Irish association between woman and land, and by ascribing a female motherly voice that speaks on behalf of an oppressed community. The *Aisling* poetic genre and figures such as The Old Woman of Beare, Shan Bhean Bhocht, Cathleen ní Houlihan, and Dark Rosaleen will be recovered under political aims by poets such as James Clarence Mangan in "Dark

Rosaleen", Patrick Pearse in "I am Ireland" and "The Mother", and Francis Ledwidge in "Poor Old Woman" (Kennelly 1970: 149, 295-296, 305). In this rhetoric of nationalism, Christian allegories such as the Virgin Mary are linked to pre-colonial myths. The nation is typically portrayed as a poor old woman begging for the courageous protection of Irishmen to finally return her purity or dignity to her, of which she has been shamefully deprived by the English. Her invocation of God and religious imagery, especially blood sacrifice, are essential aspects in her discourse. In this sense, whereas England is commonly depicted as a male rapist, Ireland is simply represented as "the female victim whose sexuality is never joyful, but always painfully distasteful" (Armengol 2001: 10).

The interconnection of Woman/ Ireland/ Nationalism/ Catholicism continues to be strong in the period after the foundation of the Irish Free State. When Eamon de Valera became President of Ireland and Fianna Fáil leader, the role of women was further restricted and idealised. Article 41 of the 1937 Constitution offered a narrow and specific view of womanhood. The Irish woman was immediately associated with motherhood and domesticity:

> Article 41
> 2.1. In particular, the State recognises that by her life within the home, woman gives to the State a support without which the common good cannot be achieved.
> 2. The State shall, therefore, endeavour to ensure that mothers shall not be obliged by economic necessity to engage in labour to the neglect of their duties in the home. (Foley & Lalor 1995: 122-123)

This article declared the family as the most fundamental social unit, and women's primary role as that of wife and mother. By reassuring mothers not to be "obliged by economic necessity to engage in labour to the neglect of their duties in the home," de Valera reinforced women's relegation to the private sphere. Their world, as envisaged by the State and the Church, was supposed to revolve "around the twin poles of Altar and Hearth" (Hywel 1995: 25). Women's ideal model to follow was the Virgin Mary, who embodies virginity, sanctity, and submissive suffering. Therefore, they were strongly connected with spirituality, not physicality, and their individual sexuality was replaced by attributes of fecundity. Similarly, all those activities which could contribute to their personal, intellectual, and social fulfillment were discouraged, and the only feminine superiority widely accepted was as regards moral issues.

Taking into account these factors, it is not surprising that the Irish male poet Séan Ó Ríodáin (1986: 45) has expressed his surprise at the very concept of "Woman Poet". In "Banfhile", he explores the fact that poetry is widely considered as a male activity, requiring strength and fatherhood:

> Is it that the feminine turns masculine
> When a woman turns into a poet?
> A woman is not a poet, but poetry.

Ó Ríodáin's phrase "[a] woman is not a poet, but poetry" encapsulates Irish women situation within the Irish literary panorama. As Boland (1995a: xi) reflects in the preface to *Object Lessons*, she begins to resist the apparent splitting of poet from woman, two separate kingdoms of experience and expression:[3]

> I know now that I began writing in a country where the word *woman* and the word *poet* were almost magnetically opposed. One word was used to invoke collective nurture, the other to sketch out self-reflective individualism. Both states were necessary – that much the culture conceded – but they were oil and water and could not be mixed.

Moreover, Boland has to accept that there is not a well-established female tradition in poetry: "Much of [women's] actual experience lacks even the most rudimentary poetic precedent. 'No poet', says Eliot, 'no artist of any kind has his complete meaning alone'. The woman poet is more alone with her meaning that most" (Boland 1995a: 242). Boland observes how Irish poetry, with a few exceptions such as Emily Lawless, was largely male and bardic in formation (p.

134). In this sense, she regrets the lack of a female literary tradition in Ireland, the absence of "an expressed poetic life" of women (ibid).

Boland's impossibility to find female poetic precedents might result from her inability to read native poetry written in Gaelic; this has created what Sewell (2003: 161) has called a "deaf and blindspot" between herself writing in English and those writing in Irish, such as Mhac an tSaoi, in whom Boland would have certainly found an "encouraging example". As Montague (1974: 21-22) has argued, one of the great tragedies for Irish poets who can only write in English is their realisation that "the larger part of [the Irish literary] past lies in another language". On the other hand, Boland's inability to find any precedent in previous Irish women poets is also due to the fact that access to the work of earlier Irish women writers was, and still is, barely adequate (Haberstroh 2001: 11). Nevertheless, one should bear in mind that women's literature in Ireland is starting to be known at present and that increasing research in the last decades of the twentieth century has tried to uncover this work. A close reading of Kelly's 1987 anthology of verse by Irish women shows that women's poetry has always existed since medieval times.[4] This compilation has been able to offer contemporary women poets in Ireland a rich amalgam of very different women writers, whose work reflects in various ways Irish social and political history. Therefore, one might consider that Boland omits and ignores important and valorous voices who widely recorded the anxieties of their sex and who conducted a savage social criticism which was quite subversive at the time.[5] This fact prompts Gerardine Meaney's critique of Boland. Meaney (1993: 144) attacks Boland for ignoring those poetic foremothers that appear in Kelly's anthology, for instance, and argues that, by excluding her female predecessors, Boland "comes dangerously close to deference to the cult of the great man, the [male] poetic personality". This attack has perhaps been sharper by other Irish critics such as Ní Fhrighil (2003), who rebukes Boland for ignoring past and present Irish women poets writing in Irish, such as Eibhlín Ní Chonaill, Máire Bhuí Ní Laoghaire, or, indeed, Máire Mhac an tSaoi, who was an established poet when Boland was beginning to write.[6] Nevertheless, it is essential to bear in mind some contextual factors: first of all, the fact that Boland experiences an extra handicap, as a woman poet who does not master the Irish language and therefore cannot read much of the native literary tradition; and secondly, the fact that much past Irish women's work has only be recovered lately, after Boland started to write in the late 1960s.

The social and ideological constraints imposed on Irish women writers and her inability to find female predecessors in Irish poetry prompt Boland to adopt an uncritical (or rather submissive) attitude at her first stage in her literary career. Boland wrote her initial volumes of poetry when she was attending Trinity College, Dublin, in the 1960s. At that time, women in Ireland were still relegated to the private domestic sphere, and their educational and employment opportunities were significantly limited. As Shannon (1997: 258) notes when recalling her days as a graduate student at University College Dublin:

> The impact of social conditioning was clearly apparent at University College Dublin, where female undergraduates were only 28 percent of the student body. Most were from upper middle-class backgrounds [...], and spent more time worrying about getting a man than in using a very unique and privileged opportunity to obtain a university degree in preparation for a career. (Shannon 1997: 258)

Although Boland was studying at a different institution, she surely experienced this same atmosphere of powerlessness. As her first volumes illustrate, she prefers to make for herself a place among the well established (male) literary canon, by adopting conventional poetic features, rather than by defying them, and so asserting herself as a female poet.

Showalter (1999: 13) argues that the first phase in the literary work of a woman artist is characterised by the imitation of the predominant modes of the hegemonic tradition and the internalisation of its values. This stage of evolution, or 'Feminine' phase, bears great resemblance to the initial phase anti-colonial intellectuals such as Memmi (1990: 168) and Fanon (1990: 178) identify in the process of decolonisation. Memmi (1990: 168) argues that there is first a phase of "assimilation" or "petrifaction", according to which "[t]he first ambition of the colonised is to become equal to that splendid model and to resemble him to the point of disappearing in him" (ibid). In this phase, there is a systematic self-denial, because the colonised does not only try to resemble the "white" man but also he rejects "his true self" (p. 187). According to Memmi (1990: 190), this attempt is proven unsuccessful, for the colonised can never entirely resemble the coloniser. This phase corresponds to Fanon's (1990: 31-32) initial stage of "oppression". Unlike Memmi, Fanon applies more specifically this phase to the literary career of a colonised subject. He argues that, in this first phase, "the native intellectual gives proof that he has assimilated the culture of the occupying power" (Fanon 1990: 178). This is a period of unqualified assimilation, where the writer, in an attempt to overcome his/her marginalised status and become "whiter" or "blackless", is more influenced by the culture of the coloniser than by his/her own distinctive culture. As Fanon (1990: 176) explains: "He will not be content to get to know Rabelais and Diderot, Shakespeare and Edgar Allan Poe; he will bind them to his intelligence as closely as possible".

Boland's initial work, in particular *Eavan Boland Poetry* and *New Territory*, published in 1963 and 1967 at the age of nineteen and twenty-three, is an instance of Showalter's 'Feminine' phase and Memmi and Fanon's 'Assimilationist'/ 'Occupation' phase.[7] Both volumes of poetry show Boland at her most uncritical stance, as she seems to internalise, both formally and ideologically, the poetic conventions of the (Irish) past. In her beginnings as a poet, she defines herself as "a sexless, Victorian" woman, as "a product of nineteenth-century ideas" (Boland 1995a: 218). Significantly enough, Showalter (1999: 13) identifies the 'Feminine' phase as the period from the emergence of the male pseudonym in the 1840s to G. Eliot's death in 1880. In fact, Boland is, as we will see, concerned with nineteenth-century ideas, such as the poet's role, her relation to society, and Celtic myths and legends which constitute the Irish identity. On the other hand, and as Fanon (1990: 178) advanced, Boland reads and tries to imitate the accepted masters of the poetic tradition. Throughout *Object Lessons*, Boland (1995a: 24, 83, 124, 138, 141, 221) recalls how, as a younger self, she 'devoured' books by English authors such as Keats, Chatterton, Byron, Arnold, the Court poets of the Silver Age (i.e. Wyatt and Raleigh); and by Irish poets such as W.B. Yeats, Padraic Colum, and Francis Ledwidge. As she has argued elsewhere,

> I read all kinds of poetry [...]. I also read about poets. I was eighteen. [...] I read about Eliot in Paris. And Yeats in Coole. I read Pound and Housman and Auden. It was the reading of my time and my place: Too many men. Not enough women. Too much acceptance. Too few questions. (Boland 1997b: 24)

All these poets, in some way or another, had simplified women's lives in their work, but they enabled Boland "to internalise a sense of power and control" (Boland 1995a: 191). As a young student in Dublin in the 1960s, Boland could associate with male poets like Derek Mahon, Brendan Kennelly, and Seamus Heaney (p. 27). She could even see Patrick Kavanagh in the pubs and coffee-shops. As this woman poet asserts, "everywhere, at least to my eyes, there were signs of the command and ascendancy of poetry" (ibid). Nevertheless, within this enriching literary atmosphere, Boland could also feel some sense of exclusion:

> There were [...] depravations to be a woman poet in that situation, and I don't want to minimise those [...], especially as the depravations carried some actual dangers to identity. Although there were rich and interesting parts of [the Dublin Literary Life] climate, there was real narrowness. The oral history of poetry, which matters in every poetic community, did exist. But it didn't fit subject matter for it. The woman as poet was very alien to that way of thinking. [...] Male poets would say things like "the best thing about your work is that you would never know it was by a woman". (Interview with Allen-Randolph 1993b: 118)

Boland wants to be part of the poetic community surrounding her, but she knows that in order to do so, she has to conceal the woman in her in order to become "an honorary male poet" (ibid).

There are several significant features in the poems of *Eavan Boland Poetry* and *New Territory* which indicate that Boland is a woman writer in her 'Feminine'/ 'Assimilationist' phase:

(1) Showalter (1999: 19) points out that women, at the first stage in their literary career, do not see their writing as an expression of their female experience. The direct conflict between their vocation as writers and their status as women prompt them to hide their womanhood, sometimes by the use of a male pseudonym, or under the masquerade of a male persona (ibid). This is a feature of Boland's initial work. As Boland (1995a: 65) explains, she adopts in her initial poetry "the properties of the hero", the male voice recurrent in Western literary tradition. Gilbert and Gubar (2000: 15) have argued that the initial stages of a writing career for a woman start in her "searching glance into the mirror of the male-inscribed literary text". This is precisely what Boland does in *Eavan Boland Poetry* and *New Territory*, creating a "male-inscribed literary text". She begins to use her writing as an artistic mirror of the poetic conventions she inherits, rather than as "a method of experience" (interview with Wilson 1990b: 82). With the exception of "Malediction" and "Athene's Song" (*New Collected Poems* 2005: 13, 23),[8] Boland avoids the use of the feminine persona. Since there is no sense of self-awareness in her poems, she tries to conceal her womanhood under an apparently neutral "I" who is in the end male rather than female.

(2) Showalter (1999: 20) has demonstrated that in the 'Feminine' phase, women writers' main focus is to participate in the mainstream of culture, which involves having an uncritical attitude towards their own (oppressive) situation as women. In her initial work, Boland does not only disregard her own female reality, but also perpetuates traditional depictions of Irish women. Her initial poems describe powerful dangerous female creatures (such as Aoife in "Malediction", *Collected*, 13), or passive female objects, ideal icons of eternity

and beauty (such as Étain in "The Winning of Etain", *Collected*, 24-31). In her indulgent stance, she remains faithful to the literary aesthetic tradition, ignoring what she will later call "the real myths" of the Irish woman (Boland 1995a: 12).

(3) Boland also hides her own female identity with the employment of traditional epic topics and conventional poetic concerns. She describes her initial poetry as "a hybrid: half British movement and half Irish lyric" (Boland 1995a: 104); in other words, she internalises two different kinds of poems which were dominant when she began writing in the Dublin of the 1960s. The first "half British movement" poem refers to the metropolitan poem which was influenced by the romantic movement in the nineteenth century (Boland 1995a: 92). This poem, which was "an outcome of British civilisation", proposed a radical relation between an inner and an outer world, becoming "a commanding text of an interior life" (pp. 92-93). At this initial stage in her career, Boland internalises the romantic concept of the poet as "a person set apart from ordinary life", who, as Allen-Randolph (1993a: 6) argues, is specially endowed with "powers of vision and articulation". As we will see in "Appraisal" (*Eavan Boland Poetry*, 7-10),[9] "The Poets", "New Territory", "Mirages", and "Migration" (*Collected*, 7, 9-11), Boland represents poets as powerful "hero[es]", "lions", "birds", or "strenuous sailing men" who inhabit the realm of the stars and constellations.

The second kind of poem Boland (1995a: 104) refers to as "half Irish lyric" is "sharper and more bitter". This kind of poem is more concerned with the external meaning of the poet's life, which Boland describes as follows:

> It was the history of the bard, the prince's friend, the honoured singer. Who made his way from village to village, shifting from praise to invective as the occasion demanded. [...] Who became, reluctantly, a witness to the totality of the British conquest and the loss of the vital language. (Boland 1995a: 92)

In *New Territory*, we also come across this second kind of poem, which is "deep in Irish life" (p. 93). Boland internalises the conventional Irish literary strategy of sublimating and aestheticising the national turmoil. We will see how in "After the Irish of Egan O'Rahilly" (*Collected*, 20-21), for instance, Boland develops the traditional Irish political poem. The communal voice is speaking on behalf of a dispossessed Irish people; it addresses the enemy, the Protestant English, who is destined to be driven from Ireland. Boland recurs to important events in Irish history, such as the overthrow of the Gaelic order ("The Flight of the Earls", *Collected*, 20), the Easter Rising ("A Cynic at Kilmainham Gaol", *Collected*, 16), or the Irish Civil War ("Yeats in Civil War", *Collected*, 19). The "history of the bard, the prince's friend, the honoured singer" Boland (1995a: 92) refers to makes its appearance in the troubadour searching for his patron in "The King and the Troubadour" (*Collected*, 21-22), as well as in those mythical Classical and Celtic figures (such as Oedipus, Isaiah, Paris, and Lir's son) in "The Pilgrim", "New Territory", "The Flight of the Earls", and "The Dream of Lir's Son" (*Collected*, 8-9, 12, 20).[10] Boland's consistent choice of conventional themes and figures of the dominant aesthetic tradition reflect her desire to achieve, not only genuine excellence as a poet, but also the acceptance of Dublin's literary community.

(4) Showalter (1999: 27-28) argues that women writers at this stage develop "innovative and covert ways to dramatise the[ir] inner life", in order to give expression to their repressed feelings. In fact, Boland develops covert ways to dramatise (or give voice to) her inner anxiety. As a woman, she feels she is writing in a denied territory, and therefore, she experiences a fear of failing as a poet. Precisely because of this, the poetic figures in *New Territory* usually encounter difficulties when expressing their own thoughts. Although they are successful in the end, their journey towards artistic expression is, as we will see, continually fraught with difficulty.

(5) Another important feature of *Eavan Boland Poetry* and *New Territory* is the importance Boland attaches to her literary forefathers. Eight of the twenty-one poems in *New Territory* are dedicated to well-recognised poets at the time (Derek Mahon, Michael Longley, Eamon Grennan, Philip Edwards, and Brendan

Kennelly). With the exception of "On Giving a Cyclamen 1961" (*Boland Poetry*, 6) and "Athene's Song" (*Collected*, 23), dedicated to her mother and father respectively, significantly all her poems are written with a particular male-poet addressee in mind. At the same time, some of these poems praise canonical literary writers, such as Yeats (in "Yeats in Civil War", *Collected*, 19) and Shakespeare (in "Shakespeare" and "The Comic Shakespeare", *Collected*, 18-19). These two aspects indicate Boland's anxiety to be included in Ireland's (andocentric) literary canon. As Derek Mahon (to whom "Belfast vs. Dublin" is dedicated to) argues, Boland's praise of male writers indicates her need "to assert herself in what she correctly perceived to be a male-dominated literary culture" (Mahon 1993: 24).

(6) Boland's conservative stance is also reflected in the structure and language of the poems. In her first years of poetic career, Boland's formalism is part of the strategy to show certain artistic 'masculinity'. Boland attempts to master the poetic language of canonical poetry, to achieve the "exhilaration of language" of male poets (Boland 1995a: 27).[11] It seems, as Fanon (1991: 18) asserts, that dominating the oppressor's language affords remarkable power: "The Negro of the Antilles will be proportionately whiter – that is, he will come closer to being a real human being – in direct ratio to his mastery of the French language". According to Fanon (1991: 38), the colonised subject attempts to gain a mastery of the imposed language in order to overcome his/her marginalised status. Similarly, it seems that Boland will be a greater poet by showing her command and assurance with the language of her male poetic ancestors. Writing within a constraining tradition means sticking to well defined poetic forms. Therefore, there is a recognisable regularity in *New Territory* of traditional metrics and rhyme schemes. These poems are usually rhymed, always stanzaic, and they follow the traditional plot structure (a beginning, middle, and ending). As Boland (1995a: 77) states, her initial work was concerned mostly with form, with the shaping of the stanza and the pure line, with the fitting of the rhyme and with finding "a real music for the cadence":

It was a very intense book to write. I understand the impatience some people have expressed about it being formalist and so on. On the other hand, it's too much of a received truth of poetry critics to talk about formalism in a young poet as something negative, or as necessarily covering an evasion of feeling. I don't quite see it that way. There is a fear of feeling in almost every emerging poet. You're not sure what's the proper self and what's simply untransmuted egotism. Somehow the engagement with form helped me to know one from the other. (Interview with Allen-Randolph 1993b: 120)

In order to exemplify the features that characterise what I have called Boland's 'Feminine'/ 'Assimilationist' phase, I have written the following sections which approach her work more deeply. But, before that, I think it is necessary to analyse the ways in which Irish poets, especially W.B. Yeats, influence the initial years of Boland's literary career.

Yeats, as Haberstroh (1996: 60) rightly asserts, has a remarkable influence on Boland's initial work in various aspects. Derek Mahon (1993: 25) explains that when he first met Boland in Dublin, she seemed to be "obsessed" with Yeats, "as if she had to come to grips with this man, in combat or in love". The influences this poet exerts over Boland are numerous. First of all, Yeats attempted to create a national culture by relying on the legendary and mythological past of Ireland. His fascination with Irish myths is represented in lyrics such as *Crossways* (1889), *The Rose* (1893), and *The Wind Among the Reeds* (1899) (volumes collected in Yeats 1889, 1991), in which Yeats shows his interest in Celtic folklore and the oral tradition of ballads.[12] One of Yeats's objectives in his employment of myth was to give voice to a distinctively Irish literary tradition. According to this poet, the Irish themselves scorned their own distinctive culture, because, in their coercive colonisation, they had learned to consider it from an English point of view: "[f]orms of emotion and thought, which the future will recognise as peculiarly Irish, [...] are looked upon as un-Irish because of their novelty in a land that is so nearly conquered that it has all but nothing of its own" (cited by Webb 1991: xxxiv). Thus, he saw an imperative prerogative for the Irish writer to recover those legends of an ancient Gaelic past in order to create an 'authentic'

Irish poetry of its own. Boland resembles Yeats in her constant evocation of Celtic myths, topics, and characters. She retains the magnetic splendour of Celtic legends, such as the myth of the Children of Lir and the legend of Étain. At the same time, she also shows her interest in the Irish oral tradition, with ballads such as "Lullaby" and "The King and the Troubadour" (*Collected*, 14, 21-22). Yeats's attempt to capture Irishness was of essential importance for Boland. She spent most of her childhood living in London and New York because her father was an Irish diplomat. She did not return to Ireland until she was fourteen. In her essay "Imagining Ireland", Boland (1997c: 17) recalls how she felt detached and estranged from her country and her subsequent need to feel Irish. In order to overcome this physical and emotional displacement, she had to reconstruct her childhood and this implied gaining some insight into what to be Irish meant: "The word *Ireland* should have become the name of my childhood. Instead it became the name of my hope, my invention, my longing" (ibid). Thus, Boland felt the need to go back to the literary tradition of Ireland, in order to find her own identity. Yeats, in his aim to portray Irishness, was a powerful model for Boland to follow.

Secondly, Boland inherits Yeats's romantic idea of the poet: the poet is a bard, a special individual with visionary powers. Yeats was a self-declared romantic: his poetry focuses on the individual's expression of emotion and imagination. He viewed the poet "as [a] craftsman and as [a] hero" who has to confront reality by using the creative power of the mind (Webb 1991: xxii). As Webb (1991: xxxvii) explains, Yeats's posture is best described as bardic in "the grand declarative gestures of his rhetoric". He believed in a sense of personal nobility, and built his art around it. In her aspiration to become a well recognised "honorable male poet" (interview with Allen-Randolph 1993b: 118), Boland finds in Yeats's example an appropriate influence.

Besides the concept of the poet, Yeats's influence upon Boland is also observed in her dedication to poetic technique. In "A General Introduction for my

Work", Yeats (1924) explained the importance of form and defended his use of traditional verse forms as follows:

> If I wrote of personal love or sorrow in free verse, or in any rhythm that left it unchanged, amid all its incidence, I would be full of self-contempt because of my egotism and indiscretion, and foresee the boredom of my reader. I must choose a traditional stanza, even what I alter must seem traditional. [...] Ancient salt is best packing. (Quoted in Webb 1991: xxv)

In the same way, Boland develops the strictly regulated and received verse form. Her emphasis on artifice is a legacy of Yeats's formalism, a formalism he justified by saying: "Art is art because it is not nature" (cited by Webb 1991: xxi). This self-imposed discipline as regards poetic technique is recognised by Boland herself, when she explains her initial obsession with poetic form, with "the rhetoric of a callow apprenticeship", "the dissonance of the line and the necessity of the stanza", the fact "that the poem is pure process, that the technical encounter is the one which guarantees all others" (Boland 1995a: 132).

Apart from poetic technique, Boland inherits another feature of Yeats's poetry: the frequent distance he adopts from the speakers of the poems, whether imagined, mythological, or historical. In *New Territory*, for instance, Boland employs several well-known classical and mythological characters (Oedipus, Paris, Lir's Son, Aoife, and Isaiah). By depicting characters of recognised superiority, Boland tries to acquire the poetic authority which she herself lacks as a woman writer at this first stage.

2.2. The poet as hero set apart from ordinary life

Boland's main concern in *Eavan Boland Poetry* and *New Territory* is to explore the poet's role, and to highlight 'his' powers of vision and elocution. Her poetic figures are raised to metaphysical status by their ability to have access to a knowledge that is hidden to ordinary human beings. Boland (1995a: 191) has argued that in her initial years as a writer her reading of the "accepted masters of the tradition" prompted her internalisation of "a sense of power and control". In fact, Boland inherits from Irish poetry its authoritative stance, the inflexible association between poetry and privilege; that is, what she calls "the shadow of bardic privilege", a belief which gave Irish poets "an authority long taken from and renounced by their British counterparts" (ibid). As we have seen, Yeats perpetuated this idea of the romantic poet, in order to portray him both as a visionary and a representative of an ancient, traditional, and mystical past, a more 'authentic' Irish past. Yeats's notion of the Irish artist takes us back, in this sense, to the figure of the druid in Ancient Ireland, a prominent figure within Celtic society who enjoyed high status as a royal adviser and, in some instances, even as a ruler. As Green (1997: 7) explains, Irish druids "were involved in politics, sacrificial rituals, prophecy", the practice of magic, and "the control of the supernatural world". As faithful keepers of the oral tradition, they were considered to be the tribe's history and its identity. In this sense, their role was often intermingled with that of the Bard and Filidh, lyric singers and seer-poets (p. 15). Yeats's romantic vision of this Irish bard/poet exerts a tremendous influence over Boland at this period in her writing. In the poems I am about to analyse, Boland takes us back to a time when bards enjoyed high prestige. Her intention is to portray poets as prominent figures of high status, with a great responsibility towards their society.

In poems such as "Appraisal", Boland inherits this romantic figure of the male Irish bard. As the very title indicates, Boland is going to carry out an official valuation of the role of the poet. Her main concern in poems such as this one is to describe the whole process of writing as difficult and painful, but successful and illuminating in the end:

> The climb
> To consciousness is slow, not to discuss
> The pain. And you must have great patience now
> With my evidence and hero. He is preoccupied
> With waking up, escaping from the truss

Of sleep he has inherited: You must allow
Him youth, and freedoms hitherto denied. (*Boland Poetry*, 7)

As is typical of Yeats, Boland maintains a detached position from the poetic figure she represents. The narrative voice distances itself from the male poet: a figure described as a "hero" who wishes to escape from the constraints of humanity itself, "the truss/ of sleep" in which his community has fallen. The voice demands the national tradition to be patient with this figure, for his access to poetic vision is slow and painful. Boland emphasises that achieving artistic expression and perfection is difficult. That is why the act of writing poetry, like in other poems from this collection, is allegorised in terms of designing and constructing large buildings. Like in "Conversation" (*Boland Poetry*, 12), where the poet "has still responsibility to architect/ His own survival", in "Appraisal", he is represented as a young amateur "in this new and hard cathedral". In both cases, poets are represented as 'architects', professional figures who must mould their poems according to a pre-ordained design or pattern. Poetry is conceived as an art that must follow an orderly arrangement, a skill that is prescribed by its necessity to rely on aesthetic pattern and organisation. In this sense, form acquires great importance for this figure:

He knows that rhymes
Must replace the rhythm, petty words the fair,
Free, elegant confusion, a dripping tap the maelstrom.

Now all his past observances recoil
Upon him. He must understand for
Every scribe and singer with his toil
Of destiny, that incoherence, though the core
Be purest vision, is as impermissible
As silence and less beautiful. (*Boland Poetry*, 8)

The preponderance of a modal indicating obligation, typical in Boland's initial work, indicates that the poet feels compelled to write according to well-defined aesthetic parameters. Form and "rhymes" give harmony, cohesion, and "beauty" to what is apparently confusing and incoherent. Boland conceives the poet as a powerful creature who is able to express a chaotic reality. This figure shows his mastery by expressing his thoughts in a clear and orderly manner. In fact, Irish bardic poets were regarded as skilled and persuasive rhetoricians (Green 1997: 44). For this poetic figure in "Appraisal", verbal skill is also very important. Rhetorical emphasis, the capacity to use language effectively and persuasively, is an achievement. On the contrary, "silence" is "impermissible", for it would be understood as a weakness. In her mature poetry, Boland will highlight more the poet's silences than her ability to achieve declamatory force in her verse. Her objective will be to express a powerless and non-authoritarian poetic voice, whose vision can only be incomplete and partial. Nevertheless, in her initial phase, she feels compelled to rely on form, on what is rhetorically sanctioned.

In his ability to use language effectively, the figure in "Appraisal" distances himself from ordinary people. Poetry is viewed as an art entirely restricted to a professional and learned class. Green (1997: 31) notes how druidic poets were "trained specialists (taking as long as twenty years to learn their craft), set apart from the common people". This special 'knowledge' that characterises Boland's poetic figures runs throughout all the poems in Boland's initial work. Poets are represented as druids endowed with a power of prophecy and bound to fulfil a divine duty. "For what his spirit saw", as Boland argues in "Appraisal", "no word was made" (*Boland Poetry*, 8). Highlighting the difficulties the poet encounters in his journey towards artistic mastery is a mechanism to extol his tremendous achievement.[13] Boland employs the traditional metaphor of darkness in her depiction of a poet, who, enclosed in his room, strives ambitiously with the lines and stanzas of his poem:

> When the room flicks to dark
> And his wrist flicks away the first glass light,
> He cannot see the room inside its run
> Of walls, nor faraway the covers and the mark
> He left upon a waiting page; he has no sight.

> Only a minute goes before, impatient
> And quick-fingered, he unseals the tomb-
> The new bulb fitting tightly in its socket
> The light flares round into the hidden room;
> Then he takes up the book and reads the twice
> Beloved lines, and feels the whetted appetite
> Inside him, gradually loses consciousness
> Until he reads the memory of the lights
> Away into a trivial past of things.
> There is the lesson of that man, who placed his great
> Experience into the pitiless contraction
> Of a chosen word, and watched it wring
> His vision out like drops from cloth: Late
> Is the night, and late his pain before reaction
>
> Comes to him. (*Boland Poetry*, 9-10)

The poet in "Appraisal" "cannot see the room", "he has no sight" and therefore, he is presented as someone limited both physically and also apparently intellectually. As Boland (1997/1998: 156) has argued, "the blind poet is at the heart of the myth of the poet. As far back as Homer, the blind poet is an allegory, not only of outer limitation, but of inner vision". This myth of the blind poet, as Boland explains, is not only a legacy of the Greek epic poet Homer, but it is well rooted in Irish culture. She mentions, for instance, Antoine Raftery, one of the most important poets of the oral tradition at the end of the eighteenth century and the beginning of the nineteenth. According to Boland (1997/1998: 155), blindness was "at the heart of his identity", and this explains "the fame which attended his recovery by the Irish Revival". In "Appraisal", Boland perpetuates this allegory of the blind poet, in order to highlight the strength rather than the weakness of poetic vision; in other words, with a view to stressing "the poet's privilege, the poet's power" (p. 157). The poetic figure in this poem seems to claim, by his blindness, what Boland will sharply criticise as a mature poet:

> See me, the poet seems to say. See me, because I cannot see you. Yet even without this essential quality, I am powerful. Even without the human faculty of sight, I have the divine power of vision. There is a hubris

concealed in the legend which has always made me uneasy. (Boland 1997/1998: 157)

It is this lack of sight ascribed by Boland to her poetic figures that makes them both authoritarian and mystical. Darkness is associated with the poet's lack of external vision and also, paradoxically, with his strength of internal vision. In this sense, it is precisely this physical handicap that makes his later achievements more precious:

> And then when all his hope
> Is fleeced away, and he is bare-backed
> As the first complaining ewes, who meet
> The Spring with sacrifice, he sets his sacked
> And plundered mind to read the words. Ah there
> Is nothing to resemble what he knows
> When lines he wrote in darkness start to flare
> Around his bones, with all the genius of speed
> That words have shouted down a hill in summer. (*Boland Poetry*, 10)

The moment of sudden revelation is represented by an abrupt eruption of lightness. The lines the poet wrote in a dark room begin "to flare" and with them, his "genius" reaches its summit. Poems such as this one emphasise the poet's movement from darkness towards spiritual enlightenment and poetic vision.[14] As Boland (1995a: 101) states, at the beginning she holds the belief that poetry is "magic", and that "to name the lighting is to own it". Although the ultimate fate of the poet is to discover this 'magical' realm in isolation, he is linked in his creative discernment with a literary community that both supports and inspires him. The poet at the end of "Appraisal" reasserts his own value by restoring his sense of kinship and "affinity" with every artist:

> He has been right he finds; he thinks of anglers
> Catching princes of the loch with worms,
> He feels affinity with every mummer,
> And his lines, by rote, his paint, the wranglers

> And the clowns, the wooden stage, where truth is reaffirmed. (*Boland Poetry*, 10)

As is usual in Boland's initial work, "Appraisal" is a narrative poem clearly written with a beginning, middle, and end. The thought is compressed in the metrical framework; that is to say, each stanza contains one description or narrative event. "Appraisal" is written with nearly end-rhyme schemes and it follows the traditional lay-out. In contrast to what I will call Boland's 'Feminist'/ 'Cultural Nationalist' phase, where there is a clear lack of punctuation marks, punctuation is explicit and lines are syntactically complete. On the other hand, there are no enjambments between stanzas, as opposed to Boland's mature work, where sentences will unfold down the page. The use of the present tense, usually simple present, is also a common feature of her initial work. Boland uses it not only to give vividness and dynamism to her account of the poet's journey towards artistic vision, but also to state what she believes to be a universal 'truth'. As Quereda Rodríguez-Navarro (1997: 111) explains, this basic verb form is sometimes employed when the speaker wants to emphasise that his/her statements are timeless: "[t]he facts stated are usually valid all the times", and consequently they have "a universal validity". Boland's use of the simple present is deliberate. She is talking about the role of the poet, a role which is socially and culturally pre-established. In this sense, she is making a universal 'appraisal' which is "valid all the times" and which should be considered as axiomatic and absolute.

As we have seen, the end of "Appraisal" depicts a poet who is firmly integrated within the literary establishment. This emphasis on a male literary community becomes the main topic of "The Poets", the poem which opens *New Territory*. Like in "Appraisal", this poem follows an interesting movement. The speaker begins by depicting the limitations poets encounter when writing, if only to highlight at the end their strength and authority:

> They, like all creatures, being made
> For the shovel and worm,

Ransacked their perishable minds and found
Pattern and form
And with their own hands quarried from hard words
A figure in which secret things confide. (*Collected*, 7)

Poets are initially presented as normal human beings, "like all creatures",
bound to live and perish. Like in the previous poem, their artistic endeavor is
everything but simple, because finding their exact words for their poems is a
laborious task. Nevertheless, these poets are set apart from ordinary life by their
virtue to find "pattern and form", and by their power to see "secret things". Their
special status is reinforced by placing these poets in the realm of the
constellations, rather than in an earthy and human landscape:

They are abroad: their spirits like a pride
Of lions circulate,
Are desperate, just as the jeweled beast,
That lions constellate,
Whose scenery is Betelgeuse and Mars,
Hunts without respite among fixed stars. (*Collected*, 7)

This second stanza equates poets to "lions" and "beast[s]", traditional
symbols of power and strength. Rather than isolated creatures, they are united
cohesively in their project. Their strong sense of literary community is
emphasised by the metaphor of the constellation: poets form a group or cluster of
stars that are orderly arranged in a specific configuration. The use of the
constellations in Boland's initial work is not accidental. As Green (1997: 10)
explains, druidic poets had much knowledge of "the stars and their motion, of the
size of the world and of the earth, of natural philosophy". This link between poets
and astrology is made evident in "The Poets". The process of writing is an act of
deciphering, of knowing how to read the position of the stars. Nevertheless, this
image also suggests confinement. Poets can only write within a poetic tradition
whose tenets are already "fixed", established, and where no experimentation is
allowed. Boland emphasises how, by inhabiting such a closed system, their

access to an 'original' vision is achieved with difficulty. It is precisely because of their imprisonment of insight that their final achievement becomes more valuable and precious:

> And they prevail: to his undoing every day
> The essential sun
> Proceeds, but only to accommodate
> A tenant moon,
> And he remains until the very break
> Of morning, absentee landlord of the dark. (*Collected*, 7)

In the last stanza, Boland identifies poets as suns, stars which will not only survive but will sustain life on earth, as everlasting sources of heat and light. Like the sun which is at the centre of the planetary system, the poets' power, importance, and influence will not diminish with the passing of time, but quite the contrary. Their poetry will remain like an "absentee landlord of the dark", until the "break/ Of morning", when another poet or reader revives their work. The overlexicalisation of terms referring to land and its occupation in this poem are powerful metaphors which bear witness not only to the poet's role in society but also to Ireland's history. Land ownership has been a dominant issue in the colonial situation of Ireland. The plantations this country experienced in the sixteenth and seventieth centuries were re-enacted at the end of the nineteenth century, when the British government carried out plenty of evictions in several counties such as Donegal and Mayo (Quinn 1997: 51). Irish tenants were obliged to abandon their lands and properties, which were occupied by British landlords. Eagleton (1995: 4) explains that, as a consequence of their distinctive historical circumstances, Britain and Ireland have a different way of perceiving land. Whereas in England land is treated as an aestheticised object, in Ireland land becomes rather a political and economic category, as well as a sexual subject (the torn victim of imperial penetration):

The word 'land' in England has Romantic connotations, as befits a largely urbanised society [...]. Ireland also witnesses a romanticising of the countryside, in contrast to the morally corrupt, English-oriented metropolis; but this is more an ethical than an aesthetic matter. 'Land' in Ireland is a political rallying cry as well as a badge of cultural belonging, a question of rents as well as roots. (Eagleton 1995: 7)

Land in "The Poets" is also perceived as a politically and socially relevant category. Boland employs images of land labour and land occupation to explore issues of power and superiority, in short, to examine the sources of poetic authority. In the first stanza, poets are presented as "quarr[ying]", digging, and excavating the land with their "shovel". By owning and dominating this external landscape, they exercise their literary power.[15] That is why they become at the end of the poem powerful "landlord[s]" who "accommodate" a "tenant moon". Boland conceives poetry as a highly hierarchical terrain, an art that is dominated by literary masters ('landlords') to whom mere apprentices ('tenants') such as herself show her devotion. This is well observed in poems such as "Shakespeare" and "The King and the Troubadour" (*Collected*, 18, 21-22), where poets are described as minstrels, "siblings/ Of the court" singing and praising their masters.[16]

This notion of the artist as a person removed from ordinary life is also made explicit in the title poem of *New Territory*, where the poet is allegorised as an ancient seafarer who must dangerously travel to his own destination, "land hove". "New Territory" recovers the Irish genre of *Immram*, which flourished in pagan Ireland, and consists of stories of journeys of discovery and exploration, generally fantastic navigations to the world beyond.[17] In contrast to "Appraisal" and "The Poets", the poetic voice does not maintain a detached position from her poetic characters. From the very first line, the speaker includes herself as one of the men on board:

Several things announced the fact to us:
The captain's Spanish tears

Falling like doubloons in the headstrong light,
And then of course the fuss –
The crew jostling and interspersing cheers
With wagers. Overnight
As we went down to our cabins, nursing the last
Of the grog, talking as usual of conquest,
Land hove into sight. (*Collected*, 9)

Boland's desire to be recognised as a 'national' poet forces her to hide her gendered identity, and adopt the masculinity of the traditional poet. Nothing in the first stanza (nor in the whole poem) tells us that this is a woman talking, quite the opposite: she jokes with her male comrades in the ship, and she gambles and shouts with them in unison. The Atlantic Ocean embodies a savage, wild, natural, and nomadic life, the strength of the poet in the beginning of a sea-journey towards vision, truth, and articulation. Boland views poets as prophets who, like "Isaiah of the sacred text", are "eagle-eyed" to peer down "the unlit centuries" and to "glimpse[…] the holy boy" (*Collected*, 10).

The symbolic portrayal of poets as mariners is recurrent in Boland's initial work. In "Mirages" (*Collected*, 10), Boland also equates poets with "strenuous sailing men" who are able to see "creatures of myth/ Scattering light at the furthest points of dawn".[18] In their sea-journeying and consequent adventurous exploration, mariners and poets are more in touch with the divine, with the unseen. In this poem, like in some others such as "Conversation" (*Boland Poetry*, 11-12), Boland asserts the viability of the existence of mirages and therefore, poets' reliance on magic. Poets should be credited, for they just decipher what, though unseen to most people, is highly relevant to our daily experience. They are figures which believe magic and have "touch[ed] the Grail", but who are unable to offer actual evidence to confirm this mirage. In this way, Boland explicitly equates poetry with magic. As she has argued in her essay "Virtual Syntax, Actual Dreams", "[t]he first poets were certainly magicians. Keepers of secrets. Makers of encantations. Coaxers of rain and harvest. Holders of spells. But the dream did not die with the keepers of it" (Boland 2003a: 26). Certainly, in poems such as

"Appraisal", "The Poets", "New Territory", and "Mirages", Boland keeps this dream of the Irish native poet alive. The poet's access to magic results from his ability to use language efficiently. As Boland (2003a: 26) puts it:

> The idea of the poet, under an arc of stars, at the edge of a harvested field, at the centre of society has a true charm. But the idea of the poet in possession of a particular language to control all these has more than that. Furthermore, the idea that the poet will find the right name for these constellations, will keep the rain away from the harvest or guarantee a firstborn son is compelling. Not because these things give the poet access to magic. But because they give access to power.

In this quotation, Boland is explicitly portraying the poet as a powerful druid who is able to have nature at his mercy by his ability to master language. In her initial work, the woman poet appears as a faithful inheritor of Romanticism, not only in her view of the role of the poet in society but also by following a conventional poetic language and style.

2.3. The poet as pilgrim

As the poems above exemplify, Boland presents poets as heroic figures, as lions and mariners who are bound to travel mysteriously through "trenchant constellations" and dangerous oceans. In this sense, she also portrays the artist as an incessant pilgrim, internalising an important tenet of the Irish literary tradition. As Kiberd (1996: 580) has explained, the Irish Renaissance fostered a concept of the artist as someone "at war with social consensus", "a crusader for some ideal which existed more often in the past or in the future, but rarely in the present". In Beckett's *Waiting for Godot*, for instance, the poet figures as a tramp (p. 537). Synge signed his letters to a friend as "your old tramp" and in plays like *In the Shadow of the Glen* and *The Tinker's Wedding* he also portrayed his characters as rootless 'pilgrims' (ibid). In Yeats's poetry, the speaker usually personifies a displaced Anglo-Irish, "caught wandering across no-man's-land between two cultures" (ibid). The main character in Boland's initial work is a rendering of this wanderer, this pilgrim, who frequently appears in Western epic literature, and particularly in Yeats's poetry. As Haberstroh (1996: 60) explains, Boland's figure bears great resemblance with "the Yeats-inspired voyager" or "the traditional religious pilgrim seeking a way to deal with death". In "Appraisal", for instance, Boland perpetuates the myth of the Irish poet as romantic pilgrim, a "tripper",

> Who has stopped at small, unthought of towns
> Upon his journey. Now he sets his sights again
> Thinking he must watch among the browns
> And grays and scenes of winter pain,
> Until he too is fitted in the scheme – told
> In a secret mystery what is his part
> In this. [..]
>
> He travels in the hills, and there the trees
> And birds, the frozen animals the grass
> Sway with a dancer's rhythm and the ease
> Of centuries. His eyes dim with the pass
> Of cavalcades of harmony, until
> No single thing distinguishes itself
> From any other, not from him: The still
> Hollow, ecstatic time is come – the pelf
> Of genius. (*Boland Poetry*, 8-9)

As a free spirit, Boland's poetic character can harmonise more easily with the forces of nature than with any member of the settled community. The speaker portrays a landscape which is highly romanticised, an Edenic place where the poet can find "the pealf/ Of Genius". Boland portrays an ideal land, a profoundly loved and cherished territory where the poet achieves 'his' self-fulfilment. Nevertheless, in most poems, land is also depicted as a place where the poet cannot live. He feels compelled to emigrate, to go into exile to another landscape where he is to keep his integrity, where his artistic creativity can flourish.

In this sense, Boland's poems recall the voluntary exile of those Irish writers and intellectuals throughout the twentieth century who felt the need to leave a country strongly conservative both culturally and religiously, in order to be creative and defend their ideals. When Eamon de Valera won the 1932 election, he proceeded with a Republican agenda founded on traditionalism, as opposed to Britain's cosmopolitanism/modernisation. De Valera identified with the rural areas as a source of authenticity: rural and Catholic Ireland was 'real' Ireland. With the decision to remain officially neutral in World War II, life in Ireland consequently became even "more inward-looking" (Kiberd 1996: 471). Ireland tried to formulate a foreign policy quite independent from Britain. But at the cultural level, it isolated Irish intellectuals internationally. The 1929 Act of censorship, for instance, tried to prevent innovative thought (Smyth 1998: 96). It was a symptom of a wider censoriousness which attempted to keep a whole culture uncontaminated by foreign influence. This cultural isolation was enhanced by the Censorship of Publications Act in 1946, which aggravated censorship practices (p. 148). As a result of this social and cultural stagnation, many artists and intellectuals left Ireland because they realised that the country was using old imperialist mechanisms in the name of a nationalist revival (Kiberd 1996: 264-265). This is the case of James Joyce and Samuel Beckett, who emigrated to Switzerland and France respectively, among many other Irish writers such as Oscar Wilde, Sean O'Casey, Brian Moore, George Moore, Louis MacNeice, and John Hewitt, for instance (Hurtley et al. 1996: 100).

Emigration becomes the main topic of "The Pilgrim", a poem dedicated to one of the fellow poets Boland met during her university years: Eamon Grennan. This lyric revives the conventional idealist figure of the poet in the Irish Renaissance period, as it presents an artist who must travel alone, sharing the fate of all those birds which are bound to emigrate yearly:

> When the nest falls in winter, birds have flown
> To distant lights and hospitality.
> The pilgrim, with his childhood home a ruin,
> Shares their fate and, like them, suddenly
> Becomes a tenant of the wintry day.
> Looking back, out of the nest of stone
> As it tumbles, he can see his childhood

Flying away like an evicted bird. (*Collected*, 8)

Boland's initial work, as we have seen in "The Poets", is loaded with land imagery, and concepts involving land ownership, property, and spiritual and physical exile. In this poem, the pilgrim is portrayed as "a tenant" in "eviction" who has to abandon his country in search of "distant lights and hospitality". Boland's portrayal immediately reminds one of the landlords and earls who were banished from Ireland from the seventieth century onwards, an image which will be made more explicit in poems such as "The Flight of the Earls" (*Collected*, 20). In his fortitude, the pilgrim is compared to the conventional male hero Oedipus, a classical figure commemorated also in Yeats's poetry.[19] Like him, the poet is tragically doomed to wander restlessly in search for atonement.

The image of poet as pilgrim reappears in "Migration" (*New Territory*), where Boland depicts a community of birds which are moved by the necessity to "embark on every wind". The bird has been a traditional icon used for patriotic motives. Francis Ledwidge was one Revival poet, together with Patrick Pearse and Joseph Plunkett, who strongly engaged in national issues. In "The Blackbirds", Ledwidge recurs to the well-known allegory of the Poor Old Woman in order to incite patriotic feelings (Quoted in Kennelly 1970: 305). This poem illustrates the easy blend of the feminine and the national in the Irish Literary Revival, as it portrays a helpless woman summoning the blackbirds (i.e. the Irish rebels and patriots) to fight for her and save the country from the colonisers. In "Migration", Boland retains the allegorical image of birds to signify the Irish community of poets. Although she slightly changes the notion of Irish rebellious patriots as it appears in "The Blackbirds", the poets/birds of "Migration" are in some sense patriotic figures as well, "literary patriots" as Boyce (1991: 233) would call them. They are depicted as figures which must support and defend the culture of their community. Nevertheless, their uprooted intellectuality causes them to feel uneasiness in the place where they live. That is why they are represented as migrant birds, inner émigrés escaping "towards the sea at night":

Daredevil swallows, coloured swifts go forth
Like some great festival removing south.

Cuckoo and operatic nightingale
Meeting like trains of thought
Concluding summer, in complete agreement, file
Towards the sea at night (*Collected*, 11)

In spite of their heterogeneity and difference, "daredevil swallows", "coloured swifts", "cukoo[s]", and "operatic nightingale[s]" are able to form a cohesive group. Boland's emphasis on a singular and homogeneous community of Irish poets is linked to that cultural nationalist attempt to 'invent' a national literature which integrates differences and unites the Irish people in a social bond. As Lloyd (1993: 43) has explained, according to cultural nationalists such as Daniel Corkery, the writer must be "the people's representative", in other words, he must represent the common identity of the Irish people. He envisages a literary culture which is "the prime agent and ground of unification" (p. 16). The terms of mid-nineteenth-century nationalist discussions are reproduced half a century later in the Irish Literary Revival. Yeats devoted three decades of his life to cultural nationalism. His earlier writings exemplify an attempt to found and forge a nation. Nationalist allegories such as Cathleen ní Houlihan, which Yeats for instance used in his famous 1902 play, are employed in order to convey what Lloyd (1993: 17) names "political coherence", a common identity which overrides class and ethnic differences and unites people in a unique goal: achieving an independent nation. In "Migration", Boland captures this notion of collective kinship. The community of birds record a national unity, what Bhabha (1995: 141-147) would call a "pedagogical" formation of identity that seeks to turn "People into One".

Emigration, exile, the tendency of the Irish spirit to abandon home are observed in the adventurous nature of almost all poetic figures in Boland's initial work: in Yeats's escape "aboard a spirit-ship" ("Yeats in Civil War", *Collected*, 19), in the Gaelic landlords' flight to Europe in 1607 ("The Flight of the Earls", *Collected*, 20), in the minstrel "cross[ing] the world" in search of "his king" ("The

King and the Troubadour", *Collected*, 21-22), or in Derek Mahon's portrayal as a homeless pilgrim with "a rag tied to a stick" ("Belfast vs. Dublin", *Collected*, 14-15). The Romantic movement represents a departure from the attitudes and forms of classicism, and a rebellion against social rules and conventions. These poems develop precisely this image of poets as romantic dissidents, "immoral/ Courtiers in unholy waste" ("Belfast vs. Dublin", *Collected*, 15), whose ethics are contrary to society's established principles, and who therefore feel uneasy in their own country.

2.4. The poet's affinity with nature

Apart from developing the image of the poet as an uprooted traveller, in her initial work Boland also idealises the natural landscape. In the two poems I am going to comment on, "The Dream of Lir's Son" and "Lullaby" (*Collected*, 12, 14), the poetic speakers, clearly male, establish a very close and emotional relationship with nature. In both cases, the natural surroundings are not only personified, but they are also viewed as something which exerts a powerful influence on human beings. In this sense, Boland's initial work perpetuates the idealisation of nature in early Irish poetry and more recently in the Irish Renaissance literature.

Early Irish literature offers a large amount of "nature poems", which, as Heaney (1984b: 181) explains, exalt the untouched and unpolluted beauty of Irish landscapes.[20] These poems exemplify the profound love and admiration early Irish poets felt for nature, and which might have its origin in the sacramental value the Celts attributed to landscape (Green 1997: 24). Although bardic poetry declined under the Elizabethan and Tudor reconquests of Ireland, their tradition did not completely die. There were still Gaelic poets in the eighteenth and nineteenth centuries who gathered in rural communities in the so-called "courts of poetry", where they recited poetry and interchanged material (Praga 1996: 217-218). In the late nineteenth century, this native tradition was brought back by writers of the Irish Renaissance. Yeats, Synge, and Lady Gregory initiated a movement to revive native tradition and folklore (Kiberd 1996: 107). They devoted their writings not only to recovering the heroic legends of Cuchulain and ancient heroes, but also to creating "a vision of the western peasant as a secular saint and Gaelic mystic" (p. 171). The emphasis the Revival movement laid on locality aimed at restoring the confidence and pride in the Irish landscape. Revivalists such as Yeats, Synge, and Lady Gregory were moved by the belief that to know who you are is to know the place where you come from. Yeats's ritual invocation of places is well known. He found his poetic inspiration in what Heaney (1984a: 136) denominates "the local spirit of place", the potentiality of a rural and natural world: "Yeats's sense of the otherness of his Sligo places led him to seek for a language and an imagery other than the ones which were available to him in the aesthetic modes of literary London" (p. 135). In "The Lake Isle of Innisfree", Yeats expresses his longing for a peaceful life close to nature:

> I will arise and go now, and go to Innisfree,
> And a small cabin build there, of clay and wattles made:
> Nine bean-rows will I have there, a hive for the honey-bee.
> And live alone in the bee-loud glade. (Yeats 1992: 35)

This ritual invocation of Innisfree exemplifies the Renaissance trend to romanticise the Irish landscape, especially the western regions of the country, and the world of peasants, farms, and cattle. The pastoral was an urban creation, not only by artists like Yeats, but also by politicians such as Eamon de Valera and Michael Collins. De Valera's nationalist politics sanctified rural life with a view to locating Ireland's national identity in the agricultural community (Butler 2001: 215). He fostered an ideal of Ireland as a pastoral community, Gaelic speaking, and Catholic. This utopia became essential for subsequent Irish politics: "rural Ireland was real Ireland, the farmer [was] the moral and economic backbone of the country" (Kiberd 1996: 492). That is why the Irish national movement for political and cultural liberation has been generally characterised "as more a rural than an urban phenomenon" (p. 481).[21] The revival of the pastoral genre of the bardic tradition and its subsequent idealisation of nature responded to several cultural and political reasons. As Kiberd (1996: 482) explains, the myth of a rural nation intended to undermine the differences in rural communities (mostly between labourers, the gentry, and the new land owners), intensified after the Land Acts of the 1880s. By 1916, a new group was added to the list of victims: the urban poor community negatively affected by "the rising food prices and contracting job opportunities" (p. 491). Later, the object of this rural, Gaelic myth was to forget the atrocities committed in the Civil War "by touching base with an identity perceived, however mistakenly, as native and authentic" (Butler 2001: 215).[22]

Boland's initial work follows the Irish cultural nationalist tendency to romanticise and idealise the natural and rural landscape. In contrast to her mature poems, where Boland will focus more on urban and particularly suburban landscapes, at this stage in her literary career, she is exclusively concerned with a pure and Edenic landscape, which is almost untouched by civilisation. The only poems in which Boland explicitly focuses on urban landscapes are "On Giving a Cyclamen 1961", "February 1963" (*Boland Poetry*, 6, 13), and "Belfast vs. Dublin" (*Collected*, 14-15). Yet, in these poems, towns and cities such as Kilternan and Dublin are highly idealised as places full of "magic" and "reverence", filled with "coloured streets", a "gentle crowd" and "chatter of romance". On the contrary, rural and natural landscapes predominate in her initial work. With the exception of "Yeats in Civil War" and "A Cynic and Kilmainham Gaol" (*Collected*, 16, 19), where the speaker refers to a "wasted place" and "the broken/ Countryside" respectively, Boland offers an idealised image of Ireland, as a place of unpolluted farmlands and wild woods.

This pastoralism of Boland is observed in "The Dream of Lir's Son", one of the best examples of Boland's initial adherence to Irish traditional poetry, not only as regards style, but also as regards content. Following the line of the poets of the Revival, Boland relies on Irish myths, in order to establish continuity with a presumably authentic Irish Celtic past. "The Dream of Lir's Son" is based on the mythic legend of "The Fate of the Children of Lir".[23] Lir, a Danaan deity, married in succession two sisters (Rolleston 1998: 139-142). Although his second wife Aoife was childless, Lir's former wife had given him four children. The ardent love Lir felt for the children made the stepmother jealous and she ultimately decided to transform them by spells of sorcery into four white swans. According to the fate cast by Aoife, they had to spend nine hundred years travelling incessantly from one place to another. The eldest of the four children is the girl Fionuala. Interestingly enough, she is the one to take "the lead in all their doings", nurturing the younger children in the most tender way, and "wrapping her plumage around them on nights of frost" (p. 141). Fionuala is also the one taking the most important decisions. When their unfortunate fate is finished and they turn back to their human shape, they are about to die, due to their vast old age. Fionuala is the one speaking for the four of them, and explaining how she wants to be buried: "Lay us in one grave, and place Conn at my right hand and Fiachra at my left, and Hugh before my face, for they were wont to be when I sheltered them many a winter night upon the seas of Moyle" (p. 142). Murphy (1997: 99) explains in more detail the significance of the literary image of Fionuala:

> Fionuala has the power of speech, and it is she who confronts her stepmother and negotiates the terms of the children's enchantment. She explains the predicament to their father, and it is her voice that articulates the desolation of their exile and that counsels her brothers to draw on faith to endure their suffering.

In "The Dream of Lir's Son", Boland adopts the role of one of Lir's sons whose name is not specified (it should be either Conn or Hugh), rejecting the assertive and self-confident voice of Fionuala. Boland is like the Children of Lir, hidden as a poet under someone else's appearance. The speaker narrates a dream he has had of a bird singing. As he himself will be transformed into a swan by the spell of his step-mother, he unconsciously predicts his coming future. The dream begins in summer, when everything is highlighted by its very abundance:

> I saw a country tree as green as grass
> Clasp the simple daylight in its boughs
> Like love; at last it swelled with fruit
> And to its fertile house a bird brought
> Its house, and sang aloud in leafy splendour
> Until my ears were dazed at its air,
> My human eyes dazzled at its lodging. (*Collected*, 12)

The speaker is praising the natural surrounding: an ideal place where nature flourishes incessantly, and where birds can constantly be heard to the delight of all listeners. Boland is being loyal to those early Irish "nature poems", poems that praise, as Heaney (1984b: 181) explains, a "pristine world full of woods and water and birdsong". This wealthy nature appeals to the senses in such a way that emotions are highly stirred: the speaker's ears are "dazed" and his eyes "dazzled". This is an untouched and unpolluted setting, unaffected by social change and civilisation. Boland uses animistic and humanising metaphors and similes to reinforce the speaker's exaltation of nature. The tree is able to "clasp" lightness "in its boughs" just as the bird brings "its house" to the tree.

The employment of this myth is quite canonical. Boland is writing about conventional topics, as she has made explicit in a passage in *Object Lessons*, where she recounts the exact moment when she wrote poems like this one:

> It is late at night. The room is airless and warm. The overhead light is on, and the coffee jug is empty. I am just a few days short of my twentieth birthday. When I sit down to write, I have an uncanny sense of spoiled identity and uncertain origin. I start to write about a swan. It is a legendary image at first, cloaked in the resonance of a myth. I try the stanzas, the structures. I write down nouns and adjectives. [...] Finally, only when most of what I write has been scrapped, I see the image for what it is. I see a swan that has never been imagined, only received. (Boland 1995a: 105)

The style is equally traditional. The poet chooses her usual combination of trochees and iambs. Furthermore, the poetic language is highly rhetorical. Boland uses what Mahon (1993: 25) denominates "quaint language", that is, an attractively old-fashioned style.

In another poem from *New Territory*, "Lullaby", Boland develops even further the speaker's closeness with nature. As a conventional schoolgirl versifier, Boland follows the pattern of traditional nursery rhymes. "Lullaby" is built upon a nearly regular rhyme scheme (*aabbccdeffgghijj*), similar to that used in the heroic couplet. In this poem, Boland enacts the role of a "young and naughty" boy who is in a process of discovering the suggestive power and strength of nature:

> O nurse, when I was a rascal boy, bold
> February winds were snaffling gold
> Out of the crocuses; there in grief
> For the pretty, gaudy things I'd cry: "Stop thief"
> And you would grumble: "Child, let be, let be."
> Or we would come across a sapling tree
> To discover frost sipping its new blood:
> I'd join my arms around its perished wood
> And weep, and you would say: "Now child, its place
> Is in a merry hearth, not your embrace."
> And one April morning that was filled
> With mating tunes, a nest of finches spilled
> Which slipped its flowering anchor in a gale.
> I cupped one in my fingers, dead and small.
> But late that night you stole to me on tiptoe
> And whispered: "Child, child, the winds must blow." (*Collected*, 14)

The vocative which opens the poem is greatly significant, for it reminds one of those traditional evocations to the poetic muse, or to the beloved maiden of the male artist: Shakespeare's "Oh mistress mine!", William Blake's "O Rose, thou art sick", John Keats's "O Goddess! Hear these tuneless numbers", Lord Tennyson's "O love, they die in yon rich sky", Edward Lear's "O lovely Pussy! O Pussy, my love" are just a few of a long list of examples.[24] In this sense, Boland is imitating the conventional poetic way of evoking someone on whom the speaker is emotionally dependent. Like in this previous poem, animistic metaphors abound. The boy discovers that February winds are dangerous, because they are stealing "gold out of the crocuses"; he finds frost "sipping" the "new blood" of a sapling tree and believes gales to be intentionally destroying "a nest of finches".

This is an Edenic paradise, filled with "flowering anchor[s]" and "mating tunes", but also a cruel and merciless nature which enacts its rage against the weakest. The child's anguish and initiative to defy nature is soothed by his nurse, who continuously calms the boy by telling him that he must keep aside, for "the winds must blow".

Boland's enactment of a male character, the boy, is highly significant. The childlike stance is a noteworthy feature of nineteenth-century poetry by women. Gilbert and Gubar (2000: 591) explain that some women poets such as Emily Dickinson adopt striking distorted images in their poems, as child figures, because of their confusion about their own sense of identity as women writers. Enacting the part of a child, these critics suggest, enables Dickinson to forget her female adulthood and to escape from the responsibilities of women at home behind the mask of a playful and high spirited child (pp. 591-593).[25] In the case of Eavan Boland, it is her sense of female powerlessness, her impossibility to define herself as a woman, even less as a woman writer, which may provoke her childish enactment. In this poem, the child is described as having a tremendous imagination which is constantly thwarted by his nurse. His ingenuity and creativity might be read as an allegory of the author's womanhood: the child's desire to carry out his own intentions may unconsciously hide Boland's own wish to give voice to her own experiences as a woman. The child's ambition is restrained by the nurse, in the same way as Boland's aspirations are silenced by a constraining literary tradition. As the very same title, "Lullaby", indicates, this poem aims to lull the child to sleep. Similarly, Boland's self, her own female identity, is slumbered by this soothing song.

On the other hand, we should also bear in mind that by enacting the role of a child, Boland shows, once again, the great influence Yeats exerts on her initial work. Yeats equated childhood with an ideal of peasantry: both of them were recommended as "zone[s] in which the older forms of culture now jeopardised by modernity are preserved in oral tradition" (Kiberd 1996: 104). Thus, it is not surprising to find that one of this poet's favourite rhymes is "wild" and "child" (p.

102). Boland also establishes a parallelism between childhood and everything which is pure. The child teaches us that the natural thing is to feel affinity and closeness with nature. The boy's world in the poem is the adult poet's heart desire: she would like to live on "one April morning [...] filled/ With mating tunes" with the same childlike intensity.

In "The Winning of Etain", the long final poem in *New Territory*, Boland keeps with the mood of idealising the countryside, as when dramatising the love encounter between the Irish mythological figures of Étain and Aengus: "All about them acorns and dried leaves/ Lay close as gold and silver at a feast,/ Friendly trees shaded them like slaves/ And the sun rising was their priest" (*Collected*, 29). Boland envisages an idealised couple living in a timeless and purified landscape, a perfect and sacred Eden unaffected by social change. In this sense, land is perceived in Boland's work as a place impossible to inhabit, a place the speaker has to leave, to emigrate from. Poets are like Lir's sons, doomed to wander the seas with much suffering and distress. This view of the Irish landscape is counteracted by its romantic depiction as a utopian paradise, a delightful place where the poet can find innocence, bliss and, ultimate happiness.

2.5. Two kinds of Irish political poems

In his exhaustive study, *Nationalism in Ireland*, David George Boyce (1991: 228-258) summarises the three most important forms of cultural nationalism that operated in Ireland from 1882 onwards. The first group Boyce identifies is the "Literary Patriots". One ardent representative of this group was Sir Samuel Ferguson, a member of the Anglo-Irish professional middle class. Ferguson's main interest was to encourage all Irishmen, especially Protestants, to become concerned with the history and antiquities of Ireland, in order to lay the foundations of a worthy national literature. His effort was directed towards fostering Irish literature for literature's sake, and not for nationalist aims.[26] The Irish Literary Revival, as Boyce (1991: 233) explains, followed the steps of literary patriots like Ferguson. This revival was inspired by a concern that the Irish identity (its art, culture and language) was in danger of disappearance. In this sense, their project was to promote the study of the legends, folklore, and literature of Ireland. One clear exponent of this Revival was Yeats, a profound admirer of Sir Samuel Fegurson, whom he described as "the greatest poet Ireland has produced, because the most central and most Celtic" (quoted by Boyce 1991: 234). Yeats and his colleagues (Lady Gregory, George Moore, and Edward Martyn, for instance), wanted Ireland to make a distinctive contribution to the common European cultural heritage.

The second group Boyce distinguishes is the "Literary Nationalists". The leader of this form of cultural nationalism was the Irish protestant Thomas Davis. In contrast to the literary patriots, this romantic nationalist group used language and literature for nationalist ends. Art was only justified as a medium to promote and foster a sense of nationality among the people. According to Davis, the Irish nation was to be defined by its culture, by which he meant its literature, history, and above all, its language. The Young Irelanders were fervent supporters of education, and approved strongly of a school system that taught Irish children all their glories of their past, as well as Irish language and literature. Because literature was only conceived as a means of teaching nationalism and national self-awareness, inevitably, "the nationalistic aspect of such literature dominated and shaped its artistic content. *The Nation*'s poems, ballads and stories were charged with feeling rather than style" (Boyce 1991: 162). In this sense, the political poem was almost limited to the public event and its communal interpretation. James Clarence Mangan's "Dark Rosaleen" and "The Woman of Three Cows", Patrick Pearse's "I am Ireland" and "The Rebel", and Francis Ledwidge's "The Blackbirds" (Kennelly 1971: 149, 154, 295, 298, 305) are some examples of this. These writers were only concerned with public and external issues as subject matters for their poems and their work aimed at inciting patriotic feelings in their readers.

Finally, Boyce (1991: 235) identifies a final group, formed around the Gaelic League, which includes those members who advocated the revival of the Irish language. Whereas Yeats insisted on the validity of Irish literature written in English, these cultural nationalists believed that the only true national literature was that which found expression through the medium of the Irish language. The three most significant figures in this new movement were Father Eugene O'Crowney, Eoin MacNeill and Douglas Hyde, the first president of the Gaelic League in 1893. Like literary nationalists, the driving force behind the Gaelic Revival was nationalism. Hyde resembled Davis in that both believed that the only way to save Irish culture was to destroy English culture (p. 239). Nevertheless, there was an essential difference between both movements. The form of nationalism the Gaelic Union advocated became rather exclusive, in its reliance on "the Irish Ireland" (p. 242).[27]

It is the first and second form of cultural nationalism that Boyce distinguishes, "literary patriotism" and "literary nationalism", which Boland unconditionally assimilates in her initial work. First of all, Boland develops the traditional 'political' poem of "literary nationalism", a poem exclusively concerned with national affairs, such as the fight for cultural and political independence:

> When I began writing, an Irish poem was a very definite, tangible thing. It was as if there was a fixed space where the poet was expected to stand and speak. Right in the middle of the poem – the voice directed in a triangle relation with the subject and object. [...] It was a very potent mix of obligation and oratory. (Interview with Allen-Randolph 1999b: 299)

As a mature poet, Boland views Irish poetry as dangerously conscripted. The national issue, she claims, laid a whole new set of claims for the Irish poet, who had become a communal figure and an eloquent patriot at the service of Irish society (ibid). As an apprentice poet, Boland takes this pre-established role for granted. This is well observed in a poem such as "After the Irish of Egan

O'Rahilly" (*New Territory*), in which a male voice is speaking on behalf of a dispossessed Irish people. Boland adopts the voice of the seventeenth-century poet O'Rahilly (1670-1726), one of the last Gaelic poets who were trained at a latter-day bardic school (Welch 2000: 296). She creates her own version of O'Rahilly's poem "Is fada liom oíche", a heavy-hearted lament of the Irish defeat at the Battle of the Boyne on July 1st, 1690.[28] This battle was fought between the supporters of James II, England's last Catholic monarch, and William III, the Protestant English king. James II and his Irish Catholic supporters (known as the Jacobites) were defeated, and the Protestant ascendancy was confirmed in Ireland. In the kind of political poetry which emerged in the seventieth and eighteenth centuries, a communal voice speaks in the first person on behalf of the Irish oppressed people. He carries out a premonition according to which the enemy (both Protestant and English speaking) will be defeated. One of its most common literary genres was the *aisling*, poems in which the female persona of Ireland (usually represented as a fairy maiden of remarkable beauty) encounters the poet, engages in a dialogue with him, and declaims a prophecy of the return of Catholicism to Ireland.

O'Rahilly develops this kind of political poetry. Most of his work laments the physical and psychological damage inflicted upon Ireland. "Créachta Crích Fódla" and "Is fada liom oíche" were written after the Battle of the Boyne (Welch 2000: 296). "Tionól na bhFear Muimhneach" is an *aisling* describing the Jacobites military preparations in Munster for an imminent invasion. Similarly, in "Mac an Cheannaí" and "Gile na Gile", O'Rahilly depicts Ireland as a beautiful young woman who is mourning the loss of Catholic heroes (ibid).

In "After the Irish of Egan O'Rahilly", Boland reincorporates this theme. The choice of the male persona in the voice of the seventieth-century poet indicates Boland's willingness to perpetuate the bardic tradition. Boland maintains the heartbroken lament of O'Rahilly's poem, by depicting a lonely and devastated speaker who yearns to restore the original condition and privilege of his community, which long before had been usurped by the English intruders:

O if he lived, the prince who sheltered me,
And his company who gave me entry
On the river of the Laune,
Whose royalty stood sentry
Over intricate harbours, I and my own
Would not be desolate in Dermot's country. (*Collected*, 21)

The significance of the reference to Dermot should not be underestimated. As Rolleston (1998: 47) explains, Dermot Mackerval, a king ruling in Ireland in the sixth century, established for the first time an effective central authority, represented by the High King. This figure symbolised "the impulse which was about to move Irish people towards true national unity" (p. 47). By referring to this well-known legendary king of Ireland, O'Rahilly makes explicit not only his desire for an idealised king who will save his people, but also the possibility of an independent Ireland free from its oppressors. His advocacy of Dermot's return is followed by a profusion of references to other Irish heroes and brave rulers who had been defeated in the past:

Fierce McCarthy Mor whose friends were welcome.
McCarthy of the Lee, a slave of late,
McCarthy of Kanturk whose blood
Has dried underfoot:
Of all my princes not a single word –
Irrevocable silence ails my heart. (*Collected*, 21)

The different Irish heroes the speaker refers to belong to the ancient clan of the McCarthy, an Irish family ruling over the Gaelic kingdom of Desmond (south Munster). Of the three names mentioned, McCarthy Mor (the head of the royal dynasty in Desmond during the twelfth century) is the best known. This branch of the family was extinct with the death of the last of that line in 1773.[29] In this sense, O'Rahilly mourns the disappearance of his 'authentic' roots, the death of Irish legendary heroes who made their resistance to imperial rulers systematic. As a communal figure, he must not only express the sorrow of his people, but he must also predict the coming of the new 'Messiah', that "holy boy" who appeared in "New Territory" and will restore Ireland to the Irish. In this sense, his mournful speech gives way at the end of the poem to a more combative discourse, which defies the enemy more openly:

> Take warning wave, take warning crown of the sea,
> I, O'Rahilly – witless from your discords –
> Were Spanish sails again afloat
> And rescue on your tides,
> Would force this outcry down your wild throat,
> Would make you swallow these Atlantic words. (*Collected*, 21)

O'Rahilly's bitter "outcry" courageously confronts the enemy, proclaiming Ireland's liberation. In "Appraisal" (*Eavan Boland Poetry*), the poet is also envisaged as a person who has to keep alive the dream of the Jacobite armies coming to liberate his community:

> O he knows
> That days of such destruction should be passed
> In one another's arms, kissing with bold
> And lovely confidence, planting the rows on rows
> Of promises, until the winter die is cast. (*Boland Poetry*, 7)

The poet is socially and morally determined to remember those moments when the Gaelic world was at its full splendour: "he is born to" keep alive "a calm faced memory", a memory that will feed their anti-colonialist hearts. Like this figure in "Appraisal", O'Rahilly, in his prophetic overthrow of the English government, envisages the coming of "Spanish sails". As a Catholic country, Spain was of great help to the Irish landlords when fighting English rulers. King Philip III of Spain, who was at war with Britain, sent an army of 4,000 men to help the Irish (Canny 1989: 113). Though they were defeated in the Battle of Kinsale in 1601, Spain, since then, was an allied country for the Gaelic Irish. Thus, O'Rahilly, empowered by the help of the Spanish boats, foresees a free Ireland, an independent Catholic nation.

"After the Irish of Egan O'Rahilly" exemplifies Boland's attempt to connect herself with her native tradition. She writes the traditional Irish political poem, which travels back "into the rough angers, the street ballads, into the music of anxiety of a nationalist song [...], into the folk memory of bardic purpose and invective" (Boland 1995a: 104). In this sense, Boland internalises the conventional Irish literary strategy of sublimating and aestheticising the national turmoil.

Whereas in this poem Boland perpetuates the communal stance of a male poet highly engaged in national issues, her stance in this initial work is much more complicated than what it looks at first sight. In other poems from *New Territory*, such as "Yeats in Civil War", Boland questions the validity of the political poem itself. Yeats advocated a new kind of Irish poetry, one which aims to be 'national', which gives voice to Irish national identity, rather than 'nationalist', that sort of political poem which aimed at inciting rebellion. It was by relying on Celtic myths and legends that Yeats wished to locate Ireland's cultural unity. Boland admires Yeats's ability to escape from the horrors of war by his inhabiting a world of fantasy and imagination. Mostly in his older years, Yeats was open to the receipt of public affairs and he was even elected as a Senator (Boland & Mac Liammóir 1971: 97). Nevertheless, in his poetry, he distances himself from the external political conflict, adopting a non-committed perspective. This is clearly observed in his collection of poetry *The Tower* (published in 1928). In the long lyrical poem that gives the title to this volume, Yeats rejects any involvement in public affairs:

> It is time that I wrote my will;
> I choose upstanding men
> That climb the streams until
> The fountain leap, and at dawn
> Drop their cast at the side
> Of dripping stone; I declare
> They shall inherit my pride,
> The pride of people that were

Bound neither to Cause nor to State. (Yeats 1991: 133)

By shutting himself away in his tower, Yeats makes explicit his contempt towards the conflictive reality. He describes the Civil War as an incongruous event, characteristic of an age in which moral values are impaired and worn-out: "What shall I do with this absurdity –/ O heart, O troubled heart – this caricature,/ Decrepit age that has been tied to me/ As a dog's tail?" (p. 129). In this sense, poems such as "The Tower" explicitly announce Yeats's deliberate distance from political issues, from a world in which people are only "rage-driven, rage-tormented, and rage-hungry" (p. 141). Adopting this 'apolitical' positioning allows him to see with more clarity and arrive at the conclusion that the fighting patriot struggles for an unrealistic ideal, "plunges towards nothing, arms and fingers/ Spreading wide/ For the embrace of nothing" (ibid). The only way to escape from this unbearable and "senseless tumult" surrounding him is to cultivate his wits, to keep his soul alive (ibid).

Fed by the romantic ideas about Irish poetry, and under a clear Yeatsian influence, Boland writes "Yeats in Civil War", a poem that honours Yeats as "the poet-explorer of the imagination" (Haberstroh 1996: 61). By writing the poem following the verse form of the Shakespearean sonnet, Boland pays homage to Yeats, who was an occasional sonneteer (Strand & Boland 2000: 58).[30] The first quatrain portrays him as adopting a deliberated spiritual and physical reclusion in Thoor Ballylee, by "exchan[ging] the sandals/ Of a pilgrim for a Norman Keep/ In Galway" (*Collected*, 19). The speaker praises Yeats for disengaging from the quest for the sacred ideal of the State (an aspiration that moved those rebels of the Easter Rising and their subsequent followers in the Civil War), by taking refuge in his inner imaginary world:

Somehow you arranged your escape
Aboard a spirit-ship which every day
Hoisted sail out of fire and rape,
And on that ship your mind was stowaway. (*Collected*, 19)

Yeats's "spirit-ship" allows him to sail to a 'foreign' country, to another realm of existence. He is elevated, "hoisted", as those lions in "The Poets" which were lifted to "Betelguese and Mars" (*Collected*, 7). This metaphor reminds one of Yeats's "Sailing to Byzantium", in which the poet imaginatively sails the seas and goes "To the holy city of Byzantium", to a lost civilisation of "Monuments of unageing intellect" and "Grecian goldsmiths" (Yeats 1991: 128-129). While the sun ascends over a devastated and destroyed land, the poet finds comfort in "the smell of honey" "at every door and turn". By portraying Yeats's powerful imagination, his ability to find reprieve from a world of violence, Boland makes explicit, once again, her concept of the Irish poet, as a Romantic figure, a bard removed from the commonplace. Yeats exemplifies the ideal poetic figures Boland depicts in "New Territory" and "The Poets". He is raised to the highest status ever possible, as she makes explicit in the final couplet of the poem:

> [...] Whatever we may learn
>
> You are its sum, struggling to survive –
> A fantasy of honey your reprieve. (*Collected*, 19)

In this sense, Boland's attitude towards the role of the national poet is contradictory. As we have seen, she adopts O'Rahilly's eloquent patriotism in her poetry. On the other hand, she shows her indebtedness to Yeats, defending his immersion within a private world of emotions and his rejection to writing the traditional political poem. The contradictory pulls experienced by Boland can be summarised as follows: whether to follow the kind of art advocated by "literary nationalists" such as Thomas Davis, a poetry whose main aim is to foster political awareness; or whether to imitate "literary patriots" such as Yeats, whose work mainly intended to create a worthy national literature that could compete on equal terms with European culture (Boyce 1991: 321). The fact that in "After the Irish of Egan O'Rahilly" she employs the traditional political poem she rejects in other poems in the volume suggests that Boland is confused about the kind of poem she should write. In her initial years as a writer, Boland imitates the prevailing modes of the poetic tradition, but she encounters difficulties, as whether to follow O'Rahilly (in his strict nationalist political poems) or Yeats (in his rather privatised and personal speech). Nevertheless, in spite of this confusion, what is clear is that Boland maintains an uncritical attitude towards notions such as 'Irishness' and 'national belonging'. In contrast to her more mature production, the woman poet takes for granted the concept of the nation. That is why, like most of her Irish (male) predecessors, her work attempts to honour the memory of those heroes who, throughout history, have taken an active role in the formation of the Irish nation. I will analyse this aspect in the following section.

2.6. Commemorating lost heroes

As was hinted at in "After the Irish of Egan O'Rahilly", a very important constitutive aspect of Boland's initial work is the remembrance of lost heroes and defeated Irish warriors. This is more explicitly manifested in "The Flight of the Earls" and "A Cynic at Kilmainham Gaol" (*New Territory*), where Boland views poetry as a nostalgic recollection of the past history of Ireland. In both poems, the poet is conceived of as a worshipper, a voice that must honour and pay tribute to those who have fought for Ireland's independence.

In "The Flight of the Earls", a poem dedicated to Brendan Kennelly, Boland mentions one of the events which drastically changed Irish society: the expropriation of land property to all Gaelic Catholic landlords by the British government in 1603 and their subsequent flight to Europe in 1607. Its very title reminds us of Yeats's imaginary flight "aboard a spirit-ship" but, in contrast to this poet's liberating escape, the flight of the earls suggests everything but a journey in search for freedom. The most significant part of the poem is the final stanza, where Boland makes explicit her wish to mourn their death and exile:

> Whether our own were foolish or wise
> Hardly concerns us; death ran away with our chances

> Of a meeting, yet we strain our eyes
> Hoping perhaps just one with his golden flounces
> Has outwitted theft.
> So we are left
> Writing to headstones and forgotten princes. (*Collected*, 20)

Like in "Yeats in Civil War", Boland uses the plural form of the first person pronoun, in order to place herself within the Irish literary tradition and with a view to conveying a sense of poetic comradeship. But in this poem, this pronoun also indicates Boland's wish to include herself within Ireland's history, and her desire to express a common national identity. Boland mourns the "forgotten princes", the Old English and Gaelic Earls, and asserts that she, as her colleagues, cannot judge if they were "foolish" or "wise" in their fight. Although she is distanced from her own past, from her own ancestors, the poetic voice makes clear her wish to immortalise them in "headstones", by commemorating them through poetry. As she argues in "The Gryphons", "perennial stones" can survive "the prospect of a living feast" (*Collected*, 8). Her poem, in this sense, becomes a "headstone", a national monument that outlives and commemorates her ancestors. Boland is giving voice to the typical view of Irish history, in which, according to Eagleton (1995: 190), a misdeed can never be forgotten by the passing of time "but is doomed ceaselessly to re-enact itself" (Eagleton 1995: 190). Like in "The Pilgrim", in which the traveller restlessly stalks through the centuries in search of expiation, the speaker in this poem feels bound to constantly remember the expelled Irish earls. Eagleton (1995: 190) points out that a road sign in Donegal today reads 'To the Flight of the Earls', as though this event of 1607 is incessantly happening in the present. Britain, by contrast, lacks any road signs which read 'To the Execution of Charles I', 'To The Industrial Revolution', and so on (ibid). Boland seems to be consciously perpetuating this Irish concept of suspended time, in which past history and present reality are intermingled. By doing so, she keeps her national past alive, by vividly bringing to the fore of her poems certain issues which are at the heart of the national identity.

This act of worship and elegy is continued in "A Cynic at Kilmainham Gaol". In this poem, Boland shares the fate of those imprisoned and sentenced to death by their involvement in the Easter Rising. Kilmainham jail is an emblematic place of the Republican movement, a sentimental place that symbolises Christian martyrdom. Boland seems at first to agree with Yeats on viewing the shedding of blood as a useless and futile struggle. Her apparent skepticism is indicated by the fact that she identifies herself in the title as a "cynic". Nevertheless, this poem shows an ironic contrast. Like in "The Flight of the Earls", her attempt is not to judge the futility or appropriateness of their actions, but to remember and thereby commemorate these defeated leaders. In this sense, the poem is written in a highly pessimistic and melancholic tone. Boland attempts to understand the ideal which moved the rebels, to decipher their feelings and aspirations:

> For those imprisoned here this was a small
> Consoling inland symbol – how could their way be
> Otherwise discovered back to the western sea-board?
> How could they otherwise be free in prison
> Who for more than forty years have been shot through
> To their Atlantic hearts? (*Collected*, 16)

Everything in the jail reminds Boland of those prisoners from the Rising: the "gaslamp in the dark" was, she imagines, a "[c]onsoling inland symbol" for the rebels, who saw in this light imagery a sign of comfort, a slight hope that their insurrection was not futile. Boland seems to imply that these rebels were, in their nationalist ideal, a race of resurrected Gaelic heroes from "the western sea-board", the regions in Ireland where people, even at present, keep with more perseverance their Irish traditions and language. Like that figure in "After the Irish of Egan O'Rahilly" who described his words as "Atlantic", these rebels are equated with "Atlantic hearts". In both poems, the ocean evokes the invincible nature of Irish heroes, their strength and courage in their fight for national independence. Boland's employment of rhetorical questions to convey all these meanings is significant. Dramatic effect arises from the fact that no answer is provided for such questions. Nevertheless, as Lloyd (1993: 65) asserts when analysing a poem by Yeats, "[t]he triumph of rhetoric is for a rhetorical question to become an unquestioned fiat". Although Boland identifies herself as a "cynic" in the title, these lines offer support and encouragement for their engagement in the national cause. The speaker's memory is also an act of veneration, as she makes explicit at the beginning of the second stanza:

> But in this wizened
> Autumn dark, no worship, mine or yours
> Can resurrect the sixteen minds. (*Collected*, 16)

The speaker feels limited by the fact that her "worship" cannot ultimately bring these leaders back. Nevertheless, this act of faithful devotion that Boland claims to be worthless is practiced in the following lines:

> […] O those,
> Perhaps (Godspeed them) saw the guns with dual
> Sight – seeing from one eye with the tears they chose
> Themselves the magic, tragic town, the broken
> Countryside, the huge ungenerous tribe
> Of cowards – and the one laughing eye saw
> (God help them) growing from their own graves to jibe
> At death, a better future, neither tear nor flaw. (*Collected*, 16)

Under an urgent need to keep their memory alive, Boland feels bound to imagine the complementary ideals which moved the rebels to use the guns. On the one hand, these prisoners fought for a "broken countryside", for the misadventure of a country which longed to be independent. The poetic speaker accentuates their martyrdom by mentioning how they were left alone in their action. Fitzpatrick (1989: 196) explains that only a minority of activists within Sinn Féin, the Gaelic League, the Irish Republican Brotherhood, and the Irish Volunteers contributed to the army of 1916. The "ungenerous tribe of cowards" referred to in the poem alludes to the Irish majority who did not get involved in the insurrection out of fear and skepticism. The second ideal that moved these rebels to fight, Boland imagines, was the vision of "a better future", where there would be "neither tear nor flaw". They believed that the shedding of blood, in Pearse's words, was "a cleansing and a sanctifying thing" (Fitzpatrick 1989: 198) that would lead to the eventual attainment of the Irish Free State. Encouraged by this visionary future, they do not fear death. In "Myth and Motheland", Kearney (1985: 65) has explained the importance that Christian martyrdom had in fuelling the Irish nationalist struggle. Boland's sentimental veneration for the martyrs in the Easter Rising keeps this patriotic sentiment alive. Her attitude towards their quest for national liberation is ultimately uncritical. As Boland (1995a: 63) has later admitted:

> [...] the nation, at least for a time, was a definite and sharp reality. [...] I looked at the shamrocks, the wolfhounds, even the crude likeness of the 1916 patriots with uncritical eyes. I listened to and used the dialect of patriotism. *Martyr. Sacrifice. Our own.* And if there was a hidden drama, to some extent it was concealed by the sheer eloquence of the cause and my own need for that eloquence.

It is this "dialect of patriotism" that Boland maintains not only in "After the Irish of Egan O'Rahilly" but also in "A Cynic at Kilmainham Gaol".

2.7. Acceptance and servitude: uncritical representations of women

While few poems in Boland's initial work focus on women, Haberstroh (1996: 61) notes that in those that do so "Boland [has] adopted the poetic stereotype of women, which she would later argue, reduced and simplified them". In fact, Boland retains traditional depictions of Irish women in myth, as passive objects, ideal symbols of eternity and beauty, or powerful and dangerous creatures. As Gilbert and Gubar (2000: 20-30) explain, two opposed female images have prevailed in male texts. The most recurrent figure is the ideal woman, the eternal icon of female purity, an "angel in the house", who has no story to tell, and whose virtues are contemplation, selflessness, and delicate beauty (pp. 20-26). At the other extreme, we may encounter the supernatural monstrous woman, who threatens "to replace her angelic sister", and who is empowered with a bewitched and mysterious nature (pp. 27-30).

Boland maintains this first literary convention of the woman as a beautiful angelic Madonna, wholly passive, contemplative, submissive, graceful, and selfless. This is observed in the long final poem of *New Territory*, "The Winning of Etain" (*Collected*, 24-31), where Boland focuses on the beautiful, passive, and speechless Celtic figure of Étain. Written in octaves, the poem narrates the fairy battle of two men, Fergus and Aengus, to win Étain's love, ending with Aengus's victory as he and Étain escape.

On the other hand, Boland perpetuates the malevolent and monstrous female figure of the literary tradition in "Malediction" (*Collected*, 13). In this poem, based on the mythical legend of the Children of Lir, we hear Aoife's addressing one of Lir's sons, in the process of casting on her step-child a spell which gives him the shape of a white swam. Her speech is highly authoritarian and emotional; she is obviously moved by anger and hatred, jealousy and cruelty. Boland seems to feel an alluring attraction to Aoife due to her power, her bewitched and mysterious nature, and her ability to defy her husband's power. Her strength almost seems 'masculine', if we compare her to the usually passive and silent female figures of traditional Western literature.[31]

By employing passive and beautiful as well as strong and fierce female figures of Celtic legends, Boland shows her need to explore traditional female stereotypes. Before subverting the inherited myths, she needs to discover and dig into the damage which this tradition has exerted upon women. As she explains in her semi-autobiographical prose work:

> Then why did I not walk away? Simply because I was not free to. For all
> my quarrels [...], I needed to find and repossess that idea [the conservative

stereotypes of women] at some level of repose. Like the swimmer in Adrienne Rich's poem "Diving into the Wreck", I needed to find out "the damage that was done and the treasures that prevail". (Boland 1995a: 146)

In order to observe how Boland, in contrast to her mature work, maintains a highly uncritical attitude towards male representations of women in any form of artistic representation, I have chosen to analyse "From the Painting *Back from Market* by Chardin" (*New Territory*). As Boland has admitted, her mother has exerted a great influence in her poetry (interview with Allen-Randolph 1993b: 117). She was a painter, and this originated Boland's later enthusiasm with great artists such as Chardin, Renoir, Van Eyck, and Degas, whose paintings will be consistently mentioned in her poems. "From the Painting *Back from Market* by Chardin" constitutes one of the few poems in Boland's initial work, together with "The Winning of Etain", "Malediction", and "Athene's Song", to have a woman at its main topic. In contrast to a later poem which focuses on another painting by Chardin, "Self-Portrait on a Summer Evening" (*Collected*, 129-130), Boland includes the artist's name in the title, revealing his importance and authority (McGuckian 1993: 31). This woman is described from a male perspective, an "I" who gazes at the painting as Chardin had gazed at the woman. The persona does not identify with this female figure, but rather stays at a great distance. In this sense, Boland describes her from a detached position:

> Dressed in the colours of a country day –
> Grey-blue, blue-grey, the white of seagull' bodies –
> Chardin's peasant woman
> Is to be found at all times in her short delay
> Of dreams, her eyes mixed
> Between love and market, empty flagons of wine
> At her feet, bread under her arm. He has fixed
> Her limbs in colour, and her heart in line. (*Collected*, 17)

The woman, depicted as wearing a dress in "the colours of the country day", seems to be trapped in the phrase "Grey-blue, blue-grey", where the adjectives are interwoven. This antistrophe emphasises the persona's consignment. Furthermore, the woman is not portrayed as an independent person, as a subject carrying out actions, but as an object. This justifies the use of the genitive ("Chardin's peasant woman"), which implies possession. The passive construction "is to be found" reinforces the woman's submissive stance, her deprived condition to be the subject of the poem, and her status as a mere decorative object.[32] The "I", the gazer of the painting, is the one that 'finds' this woman. On the other hand, Chardin, in contrast to the female figure, appears as an active agent, fixing "her limbs in colour, and her heart in line". Mahon (1993: 25) asserts that "her heart in line" is "a good if unintentional pun: this faithful wife, domestic, whatever she is, is not about to step *out* of line". Not only are the woman's feelings and intelligence insignificant to the artist's eyes; her "limbs", that is to say, her body, is reduced to "colour". The woman's physicality is only to be seen by the gaze. Just as limbs ("hindlegs") are sold in the market, women's hearts become a sort of buying and selling property. Thus, Chardin circumscribes the woman in his work of art both physically and spiritually, and thus reaffirms the basic assumption underlying all male-dominated Western philosophical discourse that a postulating subject is capable of using the gaze in order to show his mastery (Moi 1991: 180).

This woman's solidification seems to be interrupted in the second stanza, where we observe for the first time female action:

> In her right hand, the hindlegs of a hare
> Peep from a cloth sack; through the door
> Another woman moves
> In painted daylight; nothing in this bare
> Closet has been lost
> Or changed. (*Collected*, 17)

Although this other woman is presented in motion as an agentive subject, her action only occurs in "painted daylight", and therefore her movement is determined by the painter's gaze and the degree of lightness he decides to give to his painting. Furthermore, this woman can only move in a "bare/ Closet", that is, she is exposed to view in the enclosed cabinet of the drawing. Since both women have been simplified in Chardin's painting, Boland introduces her voice for the first time, mediating on the imprisoning functions of art and myth: "I think of what great art removes:/ Hazard and death, the future and the past,/ This woman's secret history and her loves" (*Collected*, 17). Boland realises the necessity to incorporate the silent and untold lives of women, which are not portrayed in the painting. Her concern for what the poem cannot grasp, what lies outside artistic representation, will be one of Boland's most important guiding motives in her mature work. Nevertheless, Boland eventually remains uncritical towards Chardin's "great" representation. As McGuckian (1993: 31-32) explains, she simply offers her "opinion rather than a personal distortion or revision", by describing in detail the canvas for more than half the poem. In the last stanza, Boland extends the cause of the woman's simplification: it is not only in Chardin's painting where her inner life is omitted, but also in the public setting of the market:

> And even the dawn market, from whose bargaining
> She has just come back, when men and women
> Congregate and go
> Among the produce, learning to live from morning
> To next day, linked
> By a common impulse to survive, although
> In surging light they are single and distinct,
> Like birds in the accumulating snow. (*Collected*, 17)

The speaker implies that it is also in real life where this woman cannot see her desires fulfilled, where her heart is fixed "in line" and dreaming is the only possible escape. Boland incorporates men in the picture and, advancing her mature work, she asserts that it is their very ordinariness, their human "impulse to survive", which makes them "single and distinct". In any case, her description is everything but ordinary. Keeping with the mood of her initial work, the poet offers a very romantic image of these poetic figures. Men and women are living in a cruel capitalist society concerned only with the public exchange of "the produce". In this setting, they are compared to birds imprisoned in an asphyxiating snow. As McGuckian (1993: 31) notes, this final image coalesces with the animal imagery observed throughout the poem. In the same way as the "seagulls" seem to be unable to move in the canvas and the "hindlegs of a hare", which enable the animal to run fast, are enclosed in a cloth sack, the birds are confined in "the accumulating snow". This imagery of entrapment suggests the imprisoning function of art, both for men, and especially for women. Boland does nothing to subvert this imprisonment, or include these women's daily lives and experiences in her poem. Therefore, her stance towards Chardin's canvas is an indulgent one, in contrast to the subversive attitude she will take in her later poems, where she will criticise male portrayals of falsifying women.

2.8. A dispossessed and submissive female voice

As we have seen at this stage in her literary career, Boland is mostly concerned with the role of the poet and her mastery over poetic language and aesthetic tenets. Nevertheless, and as the poet admits in *Object Lessons*, in spite of "the acute sense of liberation which a command of language and technique brought to me, [this] was offset by a growing sense of oppression" (Boland 1995a: 25). In poems such as "February 1963" (*Boland Poetry*, 13) and "Athene's Song" (*Collected*, 23), we can observe this "sense of oppression". Interestingly enough, the poetic voice in these poems is explicitly female, and we can even identify it with Boland herself. In contrast to the authority and power of the male poetic voices in "New Territory" and "After the Irish of Egan O'Rahilly", here, the speaker is clearly dispossessed and/or eventually submissive.

In "February 1963", the poetic voice seems to be that of a young girl, Boland herself at the age of eighteen. Although no explicit references are given to the sex of the speaker, some contextual knowledge helps us reach this conclusion. Boland returned to Ireland at the age of fourteen, after a long childhood exile in

London and New York. Her first poetry, as she has put it, is an attempt to "say all the ambiguities, awkward regrets, and distances of [her] childhood. It wants to say a country" (Boland 1995a: 93). Boland's obsession with belonging to her own country, with being recognised as authentically Irish, needless to say, being accepted as an Irish woman poet, is all observed in this poem. "February 1963" is unique in Boland's initial work, because, in contrast to the poems mentioned above, it explicitly expresses her uncertainty and dispossession as a young girl back in her native land. The speaker is described as standing alone in St. Stephen's Green, at the very heart of Dublin. In this context, she narrates an encounter with a mysterious man who asks her to come back to him:

> For twenty days the wind blew from
> The East without a taste
> Of summer, let alone of spring. At last
> Though, April came and, unashamed for past
> Caprice, the sunlight faced
> On Stephen's Green, and it was warm.
> My lost love came across the grass,
> His head as bright as day,
> He came to me and said: 'Will you not come
> To me again, and spin a bridge from
> Frost to April, so we'll betray
> The sour tradition, that a great thing must but pass'. (*Boland Poetry*, 13)

Like in "Lullaby" and "The Dream of Lir's Son", the speaker establishes a very close relationship with nature. Her emotions are described in terms of natural phenomena such as the passing of seasons. Winter symbolises her current desolation and loneliness, whereas the coming of summer and spring brings a promise of happiness and hopefulness. The warmth of sunlight therefore parallels the miraculous arrival of the speaker's "lost love", a man who seems to possess all the power and self-confidence she lacks. By describing "[h]is head as bright as day", Boland immediately links this figure with those poets in "The Poets" and "New Territory" who were equated to the "essential sun" and who were able to "peer down the unlit centuries". Similarly, in this poem light indicates the strength and power of the (male) literary tradition. As Boland (1997c: 16-17) has argued in her essay "Imagining Ireland", because of her childhood exile, she returned to Ireland without a clear sense of where she belonged. Her yearn to identify herself as Irish is fuelled by reading the accepted masters of the Irish national tradition. Her "lost love" is therefore Ireland, that country she has 'lost' by going into exile and which she finds the need to recover, at least by reading and memorising poems by romantic nationalists such as Yeats. As Boland (1995a: 77) admits, she finds "a peculiar indignity [...] in the silence of my childhood [...]. Lacking an idiom, I had lacked a place, [...] I had been silent". When she discovers Yeats, she began to imagine what it 'truly' means to be Irish, to read poems that, for the first time, fitted into place. The man she encounters in the park, an allegory of Irish poets such as Yeats, seems to offer this young girl the sense of stability she aspires to. He urges her to keep the dream of "the great thing" alive, to defy the traditional assumption that her (Gaelic) roots are irremediably destroyed by the imperial intervention. Yeats's poetry, as we have seen, attempts to capture a native 'authenticity', a pure and uncontaminated 'Irishness'. By turning to this man, therefore, Boland might heal her injured identity:

> And I am in the park, looking for in this
> Man, (as though his eyes
> Will issue it, his hand quite suddenly uncover
> It), my eighteenth winter, so that I can discover
> Who in me once prized
> His love and every passionate, possessive kiss.
> But neither he, nor I, have found me here.
> And I must still be found:
> I am not in his memory, nor I am on
> The grass behind me nor on that I'll stand upon.
> Only on this green ground
> Alone, my head upon the breast of eighteen years. (*Boland Poetry*, 13)

The appearance of the conjunction 'and' twice in this second stanza in order to introduce verse lines is, as we will see, a very characteristic feature of Boland's mature poetry. In this poem, it emphasises the speaker's anxiety to find in this man her own sense of identity, her "eighteenth winter". Boland yearns to recognise herself in those books that she 'devoured' as a young girl, those poems by English authors such as Keats, Chatterton, Byron, and Arnold, and by Irish poets such as Yeats, Padraic Colum, and Francis Ledwidge. This andocentric literary tradition is expected to compensate her sense of dispossession. As Boland (1995a: 102) has explained, she was drawn to their ability to master poetic language, in the belief that "the idea of place [is] something language could claim even if ownership had been denied". Nevertheless, these poets had, in some way or another, simplified women in their work, either by treating them as poetic ornaments, whose 'love' must be won (remember "The Winning of Etain"), or as national emblems, mere mouthpieces and ornaments. It is, therefore, unsurprising that Boland cannot identify herself with these female images. Neither the male artist nor the woman speaker "have found me", and therefore Boland's self, what her 'I' represents, "must still be found". The appearance of this passive is significant, for it indicates that the speaker is clearly deprived of agency. Boland maintains a helpless attitude, declaring that she is not able to discover her own self, and that it is for someone else to give her both a location and an identity. The only thing the poetic voice manages to make clear is that her sense of belonging is not found in England or New York, that "grass" she has left behind, but on "this green ground", Ireland, her native country. Boland is certain that it is here where she must attempt to find her own roots. But this assertion is counteracted at the end of the poem. "February 1963" finishes by emphasising the speaker's sense of solitude and alienation, what Boland (1995a: 105) has later defined as "an uncanny sense of spoiled identity and uncertain origin". Knowing where to "stand" is not sufficient, for she has not found the clues to construct her present self through poetry.

Like in "February 1963", the female voice in "Athene's Song" similarly describes herself as strongly alienated and submissive. This poem refutes Haberstroh's (1996: 60) contention that "[w]e hear no identifiable woman's voice" in *New Territory*. The 'I' of the poem corresponds to Athene, the goddess of war, and also of art and craftsmanship (Falcon Martínez et al. 1980: 99). Boland's choice of this mythological figure is quite telling. For the first time, she is going to try to revenge herself against a constraining patriarchal tradition, as she is starting to feel confident about her artistic skills and her poetic craft. As "Athene's Song" is the only poem within Boland's initial work which is written from an obviously subversive female perspective, Boland's claim that this is the only lyric in *New Territory* that still appeals to her is unsurprising (interview with Villar Argáiz). The first stanza describes how this female deity springs from her father's head:

> From my father's head I sprung
> Goddess of the war, created
> Partisan and soldier's physic –
> My symbols boast and brazen gong –
> Until I made in Athens wood
> Upon my knees a new music. (*Collected*, 23)

Athene is born, not from her mother's womb, but from the head of Zeus, something that Boland leaves clearly unquestioned. Her body is linked to the masculine one in an uncritical stance, just as in the Genesis story, where Eve springs from Adam's rib. Thus, she rises as a creature which depends on the other sex. From her very introduction to the world, she is predetermined to please others, to devote herself to the "partisan and soldiers". Her music must follow the demands of the Irish nationalist literary tradition, and therefore its main objective is to incite rebellion by glorifying a dispossessed nation and fuelling the pride of the fighters. In this sense, Athene becomes an allegorical version of Mother Ireland, an emblem of nationhood and a woman reduced to "symbols". For the first time in her initial work, Boland attempts to challenge this submissive stance. Getting tired of war, Athene suddenly decides to subvert her status as a goddess. This transformation parallels her creation of a new "pipe of bone" with which to create a radically different melody, a music that symbolises the advent of her

88

creative mind. Nevertheless, her personal fulfillment and inner peace are threatened as soon as war breaks out:

> Peace became the toy of power
> When other noises broke my sleep:
> Like dreams I saw the hot ranks
> And heroes in another flower
> Than any there; I dropped my pipe
> Remembering their shouts, their thanks. (*Collected*, 23)

The "hot ranks/ And heroes" summon Athene to create her warlike music. In her sense of obligation towards the national cause, she remembers nostalgically the glamour of "their shouts, their thanks". The dramatic tension of the poem is therefore achieved by means of Athene's opposing desires: on the one hand, she feels compelled to be loyal to her literary tradition; on the other hand, she feels the need to escape from it by establishing her 'new music'. As Allen-Randolph (1993a: 6) asserts, "the engaging drama of the poem springs from the clash between 'the new music' of Athene's nascent feminist consciousness and her paternal inheritance of boast and gong". Athene's conscious beliefs and unconscious intentions are certainly at odds. Taking into account Boland's conformist stance in her initial work, the conflict is resolved in an expected way. Athene eventually denies her own sexuality by dropping her pipe:

> Beside the water, lost and mute,
> Lies my pipe and like my mind
> Remains unknown, remains unknown
> And in some hollow taking part
> With my heart against my hand
> Holds its peace and holds its own. (*Collected*, 23)

At the end, Athene renounces her own creativity, her music of love, and returns to her earlier self. Boland is patriarchally constrained from being disloyal. Therefore, her relationship to the tradition from which she sprung is, once again, utterly uncritical.

The importance of this poem in Boland's initial production is that, for the first time, the woman poet acknowledges the existence of an inner creative self, her femaleness, which is at odds with the literary tradition she has inherited. As Boland (1995a: 58) asserts, when "I began to write those first poems, even through the borrowed images and false gestures, I saw the existence and demand of a preliminary self". "Athene's Song" witnesses Boland's "preliminary self". This poem anticipates what will be her main preoccupation in her future poetry (what I will call the 'Female'/'Liberationist' phase): giving voice to her own experience as a woman, who, like Athene's mind, "remains unknown" in the dominant aesthetics of the literary tradition. Athene's silent pipe is only a pretence of abandonment, for it "holds" its peace waiting to be sung again. This song of love will be heard again as Boland repudiates her initial male-orientated poetry.

2.9. Conclusion

As I have attempted to demonstrate, Boland's initial work can be categorised in broad terms as belonging to Showalter's 'Feminine' phase and to Memmi and Fanon's 'Assimilationist' phase, for a number of different reasons:

(1) With the exception of "Athene's Song", "February 1963", and "Malediction", Boland avoids the use of the feminine persona. Of these three poems, only the first is feminist oriented. Boland does not use her poetry as an aspect of her female experience, or an expression of it. There is no sense of self-awareness in her poems, and she tries to disguise her womanhood under a male poetic voice. Consequently, Boland retains traditional depictions of (Irish) women: as powerful, dangerous creatures (such as Aoife in "Malediction"), or as passive and beautiful icons (such as Étain in "The Winning of Etain", or Chardin's woman in "From the Painting *Back from Market* by Chardin").

(2) Boland deals with conventional themes and figures of the dominant aesthetic tradition, such as the romantic view of the poet and the idealisation of Irish natural landscapes. Poets are portrayed as heroes, ambitious mariners conquering new territories and constantly exploring a world of violence,

mortality, and death. In all cases, they are powerful figures, and the limitations they usually encounter in their journey through life only increase the value and achievement of their literary work. As romantic figures, they are "at war with social consensus" (Kiberd 1996: 537). They are dissidents, rebelling against established social rules and conventions. In this sense, the poet is portrayed as a person who maintains a position of non-commitment in a time of war (i.e. "Yeats in Civil War"), or who challenges the existing order ("After the Irish of Egan O'Rahilly"). As a result of this, they are described as lonely and isolated creatures, pilgrims in constant emigration, but also, paradoxically, as figures who are 'rooted' in a highly cohesive literary community, a place where they find a sense of belonging and their identity as poets. This sense of kinship between male poets is captured in a variety of poems, such as "The Poets", "New Territory", and "Migration". Maintaining the legacy of her forefathers also entails writing in remembrance of lost heroes and famous events that have shaped history. The Battle of the Boyne, the Flight of the Earls, the Easter Rising, and the Irish Civil War become the main poetic themes around which poems such as "After the Irish of Egan O'Rahilly", "The Flight of the Earls", "A Cynic at Kilmainham Gaol", and "Yeats in Civil War" revolve. The tone of her poems is usually elegiac, melancholic, and sentimental, for they try to restore the values of a lost civilisation of bardic poets. The praising of some noble literary writers, such as Yeats ("Yeats in Civil War") and Shakespeare ("Shakespeare", "The Comic Shakespeare"), as well as her dedication of some poems in the volume to well recognised poets of her time (Derek Mahon, Michael Longley, Eamon Grennan) enhance her anxiety to be included in the literary canon of Ireland (an arena which in the 1960s was exclusively dominated by male writers).

(3) This choice of subject matter is reflected in the structure and language of the poems. Boland shows her concern with models, with literary conventions, with the literary tradition as the very vehicle for artistic expression. Following traditional lyric poetry, she adheres to regularly-rhymed stanzas, and if there are no end-rhyme lines, Boland recurs to internal rhymes. The stanzas are usually

isometric. She plays with dissonant lines by combining trochees (which suggest unrelieved tension) with iambs (which give a resolution). The language is exact, deliberate, and measured. On the other hand, Boland seems to rely on the traditional shaping forms of epic narratives ("Appraisal"), elegies ("A Cynic at Kilmainhan Jail"), and ballads ("The King and the Troubadour"). In tone, her poems are very rhetorical and pompous. She keeps control of her emotions throughout the whole volume. Wherever the intensity of her feeling is too high, it is the voice of a male, not a female, persona who is speaking (as in "After The Irish of Egan O'Rahilly"). In short, she shows herself to be a conventional schoolgirl poet, following the example of Irish poets such as Yeats.

Therefore, in her initial work, Boland conceals her womanhood by imitating the predominant modes of the poetic tradition, as regards not only subject matter but also style. The title of the volume, *New Territory*, reveals a lot about the poet's situation at the time. Boland tried to form part of the (male) literary canon of Dublin; she wanted to fully engage in the circle of poets, and become one of them. For her, as a young poet, this is a 'new territory' to explore. Nevertheless, *New Territory* is nothing but a well-known 'Old Territory' for women in the Western/Irish literary tradition. As Roche (1993: 1) explains, "[t]he title of *New Territory* announced an aspiration rather than an achievement". Boland does not sense then that she is truthful to her own reality as an Irish woman poet. The "uncanny sense of spoiled identity" that Boland (1995a: 105) felt in her initial attempts at writing poetry will prompt this woman poet to embark on a drastic and radical change in her poetry. It will not be until her following volumes of poetry that Boland will be conscious of the gap between the experiences she wants to record as a woman and the poetic conventions available for articulating them. By bridging this gap, she will be able to create a new ground, a more authentic *new territory*, for Irish women in literature.

Notes to chapter 2

[1] An analysis of the journals and anthologies published in the latter half of the twentieth century shows how women have been suppressed from Ireland's mainstream literature. Medbh McGuckian was the only woman amongst the ten poets included in Paul Muldoon's *Faber Book of Contemporary Irish Poetry*, published in 1986 (Hill 2003: 8). Fogarty (1999: 261) compares *The Oxford Book of Irish Verse*, edited by Donagh MacDonagh and Lennox Robinson in 1958, with *The New Oxford Book of Irish Verse*, edited by Thomas Kinsella in 1986. Surprisingly enough, the earlier volume features far more women writers than Kinsella's later selection, which only incorporates the figure of Eibhlín Ní Chonaill. Even when women writers started to be published in the 1970s and 1980s, there seems to be discontinuity. Maurice Harmon's *Irish Poetry After Yeats*, Frank Ormsby's *A Rage for Order*, and John Montague's *The Faber Book of Irish Verse* recorded either nineteenth-century women writers (Eileen O'Leary, Lady Wilde, Emily Lawless, and Fanny Parnell) or contemporary poets such as Eavan Boland and Eiléan Ní Chilleanáin (Fogarty 1999: 261-262). Furthermore, as Fogarty (1999: 263) explains, the most important literary journals (such as *The Bell*, *Envoi*, and *The Lace Curtain*, with the exception of *The Dublin Magazine*), almost entirely ignored women's poetry in their publications. The publication of *The Field Day Anthology of Irish Writing* in 1991 reinforces the continuing problems women have had in getting their works published and recognized. The little space devoted to women writers was highly controversial, because it claimed to be a comprehensive collection of Irish writing from the sixth to the twentieth century.

[2] Allen-Randolph (1999a: 207) contributes to this debate, by noting that the constraints for innovation experienced in the Irish arena stem from the particular relation of Irish poets to history and the national literary tradition. Irish poets have been "more oblig[ed] to the history of their country, than most American poets ever felt themselves to be" (ibid).

[3] In an implicit allusion to Ó Ríodáin's phrase, Boland (1989b: 24) has asserted that the achievement of contemporary women's poetry in Ireland is due to the fact that the feminine emblems of the literary tradition have acquired voices, or, in her own words, "[t]hey have turned from poems into poets".

[4] In his study on women in Celtic society, Berresford (1995: 162, 187-189) even draws upon the existence of female poets in Ireland in the early medieval period, for example Liadin (the 'Grey Lady') in the seventh century, and Gormfalith and Uallach in the tenth century. It has also been acknowledged that some of the *Love Songs of Connaught* in the seventeenth and eighteenth centuries were written by women (Kelly 1997: 11).

[5] It is indeed true that we find a female literary tradition totally uncritical of the contemporary socio-political situations and the inherited literary conventions. Kelly's 1987 anthology offers a long list of women writers in the nineteenth century and the beginning of the twentieth who yielded to the nationalist cause, by constructing a poetry entirely dedicated to expressing Ireland's aspirations of liberty. Nevertheless, it is important to bear in mind that there was also a more heterogeneous and less conformist writing, a form of literature that was not always concerned with politics and women's expected cultural roles. Boland omits other women poets, such as Mary Barber, for instance, who stands out in the eighteenth century for her struggle for women's right to have access to knowledge and writing poetry. In poems such as "Conclusion of a Letter to the Rev. C-", she defended women's coequal role in society, claiming that a husband should not "treat her the worse, for her being [his] wife", and that he should "Choose books for her study, to fashion her mind,/ To emulate those who excell'd of her kind" (Kelly 1997: 28). A century later, Katharine Tynan was an advocator of women's rights, and she defended in poems such as "Any Woman" the social importance of women's role as mothers and caretakers (p. 63). Others such as Dora

Sigerson Shorter, in "A Vagrant Heart", more explicitly denounced the conventional social laws on women and defended her right to enter "a world of passion [...] for all its dangers" (p. 73). This feeling was also shared by other women writers such as Mary Devenport O'Neill, who attempted to break the stereotype of "sentimental poetry" (p. 94).

[6] Ní Fhrighil, Ríóna (2003). "The Poetry of Eavan Boland", paper delivered in IASIL (in Debrecen, Hungary, on Thursday 10 July 2003). I am deeply grateful to Dr. Ní Fhrighil for giving me a copy of her interesting paper before it has been published.

[7] Critics tend to identify *New Territory* as Boland's first volume of poetry, ignoring other previous smaller collections such as *Twenty Three Poems* (1962), *Autumn Essay* (1963a), and *Eavan Boland Poetry/ Prose Joseph O'Malley* (1963b). These "chapbooks", as Boland defines them, are out of print (interview with Villar Argáiz).

[8] For the sake of consistency, I have taken my quotations from Eavan Boland's *New Collected Poems* (Carcanet, 2005). Subsequent references are mentioned in parentheses as *Collected* followed by the page number(s).

[9] Subsequent references are mentioned in parentheses as *Boland Poetry* followed by the page number(s).

[10] In *Object Lessons*, Boland (1995a: 95) has argued that this mingling of metropolitan and nationalist tendencies in Irish literature is personified by the city of Dublin itself. The statues of Goldsmith and Burke at the main entrance of Trinity College remind her of the metropolitan poem. On the other hand, Grafton Street is linked in her imagination to a lost world of Irish poetry, "a place where the Irish bard Aodghan O'Rathaille has seen the Gaelic order collapse and his own patrons flee after the Treaty of Limerick failed at the end of the seventieth century".

[11] Adrienne Rich (1979: 40), who will exert an enormous influence on Boland's next phase, has also admitted using formalism in her initial years of her poetic career to conceal her womanhood.

[12] See, for example, Yeats's "The Madness of King Goll", "Fergus and the Druid", "Cuchulain's Fight with the Sea", and "The Song of Wandering Aengus" (Yeats 1992: 14, 27, 29, 55).

[13] In "Shakespeare" and "The Comic Shakespeare" (*Collected*, 18, 19), Boland depicts the harsh conditions this poet and playwright had to undergo in the Elizabethan period. By so doing, she pays homage to someone who managed to produce noble masterpieces in a tough and toilsome age. As she implies in the last couplet of "The Comic Shakespeare", his achievement was a consequence of the hardship he had to go through: "Would each comedy,/ Each festival and whistle of your prime,/ Today exist if you had wept in time?".

[14] As we will see in Boland's mature work, she will reverse this movement. Her poems tend to end by highlighting the speaker's powerlessness and her immersion in darkness. Her later use of dark and diffuse lights, rather than simply a metaphor of poetic failure, will be the best context where the boundaries between past and present begin to blur, and where Boland finds the summit of her poetic inspiration.

[15] For a similar comparison between farming and the very act of writing poetry see Seamus Heaney's poem "Digging" in his volume of poetry *Death of a Naturalist* (Heaney 1966: 13).

[16] Precisely because of this, a medieval world of "kings", "princes", "troubadours", "minstrels", "sycophants", "clowns", "immoral courtiers", "mummers", and "wranglers", is constantly evoked

in almost all the poems of Boland's initial work, especially in "Appraisal" (*Boland Poetry*, 7-10), "Mirages", "Shakespeare", "The Flight of the Earls", "After the Irish of Egan O'Rahilly", "The King and the Troubadour", and "The Winning of Etain" (*Collected*, 10, 18, 20, 21, 22, 24-31).

[17] The Irish genre of *Immram* was also employed by Yeats in *The Shadowy Waters* (Butler 2001: 136), and by contemporary Irish poets such as Paul Muldoon in *Why Brownlee Left* (Praga 1996: 178) and Nuala Ní Dhomhnaill in "The Voyage" (Keen 2000: 21).

[18] In this poem, the scope of the comparison widens. Poets are also compared to "kings riding to battle", royal rulers who are in touch with the irrational and are able to see "crosses burn/ In the skylight of the winter solstice" (*Collected*, 10).

[19] See, for instance, Yeats's poem "Owen Aherne and his Dancers" (Yeats 1992: 233), where one section is entitled "From 'Oedipus at Colonus'". In this poem, Yeats honours the memory of Oedipus: "Endure what life God gives and as no longer span;/ Cease to remember the delights of youth, travel-wearied aged/ mad".

[20] Another important genre within Gaelic poetry which is related to nature poetry is the *dinnsheanchas* (meaning "knowledge of the lore of places"). As Welch (2000: 90-91) explains, early Irish literature preserves a toponymic lore, according to which "placenames are explained by reference to legends which are linked to them by means of pseudo-etymological techniques". A large corpus of this literary tradition was gathered in the eleventh and twelfth centuries, and medieval Irish poets were expected to learn it by heart.

[21] The pastoralism of Collins, de Valera, and Yeats was also partly inspired by the Romantic English movement led by Wordsworth and the Lake Poets (Kiberd 1996: 486). Irish Revivalists relied on the poetics of Wordsworth, Coleridge and, most of all, Matthew Arnold, in their idealization of peasantry and the rural world, in contrast to a degenerate urban setting. Butler (2001: 199) extends the origins of the pastoral genre farther back in history, explaining that it was initially created by urban Latin poets, like Virgil and Theocritus, "as an imaginary break from the pressures of life at imperial court".

[22] With all these idealizations of rural Ireland carried out by political thinkers and writers, it seems inevitable to find an immediate counter-movement, an anti-pastoral version of the Irish landscape. In *The Great Hunger*, Patrick Kavanagh proposes an alternative for the Yeatsian myth of romantic Ireland (Praga 1996: 63). The anti-pastoral was also put to practice by Brian O'Nolan in *An Béal Bocht* and by James Joyce in *Stephen Hero* (Kiberd 1996: 503).

[23] The mythological tale of the Children of Lir has always fascinated Boland, and consequently, it appears not only in her initial work, but also in her later work, such as in "Elegy for a Youth Changed to a Swan" and "Escape" (*Collected*, 54-55, 266-267).

[24] Lines taken from Shakespeare's "Oh Mistress Mine" (Abrams et al. 1993a: 806), Blake's "The Sick Rose" (Abrams et al. 1993b: 36), Keats's "Ode to Psyche" (Abrams et al. 1993b: 788), Tennyson's "The Splendour Falls" (Hollander 1996: 68), and Lear's "The Owl and the Pussy-cat" (Hollander 1996: 133).

[25] See, for instance, the childlike stance adopted by Dickinson in "A Narrow Fellow in the Grass" (Hollander 1996: 159-160).

[26] This form of cultural nationalism is labelled by Maley (1996: 34) as "colonial nationalism". Within this group, this critic also includes Jonathan Swift and Maria Edgeworth.

---

[27] The journalist D.P. Moran, one of the promoters of Hyde's Gaelic League, expressed the belief that, to be a member of the nation, the Irishman must also be a member of the "distinct and wholly superior" Gaelic race (Boyce 1991: 251). "Irish-Ireland" nationalism highlighted the rural and Catholic nature of Irish society. In this sense, the national narrative they promoted was narrower: 'Irishness' was equated with Catholicism, the Gaelic language, ruralism and anti-modernism. The Ireland they envisaged was rather different from Davis's more inclusive "Anglo-Ireland".

[28] Boland is one exponent of a long list of Irish poets, such as James Stephens, James Clarence Mangan, Séan Ó Tuama, and Thomas Kinsella, who have either translated or written versions of O'Rahilly's work (Welch 2000: 296).

[29] From http://www.iol.ie/~edmo/mccarthy.html and http://mccarthy.montana.com/MacCarthyMor.html. Read on January 24th, 2005.

[30] Other poems which also imitate the conventional Shakespearean sonnet include "The Comic Shakespeare" (*Collected*, 18-19). No other verse form could pay better homage to Shakespeare.

[31] A study of Irish mythology gives literary evidence that, in contrast to the literature of the Romantics and the Revivalists in Ireland, female deities are represented as enjoying a powerful role and higher status than other Western representations. Berresford (1995: 15, 43, 48) lists the gallery of vigorous, independent, fiery-hearted women who figure in Celtic myths: Maeve, Grania, Findabair, Deirdre, and the historic Boadicea, for instance. Aoife is another example of these strong and powerful figures.

[32] Boland's use of passives and genitives to portray female figures as aesthetic objects of male possession is recurrent in her initial work. In "The Winning of Etain", interestingly enough, agentive subjects are always portrayed as male (either Aengus or the Druid), whereas Étain is portrayed as a mere object, something to be won. Some examples of this are "Etain, twice a woman twice a queen/ Possessed of two lives and one love"; "the winning of Etain/ A second time by Aengus"; "Her cheeks, blanched with light, were charmed away/ Her long embracing arms convulsed, her face/ Shriveled", etc (*Collected*, 24). One notes that, in the only moment when Étain is portrayed as speaking, the agentive subject is deliberately omitted from the utterance: "Bitter words were woven into the stuff/ Of disappointment" (p. 30). It is also worth considering how Étain is perceived only fragmentally, in bodily parts, by Aengus's male gaze, as when he utters: "How can I kiss these red forgetful lips,/ This unfamiliar hand, or take this body" (p. 28). Furthermore, it is significant the preponderance of verbs such as 'watch', 'see', and 'look' in this poem. The agent of such an action is always, unsurprisingly, the male character. In this sense, Boland maintains an uncritical attitude towards women's subordination in literary and cultural representations by perpetuating this oppression in her poetry.

3

Boland's Reaffirmation of Sexual Difference

3.1. Introduction

Showalter (1999:13) proposes a second phase in women's writing which she denominates 'Feminist' phase, and whose significance lies in "the protest against [...] the standards and values [of the dominant tradition], and advocacy of minority rights and values, including a demand for authority". This phase is mainly characterised by a radical confrontation with patriarchal society, and "a cultist celebration of womanhood" (p. 181). In this phase, Showalter (1999: 4) states, American and British women writers advocated sexual separatism, recurring at times to the theme of an "Amazon utopia". In their rejection of "male society and masculine culture", feminist writing stands as "a declaration of independence", a separatist writing (p. 31). In other words, this is a writing mainly defined in opposition to the male tradition.

This 'Feminist' phase resembles the second phase in the process of decolonisation that Memmi (1990: 195) and Fanon (1990: 179) identify in *The Colonizer and the Colonized* and *The Wretched of the Earth* respectively. Both anti-colonial intellectuals agree on the fact that, in order to move away from the colonial situation, the colonised engages in a vicious and bloody phase of protest. This second violent stage in the process of decolonisation is based on a vigorous attempt to recover and assert the self, an autonomous entity. Now the colonised entirely rejects the coloniser, and defends with passion his/her own distinctiveness. This is a "cultural nationalist" stage which aims at constructing a self-defensive culture in opposition to the imperialist culture. As Memmi (1990: 95) argues, colonialism creates the patriotism of the oppressed, who attempt to affirm their exclusivity in national selfhood: "For a number of historical, sociological, and psychological reasons, the struggle for liberation by colonised peoples has taken on a marked national and nationalist look". In this phase, therefore, nationalism and native identity are the writer's main concerns.

The main feature shared by the second stage of Showalter, Memmi, and Fanon, is the radical assertion of identity. Thus, whereas the feminist writer celebrates womanhood in essentialist terms, Memmi and Fanon's colonised writer strongly defends all the distinctive characteristics of his/her native tradition. In *Black Skin, White Masks*, Fanon (1991: 16-140) dedicates one chapter, "The Fact of Blackness", to a discussion of the desperate struggle of a colonised black subject who wants to discover those aspects that constitute negritude, previously undervalued and neglected by the coloniser. Fanon explains that this kind of 'Negro' is absolutely different from the 'Negro' that wants to become white (a figure resembling Boland in her initial phase, when she is willing to become a male writer), since the Negro "now wants to belong to his own people" (p. 16). This attitude resembles Showalter's feminist writer. Whereas Fanon's voice reclaims his negritude, the woman writer at this stage wants to reclaim her womanhood, and both 'colonial' subjects (affected by the social and cultural constructs of race and gender) engage in similar 'separatist' writings.

Boland's third volume of poetry, *In Her Own Image* (1980), can be included in what Showalter calls the 'Feminist' phase, or what Memmi and Fanon identify as the 'Cultural Nationalist' phase. Nevertheless, this work does not immediately follow *New Territory*, as *The War Horse* is written before, in 1975. This latter volume will be described as a transitional book to Boland's third phase, in which she repositions herself as a poet and redirects her sense of poetry (its content and linguistic features better fit Boland's mature poetry). Thus, I will deal with *The War Horse* in the following chapter, which focuses on Boland's 'Female'/'Liberationist' phase, following Showalter, Memmi, and Fanon's nomenclature. On the other hand, it is important to bear in mind that *In Her Own Image* was written at about the same time as *Night Feed* (1982). Whereas the first one grew out of Boland's experimentation with the "anti-lyric",[1] as she explains in an interview, *Night Feed* responds to Boland's treatment of "lyricism".[2] These two intermediate volumes of poetry, *The War Horse* and *Night Feed*, imply, as Showalter (1999: 13) explains, that the three phases in women's writing are not fixed categories, and as such they may overlap. Although Boland's evolution as a poet underlies a process of increasing poetic maturity (a process of initial imitation, intermediate protest, and final artistic autonomy), the departure from the inherited poetic tradition is not an easy step to take, and Boland, on her journey towards attaining artistic decolonisation, shows backward and forward movements.

As Haberstroh (1995: 21) has noted, Boland's poetry after *New Territory* attempts to place itself "outside the two types of poems she started with: the English 'movement' poem and the Irish bardic poem". In *In Her Own Image*, Boland records her own womanhood as against canonical and/or nationalist texts. In the process, she yields to the prescriptions of feminism. Her radicalism is a direct consequence of what Fanon denominates an *inborn complex*. As Fanon's "Negro", who feels the need to destroy the false statements that "Negroes are savages, brutes, illiterates" (Fanon 1991: 117), Boland also finds that there are conventional images of women that must be destroyed at all costs. In order to challenge the restrictions imposed on women's self expression, Boland embraces feminism at the aesthetic level, angrily attacking those aspects of patriarchal society she views as damaging for her own reality as a woman. Moreover, Boland finds the poetic tradition oppressive and alienating, and consequently adopts what she would later refuse as a "separatist" stance (Boland 1995a: 234). In *Object Lessons*, Boland (1995a: 145) narrates how she has been drawn to feminism:

'Start again' has been the cry of some of the best feminist poets. 'Wipe clean the slate, start afresh'. It is a cry with force and justice behind it. And it is a potent idea: to begin in a new world, clearing the desert as it were, making it blossom, even making the rain.[3]

These "separatist" appeals demand that Boland should be loyal to the Women's Movement, that she should leave aside former literary traditions, and construct her own writing criteria (p. 243). Probably because of this, and in contrast to *New Territory*, Boland refuses to dedicate her poems to male writers. Now, she does not write for "a notional *male* readership", as Mahon (1993: 24) puts it, and she engages herself in the exploration of women's experience, in a radically different poetic style.

As I intend to demonstrate, *In Her Own Image* is a feminist volume of poetry that signifies a breakthrough in Boland's poetic career.[4] I think it is convenient to highlight the words 'protest', 'advocacy' and 'reclaim' from Showalter's (1999: 13), Memmi's (1990: 195), and Fanon's (1990: 179) assertions, because these are present unequivocally in *In Her Own Image*:

(1) In contrast to the uncritical stance adopted in *New Territory*, Boland *protests* against patriarchal literary standards, in an outspoken and subversive manner. She angrily departs from conventional depictions of women. The beloved lyric muse of male artists is attacked in "Tirade for the Mimic Muse" with assertions as follows: "I know you for the ruthless bitch you are:/ Our criminal, our tricoteuse, our Muse-/ Our Muse of Mimic Art" (*Collected*, 71). Similarly, the patriarchal dichotomy evil witch/ submissive wife is strongly criticised in poems such as "Witching" and "In His Own Image" (pp. 82-84, 74-75). This act of exposing the damaging consequences of negative stereotypes on the (gendered) colonial subject has also been identified by Fanon (1991: 113) as central to this second phase of decolonisation.

(2) Boland *advocates* her right to be the author of a creative work, to be in control of her subjects in the poem. The title of the volume, *In Her Own Image*, is itself clearly subversive of the dominating male poetic discourse. As González

Arias (2000a: 37) notes, Boland overturns the Biblical passage that explains how God created humankind *in his own image*. Boland is suggesting a goddess who is able to create humanity, and by extension womanhood, in her own image. At the same time, she implies that women poets are able to write poetry in their own image (with their own experiences), without having to imitate a previous tradition which simply ignored them.

(3) Boland *reclaims* her right to describe taboo areas of female experience, such as anorexia, menstruation, mastectomy, or masturbation. The fact that *In Her Own Image* was published by Arlen House, "the pioneering Irish feminist press of the early mid-eighties" (Roche 1993: 1), is no surprise, given the radical tone of the book.[5] Boland demands the authority to create a new literary tradition and defends her creative potential by approaching subjects that were new in Ireland. Haberstroh (1996: 22-23) points to the emergence in the 1980s of a whole body of poetry by Irish women defying sexual taboos and offering alternative images to female anatomy:

> Female sexuality [...] became a focus of self-identity. In 1980, Eithne Strong published *FLESH... The Greatest Sin*, which might be read as a female version of Patrick Kavanagh's *The Great Hunger*; in the same year Eavan Boland's *In Her Own Image* explored the effects of conventional sexual images of women; and in 1982, Mary Dorcey's *Kindling* ignored the homosexuality taboo to depict lesbian experience.

Boland is one voice among many others who, in the 1980s, rely on body imagery. The woman poet produces an avant-garde work of art rooted in the female body, very similar to the one that French feminism has advocated.

French feminists like Hélène Cixous and Luce Irigaray have encouraged women to rely on their own potential and personal experiences. Hélène Cixous's name is most often associated with that of "écriture feminine" or "feminine writing". For Cixous, the best means to transform the prevailing socio-symbolic system is by means of inscribing women's sexuality in a particular form of writing called "écriture feminine".[6] Like Cixous, Irigaray defines woman's language in its relation to their sexuality. Irigaray envisages the possibility of a different, non-masculine discourse, a revolutionary and iconoclastic woman's language, what she calls "a feminine syntax" (1991: 136) or "a speaking (as) woman" (1991: 137).[7]

This French attempt at a feminist writing has its equivalent in Adrienne Rich's American advocacy of the expression of women's lived experiences. Several critics have singled Rich out as a significant influence on Boland's feminist volume.[8] Albert Gelpi (1999: 210) explains that Boland read Rich's *Diving into the Wreck* and *The Dream of a Common Language* in the final 1970s, before she began writing *In Her Own Image*. Nevertheless, it was Rich's essay "When We Dead Awaken: Writing as Re-Vision" what exerted the greatest influence on Boland's departure from her earlier 'Feminine'/'Assimilationist' phase. As Boland explains in an interview, "it was an enormous rush of oxygen to read Adrienne Rich's "When We Dead Awaken"" (Allen-Randolph 1999b: 300). In a previous prose work, Boland asserts: "Adrienne Rich is a wonderful poet and her essay "When We Dead Awaken" […] is a central statement in contemporary poetry. It should be read by every poet" (Boland 1995a: 244).[9]

After having read "When We Dead Awaken", it is easy to understand why Boland was so fascinated with this essay. Adrienne Rich's own life (as described in her essay) coincides in more than one way with Boland's life at that time. Rich (1979: 38) explains how she was encouraged by her father to read and write. In her early years, she began writing to please him, "the literary master", in a kind of respectful conservatism which demanded her to be "maidenly, elegant, intellectual, [and] discreet" (p. 39). Her life radically changed as she married in her early twenties and had three children before her thirties (p. 42). Since then, she had to share her time between fulfilling her domestic duties and writing poems. She found out that she felt dissatisfied with the poems she had written, for they seemed "mere exercises for poems I hadn't written" (ibid). Rich gradually realised that "to be maternally with small children all day in the old way, to be with a man in the old way of marriage" required her to put aside some of her desires to write her own sense of herself, her female experience (p. 43). Surely, Boland identified herself with Rich when she claims: "I am aware of the women who are not with us because they are washing dishes and looking after the children" (p. 38).

Like Rich, Boland began as a conservative young formalist, but, at the time of reading Rich's essay, she had a similar change of life that will radically transform her as a poet. At the end of the 1970s, she moved from the University culture in Dublin, where she had become "a sort of honorable *male* poet" (emphasis added), out to the suburbs (interview with Allen-Randolph 1993b: 118). She married and had two children. Gradually, she began to feel that the traditional Irish canonical poem could not account for the 'ordinary' life she had started to live. They were poems where "you could have a political murder but not a baby. Or the Dublin hills and not the suburbs under them" (Boland 1995a: 119). As her life as a woman in a Dublin suburb with small children was not part of Irish poetry, Boland felt the need to subvert the poetic tradition she had inherited. In this sense, her change of lifestyle meant for her the sort of "awakening [of] consciousness" Rich (1979: 35) talks about in her essay. According to Rich, women have to 'wake up' to the fact that they have been culturally oppressed in a male-dominated society. The challenge for women writers, she goes on, would be to rebel against this repressive reality, to search for their own identity, to explore "a whole new psychic geography", a geography which could bear witness to women's reality (ibid).

In order to approach Boland's *In Her Own Image* as an intermediate volume in Boland's evolution, I intend to apply not only Showalter, Memmi, and Fanon's theories as regards the gendered/colonised subject, but also other feminist and/or postcolonial critics. As I aim to demonstrate, Rich, Cixous, and Irigaray's feminist tenets are carried out faithfully by Boland in *In Her Own Image*. On the other hand, Spivak (1993: 3-17), among other feminist postcolonial theorists, will be helpful for an understanding of this volume's essentialist and separatist stance.

With a view to discussing the main features that clearly distinguish *In Her Own Image* as a volume of oppositional poetry, I will rely on its internal evolution. As Allen-Randolph (1991: 49-53) has also noted, the first half of the volume offers a negative analysis of society: child abuse ("Tirade for the Mimic Muse", *Collected*, 71-72), wife abuse ("In His Own Image", *Collected*, 74-75), and anorexia ("Anorexic", *Collected*, 75-76). The second half of the volume moves from a negative analysis to an exploration of a form of writing rooted in female sexuality. In this sense, the poems move from women's oppression to a celebration of womanhood in essentialist terms. It is in poems such as "Menses", "Solitary", "Exhibitionist" and "Making up" (*Collected*, 78-81, 84-88) where Boland recognises the link between sexuality and textuality as theorised by Cixous and Irigaray.[10] The following sections are aimed at demonstrating that Boland is, in 1980, at her second phase in her search for artistic autonomy.

3.2. Anger and revenge: a 'tirade' against patriarchal representations of women

A clear indication that *In Her Own Image* has not yet reached the ultimate artistic autonomy stage characteristic of Showalter, Memmi, and Fanon's final phases is that its women are moved by anger and revenge. Fanon (1990: 27) argues that a subjugated writer necessarily has to go through a period of distress, difficulty, and unrepressed anger in order to achieve artistic liberation. He shows that the destruction of the colonial world is only possible by the fierce abolition or substitution of the coloniser for the colonised:

> National liberation, national renaissance, the restoration of nationhood ... whatever may be the headings used or the new formulas introduced, decolonisation is always a violent phenomenon, [...] a whole social structure [is] changed from the bottom up. (Fanon 1990: 27)

The very first process of colonisation, Fanon goes on, was brought about by the violent exploitation of the native by the settler, when the figure of the colonised consequently becomes the invader's own creation: "it is the settler who has brought the native into existence and who perpetuates his existence" (ibid). Therefore, decolonisation is not only a total and absolute substitution of power, but also the colonised's search for their own distinctiveness, what Fanon suggestively recalls as the "veritable creation of new men", who re-introduce their own language, their own traditions, and who become "human in the very process by which they liberate themselves" (p. 28). In the process, the very violence of the colonial regime is adopted by the native (p. 31). As Sartre (1990: 18) explains in the preface to *The Wretched of the Earth*, "[w]hen [the native's rage] boils over, he rediscovers his lost innocence and he comes to know himself in that he creates himself". According to Fanon's theories, anger and self-creation go necessarily together, something that Rich (1979: 48) has also identified in women's writing:

> The awakening of consciousness is not like the crossing of a frontier – one step and then you are in another country. Much of woman's poetry has been of the nature of the blues song: a cry of pain, of victimisation, or a lyric of seduction. And today, much poetry by women [...] is charged with anger. I think we need to go through that anger [...] if not we will betray our reality.

By reading Fanon and Rich, one understands how Boland's rage in *In Her Own Image* is a necessary step in her radical defence of those womanly aspects that have been denigrated by Irish historical and literary accounts. In the opening poem of *In Her Own Image*, "Tirade for the Mimic Muse", Boland rebels with anger against her cultural oppression and uses ferocious metaphors to address the traditional feminine muse beloved by male poets: "You slut. You fat trout"; "Anyone would think you are a whore-/ An ageing-out-of-work kind-hearted tart" (*Collected*, 71). This poem shows Boland at her most aggressive and direct stance. The poetic voice addresses the mimic muse by means of colloquial language, traditionally regarded as "unpoetical" (Leech 1969: 23): "I've caught you out", "Your luck ran out", etc. (*Collected*, 71, 72). This, together with insults such as "slut", "fat trout", "whore", "tart", and "ruthless bitch" amaze any reader who has in mind Boland's rather conservative stance in *New Territory*. As Hagen and Zelman (1991: 448) explain, the speaker begins by holding up a mirror to compel this old epic muse to confront herself. Her intention is, above all, to uncover her superficial image:

> Eye-shadow, swivel brushes, blushers,
> Hot pinks, rouge pots, sticks,
> Ice for the pores, a mud mask-
> All the latest tricks.
> Not one of them disguise
> That there's a dead millennium in your eyes. (*Collected*, 71)

The image of makeup is quite recurrent in *In Her Own Image*. As González Arias (2000a: 38) points out, this imagery reinforces, on the one hand, the fictitious and artificial nature of female stereotypes and, on the other hand, women's tendency to 'kill' themselves artistically in order to appeal to men. The passive and conformist stance of a woman wearing all sorts of (lifeless) masks is confronted by a fierce woman who seeks to destroy all patriarchal structures. As a woman extremely conscious of her creative potential, the woman in the poem resembles those mad and monstrous creatures of nineteenth century literature who mean a threat to the well structured (male) society.[11] Boland literally becomes that figure of the madwoman in the attic that Gilbert and Gubar (2000: 85) mention. As these critics explain, this character is the author's double, because it is

> through the violence of the double that the female author enacts her own raging desire to escape male houses and male texts, which at the same time it is through the double's violence that this anxious author articulates for herself the costly destructiveness of anger repressed until it can no longer be contained (ibid).

In a direct confrontation against the national muse of the Irish tradition, the narrator debunks conventional "drums and dances", canonical "[r]ituals and flatteries of war" (*Collected*, 71). The image of Mother Ireland, a "looking-glass" for male poets, is blamed for escaping from the real (at times harsh) conditions of life:

> The kitchen screw and the rack of labour,
> The wash thumbed and the dish cracked,
> The scream of beaten women,
> The crime of babies battered,
> The hubbub and the shriek of daily grief
> That seeks asylum behind suburb walls-
> A world you could have sheltered in your skirts- (*Collected*, 72)

Although this muse "could have sheltered" this world in her "skirts", she prefers to "protect" herself "from horrors", and use "all the latest tricks" (such as makeup) to disguise "that there's a dead millennium in [her] eyes" (*Collected*, 71). The woman's rage is reinforced by the recognition that she "had [once] waited on [her] trashy whim". But as the speaker mazes "her way to womanhood", she realises that thanks to the details of her ordinary life ("in a nappy stink, by a soaking wash/ Among stacked dishes"), the muse's "glass cracked" (p. 72). The image of the mirror is a powerful metaphor. As Virginia Woolf (1974: 53) points out, "[w]omen have served all these centuries as looking-glasses possessing the magic and delicious power of reflecting the figure of man at twice its natural size". It is Boland's intention to reveal the real image of the mimic muse and show her "true reflections", so that her muse, more inclusive now, can bear witness to the reality of women's lives:

> Make your face naked,
> Strip your mind naked,
> Drench your skin in a woman's tears.
> I will wake you from your sluttish sleep.
> I will show you true reflections, terrors.
> You are the Muse of all mirrors.
> Look in them and weep. (*Collected*, 72)

What the speaker suggests is that, although this woman has been a prisoner of the mirror/ text's images, she has the ability to break her former mirror and look at last at her "true reflections", her own womanhood and her own autonomy. Gilbert and Gubar (2000: 17) explain that "before the woman writer can journey through the looking glass towards literary autonomy, she must come to terms with the images on the surface of the glass". In other words, this woman must contemplate herself in the mirror of the male-inscribed literary tradition, in order to kill the aesthetic ideal through which she has been 'killed' into art. In this sense, Boland's poem shares this powerful metaphor of the mirror-looking woman with Mary Elizabeth Coleridge's "The Other Side of the Mirror", where the poet encourages the woman to break the glass and be free of it:

> Shade of a shadow in the glass,
>   O set the crystal surface free!
> Pass – as the fairer visions pass –
>   Nor ever more return, to be
> The ghost of a distracted hour,
> That heard me whisper, 'I am she!' (Quoted in Gilbert & Gubar 2000: 16)

As with Coleridge's poem, similarly, in "Tirade for the Mimic Muse", Boland seems to have opened her eyes to female realities within and around her. Before asserting herself in essentialist terms, as she will do in the second half of this volume, she must come to terms with those male constructs which are reflected in the mirror. As Gilbert and Gubar (2000: 17) assert, "self-definition necessarily precedes self-assertion: the creative 'I AM' cannot be uttered if the 'I' knows not what it is".

Boland's new aesthetics is perceived formally in the poem. She changes the conventional verse technique of her first poems by writing ten-line stanzas with no regular meter and rhyme. Her aggressive and assertive stance is reflected in the use of vocatives and imperatives, devices which denote the authority of the poetic voice. Her empowerment is reinforced by the modal volitional 'will', which expresses her intention to carry out actions: "I will wake you from your sluttish sleep./ I will show you true reflections, terrors" (*Collected*, 72). It is this use of the volitional modal, as we will see, which clearly distinguishes *In Her Own Image* from other volumes of poetry. Lack of coherent form is also observed in the deviated syntax of the poem. There are midline caesuras created by commas, fragmentary lines, and incomplete sentences. Deviation at the level of graphology is also significant. Orthography becomes an expressive device in this poem. Note the lack of punctuation at the end of the third line:

> Hoping your lamp and flash,
> Your glass, might show
> This world I needed nothing else to know (*Collected*, 72)

All these linguistic deviations commented above may indicate that Boland is giving verbal expression to the revolution of discourse advocated by French feminism, most notably by Hélène Cixous and Luce Irigaray, which I will develop later on. French feminism defends a form of language that manages to surpass "the coded, clichéd, ordinary language", as Andermatt (1984: 5) explains. Although Kristeva's theories will be most appropriately addressed in Boland's mature work, some of her assertions come close to Cixous's and Irigaray's. In "Oscillation du 'pouvoir' au 'refus'", Kristeva (1981: 165-166) argues that women's writing has to be the work of the avant-garde which produces linguistic innovations:

> [I]n a culture where the speaking subjects are conceived of as masters of their speech, they have what is called a "phallic" position. The fragmentation of language in a text calls into question the very posture of this mastery. [...] If women have a role to play in this on-going process, it is only in assuming a *negative* function: reject everything finite, definite, structured, loaded with meaning, in the existing state of society.

According to these feminists, language is masculine, in a system entirely based upon one fundamental signifier: the phallus. When women begin to speak confidently of themselves, they manage to find what they think of as their true voice, a "feminine syntax". Boland's language certainly disorients the reader for its incoherent form and fragmented language, for its angry stance and chaotic emotional state.

As we will see in the following section, Boland's 'feminist' women, in their demolishing discourses, reflect more dispossession, self-hatred, and anger than relaxed authority and artistic freedom. As Virginia Woolf identified, there are risks in reacting with anger and bitterness toward one's reality. When talking about Charlotte Brontë, Woolf (1974: 104) argued that it was her indignation that distanced her from the freedom to think by herself:

> [O]ne sees that she will never get her genius expressed whole and entire. Her books will be deformed and twisted. She will write in a rage where she should write calmly. She will write foolishly where she should write wisely. She will write of herself where she should write of her characters. She is at war with her lot.

It won't be until Boland leaves aside her anger that she will come to terms with her own poetic voice and she will write her finest poems. As she will later assert, "I do not believe we will reach the future without living through the womanly angers which shadow this present" (Boland 1995a: 254).

3.3. Ambivalent impulses: a fractured and confused self

3.3.1. A split poetic voice in "Anorexic"

As Fanon (1991: 110) and Showalter (1999: 191) have explained, the rage that invades the gendered and colonial subject in the second phase of artistic decolonisation is linked to increasing ambivalent impulses and antagonistic feelings about the self. Fanon (1991: 110) describes how the colonised black figure is constantly assailed by profound contradictions concerning his/her own identity:

An unfamiliar weight burdened me. The real world challenged my claims. In the white world the man of colour encounters difficulties in the developing of this bodily schema. Consciousness of the body is solely a negating activity. It is a third-person consciousness. The body is surrounded by an atmosphere of certain uncertainty.

Fanon's character suddenly feels insecure about his own body, confused by the acknowledgment that, for the white man, "[t]he Negro is an animal, the Negro is bad, the Negro is mean, the Negro is ugly" (Fanon 1991: 113). Instead of ignoring this aspect of his (culturally constructed) identity, the colonised subject demands that "notice" be taken of this current image (ibid).

In *In Her Own Image*, under the threatening male gaze, Boland experiences this sort of uncertainty and "corporeal malediction" that Fanon (1991: 111) identifies. Although Boland, as a feminist writer, openly talks about her sexual attitudes, in the process, she reflects profound conflicts and contradictions. This is observed in the clear splitting of identity that the poetic voices in some of the poems experience. In most of them, we come across double selves in constant struggle ("In Her Own Image", "Anorexic", "Menses", *Collected*, 73, 75-76, 80-81) or distorted minds which turn this self-hatred into self-destruction ("Witching", *Collected*, 82-84). This self-annihilation observed in *In Her Own Image* resembles Boland's mature dissolution of her poetic images. Nevertheless, the cause and effect is different. In her mature poetry, the woman poet will represent the self in terms of dissolution, the aim being to show the fallacy involved in defending essentialist definitions of identity. In this volume, Boland ironically destroys herself with a view to reflecting the myth that the cost of female wisdom is self-extermination, or, at best, insanity. On the other hand, the movement towards self-annihilation that these poems exemplify might be caused by Boland's "anxiety of authorship". This term, coined by Gilbert and Gubar (2000: 49), signifies a woman artist's fear that she cannot be an artistic creator and that, if she ever writes, she will be destroyed, or, at best, she will be forced to live in isolation.

112

A significant case of this is found in "Anorexic", where Boland portrays, as the very same title indicates, what Gilbert and Gubar (2000: 53) consider as one of the most common "female diseases" portrayed in women's writing: anorexia. This poem describes a woman acting in self-destruction, by her internalisation of the patriarchal duality established between purity and sexuality, as epitomised by the Virgin Mary (an ideal of intellectual virtuousness) and Eve (an allegory of sinful sexuality): "Flesh is heretic./ My body is a witch./ I am burning it" (*Collected*, 75). Boland associates anorexia with traditional conceptualisations of female sexuality, as recorded in historical, literary, and religious texts. In this poem, a male wish is fulfilled by a woman who seems to have accepted her role fully. Taught by patriarchal conventions to be a beautiful and virginal object, this woman feels anxious about her own flesh. Thus, the feeling underlying this poem is one of masochistic violence. Drawing attention to her deformed figure, the speaker proceeds to act in self-destruction, by renouncing to eat and burning her own body:

> Yes I am torching
> her curves and paps and wiles.
> They scorch in my self-denials.
>
> [...]
>
> I vomited her hungers.
> Now the bitch is burning. (*Collected*, 75)

In a reversal of the myth of origins in which Eve is condemned for having eaten the apple, the poetic persona, "thin as a rib", deliberately punishes herself with starvation. In attempting to mould her identity in man's idealised image, she internalises what Hélène Cixous (1994: 37) denominates the "dual, hierachized oppositions" of the male discourse:

> Where is she?
> Activity/ passivity

Sun/ Moon
Culture/ Nature
Day/ Night

Father/ Mother
Head/ Heart
Inteligible/ Palpable
Logos/ Pathos
Form, convex, sep, advance, semen, progress.
Matter, concave, ground –where steps are taken, holding – and dumping – ground
Man

Woman

The "couple" man/woman is inserted within this opposition as irreconcilable opposites. In this hierarchical distribution, male is privileged and the feminine is subordinated to the masculine order. Cixous argues that this oppositional practice has become endemic to the extent that it appears "eternal-natural" (ibid). In this poem, Boland adopts the anorexic's point of view in order to denounce how easy the labels and categories of (masculine) thought can be understood as 'natural'. To the opposing dualities Cixous mentions, we may add one that directly affects the speaker: flesh vs. soul. Only by remaining "foodless" and rejecting her female flesh, can she attain the male soul or the desired purity associated with the Virgin. As Mary Condren (1989: 5) explains in her study of religious female images:

> Women have been identified with Eve, the symbol of evil, and can only attain sanctity by identifying with the Virgin Mary, the opposite of Eve. But this is an impossible task since we are told that Mary herself "was conceived without sin" and when she gave birth to Jesus remained a virgin. To reach full sanctity then, women have to renounce their sexuality, symbol of their role as temptresses and the means by which they drag men from their lofty heights. [...] Sex and spirituality have become polar opposites in Christian teaching.

Internalising the patriarchal discourse, Boland's Eve, viewing her identity split into polar opposites, perceives masculinity as the ideal state. That is why the poetic persona seeks to return to Adam's body where she can grow "angular and holy". She desires it so intensely that spatial imagery becomes obsessively depicted:

> I will slip
> back into him again
> as if I had never been away.
>
> Caged so
> I will grow
> angular and holy
>
> past pain,
> keeping his heart
> such company
>
> as will make me forget
> in a small place
> the fall
>
> into forked dark,
> into python needs
> heaving to hips and breasts
> and lips and heat
> and sweat and fat and greed. (*Collected*, 76)

As Allen-Randolph (1991: 52) rightly notes, here, verse imitates content. As the penultimate stanza "falls" into the final one, the speaker tries to invert the "fall" from the grace of the male body into a female body of "python needs", "hips", "breasts", "lips", and "sweat and fat and greed". It is significant how the woman avoids employing possessive constructions in the first person when referring to her body, preferring to use no possessives at all, or the third person possessive. With linguistic techniques such as this, Boland explicitly denounces the corruption exerted by male-centered myths. In an interview with Wilson

(1990b: 82), Boland explains her interest in adopting the speaking voice of one of the patriarchal victims, the anorexic:

> I have to say that I think *In Her Own Image* is a misunderstood book [...]. I wrote it with a puritan perspective, but it was taken to be a confession of a number of diseases which I had and neuroses which I was clearly giving evidence of! There are certain areas that are degraded because they were silent. They need to be re-experienced and re-examined. Their darker energies need to be looked at. That is exactly what *In Her Own Image* is about, seeing the image by looking at it.

In this sense, Boland looks at the trauma of anorexia from a feminist critical stance. Fogarty (1994: 97-98) draws a very interesting comparison between Paul Muldoon's "Aisling" and Boland's "Anorexic". Her analysis of two poems dealing with anorexia provides a useful insight into the different uses of feminine images by contemporary Irish male and female writers. She concludes that, whereas in Muldoon's poem anorexia acts as "an allegory of the futility of the actions of Irish republican prisoners on hunger strikes", in Boland's poem, anorexia is not used to talk about apparently public and political issues (p. 98). Boland's lyric 'I' is no longer a "transcendent and universalising" male voice, but rather a voice that treats a concrete experience with "ironic closeness and familiarity" (ibid). Thus, Boland places the anorexic at the centre of a private experience. As González Arias (2000a: 38) explains, "The Beauty Myth" is the only way contemporary society has to imprison women, as former myths about chastity, maternity, and passivity have lost most of their effectiveness. Boland questions the portrayal of anorexia from the inside of its victim's mind, showing how the acceptance of the male ideal of women as beautiful objects only leads to self-inflicted torture.

Other poems in this volume continue exploring the tragic consequences when women accept imposed patriarchal systems of representation, by reflecting a fractured and split identity which results from woman's internalisation of the conventional roles of mother and wife. The following section analyses this aspect more thoroughly.

3.3.2. Ambivalence towards motherhood

As has been hinted, Showalter (1999: 191) also identifies the ambivalent impulses and contradictory feelings that Fanon (1991: 110) diagnosed in the second phase of artistic decolonisation. This American feminist critic explains how the celebration of motherhood and maternal love can at times be combined with an extreme aversion to the actual process of sexual intercourse and childbirth. In the title poem "In Her Own Image", Boland puts the reader inside a woman's mind that ends up killing her own child. The narrator's rejection of motherhood results from her uneasiness with the social conventions regarding women as mothers. In a country where a nationalist tradition has often recurred to the symbolic identification between Ireland and the Mother, and where the precepts of the 1937 Constitution have relegated women to the exclusive roles of mothers and housewives, feminist counter-statements such as this are quite revolutionary. The act of rejecting motherhood does not necessarily imply a rejection of female procreativity, but an escape from the traditional role of mothering that women have been subjected to. In "In Her Own Image", the mother kills her own daughter in order to avoid her experiencing the same victimisation that she has suffered from. By destroying her offspring, the woman speaker avoids the perpetuation of male stereotypes. From the very beginning, we come across the internal confusion of a woman who has just strangled her own child: "It is her eyes:/ the irises are gold/ and round they go/ like the ring on my wedding finger" (*Collected*, 73). The initial lines of the poem show how the woman speaker is alienated by the roles of mother and wife. She compares the gold irises of the dead child's eyes with her wedding ring. Both are metaphors of the timelessness that have entrapped the speaker in an image which portrays her as eternally beautiful and immortal. As Rich (1979: 34) has noted, woman's "awakening of consciousness" can be "confusing, disorienting, and painful", for realising the oppression you have been exposed to is not pleasant at all. The woman in "In Her Own Image" similarly feels confused and disconcerted at her awakening to the oppression she has been suffering. Her inability to define herself leads her to an act of self-negation:

> She is not myself
> anymore, she is not
> even in my sky
> anymore and I
> am not myself. (*Collected*, 73)

The schizophrenic personality of the anorexic acquires here the shape of a woman who revolves around double selves. These lines show a fragmented self, which, as Allen Randolph (1991: 51) explains, only knows how to define herself in negative terms, by "what-she-is-not". She cannot perceive herself as a stable and fixed subject. Unable to disentangle her sense of herself from her sense of her daughter, she ends up confusing her own body with that of her child. As in "Anorexic", the narrator tries to kill that part of herself she feels is oppressing her. But, instead of proceeding to act in self-destruction, she ends up killing her own daughter:

> I will not disfigure
> her pretty face.
> Let her wear amethyst thumbprints,
> a family heirloom,
> a sort of burial necklace (*Collected*, 73)

The end of the poem portrays a dead daughter who wears a "family heirloom" of "amethyst thumbprints". Family is understood as a socially and culturally sanctioned structure in which violent parameters towards women are perpetuated. Unable to escape from this destructive heritage, killing her own child and liberating herself from a possible offspring are the only means the speaker can have access to her own identity. The poem ends with the persona burying her "second nature", and adopting a "compromise" to "bloom" *in her own image.* This promise of a future, compromised identity, a healed fragmented self, will be fulfilled in poems such as "Solitary" and "Making Up", where the body will be an essential element for the woman's united and unbreakable identity.[12]

Boland's rejection of motherhood as a social institution is continued in poems such as "Witching". As Fanon's 'Negro' (1991: 130), who finally decides to embrace a mystical past, a valid historical place where accounts of "learned blacks" might restore "the dignity of his race", Boland similarly embraces in "Witching" a mystical past inhabited by those elderly sisters who had a magical power fearful to men. The witch in this poem becomes a liberating symbol of an oppressive masculine culture. For feminists as well as contemporary women writers, witches stand for female creativity with their highest potential. As French feminist Gauthier (1981b: 199-201) asserts:

> Why witches? *Because witches sing* [...]. In reality, they croon lullabies, they howl, they gasp, they babble, they shout, they sigh. [...]
> Why witches? *Because witches are alive.* Because they are in direct contact with the life of their own bodies and bodies of others, with the life force itself. [...]
> Why witches? *Because witches are rapturous* [...]. Their pleasure is so violent, so transgressive, so open, so fatal, that men have not yet recovered.

This reliance on witches in the second stage of decolonisation has also been identified by Showalter (1999: 193). This feminist critic has noted that, in their allusions to physical victimisation and sexual exploitation, feminist writers usually identify with fearful figures, such as the witch or the prostitute, who albeit despised by patriarchal society are very helpful for the purposes of subversion. In this poem, Boland recurs precisely to this figure in order to subvert what has traditionally been a sacred role for women. Rather than something desired, motherhood is connected here with those women who repeat male standards, and also with the damaging allegorical image of Mother Ireland. Directing her speech towards those "nursery lights", the witch describes them in rather negative terms:

> these my enemies [...]
>
> who breed
> and breed,
> who talk and talk –
>
> birth
> and bleeding,
> the bacteria of feeds. (*Collected*, 82)

By connecting childbirth and bleeding, the speaker links motherhood with that nationalist speech that advocates blood sacrifice in the fight for the mother country. The "nursery lights" signify, as Kelly (1993: 53) puts it, those "national-muses [who provide] nurturing milk for the male oral tradition". These apparently harmless lights are constraining images of womanhood that "shine", "multiply", and "douse" the witch's own light. Only by burning her own body, can she create her own light, a light which is not the reflection of any looking-glass, any "nursery light":

> I will
> reverse
> their arson,
>
> make
> a pyre
> of my haunch
>
> and so
> the last thing
> they know
> will be
> the stench
> of my crotch. (*Collected*, 83)

In this sense, the woman in the poem becomes a figure of her own creation: she turns out to be a self-burnt witch, rather than a witch burnt at the stake by others. As in "In Her Own Image", childbearing is understood as an impediment to achieving one's identity. The witch-figure denies the possibility of bearing a child, reacting to an inherited tradition in which women were most valued for their sole role in motherhood. By burning her "haunch" (a metonymy of motherhood), the witch destroys not only her potential to be pregnant, but also those traditionally Irish icons of female domesticity. In this sense, destruction and creation are intrinsically linked. By destroying the mythical mother of the Irish tradition, the woman in the poem creates her own distinct identity.

Boland's scathing rejection of maternity in "In Her Own Image" and "Witching" is counteracted in "Menses", a poem that contains the only passage in the volume where motherhood forms an indispensable part of the woman's identity. Although this belongs to the second half of the internal evolution I earlier identified in *In Her Own Image*, I think it appropriate to include it here. This poem will provide useful introduction for the following section, for it puts forward one of the most positive affirmations of Boland's womanhood in this volume.

In "Menses", Boland exposes to public view something which has not only been ignored, but also hidden as shameful in society: menstruation. As González Arias (2000b: 129-130) explains, menstruation is understood, both in the Bible and in early Irish texts, as a divine punishment for women. By focusing on this womanly experience, Boland overturns this belief, transforming what has traditionally been considered a penance into a liberating source of woman's creativity. "Menses" starts by describing a woman who initially feels angry and disgusted at the experience of menstruation, especially because she is under the control of the moon. Rather than standing as a symbol of female power, the moon both paralyses the woman, in an endless cycle of biological menstruation, and condemns her as a sinful Eve, "a fallen self" punished with period pains:

My days are moon-dials.
She will never be done with me.
She needs me.
She is dry.

I leash to her,
a sea,
a washy heave,
a tide. (*Collected*, 80)

The narrator here is doomed and dominated by the coming and going of
fluids inside her body. Internalising the patriarchal duality flesh vs. soul that
appeared in "Anorexic", the speaker negates the "tides" of her body as a source of
creative potential, and argues that "[o]nly her mind is free" to analyse "the ruffian
growths,/ the bindweed/ and the meadowsweet,/ the riff-raff" of her garden
(*Collected*, 80). These plants are allegories of her own female potential. They
symbolise, as Kelly (1993: 52) would put it, "the woman's own artistic drives", to
leave aside her own bodily discomfort and engage in a liberating creative activity.
The narrator here adopts a separatist stance, by envying the plants which are not
bound to sexual intercourse in order to experience childbirth:

How I envy them:
each filament,
each anther bred

[...]

They are street-walkers,
lesbians,
nuns.
I am not one of them (*Collected*, 80-81)

In this sense, the speaker quarrels with the negative influence that the moon exerts
over her own body, and therefore, over her own artistic potential. Nevertheless,
the final part of the poem reorients the woman's stance towards the moon-mother
by reconstructing menstruation as a source of her creative potential. It is in her

own inner self, her potential for motherhood, and sexual desire, where she must find her own 'true' creative self:

> Another hour
> and she will addle me
>
> till I begin
> to think like her.
> As when I've grown
> round and obscene with child,
> or when I moan
> for him between the sheets,
> then I begin to know
> that I am bright and original
> and that my light's my own. (*Collected*, 81)

Motherhood is not perceived anymore as a confinement for women's creativity. On the contrary, it is in the positive reconstruction of an identity grounded in motherhood where the woman speaker finds her artistic inspiration. By her ability to be a mother, the speaker becomes a god-like creature with significance of her own.

3.4. Reaffirming sexual difference: the woman's body on the foreground

In contrast to previous poems like "Anorexic" and "In Her Own Image", where identity was perceived as something unstable, in the second half of this volume, the poems move towards an assertion of the self in essentialist terms. We have seen something of this in "Menses", where the woman found her distinctive identity in her biological pull towards motherhood. The negative analysis of culture and victimisation which underlies the first poems[13] gives way to a praising description of womanhood in terms of the female body. Before explaining how Boland states her identity from the perspective of the female body and sexual pleasure, it is essential to explain the main reasons that drive her to emphasise women's 'Otherness' through writing. In order to do so, I will rely on Cixous's and Irigaray's advocacy of a woman's liberation based on what they call "sexual difference".

Cixous (1994: 38) and Irigaray (1991: 24) argue that women must have access to a full identity of their own, distinct from men. One of the main differences between feminists such as Simone de Beauvoir, on the one hand, and Hélène Cixous and Luce Irigaray, on the other, is that whereas de Beauvoir fights for women's equal rights, Cixous and Irigaray opt for difference, specifically sexual difference. As I am addressing Cixous's theories in subsequent sections, and due to the similarity of their approaches, I will focus particularly on Irigaray's theories. In an essay called "Equal or Different?", Irigaray (1991: 23-29) develops this point. For this feminist critic, de Beauvoir's defence of equality is erroneous, as "equal" tends to mean "equal to men". It is her view that women need an identity as women, and that there should be "*woman*kind as well as *man*kind" (p. 24). Whereas de Beauvoir emphasises access to the world of men (and thus *equality*), Irigaray is suggesting instead the creation of a world of women. In Irigarian terms, woman has always been defined as man's 'Other', what she terms the "other of the same", the necessary negation of the male subject. In order to cease being the "other of the same", this 'Other' must stress her otherness and difference, what is unique in herself. Only by doing so, a self-defined woman with 'real' social and symbolic representation can emerge (p. 32). In this sense, woman would become "woman-for-herself" rather than the "other of the same" (p. 159). As Irigaray (1991: 151) has put it: "For women, it is [...] a matter of learning to discover and inhabit a different magnetism and the morphology of a sexuate body, especially in its singularities and mucous qualities". Sexual difference is envisaged as both liberating for the two sexes and preserving what is unique and distinctive in each sex. Irigaray envisages a possible female imaginary in which the language of the female body is inscribed. Her advocacy of sexual difference would imply "an autonomous and positive representation of [women's] sexuality in culture" (p. 42).

This notion of sexual difference defended by French feminism is very similar to Gayatri Spivak's advocacy of "strategic essentialism". As Spivak (1993: 17) has admitted on several occasions, adopting "a strategic use" of essentialism has enabled her project as a feminist. In other words, essentials must be employed in certain situations, as she asserts in a conversation with Elizabeth Grosz (1990: 11): "I think we have to choose again strategically, not universal but essentialist. [...] I must say I am an essentialist person from time to time. There is for example, the strategic choice of a genitalist essentialism in anti-sexist work today". In her essay "Feminism and Critical Theory", for instance, Spivak (1988a: 77) asserts that the word "woman" must be defined in terms of the word "man":

> [D]efining the word "woman" as resting on the word "man" is a reactionary position. [...] The only way that I can see myself making definitions is in a provisional and polemical one: I construct my definition as a woman not in terms of a woman's putative essence but in terms of words currently in use. "Man" is such a word in common usage.

Although this feminist postcolonial critic asserts that essentialism is not the right stance, she defends it as a necessary step and strategy: "women today may *have* to take 'the risk of essence' in order to think differently" (Spivak 1993: 3). In this sense, Spivak reminds one of Irigaray, who warns, as Whitford (1991: 13) explains, against deconstructing (or replacing) the male/female opposition before women have access to "identity and subjectivity".

Cixous's and Irigaray's defence of sexual difference and Spivak's occasional return to essentialism is observed in Boland's *In Her Own Image*. Boland becomes an essentialist in the strategic sense Spivak talks about, as a necessary way of fighting back at a certain point. It is in this phase where Boland discovers the possibility of a feminist discourse, and in this first flush of feminist thought she becomes the most energetic essentialist, as I will discuss in more detail.

In all the poems of *In Her Own Image*, there is a strong connection between body imagery and personal identity. That is why Boland might be located within that phase of feminism which endorses sexism, and "women write as a biologically oppressed group" (Ashcroft, Griffiths & Tiffin 2002: 174). This reliance on the body is identified by Fanon as a distinctive and necessary feature in the process of decolonisation. Fanon's colonised subject states at a certain point: "I was responsible at the same time for my body, for my race, for my ancestors. I subjected myself to an objective examination, I discovered my blackness, my ethnic characteristics. [...] I made myself an object" (Fanon 1991: 112). In a similar way to Fanon's colonised subject, Boland proceeds to analyse her body, making herself an object of analysis. *In Her Own Image* shows, above all, Boland's quest for autonomous self-definition based on the potential of her female body. Ostriker (1986: 92), noting that contemporary women poets employ anatomical imagery far more frequently than male poets, asserts:

> One of the ways we recognise a poetess – which is to say a woman poet locked into sentimentality by her inhibitions – is that she steers clear of anatomical references. [...] One of the ways we recognise that a woman poet has taken some kind of liberating jump is that her muted parts begin to explain themselves.

The poems in the second half of *In Her Own Image* might be read as a sign of liberation for the female writer, in Ostriker's own words (1986: 91), a "release of anatomy". Patrick Kavanagh (1967: 27) asserts in *Collected Prose* that "the body with its feelings, its instincts, provides women with a source of wisdom, but they lack the analytic detachment to exploit it in literature". In contrast to this view, Boland's poetry shows a woman who is able to perceive through her body. It is in the female body where the poetic voices in this volume find their name and identity.

That is why Cixous's and Irigaray's theories are appropriate for approaching *In Her Own Image*. In their advocacy of sexual difference, these

French feminists connect writing with women's bodies in a direct and intrinsic way. In "The Laugh of the Medusa", Cixous (1981: 245-246) stresses the importance of writing about the female body, insisting that women's creativity is and should be intrinsically sexual and carnal:

> Woman must write her self: must write about women and bring women to writing, from which they have driven away as violently as from their bodies. [...] And why don't you write? Write! Writing is for you; you are for you; your body is yours, take it.

Irigaray shares Cixous's dependence on the female body.[14] The language that she envisages in "When Our Lips Speak Together" directly connects female sexuality and writing:

> if we don't invent a language, if we don't find our body's language [...] [w]e shall [...] leave our desires unexpressed, unrealised. Asleep again, unsatisfied, we shall fall back upon the words of men – who for their part, have "known" for a long time. But *not our body*. (Irigaray 1985: 214)

The invention of language parallels the rediscovery of the body which has its own language, a feminine language that must be heard. For Irigaray (1991: 200), it is necessary to elaborate "an art of the sexual", a place where women can explore their autoeroticism.[15]

This writing deriving from the body emerges for the first time in *In Her Own Image*. Boland writes herself, her bodily feelings or the imaginary carnal experiences of other women. In the process, she destroys traditional poetic standards, for it is women's real lives which defy the laws of patriarchal texts. In contrast to the women in Irish legends, who have been denied their right to act as agentive subjects (Haberstroh 1996: 192), *In Her Own Image* is revolutionary, because it introduces women who speak through their own body, in their own voice, disrupting their imposed silence. By analysing their bodies as if it were the first time they examine them and by fulfilling their sexual desires, these women try to attain their own identity. In this sense, Boland carries out a celebration of womanhood, which is mainly defined by sexuality, by those biological features that distinguish women from men. This stance has been described as "biologism", the belief that there is a given 'female' nature, "an essence which is biologically given" (Moi 1997: 108-109).

In order to introduce this aspect of Boland's work, I will briefly analyse "Mastectomy", a poem included in the first half of *In Her Own Image* for its emphasis on the tragic consequences cultural impositions have on women's bodies. As in the poems considered later on, this poem reflects a strong connection between the body and the personal identity. The violence and aggressiveness that invaded the woman in "Tirade for the Mimic Muse" is observed in this poem, where the poetic speaker angrily attacks the male surgeon who has usurped her breast, a symbol of her identity as a woman. This poem advances the separatist stance that we observe in poems such as "Solitary" (*Collected*, 78-79), by setting a sharp contrast between the woman speaker and a male 'Other'. In contrast to "Tirade for the Mimic Muse", "Anorexic", and "In Her Own Image", where the 'Other' was perceived as the woman's double self, "Mastectomy" places this division in terms of sexual difference. The "other of the same", as Irigaray (1991: 159) would put it, is connected with a masculinity, described in negative and accusing terms, since the "he" is a violent subject who satisfies himself by engaging in war and usurpation. He is described as a "blade-handed" surgeon, a "specialist/ freshing death/ across his desk" (*Collected*, 77). Boland establishes a symbolic connection between the male victimiser and the patriarchal discourse, which claims authority over the woman's body. The female body becomes the site where all sorts of male atrocities are committed:

> I have stopped bleeding.
> I look down.
> It has gone.
>
> So they have taken off
> what slaked them first,

what they have hated since (*Collected*, 77)

For Boland, the breast is a symbol, not only of procreation, metonymic for her function as mother (as the bosom nurtures her child), but also of female potential and sexual pleasure for both. Boland turns upside down the Freudian thesis of the penis-envy (according to which the woman desires what she can never have), since here, it is the man who lusts after the woman's breast. Boland's critique resembles Irigaray's attack on psychoanalytic theories. In her second book *Speculum* (originally published in 1974) and in essays like "The poverty of psychoanalysis" (1991: 79-104) and "The Power of Discourse and the Subordination of the Feminine" (1991: 118-132), Irigaray stands as an outspoken feminist and critic of Freud and Lacan. According to their theories, female sexuality is conceptualised according to masculine parameters. The constitution of women's sex means "deficiency", "lack", "atrophy" of the male sex, and even "penis-envy" (Irigaray 1991: 119). In this sense, women are left within the symbolic in a perpetual "exile", "like ghosts" in the masculine phallic imaginary (p. 91). Boland is able to reverse this belief. It is now the male sex that is described as 'lack', as an 'Other' which cannot have the female breast. In their envy, the surgeon and specialist deprive the woman of what "slaked them first", "the wetness of their dreams".[16] Because of the male destructive power directed towards the woman's sexuality, the speaker's identity is, in this way, damaged:

> I flatten
> to their looting,
> to the sleight
>
> of their plunder.
> I am a brute site.
> Theirs is the true booty. (*Collected*, 78)

As she implies in the last line of the poem, the body is the *truth* of the woman's self. In this volume, womanhood is best defined by bodily imagery, in contrast to those traditional allegorical notions (such as Mother Ireland) where carnal references are usually occluded.

This reliance on the female body continues in "Solitary", where Boland, by writing about the experience of masturbation, connects female pleasure with artistic expression and female speech, something that Gilbert and Gubar (2000: 568) have identified as common in women's writing. In worshipping, as we will see, her own power to touch herself, Boland links her own writing with that woman's language advocated by Irigaray (1991: 126) which privileges touch rather than sight. Subverting the dominance of the male gaze in patriarchal Western constructions, this feminist critic conceptualises female relationships in more physical terms:

> [What women] have to do is touch one another, listen to one another, smell one another, see one another – without necessarily privileging the gaze, without a beautiful mask, without submitting to a libidinal economy which means that the body has to be covered with a veil if it is to be desirable! (Irigaray 1991: 101)

The female eroticism that "Solitary" advocates disrupts those Western constructions in which women have been consigned to passivity and become beautiful objects of contemplation. Describing her experience as sacramental, the speaker depicts herself as a "votary", "worshipping" the shrine of her female genitalia:

> Night:
> An oratory of dark,
> a chapel of unreason.
>
> Here in the shrubbery
> the shrine.
> I am its votary,
> its season. (*Collected*, 78)

The initial word of the poem is telling. As Cixous (1994: 37) shows, night has traditionally been a female term in the binary logic. In "Solitary", it becomes clear that the speaker is carrying out her activity in the realm of the unknown, under the shadows, in the domain of the mysterious power of the moon and the spell of witches. In this way, "Night" immerses us in a female universe which stands in direct opposition to the male world. The speaker establishes this contrast by confronting the male gods who have the privilege of giving her sexual pleasure. Taught that "You could die for this/ The gods could make you blind", the speaker, nonetheless, lets herself be carried by "these incendiary/ and frenzied ways" (*Collected*, 78-79). Female sexuality is depicted as a sensual and erotic experience which, briefly after reaching its summit, rapidly descends. By showing she is not sexually inactive (as traditionally acknowledged), she defies the orthodox gods. In this sense, masturbation becomes an act of worship of the self, a celebration of female sexuality very much in the mood of French feminism. As Luce Irigaray (1985: 24) explains, whereas the man

> needs an instrument in order to touch himself: his hand, woman's genitals, language [...], a woman touches herself by and within herself directly, without meditation, without anyone being able to forbid her to do so, for her sex is composed of two lips which embrace continually.

By masturbating herself "without anyone being able to forbid her", the woman in "Solitary" is self-sufficient and powerful. Nevertheless, although French feminism has advocated a form of women's writing that is rooted in the female body, both Irigaray (1991: 171-174) and Cixous (1994: 119-128) have identified the danger involved in claiming the superiority of one's sex. They argue that in order to achieve a complete renewal after a destructive patriarchal culture, sexual difference must be combined with what they call an "amorous exchange" between a man and a woman. This "amorous exchange" is that in which one sex will not seek superiority over the other, and their relationship will be one of equality and harmony between opposites. The "amorous exchange" that Irigaray

and Cixous so strongly advocate is not manifested by the woman in "Solitary",
but rather in other poems which better suit Boland's 'female' aesthetic. In this
poem, the poetic voice refuses to engage in sexual intercourse with men, and
claims her superiority by making clear that she herself, and "only" she, has access
to "the true sensual rhythms of her own body" (Kelly 1993: 51):

> I know,
> only I know
>
> these incendiary
> and frenzied ways:
> I am alone
>
> no one's here,
> no one sees
> my hands
>
> fan and cup,
> my thumbs tinder. (*Collected*, 78-79)

In this sense, Boland maintains the opposites of sexual difference (male
sexuality vs. female sexuality), and establishes their relationship on a basis of
superiority and not equality as advocated by Cixous and Irigaray. This
egocentrism and self-admiration is a necessary step in the process of turning
upside down some masculine constructs. By praising her autoeroticism, the
woman calls into question the puritan dual view of body and mind. Whereas the
woman in "Anorexic" adopted the traditional opposing duality flesh vs. soul
common in male discourse, the persona in this poem integrates body and mind by
means of verbal parallelism:

> How my flesh summers,
> how my mind shadows
> meshed in this brightness (*Collected*, 79)

In contrast to "Anorexic", where the woman avoided using possessive constructions to refer to the parts of her body, the speaker in "Solitary" openly makes her dominion over her own body explicit: "my fingers", "my hands", "my thumbs", "my flesh", etc. This is a woman who asserts herself, and does not despise her female flesh. Her body is her identity, so fulfilling her desire is coming to terms with her own true self.

Unsurprisingly, this poem is full of imagery concerning the earth. As Fanon (1991: 126-128) has explained, one way for the oppressed subject to assert his/her identity is to defend an authentic relation with everything that is pure and absolute, something which the (white and/or male) coloniser cannot have access to. In a similar way to Fanon's 'Negro', Boland defends in "Solitary" a union with the natural and spiritual world inaccessible to the (white) man.[17] Like the woman in "Menses", the speaker here is intrinsically connected with the rhythms of the earth, and the cyclical variation of the seasons: her flesh "summers", her mind "shadows", and after "flush[ing]" and "dark[ing]" in her orgasm, she "winter[s]/ into sleep".

In this sense, Boland's main objective becomes to write a poetry that can record the fluid rhythms of her own body. The act of masturbation becomes a definite form of "écriture feminine". Irigaray's sexual lips are the woman's lips opening to utter her 'true' speech, a language that celebrates female sexuality and drives us closer to female's subjectivity:

> how my cry
> blasphemes
> light and dark,
> screams
> land from sea,
> makes word flesh (*Collected*, 79)

In a reversal of the Christian myth of creation, the speaker "makes word flesh". She becomes a goddess, producing a new artistic representation *in her own image*. Boland explicitly connects creativity and biology, text (the "word") and body (the "flesh"). On the other hand, references to "my cry" and to her act of "scream[ing]" directly link this woman's agency with her ability to perceive herself through her own body. This appreciation of the female body as a place of resistance reaches a point where Boland adopts the most extreme biological and deterministic stance. At the end of the poem, the speaker is reduced to biological matter: she becomes "animal/ inanimate" (p. 79).

The danger of falling into this sort of biological determinism the end of "Solitary" exemplifies has been identified by de Beauvoir (1981: 153), who views the female body as a menace for the liberation of the female potential:

> it's a good thing that a woman is no longer ashamed of her body, of her pregnancy, of her menstruation. I think it is excellent that she should get to know her body. But it would be an error to make of it a value and to think that the feminine body gives you a new dimension of the world. It would be ridiculous and absurd, it would be like constructing a counter-penis. The women who share this belief fall again into the irrational, into mysticism, into a sense of the cosmic.

This is what happens in "Solitary": by revalorising the body in such a way, the speaker eventually falls into "the irrational" and "mysticism". The narrator is immersed in an intense private experience of madness and delirium. She describes herself to be in "a chapel of *unreason*" and argues that she, and only she, has access to "these incendiary/ and *frenzied* ways" (emphasis added). The irrational discourse that the woman conducts in "Solitary" was also observed in "Witching", where Boland identified with the apparently mad figure of the witch. The "craft" and "bookish" gifts of the witch paralleled her evil and psychotic enterprise: to "abort the birth/ of calves/ and warts" (*Collected*, 82). Boland's connection of poetry with madness is symptomatic of a whole patriarchal belief that places womanhood more in touch with the irrational than with the rational. This traditional equation is also maintained in French Feminism. Both Cixous and Irigaray have envisaged a woman's language that draws on the resources of the unconscious and has the capacity to go beyond reason. In *La*, Cixous (1994: 59) describes feminine writing as against "reason", labelled an "enemy": "Her scene of wild writings forever escapes vigilance, armed reason, force, jealousy, death, wish, [...], the traps and bites of life's enemies" (1994: 59). Similarly, Irigaray (1985: 28-29) argues that due to the fact that women find sexual pleasure almost everywhere, their discourse touches irrationality itself:[18]

> This is doubtless why she is said to be whimsical, incomprehensible, agitated, capricious ... not to mention her language, in which "she" sets off in all directions leaving "him" unable to discern the coherence of any meaning. Hers are contradictory words, somewhat mad from the standpoint of reason, inaudible for whoever listens to them with ready-made grids, with a fully elaborated code in hand [...]. For if "she" says something, it is not, it is already no longer, identical with what she means.

By defining women's language as irrational and non-reasonable, both Cixous and Irigaray try to show the impossibility of trapping women in an exact definition, for they try to express a *"silent, multiple, diffuse touch"* that is utterly inaccessible and therefore incomprehensible to men (Irigaray 1985: 29). Nevertheless, in the process, what they do is replicate the male binary logic Logos/Pathos by which women have been undervalued as irrational and hysterical to the standards of (masculine rational) logic. This is precisely what occurs in "Solitary" and "Witching": in their irrational and mad discourses, these women refuse to escape binary male constructs.[19]

A linguistic analysis of "Solitary" significantly supports this interpretation from a French feminist perspective. The loosening of stanzaic form and the absence of a regular rhythmic pattern corresponds with the speech of a woman who strives to give voice to her own sexuality, discarding inhibitions, and moving away from the main stream of discourse. The broken and fragmented language, the lack of punctuation, and the lack of almost any cohesive conjunctions in the poem further indicate that this speaker is interested in breaking textual conventions, dislocating normal cohesive devices. Therefore, "Solitary" is written in a form of woman's language according to which, as Irigaray (1985: 300) puts it, "'she' goes off in all directions and in which 'he' is unable to discern the coherence of any meaning". As Boland goes against the logic of male reason, in her statements we come across "some chatter, and exclamation, a half-secret, a sentence left in suspense" (ibid).

The emphasis on 'writing the body' that "Solitary" reflects is perhaps more clearly put into practice in "Exhibitionist", the longest poem of the whole volume. In this poem, the woman decides not to hide the clearest sign of her identity, her body, anymore. By exposing the naked body of a woman, Boland transcends the traditional distinctions between the public and the private. Furthermore, Boland equates writing with an act of exhibitionism. Both "the text" and the poem's "aesthetic" are intrinsically connected with "this trash/ and gimmickry/ of sex", the female body:

> I wake to dark,
> a window slime of dew.
> Time to start
>
> working
> from the text,
> making
>
> from this trash
> and gimmickry
> of sex
>
> my aesthetic (*Collected*, 84)

As in "Witching" and "Solitary", Boland situates this moment in a dark setting. As in most of the poems of this volume, imagery of lightness and darkness are brought together in order to enhance this feeling of female enlightenment (interestingly referred to as 'dark') vs. the male tradition (allegorised as 'light'). When she carries out a strip show the poet is allowed to express her own art freely and unrestrainedly. Gaining autonomy over her own body, she has the power to expose "a hip first", and then "a breast" (p. 84). These images powerfully suggest

Eve's mythical rib-shaped curve. This new Eve, rather than hiding her shameful flesh (as she has been taught to), decides to get rid of all those clothes which "bushelled" her "asleep", finally waking from a liberating self-unconsciousness. The link between the female body and the woman's identity is further emphasised by the following conversion of nouns into verbs:

> I subvert
>
> sculpture
> the old mode:
> I skin
>
> I dimple clay
> I flesh,
> I rump stone. (*Collected*, 85)

By turning nouns such as "skin", "flesh and "rump" into verbs of action, she describes herself as an agent who creates her own body, rather than a mere inanimate object of male production. In this sense, the speaker becomes a new Eve who doesn't need Adam to spring from his rib. Furthermore, she does not use her own sexuality to seduce men, as traditionally believed. Rather than being an enticer, Eve draws men's attention towards her own nakedness in order to annihilate sexual craving and lust:

> Cast down
> Lucifers,
> spruce
>
> businessmen,
> their eyes
> cast down.
>
> [...]
> I'll show them how
>
> in offices,
> their minds

blind on files

the view
blues through
my curves and arcs. (*Collected*, 85-86)

The speaker deliberately enters those "files" where men have registered their representations of women. The reiterated presence of the volitional 'will', a characteristic feature of this volume, shows the narrator's determinacy and intention to carry out her revenge against patriarchal values. By burning her own body, she defeats the power of the male gaze and those stereotypical images of women as symbols of male fantasies: "Into the gutter/ of their lusts/ I burn/ the shine/ of my flesh" (p. 86). By her self-destruction, Boland 'burns off' mythical visions of women, as fallen Eves, and produces her own self, described as "the light that is/ unyielding/ frigid/ constellate". As Alen-Randoplh (1991: 56) explains, 'frigid' in this context means "unresponsive" to the male sexual organ and to male lust. In this way, the end of "Exhibitionist" connects true self, woman's identity, with a clear aversion to sexual intercourse. This separatist stance, according to which the male 'Other' is described as an unsuited sexual partner, was also observed in "Menses", where the speaker envied her garden weeds for their ability to reproduce independently, and in "Solitary", where the speaker defiantly masturbated herself.

This equation of female identity with body imagery is continued in the final poem of *In Her Own Image*, "Making Up". Here, the poet gains the freedom of expressing her own womanhood through a complex succession of metaphors that have appeared throughout the whole collection: makeup, waking up, mirrors, witchcraft, lightness and darkness, and water. The rich amalgam of literary motifs Boland recurs to is symptomatic of a second phase in the process of artistic decolonisation whose style is, as described by Fanon (1990: 177),

[a] harsh style, full of images, for the image is the drawbridge which allows unconscious energies to be scattered on the surrounding meadows.

> It is a vigorous style, alive with rhythms, struck through and through with bursting life; it is full of colour, too, bronzed, sun-baked and violent... [It] expresses above all, hand to hand struggle and it reveals the need that man has to liberate himself from a part of his being which already contained the seeds of decay.

This quotation is very helpful for understanding this volume's recurring motifs. By using the images mentioned above, Boland tries to unmask her women, and liberate them from the imprisonment male texts have confined them to. In particular, makeup becomes a powerful metaphor. This image operates simultaneously as a metaphor of self-creation and a reference to women's victimisation by conventional "made up" images of femininity (Allen-Randolph 1991: 58). As the woman wakes up, she realises how her "naked face" is "dulsed and shrouded" (*Collected*, 87), suggesting the artificiality of the images of women reproduced in culture and literature. This shroud, a veil covering the face, is an image of confinement which has fascinated women and male writers ever since the nineteenth century. This veil implies the presence of power, of an inner life behind its surface. Romantics such as Blake, Wordsworth, Coleridge, Emerson, and Shelley have perpetuated a tradition which embraces the veil as a necessary concealment of guilt and sin. For these male writers, the veil has been an emblem of the "obscure potential" associated to the female, "a mysterious [and inaccessible] otherness" (Gilbert & Gubar 2000: 471). The woman in "Making Up" experiences herself behind a veil, a "shrouded" face; she feels under "a cloud" in "a dull pre-dawn". Suddenly, she decides to lift this veil and disclose the obscure potential behind it. She does so by creating her own makeup:

> But I'll soon
> see to that.
> I push the blusher up,
>
> I raddle
> and I prink,
> pinking bone
> till my eyes

are
a rouge-washed
flush on water. (*Collected*, 87)

Demystifying Romantic myths, the speaker lifts the patriarchal veil, cleanses the male makeup, for more "rouge-washed" colours. This is a woman creating her own painted face, with a desire to celebrate her own creativity. Her new assertive stance is observed in the choice of syntactic constructions, in which an agentive subject is followed by verbs of action, something typical in this volume of poetry. Now that her "face is made", and the woman reclaims her status and control of her image, she warns:

Take nothing, nothing
at its face value:
Legendary seas,
nakedness,

that up and stuck
lassitude
of thigh and buttock
that they prayed to -

it's a trick.
Myths
are made by men. (*Collected*, 88)

By admitting that all identities are necessarily fictional constructions, the narrator argues that both her new makeup and the "nakedness" that identified her former sister in "Exhibitionist" are merely repetitions of male persuasive myths. In this sense, she would be moving away from that essentialist stance that pervaded previous poems. Nevertheless, in the following lines, the speaker contradicts this assertion. Once again, she adopts a biological stance by defending, through her own body, the 'real':

The truth of this

> wave-raiding
> sea-heaving
> made-up
> tale
>
> of a face
> from the source
> of the morning
> is my own:
>
> Mine are the rouge pots,
> the hot pinks,
> the fledged
> and edgy mix
> of light and water
> out of which
> I dawn. (*Collected*, 88)

The victorious awakening of this new self at the end of the poem, a self that proclaims her superiority by *making up* her own image and successfully "dawn[ing]", refutes the previous deconstruction of identity-claims. At the end of the poem, the speaker reclaims the truth, the tale, and the rouge pots as her own. This belief that the 'true' essence of herself is found in her body (in this case, her painted face) is observed in the numerous times in which 'truth' is repeated in this volume, mainly in those cases where the poetic voice is referring to the body. As we saw in "Mastectomy", the speaker accused the male surgeon of stripping her breast, described as "the *true* booty" (*Collected*, 78). The woman's genuine essence that men appropriated in this poem becomes the source of resistance in "Tirade for the Mimic Muse". The statement of intent in this opening poem, "I will show you *true* reflections" reflects the aesthetics of a woman poet who advocates her perception of 'real life' as experienced by the female body (*Collected*, 72). This belief in the 'real' and in its advocacy by the woman writer pervades Cixous's writings too. As we saw in "The Laugh of the Medusa", this feminist writer advocated that women must break out of their silence and write their bodies (Cixous 1981: 245-246). Only by doing so, they come onto the stage of the "real", as Andermatt (1984: 56) explains. Similarly, Boland defends that a writing that gives voice to the woman's body stands in a direct relation to life and to reality. This conviction stands in contrast to Boland's later poetic production, where notions such as 'truth' and the 'real' will be constantly put into question, in the most poststructuralist fashion. As we will see, her mature work will identify the 'real' as a social construction. By showing the impossibility of solidifying her artistic images within the poem, Boland will show the fallacy of essentialist attempts (such as those by feminist, nationalist, and imperialist ideologies) to define a 'real' and 'true' identity.

But, at this early stage in her career, Boland cannot help adopting an emancipating project that defines womanhood in essentialist terms. In this way, Boland experiences the same dilemma as Cixous and Irigaray. As Whitford (1991: 12) argues, these French feminists are confronted by the modernist/postmodernist debate: on the one hand, their emancipatory force is grounded precisely in the very "modernist category 'woman' with essentialist implications"; on the other hand, they try to avoid the perpetuation of oppressive structures by envisaging new forms of resistance that overcome the Western patriarchal binary thought.

Cixous's and Irigaray's conception of sexual difference, for instance, exemplifies this feminist dilemma. On the one hand, they advocate defining women as sexually different from men, and the existence of boundaries that preserve what is unique and distinctive in each sex. As Irigaray (1991: 115) puts it, the difference between the sexes "contrives a space or site of liberty between two bodies, two flesh, which protects the partners by giving them boundaries". Cixous's and Irigaray's need for a separate woman's identity requires the existence of boundaries that prevent the fusion between the male and the female, or the incorporation of one category into the other. On the other hand, Cixous and Irigaray argue that women are merely characterised by fluidity, and that it is this fluid nature which allows them to escape all binary oppositions. Here, one might ask, how can the female, if it is merely defined by fluidity, be held behind some boundaries? Wouldn't women's fluid nature overcome these boundaries that separate the sexes? In short, the belief that there is a woman's essence clearly distinguishable from man's, a "womanness" as Rooney (1993: 2) would put it, contradicts the French feminist belief in a woman's language that "can only go on and on, without ever inscribing or distinguishing contours" (Cixous 1994: 44), a writing mainly defined by fluidity and infiniteness.

Boland exposes a similar contradiction. On the one hand, she defends sexual difference in poems such as "Mastectomy", "Solitary", and "Exhibitionist", in which a distinguishable woman's body and sexuality stands in contrast to a male 'Other'. In "Making Up", this new woman will create her aesthetic *in opposition* to those "myths made by men", myths in which women have been "stuck" in a "lassitude", in which their "thigh[s]" and "buttock[s]" only serve to fulfil male's desires (*Collected*, 88). On the other hand, Boland re-situates this new woman as a fluid entity that is able to overcome categorisations. The fluid definition of the woman in "Making Up" is attained by means of water imagery. Her eyes are described as "a rouge-washed/ flush on water", a "mirror set" of "ocean shine", and her face projects visions of "wave-riding" and "sea-heaving" (pp. 87-88). In contrast to the "Legendary seas" of patriarchal tradition (in which women have been edible seaweeds, "dulsed"), the woman's sea is a sort of liberating ocean, a rising, insurrectionary combination of bright colours and liquids that manages to escape male simplistic representations. The "edgy mix/ of light and water" that makes up her own face is unstable; it escapes masculine 'contours' (p. 88). The image of the woman is as variable as the makeup that covers her, makeup that is liable to change, depending on the light or the sea tides during the day. The new muse's identification with water links her with the idea of perpetually renewed fertility, with a constant ability to make herself up differently *in her own image*. In this sense, Boland combines sexual difference while attempting to offer an image of womanhood that refuses simplification by male standards. It won't be until her mature work that Boland will more successfully represent her women as escaping artistic solidification, as she will leave aside this emphasis on sexual difference and will be able to achieve the desired effect, by bringing her own women to dissolution.

3.5. An experimental language

Although Allen-Randolph (1991: 53) recognises the volume's link between the female body and textuality, he argues that Boland's project distances itself from French feminism by operating not at the level of style, but at the level of content: "While Cixous envisions a new language based upon the rhythms of the body, Boland envisions a new aesthetic which reconceptualises the body as a subject for poetry and as a mode of knowing".[20] I disagree with this critic, for I think that Boland manages to give voice to "the rhythms of the body" by means of linguistic techniques, techniques which manage to subvert the "coded, clichéd, ordinary language", an endeavour, as Andermatt (1984: 5) explains, at the centre of Cixous's and Irigaray's theorisation of "écriture feminine". In order to reclaim her womanhood, Boland departures from the prevailing modes of the literary tradition and attempts to experiment with what she calls the "anti-lyric" (interview with Allen Randolph 1993b: 122). There is a shift of poetic language as regards her earlier phase, the 'Feminine' and 'Assimilationist' phase. *In Her Own Image* exposes a more fluid poetry, not so constrained as the first.

First of all, Boland deliberately breaks with the male-orientated linguistic style. Accordingly, she leaves behind the logical patterns of meter and rhyme. *New Territory* showed how poets were merely concerned with "pattern and form" and how they hunted "among fixed stars" ("The Poets", *Collected*, 7), that is, among a well-established poetic canon. Now, Boland abandons the need to organise sound in beautiful and logical patterns, creating a disruption in the patriarchal order. There is no regular rhythmical pattern whatsoever, and if there is some occasional rhyme and musicality, it is created by lexical repetition. Haberstroh (1996: 66) argues that "this loosening of form represents a departure for Boland from those conventional models which had dominated her earlier volumes". In *In Her Own Image*, everything is loose: we find a lack of coherent form and no conventional verse techniques. With the exception of "Tirade for the Mimic Muse", all the poems break even orthographical conventions, by beginning in lower case. In some interesting cases, as in "In His Own Image", there is an interchange of lower case and upper case, in order to break conventional poetic patterns. In contrast to her earlier production, Boland gives preference to tercets, as in poems such as "Mastectomy", "Exhibitionist" and "Witching". With poems such as "In His Own Image" and "Menses", Boland starts to experiment with the loosening of stanzaic form, something unobserved in her earlier poetic production.

Secondly, deviated syntax abounds in this volume: the blurring of personal pronouns (as in "In Her Own Image") and the presence of midline caesuras (as in "Tirade for the Mimic Muse") are quite common. Fragmentary lines and incomplete sentences, sometimes with no predicates are also recurrent (as in "Solitary" and "Tirade for the Mimic Muse"). We also come across clipped stanzas, some of them created by only one word and others by complete sentences. The length of the verse lines as well as the length of the sentences greatly vary in poems such as "Exhibitionist" and "Making Up". With the exception of "Tirade for the Mimic Muse", it is quite typical to find very short sentences, mainly when the 'I' is the focus of attention. This, together with the fact that there are no strong hyperbatons (in contrast to Boland's initial production where rhetorical emphasis was favoured), supports the view that Boland wants to make her message clear.

Thirdly, Boland's experimentation with language is also observed in the lack of punctuation, which clearly distinguishes *In Her Own Image* from earlier and later volumes (note in particular "Solitary", "Witching", and "Making Up"). This lack of punctuation is reinforced by the fact that there is, in some poems, a total absence of cohesive devices. In other poems, by contrast, we come across a proliferation of additive conjunctions ('and') following one another in the same sentence (usually enumerations). In poems such as "Anorexic" this technique suggests that this woman is emotionally carried by her own thoughts, and it further emphasises her anxiety over her own flesh. Although the presence of the additive conjunction is typical in Boland's mature style, it usually appears after long sentences, sometimes after a full stop, and not indiscriminately after one another in the very same sentence as in this volume.

Fourthly, excessive repetitions of the first person pronoun indicate that the woman in *In Her Own Image* is constantly trying to analyse and define herself, to let her voice be heard and not reported (in contrast to *New Territory*, wherein these type of pronouns hardly appear). Furthermore, there are constant references to the female body, most of them, interestingly enough, preceded by 'my', indicating self-possession. These references vary, from the most common ones (skin, flesh, body, face, eyes, cheek, hips, thigh) to more subversive ones (nipples, curves, paps, wiles, breasts, haunch, and crotch).

Fifth, the women in these poems are restlessly struggling to assert themselves, as exclamatory sentences and emphatic auxiliaries indicate. The presence of these constructions in almost all the poems also indicates that the woman in this volume wants to be carried away by her own thoughts, her own emotions. In this sense, Boland deliberately perpetuates the binary logic by which women correspond to pathos and men to logos, as I analyse below. On the other hand, there are plenty of free intermittent lexical repetitions ('ploces') that indicate that these women want to emphasise what they are actually saying.

Finally, the highly rhetorical language so significant in Boland's initial poems is now substituted by colloquial language. There are plenty of common insults (which will not appear in Boland's later production), some significant neologisms, and conversions of nouns into verbs that emphasise the link between the female body and the speaker's identity and agency (as we have seen in "Exhibitionist").[21]

3.6. Conclusion

Boland's emphasis on the union between sexuality and textual creativity is an essential step she takes in the process of dismantling the dominant male discourse.

As I have tried to show, this stance might be interpreted through Cixous's and Irigaray's advocacy of a "sexual difference" that encourages women to have access to a full identity of their own, distinct from men. Precisely because of this, Boland's revolutionary project evinces a biological essentialism according to which the poet reveals, by writing the body, what is 'real' and 'true'. Her unquestionable defence of the sexual individuality and pleasure of her poetic voices prompts the reader to identify these women with universal prototypes that incarnate the ultimate definition of womanhood. In *In Her Own Image*, the body seems to embody the essence of woman literally. In returning to the body, what Boland actually does is assert her own identity as different from the male 'Other', and voluntarily replicating, therefore, the patriarchal mode of thinking (according to which the male subject predicates his control and domination upon those designated as different) in order to subvert women's position within this logic. As Rooney (1993: 2) explains in a conversation with Spivak:

> The body is of course essentialism's great text: to read in its form the essence of Woman is certainly one of phallocentrism's strategies [...], feminism's return to the body is only in part a rejoinder to the resilience of anti-feminism's essentialism.

Other postcolonial feminist critics like Christian (1990: 45), Minh-ha (1989: 38), and Donaldson (1992: 11) have similarly identified the danger of forging feminism from such "univocal" terms such as sexual difference and 'sisterhood'. Laying claim to the specificity of women's sexuality is both limiting and deceiving, because it reduces "the Other to the same – an impulse at the heart of the colonialist project" (Donaldson 1992: 11).

Therefore, Boland in *In Her Own Image* does not manage to decentralise binary positions. Her poetic voices are radical feminists: they are moved by anger and revenge, and they reject any sexual intercourse with their male counterparts, defending their independence and their capacity to give themselves sexual pleasure and be creative forces. The couple man/woman that Cixous (1994: 37) identifies as irreconcilable opposites in Western thought is reiterated in this volume, in which Boland usually places her women in opposition to the male 'Other'. Central to Boland's work in this phase is the principle of duality. In *In Her Own Image*, there is always a split, a clear boundary between the 'self' and the 'Other'. It is worthwhile noticing the repetition of 'self', 'myself', and 'yourself', noun and pronouns that emphasise those essential qualities distinguishing one individual from another. Boland's emphasis on individuality inevitably leads to a clear and binary demarcation between the 'self' and the "other than the self", to use Irigaray's term (1991: 159). This 'Other', described as opposite to the 'self', acquires different forms in *In Her Own Image*: although it is usually the male 'Other', it can also be the mimic muse, the moon, the nursery lights, or the sinful Eve. This compartmentalisation of distinguished identities will disappear in Boland's mature work, where she will constantly fuse the 'I' of the poem (the poetic self) with those images she represents (usually a 'she').

The main problem with the egalitarian and non-oppositional notion of sexual difference that Irigaray (1991: 171-174) and Cixous (1994: 119-128) envisage is that it is very difficult to assert sexual difference without invoking one of the parts of this difference as superior. It is not only that both Irigaray and Cixous conceive of woman's language in terms of biological determinism, but that they also seem to be privileging women's sexuality over men's. As we have seen, Irigaray (1985: 24) overvalues woman's ability, in contrast to men, to touch herself without any recourse to instruments: her sex "touches itself all the time". Furthermore, Irigaray has stated that "[n]othing is more spiritual than female sexuality" (1991: 190). Statements such as this endow women with a higher value than men, contradicting the belief in an "amorous exchange" that avoids theorising the superiority of one sex over the other.[22] Irigaray does not avoid the reversal of hierarchical values of one sex over another that she tries passionately to dismantle. This is the modernist/postmodernist debate that feminists have to confront, something that Whitford (1991: 12) has already taken into consideration: the difficulty of envisaging sexual emancipation without claiming women's superiority, or without advocating their uniqueness.

This is one of the dilemmas that Boland encounters in *In Her Own Image*. By constantly praising her poetic voices for their superiority to talk (or write) about their sexual life, about their bodies and womanly experiences, Boland replicates the pattern of authority present in the male discourse. In the dualistic opposition that Cixous (1994: 37) most drastically attacks, the strong, high, and active place is occupied by men, and the other by women. Boland does not escape this opposition, and attempts through the act of writing to acquire a strong and powerful position similar to the masculine one.

The presence of an authoritarian and rhetorically powerful self is observed in the predicates that Boland employs in these poems. First of all, the use of imperatives is recurrent, always addressed to the 'Other': the mimic and national muse of male poets (as in "Tirade for the Mimic Muse" and "Witching"), or the male 'Other' (as in "Exhibitionist"). Secondly, the presence of the volitional 'will' is distinctive and unique in this volume. At times this use of the modal is combined with the modal 'will' of certainty (as in "Witching"). Nevertheless, whereas Boland will continue to employ modals indicating certainty, the use of the volitional 'will' is significantly rare in later productions. In poems such as "Tirade for the Mimic Muse", "In Her Own Image", "Anorexic", "Witching", "Exhibitionist", and "Making Up", this use of the modal 'will' indicates that the speaker is involved in the act or instance of making a conscious choice or decision. The fact that three of these poems end with these uses of the modal shows that Boland favours the movement from oppression towards a liberationist project in which the woman exerts her own agency.

Thirdly, the poetic speaker, eager to make clear that she is in command of the experience she is talking about, reassures her right to act as a spokesperson for women's experiences by the, sometimes overused and repetitive, presence of the verb 'to know'. This verb, exclusively attached to the first person pronoun 'I', indicates that the poetic speaker can perceive directly, can grasp 'reality' with clarity and certainty. Some examples of this are found in "Tirade for the Mimic Muse" ("I know you for the ruthless bitch you are", "[A world] well I know", *Collected*, 71, 72); "In Her Own Image" ("And I know just the place", *Collected*, 73); "Solitary" ("I know,/ only I know/ these frenzied and incendiary ways", *Collected*, 78-79); "Menses" ("then I begin to know/ that I am bright and original/ and that my light's my own", *Collected*, 81); and "Witching" ("But I/ know/ what to do:/ I will reverse their arson", *Collected*, 83).

Fourthly, the significant presence of lexical verbs of action indicates that this is a woman adopting a subject rather than object position.[23] This, combined with the preponderance of verbs reflecting subversion, indicate that the woman intends to overthrow male authority. Some significant examples appear in "Solitary" ("I *defy* them"; "my cry/ *blasphemes*/ light and dark", *Collected*, 78, 79), "Witching" ("I will *reverse* their arson", *Collected*, 83), and "Exhibitionist" ("I *subvert* sculpture/ the old mode"; "*Cast down*/ Lucifers,/ spruce/ businessmen,/ their eyes/ cast down."; "the light that is *unyielding*", *Collected*, 85-86). The presence of an assertive speaker is also emphasised by the use of the verb 'to be' followed by the subject 'I' in the present form. Furthermore, the use of the adverb 'yes' three times in this volume is used to affirm what the narrator is actually saying, as in "Anorexic" ("Yes I am torching/ her curves and paps and wiles", *Collected*, 75), "Menses" ("Yes it is me/ she poaches her old face in", *Collected*, 81), and "Witching" ("Yes it's my turn/ to stack/ the twigs/ and twig the fire", *Collected*, 84). It is as if the poetic voices in this volume are answering with assurance and confidence all those who question what she is actually doing.

Finally, whereas in Boland's mature work the focus of attention will be more on what cannot be said and grasped within the poem, in other words, on the limits that the poet finds in describing the 'real', this volume of poetry focuses more on what the speaker can actually say and describe. There is nothing that she cannot address: both the source of her oppression and the creation of a new self are given voice.[24] In this sense, the woman is always portrayed in the act of speaking. In "Making Up", the narrator argues that "[my mouth] won't stay shut" and that "My face is made,/ It says" (*Collected*, 87). In "Solitary", the speaker describes how "my cry [...] makes word flesh" (*Collected*, 79). In this sense, there are constant references to the woman speaker's "mouth", "lips", and also to her "hand" and "fingers". These parts of the body are essential, for they enable the woman to exert agency by talking and writing.

By depicting her poetic voices in *In Her Own Image* as strongly authoritative and powerful, Boland deliberately maintains a hierarchical structure. As Irigaray says at the end of "This Sex Which is Not One" (1985: 33), if women's "aim were simply to reverse the order of things, even supposing this to be possible, history would repeat itself in the long run, would revert to sameness: to phallocratism".[25] As Irigaray envisages, a reversal in the hierarchies of power wherein the formerly 'inferior' term occupies the position of the 'superior' term, will not alter the nature of their relationships. It won't be until her more mature production that Boland will more successfully subvert this dichotomy, by stressing the powerlessness of her poetic voices rather than their power.

In this sense, and however defensive her assertive stance might be, Boland ends up reinstating patriarchal values and writing within those terms which have oppressed women in the first place. This is another feature that clearly distinguishes *In Her Own Image* as what Showalter would call a 'Feminist', and Memmi and Fanon a 'Cultural Nationalist' volume. Feminist critics like Moi (1997: 108) have argued that, by attempting to define 'feminine' features, feminism perpetuates traditional binary oppositions. This sort of feminism falls back into another patriarchal trap:

> we still need to emphasise that difference between male and female experience of the world. But that difference is shaped by the patriarchal structures feminists are opposing; and to remain faithful to it is to play the patriarchal game. (Moi 1997: 113)

Like radical feminism, nationalism runs the risk of 'playing the coloniser's game' by its necessity to construct a counter-ideology which at the end is constructed upon the categories of the colonising culture itself. Both Memmi (1990: 201-205) and Fanon (1990: 38-39) show a reluctance towards nationalism as a viable means of decolonisation. Even after the struggle for national freedom has succeeded, there are certain features of the former colonial power which are still maintained in the national governments. The reason for this, as Memmi (1990: 201: 197) explains, is that the colonised continues to define himself in the terms imposed by the coloniser. In relation to this, Fanon (1990: 38-39) explains that the techniques the writer employs in this phase, and which are based on an exclusive defence of his/her own identity, are not really creative, for they are merely inverted copies of the previous colonial regime. As Fanon (1990: 192) states, it was the coloniser who, in the need to reassure his power, encouraged a defensive and violent writing: "Stinging denunciations, the exposing of distressing conditions and passions which find their outlet in expression are in fact assimilated by the occupying power in a catharsis process". Thus, the native culture maintains its values within the framework of colonial domination.

Like nationalist writing, Boland's revolutionary volume of poetry does not challenge the very foundations of patriarchy. Although Boland's intention is to re-evaluate the 'feminine' categories of male discourse, in the process, she reiterates the traditional gender binary divisions Cixous (1994: 37) identifies. For Boland, it is very important to situate her women in a night atmosphere, in contrast to that lightness that surrounded the poet in *Eavan Boland Poetry* and *New Territory*. Whereas in Boland's later productions the women inhabit 'in-between' landscapes (located either at diffuse moments such as dawn or dusk), the women here are located in clearly determined and well-established ones: they inhabit the night, as the first sentence of poems such as "Solitary", "Menses", "Witching", and "Exhibitionist" make clear: "Night:/ An oratory of dark"; "It is dark again"; "My gifts/ are nightly"; "I wake to dark" (*Collected*, 78, 80, 82, 84). In this sense, her women are dominated by the moon and their realm is the night, just as in the binary logic. Although Boland's characters deconstruct some of the patriarchal binary oppositions (her women are strongly active), they keep exalting the typical feminine pathos over the conventional male logos, as we have seen in "Solitary" and "Witching". The women in the volume constantly 'talk' in a high emotional tone. They are moved more by emotion (revenge, hatred, and bitterness) than by reason.

Furthermore, Boland's poetic voices create themselves by means of the same devices that patriarchal society provides them with. Subversion is carried out by relying on traditional images such as cosmetics and mirrors. The woman poet feels the need to move within traditional (male) parameters, in order to define herself. Although the poetic voice in "Menses" asserts at one point that she is "bright" and "original" (*Collected*, 81), it will not be until later when Boland will produce more original imagery to bear witness to her female subjectivity. As a result, Fanon (1990: 192) says, this phase is characterised by a sort of "paralysed and non-creative culture". There is no over-production of literature and the writer continues writing images that are not his/her own. Like Fanon, Showalter (1999: 215) observes how the feminist phase, in its prescriptive demands, was unproductive in the terrain of literature (note that she only dedicates one brief chapter in her long study to a discussion of feminist writing): "In retrospect, it looks as if all the feminists had but one story to tell, and exhausted themselves in its narration". Following these remarks, it may not be coincidental that Boland's 'Feminist' phase only includes one volume of poetry.

Another reason justifies the fact that Boland has not yet moved into a liberating artistic autonomy. Although in *In Her Own Image* Boland implies that sexuality is a very important aspect in woman's lives, she does not give voice to other 'feminine' qualities which she will find highly gratifying and fulfilling in her next phase: her role as a mother/caretaker of her children, her love for her husband, or her need to establish a comradeship with the women of the past. Boland's artistic autonomy will not be attained until she gives voice to her own experiences as an Irish woman writer, although this will not involve achieving an 'authentic' identity, but deconstructing it (she will avoid the essentialist stance of this second phase, by calling into question categories such as 'femaleness' and

'Irishness'). Her women, although representative of a variety of female experiences, do not bear witness to Boland's personal reality: she has neither suffered anorexia, nor been battered by her husband, as she explains in an interview with Wilson (1990b: 82). Thus, this volume represents a woman trying to define herself by means of other women. Until Boland does not disentangle what her 'I' is (a mother concerned with her daughters growing up, a woman worried about getting older), she will not achieve artistic decolonisation. The identity crises suffered by the angry voices in this volume are a direct consequence of Boland's pressure on breaking away from the influence of the patriarchal tradition. In a later poem, "A False Spring" (*Outside History*), Boland will realise the need to calm down the angry woman in *In Her Own Image*: "I want to tell her she can rest,/ she is embodied now" (*Collected*, 178). This embodiment will represent for Boland her desire for "a poetry that contains the whole of her experience" (Foster 1999: 5), an experience which will be fully expressed in her next phase. It will not be until then that the woman in the poem and the woman writing the poem will become the same person.

154

Notes to chapter 3

[1] As Allen-Randolph (1993a: 10) notes, "[t]he precedents for these poems were Plath's late anti-lyrics in *Ariel*". Like Plath, Boland attempts to move away from the restrictions she felt that traditional lyric poetry had posed to her as a woman writer.

[2] In the interview with Allen- Randolph (1993b: 122), Boland explains:

In Her Own Image was a liberating book to write. Some of the poems in it were drafted or revised at the same time – even sometimes, my notebooks show, in the same week – as poems in *Night Feed*. [...] *In Her Own Image* allowed me to experiment with the anti-lyric which I saw as providing or guaranteeing the lyricism of *Night Feed*.

[3] Maguire (1999: 62) explains that the feminism Boland refers to is that early feminism of "Stalinist impulses" reflected in Ireland in the mid 1970s. According to this critic, it was the feminist theory developed within the Irish Women's Movement and the emerging Women's Studies departments.

[4] By asserting that *In Her Own Image* is a feminist volume, I disagree with O'Donnell (1993: 41) when she argues the following:

The ten poems in *In Her Own Image* were relentlessly described as 'feminist' poems. As women writers have been discovered in the intervening years, almost anything to do with women's lives is liable to be termed 'feminist', a convenient mechanism perhaps, by which the actual poetry may be critically diminished.

According to O'Donnell, the adjective 'feminist' has been too easily linked with critical denigration. It is my contention that, precisely because of its feminist stance and not in spite of it, *In Her Own Image* is a unique volume of unquestionable value in Boland's career. The themes that Boland puts forwards are an enormous and significant achievement for a woman poet who is trying to make herself heard in a country with a strong androcentric poetic tradition.

[5] Arlen House also published disregarded masterworks like Kate O'Brien's *The Ante-Room* (dealing with issues like lesbianism) back into print (Roche 1993: 1).

[6] Cixous suggests that both sexes are potentially capable of producing a "feminine writing". As Andermatt (1984: 11) explains, she believes that there are "women who write on the masculine side and men who do not repress their femininity". Nevertheless, Cixous believes that women are currently more capable of producing this kind of writing, because, by giving voice to their experiences, they have more potential to subvert the prevailing order. In her essay "Extreme Fidelity", Cixous (1994: 136) describes the work of Clarice Lispector as the best example of "feminine writing".

[7] Irigaray develops this theme particularly in her essays "This Sex Which Is Not One" (1985: 23-33), "The 'Mechanics' of Fluids" (1985: 106-118), and "When Our Lips Speak Together" (1985: 205-218).

[8] See Allen-Randolph (1995), Luftig (1993), and Gelpi (1999).

[9] Nonetheless, somewhat later, as a more mature poet, Boland (1995a: 244) criticises Rich for being "separatist" and "antitraditional", something that Maguire (1999: 61) disagrees about, by arguing that Rich is not so radical, for she consistently highlights the influence that canonical male poets exerted on her, mostly in terms of technique.

[10] It is important to note, however, that, while her writing practice in *In Her Own Image* shows a clear affiliation with the French feminist movement, Boland was not familiar with this critical school until several years after publishing this volume of poetry (Allen-Randolph 1991: 48).

[11] See Gilbert and Gubar's second chapter in *The Madwoman in the Attic*, "Infection in the Sentence: the Woman Writer and the Anxiety of Authorship", for rebellious female characters in women's fiction (2000: 45-92).

[12] The endangered selfhood presented by the speaker in "Anorexic" and "In Her Own Image" is also manifested in "Mastectomy" (*Collected*, 76-78), where the identity of the narrator is destroyed by the male surgeon's removal of her breast. Because of the poem's connection between the woman's identity and the female body, I will analyse this poem in the following section, by applying some principles of French Feminism.

[13] As in "Tirade for the Mimic Muse", "In Her Own Image", and "Anorexic", Boland attacks social standards in "In His Own Image" (*Collected*, 74-75). In this poem, Boland ironically portrays the internal confusion of a woman who is being battered by her husband.

[14] Whitford (1991: 2) thinks that it is inaccurate to view Irigaray as an "essentialist" who defends a transparent relation between women's bodies and women's true identity. According to this critic, readings such as this tend to ignore the complexity of Irigaray's work. Although it is true that Irigaray's work should be viewed in its totality, what is unquestionable is that bodily references are constantly present in her essays, and that, in her notion of woman's language, biology determines speech.

[15] Other feminist critics like Chantal Chawaf (1981: 177-178) argue for a similar woman's language grounded in the female body:
> The word must comfort the body. [...] In order to reconnect the book with the body and with pleasure, we must disintellectualise writing. [...] If a music of femininity is arising out of its own oppression, it materialises through the rediscovered body.

[16] On the other hand, Boland criticises the Freudian concept of the breast as an erotic object for the male sexual fantasies. Instead, the breast, after it has been extracted, is everything but erotic. Although it continues arousing awe and admiration ("wonder"), it is described in more realist terms, as "blue-veined" and "white-domed".

[17] Fanon (1991: 126-128) explains the colonised's union between self and nature as follows:
> Black Magic, primitive mentality, animism, animal eroticism, it all floods over me. All of it is typical of peoples that have not kept pace with the evolution of the human race. [...] Yes, we are – we Negroes – backward, simple, free in our behaviour. That is because for us the body is not something opposed to what you call the mind. We are in the world. And long live the couple, Man and Earth! [...] Between the world and me a relation of coexistence was established. I had discovered the primeval One.

[18] Just by looking at one passage in "When Our Lips Speak Together", one might get this idea of how Irigaray's discourse itself touches irrationality:
> Open your lips: don't open them simply. I don't open them simply. We-you/I- are neither open nor closed. We never separate simply: a single word cannot be pronounced, produced, uttered by our mouths. (Irigaray 1985: 209)

For other examples in which Irigaray puts this form of irrational language into practice, see her essay "He Risks who risks life itself" (1991: 213-218).

[19] In arguing this, I disagree with González Arias (2000b: 187), who argues, when commenting on "Exhibitionist", that Boland manages to dismantle the binary Logos/Pathos.

[20] Similarly, Fogarty (1994: 94) asserts that Boland's work "cannot readily be aligned with any preconceived belief in a hidden, radical dynamic in women's language". Nevertheless, I presume she is referring to Boland's later volumes of poetry, where language is everything but radical.

[21] This conversion is also observed in those poems from *Night Feed* (1982) that still show a trace of Boland's feminist aesthetic, as in "The Woman Turns Herself into a Fish", where the speaker utters "I flab upward" (*Collected*, 118).

[22] Furthermore, Irigaray (1991: 196) argues that in the world of technology women are perhaps even better than men, because "they are more patient, more obedient, and because they have a talent for more delicate, more precise gestures".

[23] The only moments in which we cannot find modal volitional 'will' and verbs of action are those poems where Boland deliberately adopts an oppressed role. In "Mastectomy", for instance, there are no verbs of action whatsoever, and the only action is carried out by the male 'Other'.

[24] In contrast to Boland's later emphasis on 'silences' and 'whispers', the only poem where silence appears in this volume is in "Exhibitionist", where the woman describes her own act of stripping down: "hush/ of hip" (*Collected*, 85).

[25] As Jacques Derrida (1981: 41) argues in another context: "To deconstruct the opposition […] is to overturn the hierarchy at a given moment. To overlook this phase is to forget the conflictual and subordinating structure of opposition" (quoted by Renza 1984: 39).

4

Boland's Artistic Decolonisation

4.1. Introduction

Showalter (1999: 13) identifies a third stage in women's writing which she denominates the 'Female' phase, and defines as "a turning inward freed from some of the dependency of opposition, a search for identity". Showalter views "female literature" as that written by women which intentionally concerns itself with the enunciation of these women's own experiences and which reflects an "autonomous self-expression", self-discovery, and self-scrutiny (p. 4). This critic argues that, at this stage, women writers stick to their own feelings, values, and dissatisfactions (p. 241). If we highlight Showalter's emphasis that the third phase involves, above all, a freedom of expression in relation to the literary mainstream, Boland's mature work can be indisputably located within Showalter's 'Female' phase. Before going any further, I would like to make it clear that when applying the concept 'Female' to Boland's mature poetry, I refer to Showalter's main definition of the term: artistic freedom or autonomous self-expression. I do not intend to imply that there is a 'female essence' in Boland's poetry, because, as we will see, Boland calls into question the very category of 'womanhood'. In her volumes of poetry following *In Her Own Image*, we can see an increasing process of self-sufficient expression, by constantly giving voice to her own experiences as a woman, an Irish citizen, and a poet. Nevertheless, finding artistic autonomy for Boland does not involve a construction of a poetic identity in essentialist terms, but rather a deconstruction of it. At first sight, this would seem to distance Boland's mature work from what Showalter identifies as 'female writing', and its interrelated emphasis on 'female' identity and women's experiences. Nevertheless, a closer look at Showalter's analysis shows that Boland's poetry is but one instance of the 'Female' phase this feminist critic talks about.

Critics such as Moi (1991: 7) have criticised Showalter for studying women's writing from the assumption that there is a female writing vs. a masculine writing. Moi argues that feminist literary analysis must turn to the poststructuralist theory of French feminism in general, and Julia Kristeva in particular, because it rejects biologism and essentialism, and deconstructs "the opposition between masculinity and femininity" (Moi 1991: 12).[1] In fact, Showalter uncritically uses terms such as "female" and "masculine" (as in p. 33) implying that there are certain features specifically found in men and women's writing distinctively. This would justify Moi's critique that Showalter perpetuates the binary logic of Western thought (i.e. masculinity vs. femininity). Nevertheless, attacks such as Moi's seem to ignore that Showalter's intention is not to look at a woman's essence, at an "an innate sexual attitude", in the female literary tradition, but at the ways in which women writers gradually achieve independent self-expression. As Showalter (1999: 12) asserts at the beginning of her study: "I am [...] uncomfortable with the notion of a "female imagination". The theory of a female sensibility revealing itself in an imagery and form specific to women always runs dangerously close to reiterating the familiar stereotypes". In this sense, Showalter acknowledges the danger of conferring specific features to women's writers, because they might be understood as natural and exclusive to them. This belief of hers moves her close to the deconstructive moves that feminism has taken, mostly after Hélène Cixous, Luce Irigaray, and Julia Kristeva, and which have emphasised the artificiality of gender differences. Furthermore, Showalter (1999: 34) even asserts that although "female writing" at this stage involves a search for identity, this does not necessarily require, contradicting other assertions she makes in her study (as in p. 4), an articulation of women's experiences: "Paradoxically, the more female this literature became in the formal and theoretical sense, the further it moved from exploring the physical experience of women [...]; female aestheticism is [...] oddly sexless in its content". In this sense, when analysing Virginia Woolf's fiction, a clear exponent of what Showalter calls a "deliberate female aesthetic", this critic highlights this writer's dream of androgyny (p. 264). Showalter understands androgyny as a "full balance and command of an emotional range that includes male and female elements" (p. 263). Although Showalter admits to being suspicious about concepts such as this, which, "like all utopian ideals [...] lacks zest and energy" (ibid), I would argue that androgyny might be understood in itself as a way of deconstructing maleness and femaleness, the binary (sexual) division identified as intrinsic to Western thought. As Moi (1991: 9) argues, Woolf practices "a deconstructive form of writing, one that engages and thereby exposes the duplicitous nature of discourse". In this sense, Woolf's sexual identity unites two polarised concepts which are identified as opposites. As this woman writer (1974: 139) argues in *A Room of One's Own*, the "ideal and free state of mind" of a good artist like Shakespeare should be androgynous. Woolf (1974: 147) defends that women must stop regarding men as "the opposing faction" in order to find harmony between both sexes and gain what she calls the "unity of mind". More than a deconstruction of identity as such, Woolf's notion of androgyny is an ideal of identity, the utopian dream of encompassing within the same personality two distinct principles, maleness and femaleness. In this sense, this ideal notion of identity deconstructs at least one aspect of it: the sexual aspect of identity. Showalter's emphasis on this "sexless" dream of women writers at their final stage, reminds one of that deconstructive movement within French feminist theory which aims to disentangle polarised concepts in the prevailing language, such as the terms 'man' and 'woman'. On the other hand, by identifying in the third phase of women's writing "a turning inward freed from some of the dependency of opposition", Showalter (1999: 13) seems to argue that, unlike the radical feminism of the second stage, women writers do not seek an inversion of the structures of domination. In this sense, 'female' identity would not operate within the discursive limits set by patriarchal discourse, and it would move away from binary oppositions such as 'man' vs. 'woman'.

Feminism in this deconstructionist phase would be part, as Ashcroft, Griffiths and Tiffin (2002: 174) explain, of the political project "to raise and transform consciousness", a project similar to the one advocated by anti-colonial intellectuals such as Albert Memmi (1990: 198) and Frantz Fanon (1990: 148). Both Memmi and Fanon believe that the second phase in the decolonising process is a prelude to a more "positive" and "liberating" movement. Memmi argues that, in the previous two phases, the colonised subject depended on the figure of the coloniser, both as a model to imitate, or as an antithesis to reject. He believes that it is only in "the decomposition of this [inter]dependence" established between coloniser and colonised that any sort of viable decolonisation is possible (Memmi 1990: 7). Like Showalter, therefore, Memmi's writings advocate liberation from the dependency of opposition. The colonised has to cease defining himself/herself through the categories imposed by the colonisers, and this would certainly imply moving beyond boundaries such as East vs. West, colonised vs. coloniser. Memmi's (1990: 217) call for "revolution" and the creation of "a whole and free man" advances Fanon's (1990: 28) later advocacy for the "veritable creation of new men". Fanon argues that, in the final phase of liberation, the colonial subject does not rely on an antagonistic resistance (p. 182). In contrast to the second phase of the process of decolonisation, the writer in this period does not seek to replace the canon, but intends to reconstruct it by rereading previous oppressive assumptions and creating his/her own writing criteria. Now, according to Fanon, colonialism and the colonised subject must vanish. The radical division into paired oppositions such as good vs. evil, true vs. false, white vs. black underlying colonial relationships, which Fanon (1991: 11) characterises as the product of a "manichaeism delirium", hinders the process of ultimate liberation. In this sense, Fanon explains that assertion of negritude is not sufficient in itself, for race is a cultural construct. By moving beyond racial boundaries, the individual achieves the ultimate freedom and liberation. As Fanon (1991: 231) explains, "the black soul is a white man's artifact", "[t]he Negro is not. Anymore than the white man. [...] Why not the quite simple attempt to touch the other, to feel the other, to explain the other to myself?".[2] In this sense, as Young (1992: 119) has acknowledged, Fanon was one of the pioneering writers to deconstruct Western thought and its binary system.

In Boland's final phase, there is also an urgent need to break national and gender boundaries. Boland's assertion of womanhood in *In Her Own Image* is one means of achieving artistic freedom, but not the ultimate end. Her poetry, as we will see, moves away from essentialist identity-claims such as Irishness, and also from those feminist attempts to construct the category 'woman' in opposition to the category 'man'. Boland explicitly moves away from feminism, because, in her own words, it only encourages the woman poet "to feminise her perceptions rather than humanise her femininity" (Boland 1995a: 245). As Boland (1996a: 142) has asserted elsewhere, women's importance in Irish poetry is not because of issues of gender or politics, but because their poetry "contains elements of human justice". According to Boland (1995a: 235), women's project is "neither marginal nor specialist. It is a project which concerns all of poetry, all that leads into it in the past and everywhere it is going in the future". The extent to which Boland's discourse resembles Fanon's 'humanist' and 'liberationist discourse' is significant, as made explicit throughout *Black Skin, White Masks* and *The Wretched of the Earth* with assertions such as "I believe that the individual should tend to take on the universality inherent in the human condition" (Fanon 1991: 12), or his belief that the writer must "use the past with the intention of opening the future, as an invitation to action, a basis for hope" (p. 187). Boland's project is not merely concerned with issues like gender; it is concerned with the transformation of poetry itself, the restructuring of the foundations on which canonical poetry has been based (such as the traditional association of 'man' as writer/poet and 'woman' as decorative object or sexual image in the poem).

Taking the aforementioned into account, I think it appropriate to apply Showalter's 'Female' phase, and Memmi and Fanon's 'Liberationist' phase to Boland's work produced between 1982 and 2001: *Night Feed* (1982), *The Journey and Other Poems* (1986), *Outside History* (1990), *In a Time of Violence* (1994), *The Lost Land* (1998), and *Code* (2001). As Fanon (1990: 192) explains, the final period in the decolonising process, in contrast to the earlier inoperative and non-creative phases, witnesses a relative over-production of literature. Boland's numerous volumes of poetry record a process of 'female' consciousness expanding and maturing. She expresses her dissatisfaction with her earlier feminine work (mostly *New Territory*), where she wrote the kind of poetry which was expected from her sex, and also with her feminist volume of poetry (*In Her Own Image*), where she defensively celebrated womanhood and adopted a separatist stance in her attempt to establish her own poetic aesthetics.

In what follows I will demonstrate how Boland's mature poetry is dominated by some specific features which construct what Showalter (1999: 33) denominates a "deliberate female aesthetic", or Memmi (1990: 148) and Fanon (1990: 182) a "liberating" writing. Instead of considering Boland's mature work in a chronological way, I have chosen a thematic criteria to explore her production from *Night Feed* onwards, as this phase does not follow a straight line of development.

The first section focuses on Boland's main source of poetic creativity: her life as a suburban married mother. I will show, principally by drawing on some poems from *The War Horse* (1975) and *Code* (2001), how Boland avoids adopting an oppositional stance by advocating what French feminism calls an "amorous exchange" that is based on an equal partnership between antagonistic opposites. Although *The War Horse* was written before *In Her Own Image* (1980), I will treat it as a prelude to Boland's third phase, for the poetic aesthetics that Boland develops in this work better fits her mature production. In these poems, Boland particularly draws on her marriage to envisage an ideal form of life that can maintain 'female difference' while not imposing this difference as superior.

The second section is dedicated to Boland's deconstruction of poetic identity, mostly in her volumes *The Journey and Other Poems* (1986) and *In a Time of Violence* (1994), and also in some individual poems from *Outside History* (1990) and *The Lost Land* (1998). It will be here where Showalter's, Memmi's, and Fanon's deconstructive theories will be better observed. Postcolonial theory (with its advocacy of hybridity and ambivalence) and French feminist theory (with its emphasis on woman's fluidity) will give us an insight into how Boland carries out this process.

The third section focuses on one of the most important aspects of Boland's poetry: her attempt to give voice to those lived experiences, mostly female, that lie unrecorded and undervalued by nationalist historical accounts. As I will show in this section, Boland avoids acting as a spokesperson, for such an act would perpetuate the nationalist relation between poet and community, and would also inevitably simplify under a homogenous voice a reality which is heterogeneous and fragmentary. The past is always for Boland an ungraspable terrain. Nevertheless, by recording her powerlessness and limitations as a poet, Boland's discourse will be non-authoritarian and therefore highly subversive. In order to analyse this interesting aspect of her work, I will rely on Spivak's postcolonial premises in "Can the Subaltern Speak?" (1994) and Kristeva's feminist postulates in "Revolution in Poetic Language" (1986a).

The fourth section focuses on *The Lost Land* (1998) and *Code* (2001) and how these volumes of poetry are shaped by Boland's mature exile in the US. As I will demonstrate, Boland stands as a more secure and confident writer, whose assured place within the Irish and American literary panoramas has allowed her to overcome her oppression as a woman writer and an Irish citizen. In spite of this, I will show how in some poems Boland still portrays herself as a powerless and non-authoritarian poetic voice, a subversive mechanism to move away from dominant discourses such as the colonialist, nationalist, and patriarchal.

4.2. Boland's marriage: an "amorous exchange" between opposite factions

As Showalter (1999: 35) states, the woman writer at her 'Female' phase "tries to unify her fragments of female experience through artistic vision". By 'female experience', this feminist literary critic means women's personal stories, their involvement in society as caretakers, wives, mothers, and housewives. This is precisely what Boland does in her mature work; she tries to defend her female reality from the perspective of a woman poet. Like Showalter, Boland (1995a: 130) has expressed her belief that women's writing is specially marked by their (female) personal experience, for they have no literary tradition to look back to: "Yet in poetry and women's writing in particular, the private witness is often all there is to go on". Her volumes of poetry after *In Her Own Image* exemplify Boland's remark. She makes her own personal experience as a woman and a poet part of her source material, putting into practice Adrienne Rich's realisation that "instead of poems about experience, I am getting poems that are experiences" (Boland 1995a: 131). In this stage of her evolution, the 'I' of her poems can be identified with Boland herself. As she admits in an interview, "the voice is me. It isn't just the voice of an 'I'" (Wilson 1990b: 81). Thus, one of Boland's great achievements in this phase is her ability to become the speaking subject of her own poems. She adopts the perspective of, and speaks as, a wife, a mother, and a housewife.

Boland's emphasis on women's experiences indicates that her poems are grounded in an oppositional politics, even though she tries to subvert them. By focusing on a woman's world of domestic interiors and night feedings, she inevitably describes it as presumably different from a male world. As Keen (2000: 28) has argued, gendered postcolonial identities are constructed upon a series of

> alienating contradictions that have to be embraced before they can be
> ended, worked through rather than merely transcended, but always with

the hope of re-emerging in a less polarised context which makes an appreciation of the heterogeneity of lived experience possible.

Although in her poetry Boland praises her lived experience as an Irish woman, she will not fall prey to the biological essentialism of *In Her Own Image*. On the one hand, Boland avoids adopting the separatist stance of this volume, by recognising the positive influence of the male 'Other'. As a married woman, Boland begins to dedicate some of her pieces of work to her husband. This is the case of "The Other Woman" and "The Botanic Gardens" (*Collected*, 39, 45-46), poems in which she specifically focuses on the new concerns of marriage life and domesticity. On the other hand, she emphasises the need to resituate sexual difference on an equalitarian relationship, not based on oppositions as in the second phase. This reconciliatory attitude in her mature work starts to be perceived as early as in *The War Horse*.

Although *The War Horse* (originally published in 1975) was written after *New Territory*, her most conventional volume as regards subject matter and poetic form, and before *In Her Own Image*, a volume with a clear feminist bias, we start to perceive in some poems of this collection an emerging female awareness characteristic of her mature style. In this sense, this volume stands as a work of transition in Boland's poetic career, something that Allen-Randolph (1993a: 8) and Brown (1993: 37) have already considered. The interesting thing about this volume is that it combines feminine submission and female awareness.[3] These contradictory pulls reflect Boland's difficulty in leaving literary conventions aside. As she has admitted in an interview with Allen-Randolph (1993b: 120-121):

> I moved from the University culture out to the suburbs. I left an apparently sustaining literary culture – although one, as I've said, that I'd already begun to question. I was really trying to find a voice within my own poems and having some puzzling experiences while doing so. [...] The learning experience of those years was essentially in unlearning received aesthetics, and in beginning to trust my instincts.

Because of these "puzzling experiences", Boland revolves around feelings of unconditional love and loathing for the legacy of the forefathers. On the one hand, she continues to connect her literary production to the patriarchal canon, by employing Irish myths and relying on traditional forms. She still writes under the masquerade of a 'male' poet in poems still constructed upon highly regular stanzas and well-recognised literary techniques. On the other hand, there are some significant poems in this volume where Boland explicitly becomes the speaking subject. In poems such as "The Other Woman", "The Botanic Gardens", "Prisoners", and "Suburban Woman" the poetic voice is Boland herself, a suburban married woman and a housewife who bases herself in her house in Dundrum (*Collected*, 39, 45-46, 63-65).[4]

Another key factor that distinguishes *The War Horse* as a work of transition is Boland's paradoxical attitude towards Ireland's fight for national independence. She claims opposite postulates: a call for war and an advocacy of peace. As in her initial phase, poems such as "Conversation with an Inspector of Taxes" and "The Atlantic Ocean" (*Collected*, 57-59, 59-60) offer an image of the poet as a male communal figure, supporting revolution and encouraging his community to fight against the oppressor. Writing is portrayed as a politically committed activity, and the poet stands as a spokesperson, as someone who must give voice to the needs of his people. The poetic voice in "After the Irish of Egan O'Rahilly" (*Collected*, 20-21) is very similar to that which appears in "Conversation with an Inspector of Taxes". Following the style of the Soviet poet Mayakovski, Boland writes a forceful and declamatory poem praising the Communist revolution. The poet supports rebellion: he is a warrior who, loyal to his "debts of honour", must follow "the Red Army, boiling across frontiers/ In a wash of Cossack stallions" (p. 58). This support and encouragement of rebellion also appears in "The Atlantic Ocean", where the poet's angry and emotional speech reminds one also of Egan O'Rahilly's discourse. Poems such as these attempt to follow a poetic legacy, such as that created by the Celtic Revival, which at times involved supporting violence and feeding a national feeling of revenge and freedom.

The call for war and support of rebellion that these poems exemplify contradicts the accusation of war and advocacy of peace in most of the poems in *The War Horse*. This shift as regards poetic sensibility is due, not only to Boland's personal change of lifestyle, but also to Ireland's political agitation at the moment. Brown (1993: 34) explains that, in the mid-seventies, the Northern Irish crisis reached its climax with "the Worker's Strike, the fall of the power-sharing executive, and the bombing of Dublin". Faced with such manifestations of violence and disagreement, Boland rejects Yeats's utopian dream of an Irish national and cultural unity. In June 1974, at the time of writing the poems in *The War Horse*, Boland published an essay in the *Irish Times* entitled "The Weasel's Tooth". This essay expresses her belief in the fallacy of the Yeatsian vision of cultural unity, because, as she explains,

> there is, and at last I recognise it, no unity whatsoever in this culture of ours. And even more important, I recognise that there is no need whatsoever for such a unity. If we search for it we will, at a crucial moment, be mutilating with fantasy once again the very force we should be liberating with reality. (Boland 1974: 56)

In *The War Horse*, Boland challenges national definitions of unity suggesting that the image of Ireland as a cultural whole has caused violence and death. In contrast to other poems in the collection, Boland does not aestheticise violence, but places it under close scrutiny. The poet shows the destructive side of war, and focuses on the wounds and deaths caused by national struggles. In poems such as "Suburban Woman", the poet presents war as a "rape on either side", showing that in any form of contemporary struggle, all parts (whether Loyalist or Nationalist) find themselves damaged (*Collected*, 63). Other poems such as "The War Horse" and "Child of Our Time" offer another perception to war, not a communal one this time, but a private and personally experienced one (*Collected*,

39-40, 41). "Child of Our Time", for instance, evokes a photograph of the body of a young child being lifted from the rubble of a bomb-blast in Dublin on 17 May 1974 (Brown 1993: 34). In other poems of this volume, the Irish troubles "parallel private family battles" within Boland's own domestic world (Haberstroh 1996: 62).[5] Boland's intention is to show how the Northern Irish conflict is, in the end, a conflict between members belonging to the same community. In "Belfast vs. Dublin" (*New Territory*), Boland presented the point of view between Northerners and Southerners as irreconcilable. This poem was dedicated and addressed to Derek Mahon, a poet born in Belfast in 1941. After realising that she, as a Dublin poet, is inevitably distanced from Mahon by "the brilliant quarrel/ Of our towns", and that they will never agree on "the living out/ Of life", Boland concludes:

> Let us then cavalierly fork
> Our ways, since we, and all unknown,
> Have called into question one another's own. (*Collected*, 15)

The woman poet here prefers to evade any possible communication between both parties. The points of view of Northerners and Southerners are not only extremely different, but also impossible to reconcile. It is not until *The War Horse*, where Boland relies on love and communication as possible solutions to all quarrels. In this sense, some of the poems in this volume put into practice Cixous's and Irigaray's advocacy of reconciling opposites in a 'love' that surpasses boundaries. Although these French feminists refer to male and female sexual opposites, their theories can be applied to Boland's advocacy of a uniting love that reconciles English and Irish warring factions.

Cixous and Irigaray envisage an alternative subject position where both the 'self' and the 'Other', although maintaining their sexual difference, can coexist in a relationship of enabling and egalitarian love. For both feminists, the orientation of Western (patriarchal) thought has been to divide, separate, and distinguish between polar opposites such as spirit and nature, mind and matter, male and female. In this dualistic stance, masculine and feminine are placed in opposition in a relation of power and domination. Their theories attempt to dismantle in this sense such rigid and hierarchical oppositions. In *The Book of Promethea*, Cixous (1994: 119-128) advocates a "love exchange" in which the 'self' will not dominate the 'Other'. This new relationship between the 'self' and the 'Other' is established between what Cixous terms "bisexuality" (1994: 40) or "feminine economy". In her essay "Sorties", Cixous (1994: 35-46) distinguishes between what she terms a "masculine" and a "feminine economy". The "masculine" is concerned with property, and with those "gift functions" that reinforce his position: "virility, authority, power, money, [...] pleasure, [and] phallocentric narcissism at the same time" (p. 44). The "feminine gift", by contrast, is given "without calculation" and for the other's pleasure. Being aware that this stance might be easily used to charge her with being biologically essentialist, Cixous (1994: 129-137) asserts in her essay "Extreme Fidelity" that the terms "masculine" and "feminine economy" are not dependent on anatomical sex, but on different modes of behaviour.[6] Similarly, Irigaray (1991: 115) advocates a sexual difference that is combined with what she calls the "amorous exchange" between a man and a woman. In this encounter between the sexes, women become desiring subjects, partners of love, instead of objects of "sexual exchange" (p. 130). The sexual relationship is understood by Irigaray as one in which one's own sex is fulfilled equally, and the different sexes can co-habit in harmony and peace, without seeking any superiority over the other. In this sense, the "sexual encounter" or what she calls "the genesis of love" would be established in a sort of horizontal relationship, and not as a "disguised or polemic form of the master-slave relationship" (p. 174).[7]

Like Cixous and Irigaray, postcolonial theorists have also identified the need to overcome oppositions by establishing a differential relationship with the 'Other'. Criticising the colonial dichotomy coloniser and colonised that is intrinsic to Western (and imperialistic) thought, Frantz Fanon (1991: 231) argues that liberation for the individual lies in the "quite simple attempt to touch the other, to feel the other, to explain the other to myself" (ibid). Similarly, critics such as Said

(1994: 277), Bhabha (1995: 13) and Spivak (1988a: 253-254) locate decolonisation in the harmonious relation and combination of the different elements, colonial and postcolonial, and stress the plurality of identity through various versions of the concept of "hybridity". In this sense, Cixous's and Irigaray's strategies of "bisexuality" and "amorous exchange" are very similar to the cultural syncreticism postcolonial theory advocates.

The advocacy of love and "amorous exchange" that feminist and postcolonial criticism argues in favour of is put into practice in *The War Horse*. Boland's main objective is, as she says in "The Laws of Love", to

> plead
>
> Another world for whose horizons,
> For whose anguish no reprieve
> Exists unless new citizens. (*Collected*, 50)

Boland envisages a world whose "new citizens" are regulated by the "laws of love". This is a world in which warring opposites no longer exist and where one must be able to "judge which is the other's source" today, to understand what drives the other party to violence (p. 23). This urgent call for peace and love is best observed in those poems where Boland explicitly adopts the voice of Mother Ireland. The main concern in poems such as "A Soldier's Son" and "Ready for Flight" (*Collected*, 41-42, 47) is not so much to turn Mother Ireland into a humanised figure or an ordinary woman (the concern of later poems such as "Mise Eire" and "Mother Ireland", *Collected*, 128-129, 261-262), but to change Mother Ireland's discourse from encouraging war and violence to proclaiming peace and love. The Goddess Athene (who first appeared in *New Territory*) starts to acquire a voice of her own, creating a "new music" with which to combat the heroic music of "song and gong" (*Collected*, 23). This new Athene is no longer a Goddess of War but a Goddess of Peace.

This Goddess of Peace appears for the first time in "A Soldier's Son". Whereas in her initial poetry, Boland remains uncritical of a national tradition that advocates violence, here the nation (and all that originates from it, such as the literary tradition) is referred to in the third person of the plural, indicating that the speaker maintains a detached distance from it:

> A young man's war it is, a young man's war
> Or so they say and so they go to wage
> This struggle (*Collected*, 41)

In this poem, Mother Ireland reveals what most people obliterate in their bloody engagement with violence: that war is, in the end, a battle that confronts fathers and sons: "knowing as I do/// That in the cross-hairs of his gun he found/ You his only son" (ibid). The narrator shows the fallacy of the binary logic of 'self' vs. 'Other' that underlies Loyalist or Nationalist discourses by presenting the different opponents as sharing the same roots and belonging to the same family. By killing his enemy, the warrior in this poem really kills a part of himself. The problem that this new Mother Ireland identifies is that the confronters stick to a very narrow definition of Irishness. Reversing the nationalist call for self-sacrifice, Mother Ireland advises her sons to move beyond war lines in order to start perceiving the enemy as a part of their identity as well, their "heritage":

> Son of a soldier who saw war on the ground,
> Now cross the peace lines I have made for you
> To find on this side if not peace then honour,
> Your heritage. (Ibid)

When crossing the "peace lines" that Mother Ireland has created, one can observe that the 'Other' that lies on the other side of the border is but an instant of the 'self', for it shares the same legacy, tradition, and ancestors.

Mother Ireland's advocacy of crossing well established boundary-lines (Loyalist vs. Nationalist, North vs. South) is also observed in "Ready for Flight". This poem shows that Boland is still greatly concerned with traditional poetic forms, because it is written in the form of a sonnet with high regular stanzas and rhythmic patterns. Nevertheless, in spite of its reliance on conventional literary techniques, "Ready for Flight" exemplifies a great shift in Boland's poetic sensibility. Mother Ireland stands as a different saviour than the one supported by the nationalist discourse. Instead of calling 'her sons' to fight for her, she promises to bring "to wasted areas the sight/ Of butterfly and swan and turtle dove/ Their wings ruffled like sails ready for flight" (*Collected*, 47). These birds are symbols of peace, of the harmonious coming together of different warring factions. The image of the birds promising liberation inevitably reminds one of Ledwidge's "The Blackbirds", where the Poor Old Woman summons her birds to rescue her (Kennelly 1970: 305). In the poem of this well-known patriotic Revivalist, writing in the end of the nineteenth century and the beginning of the twentieth, the Poor Old Woman is speaking in constant grief. She is portrayed as a victimised figure who is unable to act on her own, and thus summons the 'blackbirds' to save her from her dissatisfaction. The poem is intended to incite patriotic feelings, in order to encourage rebellion on the Irish people's part. Whereas in "Migration" (*Collected*, 11), Boland retained the allegorical image of the birds, to signify the Irish community of poets and their important national task, here Boland subverts their significance. "Ready for Flight" does not intend to provoke struggle, but quite the contrary: it offers peace and relief in the face of conflict and war. The speaker is no more the grieving Poor Old Woman, but a sheltering woman who lodges under her arms all opposing factions. On the other hand, in contrast to the angry poetic voices in *In Her Own Image*, this new Mother Ireland confesses to exerting her agency at "a more temperate place" (p. 47). Anger and revenge are alien to her project of proclaiming an alternative to war: the union of "love with love". This is the only way by which, as she says in the final couplet, "you and I would live in peace" (ibid). The woman poet is here addressing everyone, Northerners and Southerners, Loyalists and Nationalists. Nationalism is in this sense viewed as a persistent negotiation to incorporate new and varied voices of individual experience. As Gray (2000: 287) points out:

Boland's concept of nation [...] reflects contemporary concern with the complexity of subject positions – that is, the recognition that all single points of view are actually complex and fluid intersections of pressures, a recognition that consequently denies that any single point of view can claim extended hegemony over others.

In her attempt to envisage a better world, a world of peace, warring oppositions such as 'self' (the 'I') and 'the other' (the 'you' of the poem) must be overcome by an "amorous exchange" that unites "love with love". In this sense, the poems of *The War Horse* move towards a possibility of healing the scars created by the war. Even though, Boland suggests, her contemporary reality, as that reality of Irishmen and women, is wounded by the present state of affairs, there is, in some poems of this collection, a visionary hope for a better future. This stands in contrast to the pessimism that abounds in Boland's mature poetry. As we will see in the following sections, volumes such as *The Journey, Outside History, In a Time of Violence*, and *The Lost Land* place greater emphasis on the oppression and dispossession that has surrounded, and as a legacy, still surrounds the Irish woman poet.

Cixous's and Irigaray's advocacy of a sexual difference based on a relationship of equality is best observed in "The Botanic Gardens".[8] Compared to "A Soldier's Son" and "Ready for Flight", this poem proposes an alternative to the external conflict now more specifically rooted in the lived experience of the speaker: her marriage. In this poem dedicated to her husband, two lovers, ignoring for an instance the violence observed in newspapers and television screens, walk among the plants of a botanic garden:

> Guided by love, leaving aside dispute –
> Guns on the pages of newspapers, the sound
> Urgent of peace – we drive in real pursuit
> Of another season, Spring, where each has found
> Something before, new, and then sense
> In the Botanic Gardens, terms of reference. (*Collected*, 45)

The presence here of the first person pronoun in the plural form is significant. Whereas in Boland's 'Feminist' phase, the use of this pronoun was used exclusively to refer to a woman's community (as in "Tirade for the Mimic Muse"), here, as in other poems in *The War Horse*, it includes herself and her husband. The male 'Other' is no longer her adversary (as in *In Her Own Image*), but quite the contrary: the male 'Other' is her lovely husband, her companion and complement, an important part of her female identity. In this poem, both, man and woman are "[g]uided by love", and not by a desire to dominate the other. Boland's marriage is presented as an ideal relationship, an "amorous exchange" that is based on an equal relationship. It offers a "new" alternative to war, another "season", spring, where peace and love bloom. In their walk through the gardens, she recalls the time when she got married and her discovery of new sensations at that time:

> You take my hand. Three years ago, your bride.
> I felt your heart in darkness, a full moon
> Hauling mine to it like a tide. (Ibid)[9]

Love is envisaged as something which can unite two different persons in harmony, in a mysterious relationship of mutual positive influence. The image of the "full moon" encompasses mysterious forces, incomprehensible to reason, which draw her to the side of a man. Equality does not entail that one person cannot learn from another, but much the contrary, it even leads to personal enrichment. Whereas the constellations largely stood in the first phase for the mysterious realm where the poets navigated (e.g. "The Poets", *Collected*, 7), in this volume, the constellations stand for the mysterious love and admiration that unites two people together in such a special relationship.[10] The speaker's marriage symbolises the amiable union of two people, who "twine like these trees in peace and stress/ Before the peril of unconsciousness" (*Collected*, 45). Boland explicitly connects her marriage with those plants in the garden: both nature and her relationship are able to maintain peace at a time of national struggle. In this sense, the botanic gardens stand as a metonymy of Ireland, and its plants acquire political associations:

> Corsican pine, guerrilla poison plants –
> The first gardener here by foreign carriage
> And careful seeding in this circumference
> Imitated the hours of our marriage:
> The flowers of forced proximity, swollen, fed,
> Flourishing here, usually sheltered,
>
> Exposed this once. (Ibid)

As Haberstroh (1996: 64) rightly notes, the foreign gardener recalls the different invasions that Ireland has experienced and its subsequent plantations in the sixteenth and seventeenth centuries. Seeding and planting are not, as in "The Poets", a metaphor of domination (poets dominating chaos by inflicting order and form), but a reference to love. The flowers and spring stand as a symbol of peace and reconciliation between not only different communities co-habiting together (whether Irish, Anglo-Irish, Protestant, or Catholic), but also between the two different sexes. In a direct association between imperialism (by which one 'race' dominates the other one) and patriarchy (according to which men have dominated women in the conventional 'contract' of marriage), Boland envisages a way in which colonisers and colonised can co-exist peacefully, a model of peace which has its basis in mutual acceptance and understanding. The diverse plants, by "forced proximity", were compelled to survive together in a small place, in the insular territory of Ireland: "this circumference". But, as in her marriage, these plants were able to flourish in a harmonious unity. In order to achieve equality, Boland implies, the 'self' must not obliterate dissimilarity, but accept the 'Other' as different. This is what the following lines of the poem exemplify. The speaker's husband is suddenly portrayed as beyond her "reach": he moves away from the speaker in his search "for something", without noticing her "absence in the conservatory" (*Collected*, 46). Boland temporarily feels distanced from her husband, who is absorbed observing the grotesque figure of the cacti, sweating "in sandy heat", without realising she is at his side. Even though he has "overstepped" her "reach", Boland does not try to impose a definition on the 'Other', but loves him for what she cannot grasp:

> Each pumpkin history
> Turns coach at a touch of your hand.
> I watch and love you in your mystery. (Ibid)

It is the mystery of this figure, the fact that "Each pumpkin history/ Turns coach at the touch of [his] hand", which makes Boland love his husband. The emphasis of "The Botanic Gardens" is on the fact that the speaker is able to love her husband, not in spite of, but precisely because of his 'Otherness'. Irigaray (1991: 171) has argued that in this "amorous exchange", the self must feel "admiration" and "wonder" for the "unknowable other", "that which differs sexually from me". The gap between man and woman becomes enabling as long as "[w]onder might allow them to retain an autonomy based on their difference, and give them a space of freedom or attraction, a possibility of separation or alliance" (p. 172). This feeling of admiration, of seeing the 'Other' as though for the first time, as unknowable, but equally irreplaceable, is observed in this poem. Like Cixous and Irigaray, Boland is able to combine sexual difference and equality. Her poem focuses on the marriage experience of the speaker, but it also emphasises a way of life according to which one loves the 'Other' as different, without converting this 'Other' to one's own view of the world. In this sense, Boland's true and liberating marriage stands as a reconciliatory attitude between opposites. As in other poems from *The War Horse*, such as "The Other Woman" (*Collected*, 39), Boland comes to the realisation that what really matters is the closeness, the mysterious emotional bond which links both people together in marriage.

Whereas Boland's married life becomes one of the most important topics in *The War Horse*, it is significant how it remains occluded throughout her subsequent volumes of poetry, collections mainly concerned with other aspects such as her ordinary domestic life as a mother and housewife, and Ireland's oppressed and unrecorded past. It is not until her latest volume of poetry, *Code*, where marriage becomes once again the most important motif. As in *The War Horse*, in this volume there is a preponderance of first person pronouns and possessive forms in the plural (i.e. 'we' and 'our'), in order to include within the same term of reference the speaker and her husband. The main difference between the two collections of poetry is that whereas in the first one Boland's uses her own marriage in order to counteract the violence of the Troubles, in the latter one, she employs it with a view to debunk conventional love poetry. This is made explicit in Boland's prosaic poem "Against Love Poetry". By recurring to a paragraph, she expresses her wish to move away from the conventional love sonnet:

> We were married in summer, thirty years ago. I have loved you deeply from that moment to this. I have loved other things as well. Among them the idea of women's freedom. Why do I put these words side by side? Because I am a woman. Because marriage is not freedom. Therefore, every word here is written against love poetry. Love poetry can do no justice to this. […] It is to mark the contradictions of a daily love that I have written this. Against love poetry. (*Collected*, 280)

As Murphy (2003: 347) asserts, for Boland, it is not so much that "love itself is contradictory; rather it is the institution of marriage itself", conventionally established as a "social contract that defines a power relationship". On the other hand, she does not intend to write against love as such, but against the way in which love has been idealised and conventionalised in lyric poetry. Henderson (1997: 39) explains how conventional love poetry has been based on the trope of the male gazing upon his beloved. By doing so, male poets have displayed a "domineering attitude towards their [female] object of desire" (p. 56). Both in her prose account and in her poetry, Boland dismantles this convention. In *Object Lessons*, she criticises the fusion of the sexual and the erotic in poetry, because it has been responsible for the everlasting beauty, silence, and agelessness of the female object (Boland 1995a: 210). Various poets, throughout time, have perpetuated this damaging fusion, such as Edmund Spenser, Robert Herrick, and John Keats (p. 215, 218, 225). In order to overcome this pitfall, Boland becomes the speaking subject of the poem, rather than a passive and erotic object. On the other hand, she destabilises conventional love poetry by presenting the figures of a husband and wife no longer as eternal, perfect, and romanticised, but as people who experience the passing of time and the loss of beauty.

The poem that opens *Code* introduces the concern which is at the heart of the volume: the intersections of art and marriage. In "In Which Hester Bateman, Eighteenth-Century English Silversmith, Takes an Irish Commission", Boland draws on a popular eighteenth-century woman artist in order to show how art has traditionally violated and simplified the union between husband and wife:

> Hester Bateman made a marriage spoon
> And then subjected it to violence.
> Chased, beat it. Scarred it and marked it.
> All in the spirit of our darkest century.
>
> [...]
>
> Here in miniature a man and a woman
> Emerge beside each other from the earth,
> From the deep mine, from the seams of rock
> Which made inevitable her craft of hurt. (*Collected*, 279)

In Boland's poem, the man and the woman, in contrast to traditional poetry, are not associated with eternal love and beauty, but with "hurt". This couple, in this sense, represents Boland's own poetics: "a craft of hurt", an art that does not immortalise the images as ideal emblems, but a sort of anti-aesthetic art that brings to the fore of the poem all the chasing, beating, and scarring that artistic representation entails. For Boland, any sort of artistic representation relies on violence to create order and beauty. As soon as Bateman attempts to inscribe their profiles in silver, she inevitably simplifies and misrepresents their reality. This misrepresentation becomes the starting point from which Boland reflects on how marriage has been a conventional institution that establishes power relationships. The marriage that Bateman portrays in her silver spoon is further compared to the unequal relationship between England and Ireland. Her artistic representation, as Hagen and Zelman (2004: 89) explain, "emulates the colonial process" by which England has brutally attempted to remould "Ireland to an English plan". As this woman "lets cool the sweet colonial metal", both figures "inch[..] towards the light", to a place where

> Past and future and the space between
> The semblance of empire, the promise of nation,
> Are vanishing in this mediation
> Between oppression and love's remembrance
>
> Until resistance is their only element. It is
> What they embody, bound now and always.
> History frowns on them: yet in its gaze
> They join their injured hands and make their vows. (*Collected*, 279-280)

Although Ireland and England seem to be bound forever in a relationship that, as conventional marriage, unites two factions in a hierarchical way, the final lines of the poem offer an earnest promise of co-habitation on equal terms, a form of "amorous exchange" according to which two countries can live in peace and harmony. The change from past to present tense that the poem records is a typical feature of Boland's mature work. Boland constantly brings a past and remote situation to her present context, extracting all its relevance and significance. After remembering the violations of conventional love poetry and the unequal 'marriage' between England and Ireland, Boland creates a promising space in her poem where real change can be brought about. On the other hand, the short sentences, some of them incomplete, that opened the poem are substituted now by longer sentences which unfold down the page by means of enjambments. Whereas the first linguistic technique is used in order to show the violence and simplification of a 'real' marriage in art, the more fluid language at the end of the poem enhances the feeling that this violence and oppression can be got rid of. Boland envisages liberation, a possibility that the English and the Irish can co-habit on equal terms and that art and marriage can make a more accurate match. Both "empire" and "nation" start to vanish as coloniser and colonised "join their injured hands and make their vows". Although violence cannot be forgotten and wounds are still inscribed in their bodies, Boland is able to visualise a new relationship. The "remembrance" of "oppression" is therefore counteracted by "love", by a new marriage that is based on affection, mutual understanding, and forgiveness of past atrocities. The movement from dark to light that the poem exemplifies parallels this release. "[T]he spirit of our darkest century" in the first stanza suddenly "[i]nches towards the light", towards a place where Boland envisages an "amorous exchange" that maintains difference and equality simultaneously.

In other poems from *Code*, Boland more explicitly focuses on her married life in order to draw us into a liberating form of relationship between apparently contrary factions. The woman speaker in "A Marriage for the Millennium" asks her husband:

> Do you believe
> that Progress is a woman?
> A spirit seeking for its opposite?
> For a true marriage to ease her quick heartbeat? (*Collected*, 286)

Although this question is left unanswered in this particular poem, Boland's contention in this volume is that it is indeed in "a true marriage" that unites "opposite[s]" where "Progress" is found. In contrast to *In Her Own Image*, change is not brought about by isolation, but by uniting one's efforts with the 'Other'. This becomes the main topic of "The Pinhole Camera", a poem where Boland recalls a solar eclipse in August 1999 and her husband making a device in order to track the obscuring of the sun by the moon. In this natural phenomenon the speaker finds an appropriate metaphor to record her thirty-year-marriage life:

> [...] this is real –
> how your page records
> the alignment of planets:
> their governance.
> In other words,
> the not-to-be-seen again
> mystery of
> a mutual influence (*Collected*, 281)

The disruption of the lay-out is a common feature in Boland's mature work in order to represent the flowing of human lives. Boland does not wish to describe herself and her husband as eternal figures, unaffected by the passing of time, but as ordinary and ageing human beings which are bound to perish. Her husband's page, in contrast to conventional love poetry, stands out as a more accurate representation of her marriage. Rather than fixing images both in time and space, his pinhole camera is able to record the movement of celestial bodies. The speaker establishes a parallelism between "the alignment between planets", the "mystery of [their] mutual influence", and her own relationship with her husband. The cohabitation of constellations suggests the miraculous ability of being united to a separate and apparently opposite person. As in "The Botanic Gardens", the "mystery" of such a union is that, in spite of their differences, they are able to love each other. This miracle becomes explicitly manifested in another poem from *Code*, "First Year", where Boland records the initial years of her marriage:

> My talkative, unsure
> unsettled self
> was everywhere;
> but you
> were the clear spirit of somewhere. (*Collected*, 284)

Once again, her husband is portrayed as beyond the speaker's "reach" ("The Botanic Gardens", *Collected*, 46), as someone who is unknowable and therefore unreachable. But it is precisely this preservation of difference between opposites that makes marriage such a liberating relationship. Like Cixous and Irigaray, the feminist postcolonial theorist Spivak (1988a: 253-254) has argued that warring factions can only be more truthfully united when one acknowledges that he or she is separated from the 'Other' by an "irreducible difference".[11] Any attempt to grasp this "difference" runs the risk of perpetuating hierarchical relationships that are based on dominance and superiority. The speaker in "First Year" and "The Pinhole Camera" avoids understanding the 'Other' fully in her own terms. It is this "mystery", as she implies, that allows "mutual influence"; in other words, it permits opposite factions to learn from each other in positive and enriching ways. That is why marriage is envisaged in "The Pinhole Camera" as a transcendental, mystical, and superior form of relationship. Although, as we have seen, husband and wife are humanised figures whose destiny is death, Boland argues when addressing to her husband that their love will be able to outlive:

> You know
> the reason for the red berries
> darkening, and the road outside
> darkening, but did you know
> that the wedding
> of light and gravity
> is forever? (*Collected*, 281)

Constellations serve as metaphors for her marriage's endurance and survival. Whereas the suburban and ordinary landscape finds itself affected by the changes of daylight, their love will never perish and "darken". "[T]he wedding of light and gravity" that the solar eclipse shows "is forever", just as the miracle of their everlasting union.

In this sense, Boland's project resembles French feminists' attempt to challenge Western (patriarchal) thought and its dualist stance according to which the masculine and the feminine can only be related in hierarchical ways. The woman poet offers a new vision of marriage based on balance, partnership, collaboration, mutual respect, equality, and symmetry. She demonstrates that the two modes of operation, masculine and feminine, are not necessarily hierarchical and oppositional, but complementary. Both are equally important because they are essential to bringing about the wholeness of the self. That is why Boland draws on her ordinary life as a married woman in order to deal with the violent atmosphere of contemporary events (the Troubles), and also in order to establish an argument with traditional and conventional love poetry. In both cases, her marriage stands out as an ideal and true relationship that is both enriching and liberating for the speaker.

Therefore, for Boland, poetry and daily ordinary life appear as intrinsically related, as two distinct but mutually inspirational experiences. This fact would subsequently be shown in the poems that constitute mostly *Night Feed* (1982), where Boland praises her domestic landscape and her role as a mother. In this volume, the interaction between mother and child, and the resulting binding love, is also for Boland the most instructive and surprising human relationship. As Haberstroh (1996: 72) notes, the poet "shows how the intensity of a woman's experience as mother can suggest much about the universal meaning of love, life, and death". Boland emphasises how the nurturing affection between mother and child is a possible refuge from a world of violence and destruction. This is observed in poems such as "Hymn", for instance, where Boland deliberately establishes a contrast between a peaceful domestic environment and a public landscape of violence and war.

> The cutlery glitter
> of that sky
> has nothing in it
> I want to follow.
>
> Here is the star
> of my nativity:
> a nursery lamp
> in a suburb window
>
> behind which
> is boiled glass, a bottle
> and a baby all

hisses like a kettle. (*Collected*, 95)

According to the Bible, when Jesus Christ was born, three wise men set out on a journey following a nativity star that would eventually lead them to the crib where the Lamb of God was born. Boland, in the contemporary context of Ireland, has a different nativity star to follow: the nursery lamp in her suburb window. The sparkling light in the sky is only superficially attractive: its "glitter" is not real, but man-made, "cutlery". On the other hand, its brightness is a reflection of the metallic weapons and bladed swords used in combat. Kupillas (1999: 20) observes that, for Boland, "human problems are not going to be solved by some miraculous intervention of deity. Instead, the changes in human relationships will be the result of humans intervening in and influencing the lives of others". In fact, Boland implies in this poem that the solution to contemporary problems is not found in the distant stars (by invoking unreal or illusionary emblems), but in this suburban setting, in the speaker's everyday world. It is here where a promising and happier future lies. The mother's unconditional love towards her child teaches us how this change can be brought about.

This apparent indifference to the political problems in Ireland is commonly suffered by Irish women in what Hidalgo Tenorio (2000: 389) calls their "ideological exile". When using the example of the mother in O'Casey's *The Star Turns Red*, this researcher asserts that this playwright portrays a woman who wants to be unresponsive and insensitive to nationalism (p. 391). The main reason for her indifference is that, with the prospect of finding no possible reconciliation between warring factions, she opts instead to nurture personal relationships which might be more gratifying for her. Eavan Boland suffers from a similar "ideological exile". As she feels she never "owned Irish history", and "never felt entitled to the Irish experience" (Boland 1995a: 190), she refuses to adopt the ideological stance of nationalist writers who invoked the land to incite rebellion. Boland's ideology stems rather from her private sphere, from the love experienced at home. Only this can wane "the hatred that fuels war" (Haberstroh 1996: 24).

As we have seen in this section, Boland's female experience as a wife, housewife, and mother constitute very important aspects of her identity as a woman poet, and in fact, they are mentioned throughout her production. By praising and making sacramental her roles in the domestic sphere, Boland might suggest that her own private and personal experience is universal. Her emphasis on the importance of marriage and motherhood as sources of identity for the female subject would be criticised by scholars such as Spivak (interview with Threadgold & Bartkowski 1990: 118), Davis (2003: 353), Rajan (1993: 1-2), and Mohanty (1991a: 11), who believe that homogenising generalisations such as these might obliterate more heterogeneous women's experiences. All these feminist postcolonial critics have argued that any campaign which attempts to speak on behalf of all women runs the risk of eliding specific cultural, historical, and economic contexts. From this perspective, Boland might be accused of ignoring the different experiences of all those women who do not find in marriage and/or motherhood their sources of identity. Nevertheless, one should bear in mind that her poems distinctively pay homage to women's roles as wives, mothers and housewives, in order to reassess an experience which has been for long neglected (not in order to praise it above all other human experiences), and in order to unite sexual and warring opposites. On the other hand, it is also important to consider that, as Boland's work progresses, womanhood is, interestingly enough, gradually defined in terms of fluidity, erasure, and silences. The following section addresses this issue.

4.3. A deconstruction of the poetic self

4.3.1. Introduction

As Boland (1995a: 132) has admitted, she attempts to bring to the surface of her poems the two categories 'Irishness' and 'womanhood'. In the process, the very construction of identity itself (identity as an Irish citizen, and identity as a woman) is called into question. For Boland, ideas such as Irishness and womanhood, although necessary for the individual, are mere human 'constructions'. As she has recently argued, "I think all human identity is fictional in a way", and later she says that "[w]e are constructed by the construct" (interview with Villar Argáiz). Following Showalter's (1999: 13), Memmi's (1990: 7), and Fanon's (1990: 231) findings, decolonisation for the colonised subject must not be based on a politics of opposition (woman vs. man; black vs. white), and this is the main starting point from which to discuss Eavan Boland's deconstruction of identity. Of course, one might be bewildered at this assertion, for, how to construct the category 'Irishness' if not by recurring to some specific features, some essences, which distinguish the 'Irish' subject from the 'English' one, such as Irish nationalism and Celtic Revivalism have done? Or, how to construct the category 'womanhood' if not in opposition to the category 'man', such as radical feminism does? In what follows, I will show how Boland attempts to deconstruct both categories by occupying an 'in-between' space from which to counteract essentialist notions of identity.

The marginality that Boland has experienced both as an Irish person and as a woman writer has allowed her to have, as she believes, "clear eyes and a quick critical sense" (Boland 1995a: 147). The dislocation that she has felt as an Irish girl living in London is a "disguised blessing" for Boland, for, as she explains, "[i]t warned me away from facile definitions" of 'Irishness' (p. 179).[12] On the other hand, Boland (1995a: 147) also understands her invisibility as a woman writer within the Irish poetic tradition as a "disguised grace", because it has allowed her to see more clearly the simplifications and "distortions" of 'womanhood' deep in the very structure of Irish poetry. Boland has recently expressed the benefits from experiencing an "intimidatory disrespect" as a woman writer immersed in the restrictive circle of Dublin literary life: "For me, that was a subtle and painful exclusion. But it was also a motive to think more carefully about what I was doing – more carefully than I might have done if conditions hadn't been so inhospitable" (interview with Villar Argáiz). Boland's double marginalisation, as an Irish postcolonial subject and as a woman writer in Ireland, have given her "an unique vantage point" from which "to make a critique of the tradition and its resistances that helped me, and I hope might help other writers" (ibid). In this sense, her discourse is located on the margins of nationalist and feminist representations alike. Positioning herself in this border location allows Boland to act subversively, to move away from authoritarian constructions of identity.

An indication that Boland desires to move away from essentialist notions of 'nationhood' and 'womanhood' is her fierce critique of nationalism and feminism, as well as her own way of defining her poetry. Boland (1995a: 234) has extensively narrated how the contrary pulls of nationalism and feminism have threatened her project as a poet. Neither ideology helps the Irish woman poet to achieve artistic decolonisation, for they both lay powerful prescriptions "on how men and women should and should not write" (ibid). Although she admits that she doesn't find nationalism "as enabling an orthodoxy as feminism" and that "[f]eminism is a powerful, ethical ideology", she further argues that "the most enabling ethical ideologies are anti-imaginative, painful as it may be to admit it" (interview with Villar Argáiz). In this sense, Boland (1995a: 254) has asserted that she is "neither a separatist nor a postfeminist", and that, although she considers herself to be an Irish poet, she is not a nationalist writer (interview with Wilson 1990b: 84). In this sense, her project is to move her poetry away from the restrictions imposed by nationalism and radical feminism (with their authoritative views on identity).

Boland's definition of her own poetry also shows how she tries to locate her work outside the realm of definite doctrines and ideologies: "My poetry begins for me where certainty ends. I think the imagination is an ambiguous and untidy place, and its frontiers are not accessible to the logic of feminism for that reason" (Boland 1995a: 254). This definition of poetry as encompassing ambiguity responds to Boland's desire to create her work outside essentialist feminism, which (as nationalism) constructs identity on differences and opposition. Boland resists defining her work in opposition, for such action would be polarising. Thus, when writing poetry, Boland finds that all sorts of "beliefs, convictions, certainties get left on that threshold" (interview with Allen-Randolph 1993b: 125). In this sense, poetry for Boland becomes not a place of "convictions" but a place of ambiguity.

By viewing her poetry as an uncertain terrain, Boland attempts to move away from counter-hegemonic discourses and to elude the politics of polarity. This brings her close to recent postmodernist, feminist, and postcolonial attempts to envisage alternative ways for both a politics of blame and even a more destructive politics of confrontation. Postmodernist theorists such as Jean-François Lyotard and Jean Baudrillard have rejected anything that might be linked to the "metanarrative of emancipation", and advocate adopting the position of "the anti-political individual" (Sarup 1993: 155, 105). Similarly, feminists like Kristeva (1986d) have expressed reluctance to collective political action and have defended a politics of marginality. This feminist critic asserts that politically active intellectuals are hopelessly caught in the very logic of power he or she wishes to destroy. Like these postmodernist and feminist moves, postcolonial theorists like Said (1995: 73), Bhabha (1995: 9), Spivak (interview with Bhatnagar et al. 1990: 71), and Hall (1990: 230) do not view political activism as the most effective resistant attitude to adopt, because it runs the risk of perpetuating the dominant symbolic systems it seeks to undermine. As Moore-Gilbert (2000: 139) argues when talking about Bhabha, "[for him] those who oppose the dominant power on its own terms or in its own language are necessarily caught up in its logic and thus perpetuate it". In *Orientalism*, Said (1995: 73) warns of the dangers of inhaling the discourse of power employed by the West in order to manipulate and dominate the native population: "My hope is to illustrate the formidable structure of cultural domination and, specifically for formerly colonised peoples, the dangers and temptations of employing this structure upon themselves and upon others". For the four postcolonial theorists mentioned above, the only way to elude the discourse of power intrinsic in the 'identity politics' of imperialism and nationalism, is by adopting a politics of the differential, "a politics of positioning" in Hall's words (1990: 230), or "a politics of displacement" as Smyth (1998: 205) calls it. This form of politics emphasises the necessity to adopt a cultural and political pluralism that has the virtue of blurring polarisation and allows communication between the 'self' and the 'Other'. In this sense, decolonisation would be achieved by attempting "to escape from the colonialist relationship", from the antagonism "coloniser and colonised" (O'Dowd 1990: 54).[13]

Boland's explicit embracing of ambiguity as the place where her 'apolitical' poetry can be located tells us a lot about how she is going to construct her identity as an Irish woman poet. Boland consciously embraces ambivalence as the terrain in which to construct her identity. As she has asserted, "turmoil is easily negotiated into ambivalence" (Boland 1995a: 9). This ambivalence, results from the fact that her identity has always revolved around opposing and contradictory poles. Postcolonial theorists and critics as varied as Bhabha (1995: 278), Hall (1990: 230), and Boyce (1994: 36) believe that the subject, in particular the postcolonial one, is complexly constructed through different categories, of different antagonisms.[14] In her attempt to define her 'Irishness' and 'womanhood', two categories associated with fulfilled identity, Boland (1995a: 252) explains how she is constantly "assailed by contradictions". As a woman who has spent most of her childhood in England, Boland feels confused: neither feeling entirely English nor Irish, her identity is fractured.[15] Similarly, as a grown-up woman, Boland has to face a further ambivalence, which results from those contradictions found in the very deep structure of the Irish poem: the culturally and socially accepted separation between being a woman and being a writer/poet. In this sense, Boland's identity is based on what Hall (1990: 225) describes as "ruptures and discontinuities". Her work attempts to highlight, rather than heal, the conflict between these antagonistic aspects of her identity. As she has argued, her poetry intends to record the "vivid and divided world of the subject, [...] a world so volatile" that collapses and refreshes "all the other apparently stable meanings in the poem" (Boland 1995a: 189). Boland defends the notion of a "decentred subject", a project at the core, as Sarup (1993: 96) argues, of poststructuralist theory. The contradictions that she has felt as an Irish citizen and as a woman poet are productive rather than delimitating. That is why Boland (1995a: 96) has talked about "the wealth of ambiguity" around her. These contradictions allow her to embrace hybridity and ambivalence as the best strategy to construct her poetic self. As Papastergiadis (1997: 259) has argued, "[t]he positive feature of hybridity is that it invariably acknowledges that identity is constructed through a negotiation of difference, and that the presence of fissures, gaps, and contradictions is not necessarily a sign of failure". The presence of contradictions and ambiguity in Boland's poetry is not "a sign of failure", but a strategy of subversion. In this sense, Boland's work is aligned with that branch of postcolonial and feminist theory that defends hybridity, boundary crossing and fluidity as the best option.[16]

Mikhail Bakhtin's (1981) theory of linguistic hybridity, a turning point in current postcolonial debates,[17] is essential to fully understand this concept. According to Bakhtin (1981: 358), hybridity is the way in which language, even within a single sentence, can be double-voiced:

> What is a hybridisation? It is a mixture of two social languages within the limits of a single utterance, an encounter, within the arena of an utterance, between two different linguistic consciousnesses, separated from one another by an epoch, by social differentiation or by some other factors.

Bakhtin distinguishes between two types of hybridity, an "organic" hybridity which leads to fusion, and an "intentional" hybridity, which creates separation. The unconscious "organic" hybridity is described as follows:

> Unintentional, unconscious hybridisation is one of the most important modes in the historical life and evolution of all languages. We may even say that language and languages change historically primarily by hybridisation, by means of mixing various 'languages'. (Bakhtin 1981: 358-359)

From this perspective, hybridity is the fusion of two languages, an encounter between two different linguistic codes. This hybridisation is highly productive historically, for it enables "new world views, [...] new 'internal forms' for perceiving the world in words" (p. 360). In this sense, hybridity would mean "creolisation", a term coined by the Caribbean poet Edward Brathwaite (1971: 296) to suggest how, by means of borrowings and mimetic appropriation, two or more cultures or languages merge into a new one.

The second type of hybridity that Bakhtin mentions is the conscious, "intentional" hybridity. In this type of hybridity, Bakhtin explains, "[t]wo points of view are not mixed, but set against each other dialogically" (p. 360). The collision between two different points of view creates a politicised and challenging hybridity which leads to division and separation. The second form of hybridity that Bakhtin distinguishes is viewed by postcolonial critics as the one which undoes authoritative discourse, and undermines the single-voiced authority. As Young (1995: 22) highlights, "within a single discourse, one voice is able to unmask the other".

Boland's poetry can be analysed from the perspective of Bakhtin's doubled hybridity.[18] *In Her Own Image* is an instance of Bakhtin's "organic" hybridity. In this volume, Boland seeks to construct a counter-hegemony that contests dominant representations of women in male cultural and aesthetic practices. In order to do so, she homogenises women's experience under the single category 'Woman'. In this sense, hybridisation involves the fusion and assimilation of women's experiences in the belief that there exists, what French feminism has called, a distinctive 'sexual difference'.

By contrast, Boland's mature poetry is characterised by Bakhtin's (1981: 360) "intentional" hybridity. The poetic voice in Boland seems to be constituted by multiple identities that do not always make for harmony: her identity as Irish, as woman, and as poet. For Boland, the formation of identity is not the accumulation of one essence with another. It rather leads to a place where tensions are constantly recorded. By means of these tensions, Boland will open a space of hybridity and fluidity where opposites are dissolved.

The following section analyses Boland's deconstruction of identity-claims from this postcolonial and feminist perspective. Her mature work provides the prospect of a fluid identity, putting into practice the theoretical postcolonial perspective that "one is always on the move" (Spivak 1990b: 38). While her poems certainly attempt to construct a viable sense of cultural identity, they dwell more on rootlessness and non-identity than on the formation of a stable and grounded self. This postmodernist splintering of the subject results from the tensions that Boland experiences in the very process of artistic creation. Boland's mature work records all sorts of contradictory pulls: the contradictions between the stillness of art and the versatility of her life experience, the opposite poles of womanhood and poetry; and the distance that Boland finds between mythical and historical versions of Ireland.

Out of these tensions, Boland will occupy a subversive hybrid space, in which her own identity will always be represented in terms of fluidity and dissolution.[19] Nothing is stable in her mature poetry, everything is changeable, even her sense of identity. Showalter (1999: 259) asserts that one way of identifying women's 'Female' art is by their ability to "create [their own distinctive] atmospheres". Boland's mature work creates this distinctive atmosphere Showalter talks about. In most of the poems from *The Journey* onwards, Boland's temporal context is usually dusk, a time of transition when nothing is definite and everything blurs. In this context, the poet-speaker is able to shift from one sphere to another, from a real and concrete world to a supernatural or bygone world. Boland's poetic voices inhabit non-defined spaces, liminal and in-between spaces. Hers is always a landscape of rapid change: a mother walking in a suburban dusk or a woman writing at a table by an open window in a twilight setting of diffused lights. Locating herself in this transitional position allows Boland to evade facile definitions and artistic misrepresentations. In this context, self-definition engages in a gradual process of dissolution and erasure.

Very few critics, with the exception of Mills Harper (1997) and Fulford (2002a), have detected Boland's postmodernist techniques in her poetry. Mills Harper (1997: 192) has noted that Boland "occupies a region beyond subject-object definition". Fulford (2002a: 213), in the belief that identity cannot be founded on an idea of authenticity, praises Boland's dissolution of categories such as 'Irishness' and 'womanhood', because, only by so doing, she forces readers to understand the misrepresentation involved in all representations. Thanks to the versatility of her identity, Fulford highlights that Boland manages to abandon "the pathos of authenticity that has informed first-generation nationalist and feminist projects alike" (ibid). In fact, by writing from a place of liminality, Boland resists essentialisms, defies definitions of women (as those offered by nationalist and feminist ideologies), and opens a space of future potential.

4.3.2. Against the solidification of images in art

4.3.2.1. The limits of artistic representations

Boland faces a troubling dichotomy as an Irish woman poet: her desire to describe the fluidity of a life experience, and the stillness and solidification that any sort of artistic representation involves. In the following quotation, Boland (1995a: 33-34) questions her ability to record a life in a poem without simplifying or keeping it fixed. Here, her grandmother's life is symbolised by the image of the "lava cameo":

> To inscribe a profile in the cold rock. To cut a human face into what had once flowed, fiery and devouring, past farms and villages and livestock. To make a statement of something which was already a statement of random and unsparing destruction. [...] If I remembered her life, if I were to set her down – half-turned-away face in its context of ill luck and erased circumstance – would I be guilty of sarcastic craftsmanship? Would I too be making a statement of irony and corruption?

As we can see in this passage, the woman poet feels that her recovery of women's past is inadequate because she feels limited by the fact that she cannot make a statement of something which has been destroyed. But she is also doing something else: Boland is questioning her very ability to record the changes that affect women, their lived experience, without paralysing the moment. As Fulford (2002a: 206) explains,

[a]s Boland tries to work against monumental or immortal versions of identity and time, she becomes trapped within the logic of representation. Once the moment of a woman's experience is inscribed within the aesthetic space of the poem it risks becoming a frozen trope rather than living and breathing.

In this sense, Boland is faced with the task of giving voice to women's realities within a poem, without running the risk of immortalising and objectifying them any further. In order to overcome the "irony and corruption" that threatens every artist, and therefore every poet, Boland always describes her women as fluid and dissolved, and therefore, as impossible to grasp.

The danger of simplification and misrepresentation that artistic representation involves is constantly recorded in her poetry, as in poems such as "Bright-Cut Irish Silver", "An Old Steel Engraving", and "The Photograph on My Father's Desk" (*Collected*, 173, 182, 184). The first poem explicitly criticises the (Irish) poetic tradition, allegorised as silver-crafting. The speaker in this poem, attracted by the sensuality of the silver object, is induced to "take it down/ from time to time" in order:

to feel
the smooth path of silver meet the cicatrice of skill.

These scars, I tell myself, are learned.

This gift for wounding an artery of rock
was passed on from father to son, to the father
of the next son;

is an aptitude
for injuring earth while inferring it in curves and surfaces;

is this cold potency which has come,
by time and chance,

into my hands. (*Collected*, 173)

Note the clear equation of art and wounding that these lines exemplify. First of all, she attacks the fact that literature has been based on a patrilineal inheritance, from which women have been excluded. Boland is here emphasising that poetry is nothing but a male terrain, to which poets have access by "right" and "inheritance". Secondly, she denounces the conventional relationship between artistic mastery and coercion. 'Injuring' and turning women into solidified emblems is for male poets an "aptitude", a "skill". By inscribing "curves and surfaces", the artist "inscribe[s] a profile in the hard rock" (Boland 1995a: 33), transforming the hardened material in order to define and mould it. Boland implies that the artist creates 'wounds', by neglecting the actuality of women's lived experiences. The deictic demonstrative pronouns in this poem enhance the speaker's approximation to the scars, as if they were inscribed in her very same body. The relationship of power as established in Irish poetry between male subject and female object has also affected the woman speaker. The final single-line stanza, characteristic of Boland's mature style, focuses on the speaker's hands, as if, like silver, they share the same cicatrices.

Nevertheless, this poem is not only criticising the Irish poetic tradition. The end of the poem is quite ambiguous, because Boland presents herself both as a victim and an accomplice of the same artistic 'conspiracy'. The distance of the subject from the predicate gives the impression that this is a rhetorical question. Boland wonders if she is excluded from this art, or if she has rather inherited its same violence. By holding in her hands "this cold potency", Boland yields to the temptation of exerting the same power and violence over her poetic images. Although she has received this gift, not by heritage, but by "time and chance", with her hands, she can equally, in her search for order and beauty, carry out a similar misrepresentation. In this sense, and as Hagen and Zelman (2004: 88) have also noticed, Boland points to the, perhaps inevitable, diminishing and deformation that the artist, in his/her pursuit of aesthetic beauty, exerts on the objects. In poems such as "The Art of Grief", the speaker implicitly questions her own ability to reconstruct poetic images:

> An object of the images we make is
> what we are and how we lean out and
> over the perfect surface where
> our features in water greet us and save us.
> No weeping there, only the element
> claiming its emblem. (*Collected*, 240)

The first person pronoun of this passage indicates that the speaker admits to being an accomplice of an art where no "weeping" and living experiences are recorded. As "The Art of Grief" and "Bright-Cut Irish Silver" show, Boland believes that we are inevitably trapped by our own representations. In order to reverse the process, as we will see, Boland attempts to do the contrary, creating images which cannot be defined "in curves and surfaces", but that, in their very indefinite shapes, can escape both the poet and the reader's grasp.

In "The Photograph on My Father's Desk" (*Collected*, 182), Boland also reflects on the stillness and one dimensionality that, in this case, a photograph inflicts on a man and a woman. As in other poems from *Outside History*, such as "Mountain Time", "We Were Neutral in the War", and "An Old Steel Engraving" (*Collected*, 171-172, 174-175, 184), this poem is written as a third person narration. Interestingly enough, all these poems focus on 'official' and 'sanctioned' cultural and historical accounts (a mythical story, a particular historical event, or conventional artistic representations). It is as if Boland adopts the stance of an omnipresent narrator and a distant observer both to handle with more assurance her subversive movement, and also to perceive more clearly the pitfalls of traditional forms. The poem opens by describing an apparently active natural setting:

It could be
any summer afternoon.

The sun is warm on
the fruitwood garden seat.
Fuchsia droops.
Thrushes move to get
windfalls underneath the crab apple tree. (*Collected*, 182)

Although we discover a seemingly dynamic setting, the indefinite determiner 'any' indicates that the reference to the summer afternoon of the photograph is generic, and that the scene is not located within a particular time or place. The use of the present simple in these lines is significant, too. We should remember that the present simple can be used with a timeless reference, according to which the speaker states his/her facts as "usually valid all the time" (Quereda Rodríguez-Navarro 1997: 111). Since they have such "a universal validity", "they are always presented as a whole" (ibid). Similarly, in this context, Boland uses the simple present in order to show how past, present, and future are irrelevant in the photograph. Without any specific temporal reference, Boland locates this scene as timeless, at no concrete point in time. The image of the thrush also appears in "Object Lessons" (*Collected*, 167-168), a poem that similarly reflects on the stillness of artistic images, in this particular case, within the pictorial scene of a simple black mug. In this poem, the bird is portrayed as "ready to sing", but its song will be a "never/ to-be-finished aria". Whereas the bird in "Object Lessons" is constantly singing, the birds in this poem will be perpetually in movement. Nonetheless, although they are in motion, in reality their movement is static. Similarly, the sun will always be warming the garden chair, and the flower will always be drooping. This scene, frozen both in time and place, widens in the following lines, in order to include a man and a woman:

The woman
holds her throat like a wound.

> She wears
> mutton-coloured gaberdine with
> a scum of lace
> just above her boot
>
> which is pointed at
> this man coming down the path with
> his arms wide open. Laughing. (*Collected*, 182)

The woman's pose differs from the man's. While she is still, he comes with "his arms wide open" and his laughing face. The lexical verbs of action are only assigned to the male character. It is the man who has the action and is presented as moving, as the present participles indicate. The woman does not share the male's action-in-progress and her solidification is stronger in the photograph. Whereas the man is "[l]aughing", the woman in the picture is silenced and oppressed, holding her throat "like a wound". Using Boland's words in "The Art of Grief" (*Collected*, 240), it is the woman's very "indivisible act of definition which ha[s] silenced her". As we have seen in "Bright-Cut Irish Silver", Boland recurs in her poetry to metaphors of wounds and scars to suggest the violence that Irish poetry, in its desire to portray passive and beautiful female emblems, has exerted on real-and-blood women. As Foster (1999: 7) notes, the poem is constructed upon the traditional formula of "male pursuer" and "female [...] victim" which is at the heart of canonical poems such as Keats's "Ode on a Grecian Urn". Wearing gaberdine described as "mutton-coloured", the woman seems to be an oppressed lamb, a sacrificed scapegoat. The silence that characterises this image is further intensified by the end of the poem:

> The garden fills up
> with a burned silence.
>
> The talk has stopped.
> The spoon which just now
> jingled at the rim of the lemonade jug
> is still.

And the shrubbed lavender
will find
neither fragance nor muslin. (*Collected*, 182)

The photographer has not only silenced the woman, but in freezing this moment in time, has also "removed [all] life from it" (Foster 1999: 7). The previous tinkling metallic sound of the spoon has been silenced, and the lavender has even lost its fragrance. In this sense, visual representation gets rid of other senses. The faculties of hearing, smell, not to say, touch or taste, find themselves damaged, and with them, the richness of perceiving an image in all its totality. The poem ends with the modal 'will' indicating a high degree of certainty, something common in Boland's mature work in order to express the poet's conviction of how oppressive artistic representation can be.

This focus on the stillness of artistic images is continued in poems such as "An Old Steel Engraving" (*Collected*, 184). As in "Bright-Cut Irish Silver", Boland uses the engraving in this poem as a metaphor of the Irish literary tradition and also as a starting point to reflect on the dangers of "inscribing a profile" into a hard surface (Boland 1995a: 33). In the initial stanza, Boland adopts, as in "The Photograph on My Father's Desk", the position of an observer who, as an omnipresent narrator, has the authority to draw, by means of imperatives, the reader's attention to what she is interested in:

Look.
The figure in the foreground breaks his fall with
one hand. He cannot die.
The river cannot wander
into the shadows to be dragged by willows.
The passer-by is scared witless. He cannot escape.
He cannot stop staring at
this hand which can barely raise
the patriot
above the ground which is
the origin and reason for it all. (*Collected*, 184)

This poem captures a moment similar to "The Photograph on My Father's Desk". The traditional formula of male pursuer and fleeing maiden is transformed here into a hero wounded by a bayonet thrust, and a terrified eyewitness. The preponderance of the use of the modal 'can' in the negative form indicates both characters' impossibility of movement, and it enhances their stillness and petrifaction in the engraving. This impossibility or 'limited' possibility is also enhanced by the adverb "barely", and by later lexical repetitions of "nothing can move [...] nothing can stir". While the victim hangs suspended just above the ground, the passer-by "cannot stop staring" at him. As in the previous poem, Boland uses the simple present in order to express timeless reference. On the other hand, the use of short sentences enhances the imprisonment of these figures in art, something common in Boland's mature work, as observed in "Object Lessons" and "A Woman Painted on a Leaf" (*Collected*, 167-168, 241-242). At the end of this first stanza, these short sentences give way to longer ones, as with an attempt to push language to the limit, in order to overcome stillness and open a place of movement.

As this poem exemplifies, Boland's mature work, in contrast to *In Her Own Image*, addresses how Irish art/poetry had negatively misrepresented not only women, but also men. As Kupillas (1999: 19) notes, "Boland's programme for change is addressed to all". In poems such as "The Glass King" (*Collected*, 161-162), for instance, Boland has reflected on the destructive power that the Irish poetic tradition has also had on male figures. This poem explores the anguish of King Charles VI in his belief that he is made of glass. In this sense, the poet moves away from that narrow feminist focus that characterised her second phase, where she exclusively addressed women's oppression from the starting point of male destructive myths. As the woman in "The Photograph on My Father's Desk", the two male figures in "An Old Steel Engraving" are silenced by the engraver, they cannot talk, and they are imprisoned in "an unfinished action". Boland directly associates the engraving with those "mute images" of Irish poetry (1995a: 196), by calling the speaker's attention to "the spaces on the page":

More closely now:
at the stillness of unfinished action in
afternoon heat, at the spaces on the page. They widen
to include us:
we have found

the country of our malediction where
nothing can move until we find the word,
nothing can stir until we say this is

what happened and is happening and history
is one of us who turns away
while the other is turning the page. (*Collected*, 184)

In order to break this silence, the speaker calls us to "find the word", to raise our voices to talk about "what happened and is happening". Refusing to leave the scene intact, Boland implicates herself, as well as the readers, within the aesthetic experience. Rather than exerting a passive and contemplative appreciation of the engraving, the woman poet advocates the readers engaging actively with her in "finding the word" that can 'unfreeze' the scene, that can restore these characters as living entities. But this restoration of time is not a pleasant one, for it involves the death of the wounded hero and the recognition that having a nation is not a blessing, but a "malediction". Boland suggests that national stories are not composed by these frozen patriots in steel. For Boland, the nation is not something to be glorified by singing the glories of battles and the heroism of warriors, but it is about death and painful experiences, in other words, an "ordeal" (a common word in her poetry to refer to Irish history). "[T]he spaces on the page" of history must be widened, in order to include the ordinary and unexceptionable lives of common Irish people. Only by "turning away" from romanticised images of battle-cries and monumental deeds, Boland seems to suggest, can liberation from artistic representation and restrictive historical accounts be achieved. In the last lines of the poem, Boland carries out her intention to restore these engraving figures as moving and living entities:

Is this river which
moments ago must have flashed the morse
of a bayonet thrust. And is moving on. (*Collected*, 184)

The predicate that opens the final stanza is at a considerable distance from its elliptical subject. This difficult syntactical structure allows the reader to engage in Boland's creative process of reconstructing the scene in the engraving. The woman poet wants us to participate in her process of invention: what is the subject of the final stanza, is it "the country of our malediction" or is it "history"? As we lack actual facts, our reconstruction of the engraved scene is a matter of deduction, and so it is for the poet, who infers that the "morse/ of a bayonet thrust" flashed just before the scene was captured by the engraver. In this sense, Boland has to decipher what might have happened in an action described as solidified. The speaker succeeds in reversing the stillness of the engraving, by letting the scene move at the end. The simple progressive at the end counters the initial use of simple present verbs. As we will see, Boland uses the fluidity of water (in this case the river) to suggest another form of life that cannot be fossilised into any sort of artistic representation. Boland always prefers to describe her poetic images as watery rather than inflexible. In this poem, whereas ground is portrayed in rather negative terms (as "the origin and reason" for war and violence), water, by contrast, is a positive 'terrain' that allows representation but not simplification. Like the river "moving on", Boland's words at the end are left in motion, opening a place of mobility where the patriot can eventually die and the passer-by can finally escape. The verse of this last stanza, although constructed with short sentences, enhances this loose movement. The omission of the subject in ("Is this river") indicates that this sentence is but a continuation of the previous one. On the other hand, the last sentence begins with the conjunction "And". The syntactic elaborateness of the stanzas and the acceleration of the lines at the end of the poem are two frequent features of Boland's mature style. Both linguistic techniques create a profound sense of unsteadiness as the poem closes, and they parallel its movement from solidification to liberation from the restriction of artistic representation.

As we have seen in *Outside History*, Boland focuses on photographs and engravings as a starting point from which to reflect on how art exerts violence by simplifying 'real' images. This interest is continued in volumes such as *In a Time of Violence*, where maps, paintings, sculptures, figures of glass, and dolls are portrayed critically for their inability to record life in all its complexity. In "In Which the Ancient History I Learn Is Not My Own" (*Collected*, 222-224), Boland criticises the map hanging on the wall of her school in London for not displaying her own native land. But even supposedly accurate Irish maps are attacked as well. In "That the Science of Cartography is Limited", Boland recalls the moment when her husband took her to a place at the very "borders of Connacht" and pointed out a "famine road" (*Collected*, 204). As we will see, Boland constantly focuses on interstitial locations, such as edges and borders in order to suggest that there is a reality that stands on the margins of representation, outside any science of cartography. This is Boland's main criticism in this poem. What remains unrecorded on the Irish map is the past itself, the marks and wounds left on the land by those "starving Irish" making famine roads. It is this very exclusion that makes Boland call cartography into question:

> when I take down
> the map of this island, it is never so
> I can say here is
> the masterful, the apt rendering of
>
> the spherical as flat, nor
> an ingenuous design which persuades a curve
> into a place,
> but to tell myself again that
>
> the line which says woodland and cries hunger
> and gives out among sweet pine and cypress,
> and finds no horizon

will not be there. (*Collected*, 204-205)

Even in spite of the map's representation of three dimensions on the flat page, a map conveys still a flawed and simplified portrayal that does not include Ireland's past. At the end of the poem, Boland also extends the limits of the art of cartography to her own poetic endeavour. As Thurston (1999: 245) has also noticed, the "line" not only refers to the remnants of the famine road but also to Boland's own poem, which is made up of 'lines' unfolding down the page. Boland's words cannot offer an "apt rendering" of those famine roads, they simply "will not be there". Her attempt to focus on what lies outside maps is difficult, perhaps impossible, both because there is no actual evidence of their existence, and also because poetry is in some ways for Boland a limiting form of expression. Furthermore, the woman poet has argued that "the act of map-making is an act of power", and as such, it includes some geographical places at the expense of excluding others (Boland 2000a: 25). Boland tries to avoid creating a new (authoritarian) representation; in fact, she wants to create a new form of cartography that contests all acts of power. In this sense, the poem ends by emphasising the poet's own limitations to include those details of the past.

This also happens in "Lava Cameo" (*Collected*, 227-228), a poem about Boland's grandmother. Boland attempts to capture this figure's life, not "as sculpture but syntax". Whereas the sculpture compresses images, fixing the flow of life, Boland wants to "[i]nscribe catastrophe", to "arrest a profile in the flux of hell" (p. 228). This is a very difficult project, as it involves simultaneously a process of capturing and a recognition of something that cannot be held still. In this sense, Boland realises that art is a double-edged sword, as it can only apparently describe living images in solid grounds. As she has argued:

> It's an odd paradox of art that it can only work by fixing the moment –
> whether it's painting or poetry or fiction – and yet once the moment gets
> fixed, everything in expression restricts it and limits it. It's one of the most
> interesting aspects of writing a poem. (Interview with Villar Argáiz)

According to Thurston (1999: 246), this is precisely Boland's own strength, the fact that "she insistently leaves questions unanswered and problems unresolved". In fact, Boland recognises that "the limitations of the poem [...] are the strength. I've always found freedom in those limits" (interview with Villar Argáiz). Boland's work consistently points out that her own poems, just as those artistic representations like photographs and engravings, are always incomplete. This is where her power as a poet lies: by suggesting that all representations are inevitably incomplete, she manages to undermine those authoritarian ideologies (whether imperialist, nationalist, or feminist) that rely on truthful and complete images.

Nevertheless, even though Boland admits her poems are fallible representations, she believes that poetry "offers opportunities to change and dissolve time and space" (interview with Villar Argáiz). Fluidity and dissolution are subversive techniques to overturn those images sanctioned in cultural (nationalist and feminist) representations. The fluid ending that we observed in "An Old Steel Engraving" is characteristic of Boland's mature work. In "We Were Neutral in the War" (*Collected*, 174-175), Boland presents a married woman who, ignorant of all the talk of war in the 1940s, is mainly concerned with sewing and making preserves from her garden fruits. At the end of the poem, Boland offers an image of this woman dancing "the fox-trot, the two-step,/ the quick-step [...] in waltz time" (p. 175). The constant movement with which the woman is depicted at the end is Boland's attempt to counteract her earlier artistic representation of her, a representation that might run the risk of defining and therefore solidifying her. This also occurs in "The Carousel in the Park", a poem that similarly ends with an image of Boland as a young child playing on a carousel at Central Park. This young girl is presented as moving in intervals, "[u]p and down", "going high and descending", as riding a horse at a "canter" (*Collected*, 190). These two poems, like in "An Old-Steel Engraving", finish by offering fluid images which, in their constant movement, are impossible to grasp both by Boland and by the reader. In this sense, the endings of Boland's poems create a space free from the limitations, boundaries, and restrictions imposed by artistic representations. By focusing on moving images, Boland allows her figures to acquire a limitless number of different shapes. The following section will address this aspect of her work more thoroughly.

4.3.2.2. A woman who escapes artistic representation

As the previous poems have shown, Boland believes that any form of representation, whether in maps, sculptures, photographs, or poems, runs the risk of misrepresenting real images, because of its desire to capture and define them as solid and fixed entities. With a view to moving away from any sort of restrictive representation, Boland attempts to bring her poetic images to dissolution and fluidity. In order to study this aspect of Boland's work, I will draw on those French feminists' theories that conceptualise women as fluid entities in order to escape and undermine the binary masculine thought. Although, as we have seen, Cixous and Irigaray advocate sexual difference, they also urge women to gesture towards a fluid identity, one that cannot be defined and enclosed within masculine representations.

Due to her marginalised background, Cixous has maintained a very critical attitude towards all forms of oppression.[20] As an Algerian Jewish woman, Cixous has clearly understood the dangers involved in adopting any sort of ideology, which, in the long run, can be restrictive and inflexible. This is why she has attempted, through her work, to move beyond a narrowly defined feminism which relies on essentialist categories such as 'man' and 'woman'. Although in *Three Steps on the Ladder of Writing* she admits that both categories are necessarily used to defend women in a patriarchal society, Cixous (1994: 200) also expresses her view that they are deeply artificial, socially and culturally charged. The opposition man/woman is, as established, dictated by society, and therefore, it should be considered as idiosyncratic and not essential. Therefore, her writings attempt to displace this conceptual opposition:

Let's imagine we love a woman who is a man inside. This means we love not a man exactly, but a woman who is a man, which is not quite the same thing: it's a woman who is also a man, another species. These complexities are not yet audible. (Cixous 1994: 199)

In this sense, Cixous embraces the Derridean deconstruction of identity.[21] In an attempt to overcome social constructions such as 'man' and 'woman', she envisages the category of 'woman' as fluid, constantly surpassing binaries:

Let masculine sexuality gravitate around the penis, engendering this centralised body [...] under the party dictatorship. Woman does not perform on herself this regionalisation that profits the couple head-sex that only inscribes itself within frontiers. Her libido is cosmic, just as her unconsciousness is worldwide: her writing also can only go on and on, without ever inscribing or distinguishing contours, [...] she goes on and on infinitely. (Cixous 1994: 44)

As we observe here, Cixous draws a parallel between female libido and an 'in-between' writing that goes on infinitely, without inscribing outlines. As Calle-Gruber (1994: 213) argues, "Hélène Cixous' books give precisely the feminine [...] other entries to meaning; the between at work which escapes classification; a between-two, which makes three a more; a between-time which exceeds time". Cixous describes womanhood as a category that surpasses the opposition 'self'/'Other'. In their ability to be more bisexual than men, women move beyond binary oppositions. In this sense, Cixous returns to a very similar metaphor that Irigaray uses to describe women: as diffusion, liquefaction, aerial swimming before the Symbolic.

According to Irigaray (1985: 26), symbolic language has granted priority to what is organised around the phallus, the only identifiable form: "[t]he *one* of form, [...] the (male) sexual organ". This feminist critic believes that woman cannot be defined by male parameters, and consequently she is described as the negative side of man: "her sexual organ, which is not one organ, is counted as *none*. The negative, the underside, the reverse of the only visible and morphologically designatable organ [...]: the penis" (p. 26). Women present an "excess of form", or an apparent lack of (male) sexual organs. Therefore, their reality is impossible to grasp or describe by male standards (p. 11). Men fear the "open container", that which flows and is mobile, because it is not a solid ground/earth or mirror for the subject to identify with (p. 64). In this sense, they need to represent her as a closed volume, a set container, in their desire to possess, immobilise and keep her under their control.

Irigaray (1991: 56) offers a counter image to the male representations of woman: what she calls an "other woman" or "(The/A) woman". This woman "does not yet exist", but her arrival will destroy, according to Irigaray, the very "foundations of patriarchy" (p. 29). This new woman cannot be defined, represented and fixed into male representations, for she is constantly in a state of movement and flux: "You are moving. You never stay still. You never stay. You never "are". How can I say "you", when you are always other? How can I speak to you? You remain in flux, never congealing or solidifying" (Irigaray 1985: 214-215). As opposed to 'One/oneness' (le un), which signifies those unitary representations of identity within the masculine (and universal) system, Irigaray prefers to define the female subject as 'all' (toute[s]), a subject simultaneously singular and plural (p. 218). In a culture that claims to count everything, "to number everything by units", this "other woman" resists all adequate definitions, she is "[n]either one nor two", and "always one and the other, at the same time" (p. 207). Irigaray's definition of the woman in "When Our Lips Speak Together" directly reminds one of Bhabha's definition of the postcolonial migrant subject, a subject described as "neither the One [...] nor the Other [...] but something else besides which contests the terms and territories of both" (Bhabha 1995: 25). Significantly enough, Irigaray (1991: 91) also envisages this new woman as a nomad who is constantly moving and dancing, taking her own 'house' with her. Perhaps the main feature that distinguishes postcolonial theorists such as Bhabha from feminists such as Irigaray and Cixous is that, whereas Bhabha locates hybridity in the postcolonial subject's ability constantly to surpass imperialist, national, and ethnic boundaries, these French feminists more specifically locate women's fluid nature in the plurality and richness of the female sex. Irigaray (1985: 111) argues that woman's sexual organs are not countable in the male logic and, therefore, they overcome polarisation. The woman's lips, for instance, touch themselves without distinction of "one and two" (ibid). In this sense, the female body transgresses and confuses those boundaries of the male discourse:

> [The female sex] is a threshold unto *mucosity*. Beyond the classic opposites of love and hate, liquid and ice, lies this perpetually *half-open* threshold, consisting of *lips* that are strangers to dichotomy, pressed against one another, but without any possibility of suture, at least of a real kind, they do not absorb the world either into themselves or through themselves. (Irigaray 1985: 175)

In this sense, the female sex is located within no fixed boundaries. According to Irigaray, women are able to escape masculine definitions due to the various kinds of "jouissances" or pleasures they get from their sexuality. Whereas men have only one sex organ, and therefore, they can only have one kind of orgasm, women have many more sex organs, and therefore they can enjoy more plural and varied orgasms: "Fondling the breasts, touching the vulva, spreading the lips, stroking the posterior wall of the vagina, brushing against the mouth of the uterus, and so on. To evoke only a few of the most specifically female pleasures" (Irigaray 1985: 28).

In line with Cixous's and Irigaray's theories, Boland's mature work questions the view of the female subject as unified and stable. The woman in her poems is depicted as a subject "without common measure", a "volume without contours",[22] who cannot be reduced to the quantifying measurements by which she is defined and captured by male standards (Irigaray 1985: 163). From this perspective, it would be tempting to read Boland's fluid self as another feminist attempt to conceptualise the richness and plurality of the female sex. In any case, Boland avoids falling prey to this biological and deterministic notion of woman's fluidity. She conceptualises women in terms of hybridity, instability, and blurring, not because of the existence of a distinctive sexual difference, but because she suggests it is impossible to describe any living subject (whether male or female) within any sort of artistic representation. In contrast to *In Her Own Image*, her mature work offers almost no bodily references, and she does not write with a radical feminist project in mind. Although sometimes she focuses on a damaged and scarred female body, this is done in order to counteract idealistic and mythical images of women as everlasting beautiful and young. Boland's women suffer the consequences of the passing of time and the loss of beauty: they are living and bloody entities, unlike those allegorical images such as Mother Ireland.

Nevertheless, there are certain features that Boland shares with Cixous and Irigaray. Her women are presented as fluid, constantly moving. For Boland, mobility is linked with flesh-and-blood women, whereas immobility is linked with death and with those monumental and mythical images of women imprisoned in poetry. On the other hand, Boland's poetry moves to the "in-between-space" that Cixous and Irigaray talk about, when arguing that the 'in-between' is the space of women's writing, something that Meaney (1993: 141) has also identified.

This fluid notion of identity runs throughout Boland's volumes of poetry after *The Journey and Other Poems*. *The Journey* is, what I would like to call, Boland's "volume of the 'in-between'" par excellence. In this collection of poetry, the woman poet is concerned with presenting her women in constant motion; they are always located in blurred and dissolved landscapes, in diffused and tenuous lights. In order to do this, Boland develops a characteristic style of writing. First of all, the poet uses plenty of present participles and progressive verb forms referring to the poetic speaker, either in the present tense (as in "Self-Portrait on a Summer Evening", "The Bottle Garden", "Suburban Woman: A Detail", "The Briar Rose", "The Women", and "Canaletto in the National Gallery of Ireland"), or in the past tense (as in "The Oral Tradition", "The Unlived Life", "There and Back", "The Fire in Our Neighbourhood", "The Wild Spray", "The Journey", and "Fond Memory"). Her use of the progressive should not be underestimated. As Quereda Rodríguez-Navarro (1997: 123, 133) explains, the speaker uses both the present and past progressive in order to introduce us into a situation, whether within or distant from his/her present perspective, "as if it were in-the-middle-of-its-process". As these actions are always presented as in their middle of their development, they can never "be seen in their entirety, since they have not finished yet" (p. 124). This is applicable in a way to the obsessive usage of present participles in Boland's poetry. By means of these participles and progressives, Boland presents her women in constant movement, in the middle of an action that has not been completed. The fact that the reader of her poems cannot grasp these women's action "as-a-whole" also enhances the feeling that Boland's characters can never be perceived in their totality. In their constant mobility and unfinished actions, they avoid being solidified by the reader's 'gaze'. This use of participles and progressives, although maintained in other volumes of poetry such as *Outside History* and *In a Time of Violence*, is more reiterative in *The Journey*, where there is a higher emphasis on the woman speaker's movement. As the very title indicates, *The Journey* gives special importance to the speaker's act of travelling from one place to another. She is never at the origin or at the destiny of her trip, but always in the middle of a literal or imaginary journey.

Furthermore, Boland's poetic language in *The Journey* enhances the fluidity and motion of her women. Almost all the poems in this collection are constructed upon very long sentences, mostly at the end, that unfold down the page by means of strong enjambments. This technique, although present in some poems from *Outside History* and *In a Time of Violence*, will gradually disappear as we approach Boland's latest productions, *The Lost Land* and *Code*, where language will be more fractured and the poetic style will be plainer. Finally, Boland locates all her women in evening settings, when light is fading and colours become more diffused. Although some of the poems start at dawn, this landscape gradually changes at the end of the poem to dusk, in order to record the passing of time and the versatility of her images.

Boland's characteristic style responds, as explained, to a clear intention to escape the artistic (mis)representation of women in poetry, by presenting female characters who, in their constant movement, cannot be solidified in her poems. In order to study this aspect, I will analyse "Self-Portrait on a Summer Evening" (*Collected*, 129-130), where Boland focuses on a particular painting, which like those engravings, photographs, and maps of the previous poems, stands as one form of artistic representation where human images are being frozen or totally omitted. The object of attack is now Jean-Baptiste Chardin, Boland's favourite painter, as she makes explicit in *Object Lessons*:

> In the genre painters of the French eighteenth century, in Jean Baptiste Chardin in particular – I saw what I was looking for. Chardin's paintings were ordinary in the accepted sense of the word. They were unglamorous, workaday, authentic. Yet, in his works these objects were not merely described, they were revealed. The hare in its muslim bag, the crusty loaf, the woman fixed between menial tasks and human dreams – these stood out, a commanding text. And I was drawn to that text. Romanticism in the nineteenth century, it seemed to me, had prescribed that beauty be commended as truth. Chardin had done something different. He had taken truth and revealed its beauty. (Boland 1995a: 253)

Boland praises Chardin for revealing his images not as glamorous but ordinary, for showing the beauty of what is commonplace and everyday. Nevertheless, her stance on this painter's work is more complicated. We have seen how as early as in "From the Painting *Back from Market* by Chardin" (*Collected*, 17), Boland showed her interest in Chardin's paintings. In this poem, Boland maintained the painter's authority over his artistic images and merely described the woman at the market from a detached position. It won't be until two decades later, in "Self-Portrait on a Summer Evening", when Boland will adopt a more critical stance on Chardin's work.[23] Although this Romantic painter, unlike his contemporaries, did not emphasise the eternal youthfulness and beauty of his female images, his very desire to 'fix' women in his paintings involves already, according to Boland, a threatening simplification. As she makes explicit when commenting "Degas's Laundresses" (*Collected*, 108-109),

[t]he problem is, art itself is a form of restriction. And a powerful one. [...] The poem is about the painter watching the toil of these two laundresses. And how much control – almost predatory control – is needed to turn these living, shiftless, struggling women into fixed images. (Interview with Villar Argáiz)

In the first stanzas of "Self-Portrait on a Summer Evening", Boland precisely criticises Chardin's "predatory control" over the woman's portrayal:

Jean-Baptiste Chardin
is painting a woman
in the last summer light.

All summer long
he has been slighting her
in botched blues, tints,
half-tones, rinsed neutrals. (*Collected*, 129)

The painter himself is accused of prevarication, of seeing the woman only partially. The pejorative verb "slight" rhymes with "light", with the suggestion that the artist's denigration results from his perception of this woman under a limited 'male gaze'. In Moi's phrasing, "[t]he gaze enacts the voyeur's desire for sadistic power, in which the object of the gaze is cast as its passive, masochistic, feminine victim" (1991: 132). Subverting the traditional psychosexual concept of the gaze, Boland offers a counter-reading of how Chardin had gazed at the woman. Following Hagen and Zelman's (2004: 101) line of argument when discussing "The Women", the tenuous colours and dusky lights ("botched blues, tints,/ half tones, rinsed neutrals") that Boland presents in this passage are metaphors of her poetic enterprise of subverting conventional perceptions, of re-making conventional boundaries. The things that we think we see in the dusk may not be what they really are. Boland warns us that our perceptions might be constantly unreliable, and she encourages us to revise them all the time. In this sense, the 'male gaze' is only a "prism", a medium that inevitably misrepresents whatever is seen through it:

> What you are watching
> is light unlearning itself,
> an infinite unfrocking of the prism.
>
> Before your eyes
> the ordinary life
> is being glazed over:
> pigments of the bibelot,
> the cabochon, the water-opal
> pearl to the intimate
> simple colours of
> her ankle-length summer skirt. (*Collected*, 129)

Boland "unlearn[s]" Chardin's light, depriving and "unfrocking" him of the right to 'freeze' women in his artistic creation. This poem, as in most of her painting poems, indicates the damage that art inflicts on women whose ordinary life "is being glazed over" and whose landscape is, as she later argues, "reduced to detail". The use of these passives is very common in her work, as "Fever" and "The Unlived Life" (*Collected*, 133-136) exemplify. They are employed in order to emphasise the result of an action, as well as the affected subject. In this sense, they remind of the oppression, violence, and objectification involved in any form of artistic representation. "I Remember" records the moment when Boland's mother made a portrait of her, and how "an eyebrow waited helplessly to be composed" (*Collected*, 127). The focus on parts such as "an eyebrow" and later "the scattered fractions" of a face, suggests that painting cannot capture Boland's entire self. In these poems, Boland deliberately focuses on how the painter scrutinises his/her images to the extent that they are merely objectified as bodily parts. In "Growing Up", a poem about the painting *On the Terrace* by Renoir, the girls are just mentioned by "[t]heir two heads, hatted, bowed" (*Collected*, 144). "Self-Portrait on a Summer Evening" also exemplifies the painter's limited access to the ordinary woman. She is only mentioned by "her ankle-length summer skirt", and even the sky becomes to Chardin's eyes an "odd shape of apron". The totality of the woman's identity is "reduced" and fractured by the painter, who wishes to immortalise her in his work of art.

With the aim of undermining the relationship of power between male artist and female 'object', Boland identifies with the woman in the painting. As Showalter (1999: 259) has argued, one distinctive feature of the woman artist in her 'Female' phase is her desire to "animate the inanimate". The static and passive image of the previous lines suddenly becomes the poetic speaker herself, a living entity that avoids being fixed and appears to move:

> before your eyes
> before your eyes
> in my ankle-length
> summer skirt
>
> crossing between
> the garden and the house,
> under the whitebeam trees,
> keeping an eye on
> the length of the grass,
> the height of the hedge,
> the distance of the children (*Collected*, 130)

This change from third person narration to first person narration in the middle or at the end of the poem is a typical movement in Boland's mature work, as reflected in poems such as "Fever", "The Shadow Doll", "The Making of an Irish Goddess", and most often in painting poems such as "Domestic Interior" (*Collected*, 133-134, 178-179, 91-92), where Boland ends up identifying with the woman that Van Eyck has painted. In this poem, this movement is again put into practice. "Self-Portrait on a Summer Evening" blurs the division between the 'self' and the 'Other', through the speaker's established link with the woman in the painting. She is not only linked to Chardin's object of art by her vulnerability to the damaging consequences of artistic solidification. The repetition of "before your eyes" enhances the fact that both women are united by their role as mothers, as subjects who keep "an eye" on "the distance of the children". In spite of the similarities between both women, Boland offers Chardin a counter-representation. Now, the new woman is not framed inside a "cabinet picture", but outside her house, a living entity in motion. The speaker, "crossing between/ the garden and her house", presents herself in constant movement, as the preponderance of present participles indicates. On the other hand, Boland insists on the fact that the diffused dusk and faint colours (half-tones, rinsed neutrals, opague, optical greys, etc.) where this new woman is located are 'true' lights, in contrast to "the reflected light" of the "prism" and the "cabochon" of the painting. These lights keep changing even as the painter attempts to capture them. Furthermore, as Hagen and Zelman (2004: 79-80) explain, "the *length* of the grass", "the *height* of the hedge", and "the *distance* of the children" are dimensions that vary depending on the speaker's position and perspective, and as such, painting cannot offer an ultimate viable representation of them. This volatile landscape, together with the woman's indefinite shape, is something that, according to Boland, cannot be grasped by Chardin's visual representation. In "Growing Up", Boland similarly attempts to describe a landscape of constant change, in which women are "indefinite and infinite" (*Collected*, 145). This also occurs in "Listen. This is the Noise of Myth", where Boland liberates those women entrapped in mythical constructions by creating a poetic space in which "[t]he shifts and fluencies are infinite./ The moving parts are marvellous" (p. 154). Boland implies that the only way the female image can escape the artist's solidification (either in myth or in painting) is by describing her as beyond artistic representation, as outside "the bereavements of the definite" (ibid). Similarly, in "Self-Portrait on a Summer Evening", Boland works against the imprisonment of women in art, questioning artistic representation, and its desire to define an object or image. In this sense, her endeavour is aligned with Cixous's and Irigaray's theories, in which the female figure is conceptualised as fluid, outside the "frontiers" of male logic (Cixous 1994: 44; Irigaray 1985: 214). Nevertheless, this fluency Boland aspires to seems to come to a sudden stop at the end of the poem. Present participles are suddenly substituted by passive structures and diffused lights give way to the male artist's restrictive use of light:

> I am Chardin's woman
> edged in reflected light,
> hardened by
> the need to be ordinary. (*Collected*, 130)

The use of the genitive here indicates that the woman is still entrapped as an object of male possession. In contrast to the diffused and unstable setting Boland described in the preceding verse lines, the poem ends by emphasising a sharp and outlined landscape where the woman is "edged" and "hardened" by Chardin's need to define her as ordinary. Under Chardin's "reflected light", the portrait gives an illusion of a definable and static self, and of a landscape where "the boundaries between people and other objects are fixed and clearly defined" (Hagen and Zelman: 2004: 80). Boland presents a fluid woman in a dissolved and changing landscape, only to eventually describe her as entrapped and solidified in a domestic world. This movement is characteristic of Boland's mature work, and it responds to her intention to highlight at the end the woman's oppression in art rather than her liberation from it, or her inability, as we will see, to move beyond the opposing pulls of womanhood and poetry.

Nevertheless, there seems to be an "undersong" (as Boland says in "Before Spring", *Collected*, 94), beneath this final description of Chardin's woman. As in most of the poems included in *The Journey*, "Self-Portrait on a Summer Evening" is constructed with stanzas of different length and no rhyming scheme. Whereas at the beginning they are more or less short, by the end of the poem, they gradually become longer and spread out by means of very strong enjambments. This linguistic feature, together with a clear lack of punctuation at the end, intensifies the poem's loose movement. Furthermore, and in contrast to the general style of Boland's mature poems, it is significant how the conjunction 'and' does not appear even once in the poem. It is as if Boland is deliberately creating a flowing language which is not even hindered by conjunctions. All these linguistic features emphasise Boland's description of this new woman as unrestrained: the woman is as fluid and loosely defined as the very verse form of the poem. In this sense, language creates a counter-reading to Chardin's stable ordinary woman. While the final image is delimitating, the way "Self-Portrait on a Summer Evening" is constructed emphasises Boland's ability to describe a woman that escapes the artist's representation.

In this sense, Boland always represents her poetic images as fluid entities that are impossible to be grasped. The versatility and mobility that characterises her women is present throughout *The Journey*, in poems such as "The Women" and "Suburban Woman: A Detail" (*Collected*, 138-139, 141). But it is in *Outside History*, in poems such as "Doorstep Kisses", "A Different Light", and "Hanging Curtains with an Abstract Pattern in a Child's Room" (*Collected*, 194-196), where Boland more openly focuses, not only on her women's instability, but also on their very dissolution.

As the very title of "Doorstep Kisses" suggests, one of Boland's main interests in her mature poetry is to portray herself or her poetic images always on the margins of established boundaries. As Ashcroft (1994: 34) notes, postcolonial texts are always located "on the verandah", a concept which, by itself, connotes the liminality of hybrid positions. Note that "doorstep" situates the speaker at the entrance of her house: neither inside nor outside, but in a sort of interstitial location. This focus on peripheral locations is typical of *Outside History* and *In a Time of Violence*. Notice the very title of poems such as "Spring at the *Edge* of the Sonnet" (*Collected*, 192), in which Boland describes "lovers [...] out in *doorways*" (emphasis added). In other poems such as "Ghost Stories", "Our Origins Are in the Sea", and "Midnight Flowers" (*Collected*, 192, 193, 197), Boland continues to place her poetic images in an interstitial location: candles lighting in the "*doorstep*[s]" of an Iowa town, the very speaker standing "at the *edge* of our grass", or the plants in her garden "at/ the *margins* of light". This focus on marginality, which begins to be appreciated in this volume, will be continued in *In a Time of Violence*, in poems such as "Inscriptions" or "Anna Liffey", where Boland repeatedly describes herself, especially in this last poem, as a "woman at the *doorway*" of her house (*Collected*, 230, 232). Occupying these border-lines allows Boland to escape visual representation, because she is placed outside or 'in-between' definite contours. She becomes, in this sense, Irigaray's revolutionary "The/A Woman", a new entity that, by her persistent location in a "threshold", is a "stranger to dichotomy" (Irigaray 1985: 175). It is this very position that the speaker in "Doorstep Kisses" occupies. She is situated in "the last days of summer in the last hour of light". Under dusky lights, nothing is clear and distinguishable, and even the poetic speaker senses that she is becoming, like the landscape surrounding her, indistinct:

> If I stay here long enough I may become –
> since everything else around me is –
>
> the sum of small gestures, choices,
> losses in the air so fractional
> they could be
>
> fragrances which just fell from it –
>
> a musk of buddleia, perhaps, of this fuchsia
> with the drip,
> drip of whitby jet (*Collected*, 194)

The modal 'may', together with the hypothetical construction that opens this sequence indicate a certain degree of likelihood or possibility. Boland's poetry becomes, as she says in "Listen. This is the Noise of Myth", a "sequence of evicted possibilities" (*Collected*, 154). Like the new heroine Boland envisages in this poem, the woman in "Doorstep Kisses" "may or [...] may not" (ibid). Boland disturbs the view of the subject as unified and stable: her character is uncertain, and like those drops and fragrances of the plants in the garden, she is threatened with dissolution. The disintegration threatening the speaker also paradoxically liberates her from artistic solidification. Like the water dripped from the flowers, the woman is able to run free from any form of visual representation that, like Chardin's, would attempt to "harden" her.

This same emphasis on dissolution occurs in "A Different Light". This poem narrates the moment when an unexpected power cut took the speaker and her husband unawares, with "[n]o candles and no torch" (*Collected*, 195). The speaker argues how, as the light went out, "everything we knew how/ to look for had disappeared". In this context, shadows make the familiar seem foreign to the speaker's eyes:

Afterwards we talked of it for days –

how it felt at the upstairs window,
to stand and watch and still miss the moment
of gable ends and rooftops beginning

to be re-built. And that split second when
you and I were, from a distance,
a neighbourhood on the verge of definition. (*Collected*, 195)

Like the woman in "Doorstep Kisses", both the speaker and her addressee appear "on the verge of definition", just as the plants inside their house, which are described "just off-centre". This marginal location is positive rather than negative. Under such diffused lights and within this border-line, the speaker and her husband can be grasped neither by a male gaze, nor by the mature poet who is remembering this ordinary incident. The common experience of the power cut becomes an emblem of Boland's act of creation. These shadows and versatile images are the starting point from which her poetry can open up new mental images, new perceptions. The power cut allows Boland to look afresh at the familiar suburban landscape around her, and to open a new arena of signification that cannot apparently be seen in regular light. As she argues in this poem, "[a]ll depends on a sense of mystery;/ the same things in a different light" (ibid). Once again, Boland attempts to view conventional images "in a different light", forcing us to understand the danger of 'fixing' in art the complexity of lived experience.

This focus on dissolved images also occurs in "Hanging Curtains with an Abstract Pattern in a Child's Room" (*Collected*, 195-196). This poem begins by presenting a mother who looks from an upstairs window, after hanging some curtains in her child's room. The present participle of the title indicates that the action that Boland carries out is in the middle of its progress. This woman is moving rather than static, and the landscape she perceives in the "winter dusk" is equally inconstant and changeable. As we have seen, Boland defines poetry as a place of ambiguities, a place where nothing is stable and definite. She conceives that the task of poetry is to dismantle, rather than create, fixed boundaries and parameters. The curtains and their abstract pattern are an allegory of Boland's artistic enterprise. First of all, as Hagen and Zelman (2004: 83) have also considered, these curtains highlight the border line between the inside and the outside, between the domestic and the public world. In choosing the curtains, Boland is, then, deliberately occupying an intermediate terrain. On the other hand, their abstract pattern suggests Boland's wish to create an art in which women rather than being 'fixed' in pictorial and concrete representations, appear only as abstract and geometric shapes, as "signals of enigma:/ Ellipse. Triangle. A music of ratio" (*Collected*, 195). Unlike Chardin's paintings, Boland does not wish to define and "harden" images, but to open a place of potential where the creative act takes place. As Hagen and Zelman (2004: 84) argue, "words are fluid signifiers" for Boland. I agree with these critics, for I think that Boland's poetry in this phase constantly tries to deconstruct Saussurean binary oppositions. As Sarup (1993: 33) explains, Saussure saw that the signifier and the signified are related in such a way that the sign is conceived as a unit. The signifier (for instance, the sound image made by the word 'apple') always refers to an "ideal concept" (i.e. the concept apple). In Boland's poetry, there is never a one-to-one correspondence between the signifier and the signified. In this sense, she is aligned with that poststructuralist thought according to which meaning is "never tied to one particular sign" (ibid). When readers come across Boland's "signals of enigma", they can imagine her images in illimitable ways. Boland seems to suggest that one sign always leads to another sign, moving along on a chain of signifiers, to the extent that the signified can never be grasped. Boland's lack of specification when describing herself at the end of the poem not only suggests that her reality escapes any form of artistic representation, but also invites us, as readers, to become active creators in Boland's imaginative art. The woman, visualising how she would look from the road of her house, describes herself as follows:

> my blouse off-white and
>
> my skirt the colour of
> all the disappointments of a day when
>
> the curtains are pulled back on
> a dull morning. (*Collected*, 196)

The end only focuses on her clothes, "my blouse", "my skirt", which are, by the way, portrayed with diffused colours. Furthermore, the presence of the passive structure indicates that the woman poet deliberately omits herself as agentive subject, with a wish to avoid presenting her as definite and stable, as a unitary self. For Boland, in this sense, poetry is never a transparent medium that allows access to an inner truth, to her distinguishable female self. The loosening of language at the end of the poem parallels the speaker's dissolution. In this sense, the speaker becomes, just like the geometric shapes of the curtains, an abstract entity, that, in its indeterminacy, cannot be defined or established within artistic contours that would capture her.

4.3.3. In-between womanhood and poetry

As we have seen, Boland's fluidity responds to her desire to avoid the objectification that artistic representation entails. But, as I intend to show, she also attempts, by means of this fluency, to undertake a more ambitious project. Boland seeks to open an 'in-between' space, a place of potential, where she can openly talk about her own contradictions and ambivalences as an Irish woman poet, and where she can exert her own agency.

Boland begins writing within the framework of a canon which excludes her. She feels she didn't have, as a woman, the required permission to write, a feeling that was increased when she talked to male poets or when she opened a book of poetry (Boland 1995a: 109). In this context, Boland feels homeless as a woman poet. Her anxiety to repossess a tradition, a female voice in poetry, is in fact a desire to find her home as a woman poet, for, as she explains, "[i]n the middle of an emblematic nation, at the heart of a formidable tradition of writing, I was lost" (p. 111). Together with this spiritual dislocation, Boland (1995a: 156) has also recorded the physical displacement she felt when leaving the very centre of society (Dublin) and moving to the suburbs. In these initial years, she describes Dundrum as "visible and oppressive and at a distance from the love I would come to feel for it". Due to this dual (spiritual and geographical) dislocation, Boland inhabits what she calls "an interior exile [...] which is more subtle than the physical statement of leaving" (interview with Villar Argáiz). This interior exile, as she admits, is produced by her sense of estrangement when attempting to bring to the centre of her poems her own life as a suburban woman, a subject matter not particularly "sanctioned by the Irish tradition" (ibid).

According to Maguire (1999: 63), the conflict between femininity and being a poet is the dilemma Boland is more clearly interested in. Showalter (1999: 35) has argued that, like in the 'Feminine' phase, the 'Female' phase in the career of a woman writer is still concerned with the conflict involved between her life as a woman and her commitment to literature. Whereas in the first phase the writer deals with this issue by hiding her womanhood (under the masquerade of a male poetic voice, for instance), in this phase, this concern is dealt with directly, by recording the tensions involved in becoming a woman writer. As Boland (1995a: xi) asserts in *Object Lessons*,

> I know now that I began writing in a country where the word *woman* and the word *poet* were almost magnetically opposed. One word was used to invoke collective nurture, the other sketch out self-reflective individualism. Both states were necessary – that much the culture conceded – but they were oil and water and could not be mixed.

The very subtitle of Boland's semi-autobiographical book, "The Life of the Woman and the Poet in Our Time" already indicates an imminent separation between what seems to be two irreconcilable poles: it is not "The Life of the Woman Poet" but "The Life of the Woman *and* the Poet". The conjunction, more than uniting both categories at the same level, stresses their distinctive nature. Even the names of two of the chapters in this book express the troubling duality that Boland faces. In "The Woman The Place The Poet" (pp. 154-174), the categories of 'womanhood' and 'poetry' are separated by "the place", presumably Ireland. In the final chapter of the book, "The Woman Poet: Her Dilemma" (pp. 239-254), this binary is not resolved, for, although the noun phrase "Woman Poet" seems to indicate at first a resolution of contrasts, the following phrase "Her Dilemma", indicates that Boland faces a situation that requires a choice between options (womanhood or writing) that seem mutually exclusive of one another.

As Boland (1995a: xiii) explains, *Object Lessons* is constructed "in turnings and returnings", in "parts which find and repeat themselves and restate the argument until it loses its reasonable edge and hopefully becomes a sort of cadence" (p. xiii). The reason for this insistent repetition is that Boland finds it difficult to clarify, even as a mature poet, the inherent tension of being a woman and a poet, and each returning to the same subject is intended to resolve, though unsuccessfully, this conflict. As Haberstroh (1995: 20) argues, the repetitive ideas of *Object Lessons* demand that "the reader travel with the poet repeatedly over the same terrain", a terrain which, in my view, involves the distance between two supposedly irreconcilable arenas. Boland's decision to accept the title of a "woman poet" ("to be effective and useful as an Irish woman poet you have to be willing to pick up that tab", interview with Wilson 1990a: 86), is but an attempt to reconcile both separate realms. Nevertheless, Boland does not wish to establish an easy bridge between these categories. It is the unresolved tension between womanhood and poetry that is more valuable for Boland. As she states: "[i]t is these very tensions, and not their absence, and not any possibility of resolving them, which makes me believe that the woman poet is now an emblematic figure in poetry" (1995a: xiv-xv). More recently, Boland has argued: "I was a woman poet *and* I was an Irish poet. I felt both identities could interpret and re-interpret each other in some rich, demanding ways" (interview with Villar Argáiz). By recording the difficulty involved in being a woman *and* a poet in Ireland, Boland manages to change the way Irish poetry has been constructed. In this sense, the ambivalence that assails Boland is not an impediment, but offers many possibilities.

In order to justify this hypothesis, I will analyse "The Women", one of the most quoted poems from *The Journey*. This poem introduces us to the mind of a woman poet who is inside her house watching the external landscape from her window. This description of the woman looking outside is very recurrent in Boland's mature work, as we have seen in "Hanging Curtains with an Abstract Pattern in a Child's Room", and as other poems as "Midnight Flowers", "A Different Light", and "What Love Intended" (*Collected*, 193-198) exemplify. This location indicates Boland's wish to blur the boundaries between the private and the public setting, traditionally the female and the masculine domains par excellence. The borders between home and world become confused; and both arenas become part of each other. This displacement, according to Bhabha (1995: 9), forces "us [into] a vision that is as divided as it is disorienting". It is in this confusing border line location where the speaker finds her inspiration to write:

This is the hour I love: the in-between,
neither here-nor-there hour of evening.
The air is tea-coloured in the garden.
The briar rose is spilled crepe-de-Chine. (*Collected*, 141)

The first stanza draws us into a beloved "in-between" space, "neither-here-nor-there". This significant interchange of deictic forms is characteristic of Boland, as observed in "Listen: This is the Noise of Myth", where the speaker proposes her own version of an Irish myth as "not there, not here,/ not anywhere" (*Collected*, 153). The adverb 'there' in this poem indicates the mythological world, whereas the adverb 'here' is more explicitly connected to the woman's ordinary world. Boland's revision of the Irish myth intends to unite both of them, and seems to suggest that *that* mythological life and *this* actual one are not so different from each other. Whereas in "Listen. This is the Noise of Myth" Boland yearns to construct her poetry between two apparently opposite worlds (the world of myth and her own ordinary world as a woman), in "The Women", Boland explicitly locates her work in the interstices between a public space (an exclusively male domain such as poetry) and a private space (her everyday life as a housewife and mother). This blurring of well-established boundaries is also perceived in the scenery that the speaker describes: this is a landscape of diffused lights and tenuous colours, in which the air is "tea-coloured" and the silks, as she later describes in this poem, are "stove-coloured". In this setting, shapes dissolve to the extent that the simple briar rose of Boland's garden loses its consistency and becomes silk crepe. Boland is here proposing what Boyce (1994: 15-16) would call a "borderland consciousness" in which the subject, like the flowers in her garden, is in a conscious transition.[24] She inhabits border spaces that are locations of contest, flux, and change. It is in this "in-between" space where Boland achieves the summit of her creative potential:

> This is the time I do my work best,
> going up the stairs in two minds,
> in two worlds, carrying cloth or glass,
> leaving something behind, bringing
> something with me I should have left behind. (*Collected*, 141)

In this landscape of indefinite contours, Boland can express the ambiguity she experiences by her living in "two worlds" at the same time. With the realisation that womanhood and poetry occupy "two separate kingdoms of experience and expression" and with the threatening prospect of not being able to "live in both" (Boland 1995a: 114), Boland decides to occupy an intermediate position, a subversive hybrid space where both categories keep their unresolved tension. Critics such as Bhabha (1995: 13), Said (1994: 277), and Hall (1990: 235-237) believe that postcolonial agency is located in hybrid discourses. It is when the postcolonial subject adopts a liminal position and embraces rather than suppresses difference and heterogeneity, that a viable strategy of resistance is created. For Boland, poetic creation is achieved by her own ability to occupy a space 'in-between' the habits of suburban motherhood and the habits of the writer. The speaker's position in the staircase of her house situates her between these two worlds, the world of the ground floor, where she carries out her own domestic tasks, and the upper floor, where she writes her poems. Therefore, the stairwell becomes an interstitial passage between fixed identifications, 'in-between' the designations of identity. This liminality, according to Bhabha (1995: 4), "opens up the possibility of a cultural hybridity that entertains difference without an assumed or imposed hierarchy". Bhabha illustrates this notion of cultural hybridity by mentioning Renée Green, an African-American artist. These are her words, quoted by Bhabha (1995: 3):

> I used architecture literally as a reference, using the attic, the boiler room, and the stairwell to make associations between certain binary divisions such as higher and lower and heaven and hell. The stairwell became a liminal space, a pathway between the upper and lower areas, each of which was annotated with plaques referring to blackness and whiteness.

Whereas Green uses the staircase to displace the binary logic "Black/White" through which identities of difference are often constructed, Boland's employs this metaphor with a view to disturbing the dichotomy man (as writer) and woman (as mother and housewife).[25] By so doing, she occupies what Bhabha (1995: 25) calls a "Third Space", a space that disturbs the symmetry of designated male and female domains, and allows the speaker to give voice to her own creative potential:

> The hour of change, of metamorphosis,
> of shape-shifting instabilities.
> My time of sixth sense and second sight
> when in words I choose, the lines I write,
> they rise like visions and appear to me:
>
> women of work, of leisure, of the night,
> in stove-coloured silks, in lace, in nothing,
> with crewel needles, with books, with wide open legs (*Collected*, 141)

In this transitional and unstable context, the poet encounters a new landscape: neither openly public nor exclusively private, where different kinds of women "rise like visions" to Boland. The poetic muses that the speaker chooses to follow are varied: they are middle-class workers, upper class women, and also prostitutes. According to Spivak (1988a: 211), decolonisation involves, above all, a persistent acknowledgement of the heterogeneity of lived experiences. "The Women" makes explicit Boland's desire not only to write about mothers, housewives, and suburban women, but also about more heterogeneous women: "women of work" with "crewel needles", well-educated women that are free from time-consuming domestic duties, and women "of the night […] with wide open legs". Notice that Boland's title avoids generalising about those subjects: it is not "Women", but "The Women". The article does not refer to 'womankind' in general, but it emphasises a specific and concrete heterogeneous reality that Boland presumes that we, as addressees, are able to recognise. Although she has been criticised on the grounds that her work reflects a certain "class myopia" (O'Donnell 1995: 2), which results from her writing from the limited perspective of an upper-middle class Catholic family, Boland constantly attempts to bring to the fore a plurality of experiences. It is true that upper-class women are present in poems such as "The Shadow Doll" and "We Were Neutral in the War" (*Collected*, 170, 174-175), but this fact is compensated in all those poems where she attempts to grasp other realities, such as those of lower-class women, who are countrywomen most of the time (as in "The Achill Woman", *Collected*, 176-177).

In this sense, Boland's ambiguous location between her inner world as a poet and her outer world as an ordinary housewife is highly productive, as it allows her to open a place of potential inhabited by different kinds of women. Nevertheless, in contrast to the blurred and productive landscape that the poet had encountered upstairs, the poem ends, in a similar way to "Self-Portrait on a Summer Evening", by introducing us to a domestic world of well-established boundaries:

> and getting sick of it and standing up
> and going downstairs in the last brightness
>
> into a landscape without emphasis,
> light, linear, precisely planned,
> a hemisphere of tiered, aired cotton,
>
> a hot terrain of linen from the iron,
> folded in and over, stacked high,
> neatened flat, stoving heat and white. (*Collected*, 141)

Boland describes a landscape "without emphasis", "linear", and "precisely planned" that stands in opposition to the multidimensional and imaginative place her poetry has previously explored. Shapes are no longer shifting, unstable, and indefinite, but well delineated. In this sense, the domestic world is presented in all its crudeness; it is an asphyxiating "hot terrain" different to the radioactive "heat" that her poetry grasped by means of "the physical force of a dissonance". In this landscape, "cotton", "linen", and "iron" are arranged, "tiered" according to different categories and ranks. Boland's need to set a contrast between her own flowing imaginary world as an artist and her well-demarcated domestic world as a housewife is also observed in other poems such as "The Wild Spray" (*Collected*,

146). Whereas her poetry records a landscape that is moving smoothly, a "haphazard" place characterised by "the fluencies/ of colours", there is also another landscape, "a sharp" and delineated one that threatens her own poetic enterprise. By emphasising this contrast, "The Women" ends with Boland's unresolved tension between two contrary pulls: her commitment to literature and her ordinary life as a woman. As is typical in Boland's mature work, the feeling one is left with is of displacement and dislocation, of a woman who is still haunted by the contradictions of being a woman poet in Ireland.

The transformative power that Boland finds in recording her own ambivalence as a woman *and* a poet is also found in other poems from *The Journey* such as "Nocturne" (*Collected*, 142). As the narrator suggests in this poem, the "ambivalence" and "complexities" of her life as a woman poet allows her to open an in-between poetic space in which she can give voice to her own creative potential. In later poems such as "Midnight Flowers", this ambivalence between both roles is still maintained. The speaker argues, as a housewife in a domestic environment, that she "could be undone every single day by/ paradox" (p. 193). As all these poems suggest, Boland's work is therefore characterised by the sense of an enabling ambivalence.

4.3.4. In-between myth and history

As we have seen in "The Women", Boland advocates an 'in-between' space between poetry and womanhood, a place where the tension between both categories is maintained, and where she can find her source of artistic creativity. In what follows, I intend to show how Boland's poetry also moves with a subversive project in mind into another interstitial space, this time between the two polar opposites of myth and history.

Boland's mature work exemplifies the poet's ability to live in two worlds at the same time. As she asserts in *Object Lessons*, "[t]here is a duality to place", "there is the place that happened and the place that happens to you" (1995a: 154). The second place that Boland refers to is the place where she lives, whereas the first one exists more in the poet's mind, independent of the passing of time: "the place which existed before you and will continue after you have gone" (ibid). On this point, Haberstroh (1996: 21) and Praga (1996: 261) note that Irish women poets do not find their roots as easily as men do in physical and geographical locations. While male poets explore the external territory in order to clarify and reassert their identity, women poets tend to do the contrary: they explore their own self, the interior of their minds, in order to decipher their external world, their external reality. In this sense, Irish women's poetry extends the notion of place as mere geographical location, by focusing on new spaces, new territories, not necessarily physical. Boland in fact puts into practice what Heaney (1984a: 132) considers an internal exile, the ability to live in two places at the same time, either in time or in space. Thus, although Boland inhabits a suburban world, she is capable of imagining new places outside the realm of geography. This "duality to place" is constantly present in her poems. In them, Boland constantly describes Dundrum, the Dublin suburb where she lives. But there is also another world, an innovative one that haunts her:

> In my thirties I found myself [...] in a suburban house at the foothills of the Dublin mountains. Married and with two little daughters. [...] But at night the outer landscape yielded to an inner one. Familiar items blanked out and were replaced by others. (Boland 1995a: 17)

Rather than call this second place an imaginary place, I would simply like to refer to it as "a world of vision" (p. 192), for Boland has asserted that what she proposes is not as "an act of imagination", but as a "brute, choiceless fact" (p. 163). These two places are difficult to be separated, "hard to disentangle from each other" (p. 155). Whenever she describes the beauty of the landscape surrounding her (mostly by looking outside the window of her house), she is suddenly haunted by an Irish past, a bygone world no longer recoverable. Boland's poetry creates a middle space between both places, in an attempt to record "not exactly the suburbs, not entirely the hill coloured with blue shrubs, but something composed of both" (p. 172).[26] In constantly making the move to this second place, Boland's poems offer spaces of productive hybridity. Her poetry is located, as she argues, at "the very borders of myth and history" (Boland 1995a: 172), that is to say, on the margins of official mythical and historical spaces. It is in this liminal space where Boland transforms the following damaging opposition: presence of monumental images of women in myth and lack of presence of real women in history. In order to study how Boland resists the homogeneous views of both myth and history, I will refer to Julia Kristeva's theories in "Women's Time" (1986c).[27]

In this essay, Kristeva (1986c: 191) links female subjectivity to *cyclical* time and *monumental* time. Women's cyclical time involves repetition,

> cycles, gestation, the eternal recurrence of a biological rhythm which conforms to that of nature and imposes a temporality whose stereotyping may shock, but [which offers a] regularity and unison with what is experienced as extra-subjective time, cosmic time, occasion vertiginous visions, and unnameable *jouissance*.

On the other hand, as a consequence, woman's time is also monumental, in the sense that it involves eternity, an "all-encompassing and infinite [...] imaginary space" (ibid). Both types of temporality, cyclical and monumental, are linked to female subjectivity in so far as both are ways of conceptualising time from the perspective of motherhood and reproduction (p. 192). In this sense, woman's time as theorised by Kristeva is associated with the female body.

Kristeva (1986c: 192) locates women's time against 'History', characterised as *linear* time: "time as project, teleogy, linear, and prospective unfolding: time as departure, progression, and arrival". This linear time of history is also that of language, as long as this is considered as the enunciation of a sequence of words with "a beginning" and "ending", and is characterised by logical connections and linearity (ibid). In this sense, women's time remains outside language.

Kristeva distinguishes between two generations of feminists, whose identities are structured in terms of these two notions of time (time as cyclical and monumental; and time as linear). The first is composed by those egalitarian feminists who demand equal rights, and their right to occupy a place in linear time:

> In its beginnings, the women's movement, as the struggle of suffragists and of existential feminists, aspired to gain a place in linear time as the time of project and history. In this sense, the movement, while immediately universalist, is also deeply rooted in the socio-political life of nations. The political demands of women; the struggles for equal pay, for equal work, for taking power in social institutions on an equal footing with men; the rejection, when necessary, of the attributes traditionally considered feminine or maternal in so far as they are deemed incompatible with insertion in that history – all are part of the *logic of identification* with certain values. (Kristeva 1986c: 193-194)

Kristeva argues that the problem with this first generation is that, in their identification with power in order to consolidate it, these feminists perpetuate received oppressive structures. They demand the right to 'possess' the symbolic order, and their entry within linear politics and history "comes down to fabricating a few 'chiefs' among them" (p. 202).

The second generation identified by Kristeva emerges after 1968, and is formed by those feminists who emphasise women's radical difference from men and demand recognition of "an irreducible identity which has no equal in the opposite sex" (p. 194). In their wish to remain outside the linear time of history and politics, they embrace the cyclical and monumental temporality. They reject the (male) symbolic order and focus on the discovery of the specificity of the female, mostly found in the sexual (pp. 195-196). Kristeva (1986c: 202-203) also discards this radical form of feminism, because it runs the risk of turning into a counter-ideology, or an inverted form of sexism. As she argues, "the very logic of counter-power and of counter-society necessarily generates, by its very structures, its essence as a simulacrum of the combated society or of power" (p. 203).

Finally, Kristeva (1986c: 195) distinguishes a further, third generation of feminists which was emerging at the very same time she was writing. Their main task was to reconcile maternal time (motherhood) with linear time (political and historical time). It is this form of feminism that Kristeva strongly defends. She advocates, via this third generation of feminists, the addition of a female time as fluid, cyclical, and monumental within the linear progression of history, in order to subvert the patriarchal from within. As she argues, women's time as a "space-time of infinite expansion" can subvert linear versions of history (p. 192).[28]

It is this new notion of time (simultaneously female and historical) that we encounter in Boland's mature work. As we have seen, Kristeva defines woman's time as a temporality characterised by repetition and eternity, and linked to maternity. This cyclical and monumental time shapes many of Boland's poems, mostly in those where she relies on the mythical legend of Ceres and Persephone.[29] The Ceres and Persephone story is associated with the seasonal cycle of spring, summer, autumn, and winter. The female figures in this myth, furthermore, are eternal and monumental: they exist outside time, and the moral that their story communicates is for Boland, a self-evident truth, an eternal lesson that explains mother and daughter relationships. On the other hand, history is also essential for Boland. Her need to place women (whether mythological or ordinary) within the official annals of Ireland's past is of paramount importance. Therefore, her poetry, as has been explained, enters "at the point where myth touches history" (Boland 1995a: 166). Without entirely discarding either myth or history, Boland advocates the parallel existence, within the same historical moment, of all three concepts of time: cyclical, monumental, and linear. According to the woman poet, both opposing notions of time are fundamental for her subversive project of describing her women (Boland 1995a: 172).

In what follows, I focus on how Boland manages to unite these different visions of time. Firstly, I will show how Boland exploits in "Suburban Woman: A Detail" the benefits of cyclical and monumental time (*Collected*, 138-139). The speaker's fluidity in this poem helps her to be immersed in a 'timelessness' that allows her to establish a connection with those women from the Irish past. Secondly, I will show how, although Boland finds this traditional notion of woman's time highly productive, she also views the danger in identifying compliantly with mythological features, because that would mean selecting myth over history. In this sense, I will demonstrate, by focusing on "The Making of an Irish Goddess", how Boland subversively aligns this notion of time, typically female, with linear time (*Collected*, 178-179). It is here where the poet puts into practice Kristeva's advocacy of a temporality which is at once cyclical, monumental, and historical. Thirdly, I will focus on how Boland, specifically in those poems from *In a Time of Violence*, takes her poetic figures into death and erasure. In this sense, as her work progresses, she feels the urgent need to move from cyclical and monumental into linear time, that is, from myth into history. By doing so, Boland aligns herself with that first generation of feminists that Kristeva talks about, and whose main concern is to find their place as women within men's linear time. Nevertheless, I will show how, in spite of the dangers that Kristeva identifies in such action, Boland manages to avoid the perpetuation of the discourse of power. Her attempt to locate herself within history does not respond to her wish to identify with male power, but to her desire to subvert man-made representations from within.

4.3.4.1. The benefits of cyclical and monumental time

Boland never entirely rejects the traditional view of woman's time, a temporality which is cyclical and monumental. In her poetry, this notion of time, characterised by repetition and eternity, appears in order to refer to women's reality, an aspect acknowledged by critics such as Meaney (1993: 143) and Fulford (2002a: 204). Although the woman poet identifies the dangers of such a conception of female subjectivity, as it posits women as 'outside history', and therefore outside official records, her poetry exploits the benefits of such a temporal location. Repetition and eternity, two defining features of myth, can be used subversively. Boland (1995a: 172) has argued how myth is very helpful for her project of describing women's reality, because it provides "healing repetitions, the technology of propitiation", and a conciliation between past and present (Boland 1995a: 172). For Boland, women's time cannot only be recorded in a sort of lineal alignment, but also in repetitive and recurrent events. As Boland (1995a: 170) asserts, her life in the suburb is marked by repetition:

> Now here, in front of me everyday, were repetitions which had almost exactly the same effect. The crocuses under the rowan tree. The same child wheeled down to the shops at the same time everyday. A car returned home, with the same dinge on its bumper, every night. And the lamps which sprang into symmetries across our hills at dusk in November.

These repetitions Boland finds in life have their correspondence in her poetry. She comes to understand the value of "linguistic patterning" in poetry, which "both lulle[s] the mind and facilitate[s] the meaning" (ibid). For Boland, sequences and repetitions allow "deeper meanings to emerge", transcendental meanings such as "a sense of belonging, of sustenance, of a life revealed, and not restrained, by ritual and patterning" (ibid). The cadences and "melodies of renewal" that Boland finds in the suburbs, reveal women's silences, an unrecorded "unglamorous suffering" (pp. 171-172). In this sense, it is this transcendental notion of woman's time, time as circularity and monumental, that enables Boland to overcome the distance between her own present and the past of other Irish women. For Boland, women's experiences have, across time and place, some common factor. Both in her poetry and prose accounts, Boland seems to suggest that what unites women of the past to present women is their domestic roles as mothers and housewives. In this sense, womanhood, according to Boland's view, surpasses historical time; it is characterised by repetition and maternity. On this point, Meaney (1993: 143) criticises Boland for suggesting that the "continuity of female experience" can only be grounded in "the most biological sense". In fact, motherly experiences become extremely important in Boland's volumes of poetry after *Night Feed*. Nevertheless, Meaney ignores the second aspect of Boland's project: to place these women in linear time by leading her poetic figures to death and erasure, something that I will comment on in due course. By so doing, Boland manages to overcome that dream of a woman's community united in a transcendental way.

Boland's perpetuation of this traditional notion of woman's time as cyclical and monumental does not only intend to bridge the gap between past and present, but it also becomes a subversive technique with which to avoid essentialist and simplified views of women in art. Yielding to this repetitive and circular notion of time gives Boland an essential advantage. As she asserts in an interview, she is interested in "how the same thing can be seen differently over X and over again" (Schmidt 2001). In this sense, recurrence enables Boland to perceive women differently every time she describes them, moving away from the essentialist trap of definitions. Taking this into account, I disagree with critics such as Riley (1997: 25), who argue that for Boland "myths offer women limitations, not possibilities, simplistic stories rather than fluctuation narratives, thus limiting the potential for active female subjectivity". As I will demonstrate, Boland exploits the benefits afforded by myth, and its notions of time (cyclical and monumental), in order to bridge the distance between past and present and record heterogeneous images of women.

In order to explore how Boland exploits the resources of myth, I will concentrate on "Suburban Woman: A Detail", a poem included in *The Journey and Other Poems*. The first section of this poem offers a static description of a suburban environment that seems to be suspended in time and where no action is perceived:

The chimneys have been swept.
The gardens have their winter cut.
The shrubs are prinked, the hedges gelded.

The last dark shows up the headlights
of the cars coming down the Dublin mountains.

Our children used to think they were stars. (*Collected*, 138)

The parallel structure observed in the first stanza and the use of passive syntactic structures indicate that there is no motion and progression in the scene described. No linear time is recorded in this passage: the domestic world and its inhabitants seem to be immersed more in mythical than in historical time. Boland's reference to prinked shrubs and gelded hedges directly reminds one of Daphne, the Greek beautiful nymph who avoided having sexual intercourse with Apollo and was therefore transformed into a laurel tree. The women who inhabit this suburb are pseudo-Daphnes, entrapped in a monumental and cyclical time of reiterative domestic labours. But it will be this notion of time, apparently oppressing, that Boland will use subversively, as we will see. As darkness gradually disappears, the only light that is perceived is by "the headlights/ of the cars coming down the Dublin mountains". The speaker nostalgically recalls the time when her children believed the car lights to be stars in the sky. There is an impression that her children are no longer with her, that, she, like Ceres, ultimately has lost her daughter. This identification with the Earth Goddess becomes clearer in the second section of the poem:

> This is not the season
> when the goddess rose
> out of seed, out of wheat,
> out of thawed water
> and went, distracted and astray,
> to find her daughter. (*Collected*, 138)

The season this passage records is autumn, the period when Persephone was kidnapped by Hades, the King of the Underworld. Spring will be the time when Ceres will rise, as the Earth Goddess, in search of her daughter; but, at present, this goddess seems to be hidden. Like her, Boland does not embark on her search of her daughter, and more importantly, she feels dispossessed. The imminent coming of winter enhances the woman's spiritual impoverishment and alienation:

> Winter will be soon:
> Dun pools of rain;
> ruddy, addled distances;
> winter pinks, tinges and
> a first-thing smell of turf
> when I take the milk in. (Ibid)

By identifying with this Earth Goddess, Boland is immersed in a cyclical and monumental time that enables her to have access to a transcendental understanding. She has an instinctive knowledge of the recurrence of seasons and of the inevitability of her separation from her daughter. As the speaker returns from her garden after taking the milk, she describes the suburban landscape from a painter's perspective: the reddish colour of the horizon is merged with the brownish gray colour of the "pools of rain", and the pinks and tinges of her own surroundings. This description of the landscape, in which everything is seen in terms of the same range of tenuous colours (shades of red), forebodes the impending dissolution the woman is going to experience:

> Setting out for a neighbour's house
> in a denim skirt,
>
> a blouse blended in
> by the last light,
>
> I am definite
> to start with
> but the light is lessening,
> the hedge losing its detail,
> the path its edge. (*Collected*, 139)

Although she seems to be a separate entity in this landscape, her blouse blending into the last light anticipates that she is going to become indistinguishable. In

Object Lessons, Boland (1995a: 167-168) narrates the moment described in this poem:

> At what point does an actual, exact landscape – those details which are recurrent and predictable – begin to blur and soften? Sometimes [...] walking between my house and a neighbour's, past the whitebeams trees and the bicycles left glinting in the dusk, I could imagine that I myself was a surreal and changing outline, that there was something almost profound in these reliable shadows, that such lives as mine and my neighbour's were mythic, not because of their strangeness but because of their powerful ordinariness. [...] Then I would feel all the sweet, unliterate melancholy of women who must have stood as I did, throughout continents and centuries, *feeling the timelessness of that particular instant* and *the cruel time underneath its surface*. They must have measured their children, as I did, against the seasons and looked at the hedges and rowan trees, their height and the colour of their berries, as an index of the coming loss. (Emphasis added)

In this passage, Boland is explicitly fusing in a single moment cyclical and monumental, and historical time. Immersed in "the timelessness of that particular instant", the speaker feels that she is linked in a transcendental way to those mythological figures such as Ceres who went in search of her daughter. This blurring of imaginative and real worlds is common in Boland's poetry, as "This Moment", "The Pomegranate", and "Daughter" exemplify (*Collected*, 213, 215-216, 263-264). In "Suburban Woman: A Detail", the poet, once again, approaches the ordinary details of women's lives from a revisionary mythological approach. This allows her to connect her own personal experience with that of other women in the past. By linking past and present, legends and real lives, Boland implies that myth has its roots in the familial and the domestic. There is, for the poet, something about the repeated action of a woman (lifting a child, clearing a dish, and walking in her neighborhood) which reveals a deeper meaning to existence. But, as she has also argued in the passage above, she is also drawn to "the cruel time underneath its surface" (1995a: 168). Boland wants to incorporate both mythical and past women into linear time, which also implies the passing of time and the loss of beauty. Nevertheless, what Boland wants to capture in this poem is cyclical and monumental time, rather than linear time. Whereas in other poems she is more concerned with bringing her own images to the corruptive and the damaging consequences of the passing of time, in "Suburban Woman: A Detail" she is interested in recording the 'timelessness' that freezes both mythical figures and those women from a remote Irish past:

> Look at me, says the tree.
> I was a woman once like you,
> full-skirted, human.
>
> Suddenly I am not certain
> of the way I came
> or the way I will return,
> only that something
> which may be nothing
> more than darkness has begun
> softening the definitions
> of my body, leaving
>
> the fears and all the terrors
> of the flesh shifting the airs
> and forms of the autumn quiet
>
> crying "remember us". (*Collected*, 139)

Boland's feeling of shapelessness, of being a surreal and changing outline, is going to parallel her sense of timelessness. Thus, the woman-speaker does not feel anymore as if she is inhabiting a certain place at a certain time. Rather, she is suspended in time and place, as that wounded warrior in "An Old Steel Engraving". This location in cyclical and monumental time is highly subversive. Firstly, it enables her to establish a connection with past lives, with all those women who stood as she is standing right now, "throughout centuries and continents" (Boland 1995a: 168). Boland is here implying that myth and reality are intrinsically connected, that past and present, history and legend are associated by the very ordinariness of human lives. In this context, the woman senses the call of one female voice, stemming from a tree. This tree may be Daphne, transformed into a laurel tree, or Ceres, the Earth Goddess, previously out of sight, but now speaking to the woman. The fluidity that overwhelms Boland allows her to open a space where multiplicity of voices can be heard. Irigaray (1985: 209) has advocated a form of language in which "[b]etween our lips, yours and mine, several voices, several ways of speaking resound endlessly, back and forth [...]. And how could one dominate the other? Impose her voice, her tone, her meaning?". Boland's vulnerability as a subject prevents her from dominating and eclipsing other women's voices. Her own fluid speech does not overshadow the language of women in the past, but enables the emergence of different voices, without imposing one over the other. When she says to be experiencing "something/ which may be nothing", she does not only imply the rejection of historical accounts of the ordinary, whereby the ordinary is undervalued as a mere "darkness" or rejected at all as "nothing". Boland also expresses her "refusal to make grandiose claims" in her statements, as Hagen and Zelman (2004: 59) explain. Nevertheless, the resulting shapelessness and loss of self-confidence leads to a compensating gain: the remembrance of a universal community of women (mostly mothers), who have lived, or are still living, in a similar ordinary landscape. The definite shape of her surroundings disappears in order to allow this woman to enter a new place, unaffected by linear time and determined by repetition and maternity. This place is the country of the mind, the imagination, where the woman feels free to declare her solidarity with all those women who, like her, went in search of their daughters. In this sense, and although I have identified the woman with the Earth Goddess, it seems that Boland is reversing the role in the Ceres-Persephone myth by becoming a daughter in search of her (historical) foremothers.

Secondly, with the dissolution in space and time that Boland experiences, she surpasses "the fears and all the terrors" that linear time would mean for her own body. In contrast to *In Her Own Image*, the speaker's body does not involve assertion but rather the contrary. There is no connection between text/creativity and body; her female body is not the source of her woman's identity anymore. Her "flesh" reminds the speaker of her vulnerability, and therefore, she is terrified at the fact that she will grow older and lose her beauty. Instead of praising her own body, Boland brings it to dissolution, implying that the poet's creativity lies in her ability to overcome sexual boundaries. By "leaving/ the fears and all the terrors/ of the flesh", the woman senses a temporary feeling of eternity, similar to that enjoyed by Ceres.

In short, in poems such as "Suburban Woman: A Detail" Boland shows how woman's cyclical and monumental time can be used subversively. Myth allows her firstly, to establish a comradeship with an imaginative community of women and secondly, to enjoy the state of eternity, of an infinite time in which she will be able to survive, and escape the negative consequences of linear time. Nevertheless, the general tendency in her work is to insert this conventional concept of time within history. Linear time is also very important for Boland, for it enables her to locate her women 'out of myth into history'. Although Boland's poems record women as engaged in repetitive actions (such as searching for their children in a twilight setting), there is suddenly what she calls a "violent and random event" (1995a: 172) that reminds them that they are fragile subjects, affected by the passing of time and the loss of beauty. By mixing myth with history, Boland relocates women's private lives within public history. The following section addresses this aspect of Boland's work.

4.3.4.2. A revolutionary place between myth and history

In order to observe how Boland's poetry combines myth and history, by advocating Kristeva's notion of a temporality which is simultaneously cyclical, monumental, and linear, I will focus on a poem included in *Outside History*, "The Making of an Irish Goddess". In this poem, Boland seeks to redefine the unreal and mythic image of Ceres, in order to offer a more accurate image representative of contemporary Irish women. The present participle of the title refers to an action in process. In this sense, the vocabulary is of movement rather than stillness, indicating, in Fulford's words (2002b: 142), that for Boland, "real" women are "associated with the living stream rather than with the monumental". The first stanzas introduce us to the Earth Goddess who inhabits, as a mythological woman, a monumental and sacred time, in other words, she is timeless:

> Ceres went to hell
> with no sense of time.
>
> When she looked back
> all that she could see was
>
> the arteries of silver in the rock,
> the diligence of rivers always at one level,
> wheat at one height,
> leaves of a single colour,
> the same distance in the usual light;
>
> a seasonless, unscarred earth. (*Collected*, 178)

The first verse lines record the literal descent of the goddess into the Underworld.[30] When Ceres looks back, all she can see is a "seasonless, unscarred earth". The world that the Greek myth portrays is, according to Boland, an unreal world. Ceres is not affected by the passing of time and there are no seasons evolving into one another. Furthermore, it may be funny or ironical that the goddess of agriculture is unable to perceive the cycle of birth, growth, and death in nature. The mythical world is unchangeable: "the diligence of rivers" are "always at one level", the "wheat" is always "at one height", the "leaves" are "of a single colour", and there is always "the same distance in the usual light". This world seems to be frozen in time, and consequently, Ceres becomes a lifeless emblem inscribed "in the cold rock" of myth (Boland 1995a: 39). That is why the speaker cannot identify with this goddess:

> But I need time –

My flesh and that history –
To make the same descent.

In my body,
neither young now nor fertile,
and with the marks of childbirth
still on it,

in my gestures –
the way I pin my hair to hide
the stitched, healed blemish of a scar – (*Collected*, 179)

As we have seen in poems such as "Self-Portrait on a Summer Evening", this change from third person narration to first person is typical of Boland's mature work. The speaker becomes a new Irish goddess who, in contrast to the mythological Ceres, is characterised by four main factors, all of them interrelated: "[t]ime", "flesh", "history", and "scar". First of all, "time" is very important for the speaker (in fact, this noun is repeated three times in the poem). In contrast to Ceres, who is positioned in 'no time' and inhabits a "seasonless" and "unscarred earth", the speaker is a mortal and vulnerable subject affected by the passing of time. As Boland (1995a: 234) has argued, the dismantling of the traditional fusion between the erotic and the sensual in Irish poetry, offers "a radical and exciting chance to restate time in the poem". By restating time in the poem, Boland moves away from the traditional notion of woman's time as cyclical and monumental. Rather than using her poem as an instrument of timelessness (something that she had done in "Suburban Woman: A Detail"), Boland uses it to record change and decay as brought upon a woman's body which will eventually die. Secondly, "flesh" is fundamental for the poetic speaker, too. In contrast to the bodiless image of the goddess, the poetic voice is a corporeal entity. In *In Her Own Image*, Boland glorified the female body as a site of worship (remember "Solitary"); here, she tries to show its wounds and scars. Because her body is injured and blemished by childbirth, this woman is identified as a real and non-mythical being, in contrast to those legends (whether Greek or Irish) that "depend on her to be young and beautiful" ("Story", *Collected*, 236). The woman in the poem is "neither young nor fertile". She makes "gestures" which show up her "scars", what induces us to think that her image is constantly changing rather than static and timeless. Thirdly, "history" is also an essential constitutive part of this new goddess. Note the use of demonstratives such as "that history" and later "that agony", which help to indicate that Ceres is separated and excluded from official historical accounts. Whereas this goddess stands outside history, the speaker tries to become a representative voice of the past in the present, inside history. Her body is treated as a paradigm for women's history: its wounds recall the Great Famine of the 1840s and how women suffered in those times.[31] As the speaker argues, the scars of her body

> must be
>
> and accurate inscription
> of that agony:
>
> the failed harvests,
> the fields rotting to the horizon,
> the children devoured by their mothers
> whose souls, they would have said,
> went straight to hell,
> followed by their own. (*Collected*, 179)

By means of this new goddess, Boland suggests that she can make "an accurate inscription" of a national trauma. The previous perfect nature and idealised landscape of myth gives way to a more damaged and unpleasant landscape. In contrast to Boland's initial work where the poet praised the Irish landscape, her mature poetry constantly rejects the romantic view that myth portrays. The earth is portrayed as rotten and blemished as the woman's body. Just as in "Mise Eire" and "Mother Ireland" (*Collected*, 128-129, 261-262), Boland perpetuates the long-held association between earth/country and women. She portrays a non-idealised Mother Ireland: an old and injured woman who cannot hope for salvation because she is too wounded and injured by her (historical) past. In this sense, Boland manages to destroy conventional images of women by inserting them within the particular historical narrative of the Great Famine. Fulford (2002b: 147) has argued that Boland "presents herstory in terms of a material time and space peopled with the flesh of rotting corpses, and the cannibalism of 'children devoured by their mothers'". By doing so, this critic goes on, the poet is able to produce a "differential and materialist" version of history (p. 146). Indeed, Boland criticises history as a master narrative that has excluded women's stories. By presenting her body as an emblem of women's past, she includes them within Ireland's official narrative of events. In the process, myth is also attacked, for it can freeze women within lifeless emblems. Redefining the timelessness that characterises the mythical image of Ceres, the speaker locates herself at the end of the poem within a 'linear' temporality. She is a new Ceres walking in a

> March evening
> at the foothills of the Dublin mountains,
> across which the lights have changed all day,
> holding up my hand
> sickle-shaped, to my eyes
> to pick out
> my daughter from
> all the other children in the distance;
>
> her back turned to me. (*Collected*, 179)

The last lines of the poem focus on "a particular moment in time which is subject to change" (Fulford 2002b: 147). The woman, who goes to pick up her child from school, is depicted in a fluid landscape, with the effect that her image, as in the case of "Suburban Woman: A Detail", is similarly unstable and unfixed. In this sense, Boland relocates Ceres within both linear and cyclical time. In the speaker's ordinary experience of looking for her daughter in a March twilight resides the experiences of those women, those mothers who have come before her. Once again, repetition (a traditional notion of female time) appears. Collecting a child becomes for Boland, therefore, a customary act that is important both for the Irish mother and for the Greek goddess. Myth and reality, Boland implies, are linked by this mundane act. Like Ceres, this Irish mother anticipates the loss of her daughter, for her child fails to return her gaze, as "her back [is] turned to [her]".

By identifying with Ceres and also by recording a scarred and damaged female body located in a volatile landscape, Boland puts into practice Kristeva's advocacy of the parallel existence of the three notions of time. The considerable interchange of verb tenses in this poem is typical of Boland's mature production, where she constantly crosses those temporal and spatial boundaries that separate myth and the ordinary, past and present, one landscape from another. In this poem, the speaker has travelled from 'myth' (described in the past tense) to her own reality (describing her damaged body in the present tense); from 'history' (recording the Great Famine in the past tense), to her own suburban and ordinary world again (described in the present tense). By so doing, Boland locates her present reality 'in-between' myth and history. Myth and maternal time are juxtaposed with the particular historical event of the famine, and both are, in turn, connected to the ordinary suburban landscape. In this sense, both myth and history are present within a single female image, herself, a contemporary Irish woman. It is this insertion of cyclical and monumental time within the linear progression of history that, according to Kristeva (1986c: 192), is subversive. Boland manages to disrupt both myth as a timeless account, and history as a linear narrative, subverting the patriarchal from within. Rather than describing the historical event of the famine as a narrative from beginning to end, Boland interrupts this story by inserting the individual experiences of mother and daughter.[32] In this sense, the poet moves away from the idea of "an overall pattern in history", sharing the poststructuralist and postmodernist critique of historicism (Sarup 1993: 2). Poststructuralists like Michel Foucault and postmodernists such as Jean-François Lyotard attack the legitimacy of modern age myths ('the grand narratives') and draw a sharp critique of the historical notion of progress (p. 132). Sarup (1993: 59) has explained how Foucault conceives of history in terms of "genealogy":

> Whereas traditional or 'total' history inserts events into grand explanatory systems and linear processes, celebrates great moments and individuals, and seeks to document a point of origin, genealogical analysis attempts to establish and preserve the singularity of events, turns away from the spectacular in favour of the discredited, the neglected, and a whole range of phenomena which have been denied in history.

"The Making of an Irish Goddess" focuses on the singular event of picking up a child from the playground. This ordinary experience stands outside 'master' historical narratives such as those which record the Great Famine. By linking both stories within the same poetic sequence Boland (1995a: 172) is able to write of a woman "at the very borders of myth and history". This allows her to revise both the timelessness that characterises myth and simplistic and reductionist versions of history.

4.3.4.3. Out of myth into history: towards the death and erasure of the poetic self

So far, we have observed how in poems from *The Journey* and *Outside History* Boland is interested in creating a poetic space that can record both myth and history. Boland's concern with the possibilities afforded by cyclical and monumental time is continued in *In a Time of Violence*, in poems such as "The Pomegranate", where she reflects on motherly roles through the Ceres and Persephone myth, "[t]he only legend I have ever loved" (*Collected*, 215). Nevertheless, in this volume, we start to appreciate a greater focus on the speaker's linear time. Boland equates linear time with death, pain, and suffering, but she prefers this notion of time to the timelessness of cyclical and monumental time. As Boland's mature work progresses, the issues of dying and ageing become, interestingly enough, more predominant.

Mills Harper (1997: 188) has noted that Boland, unlike her poetic predecessors, consciously writes herself as a vulnerable subject, "as small and mortal, subject to absence and death". In her essay "First Principles and Last Things", this critic identifies connections between Boland and the African-American writer Audre Lorde. She explains how Boland's main poetic concerns, such as "[d]omesticity", "oral history", and "children", are linked with "illness, silence, and death" (p. 189). In order to resist the trope of 'eternal life' that has long objectified women in poetry, as everlasting young and beautiful emblems, Boland represents the self (her 'womanhood') in terms of erasure. That is why in most of the poems in *In a Time of Violence*, the theme of ageing and dying is constantly present. This emphasis distinguishes this volume of poetry from all the others. In "Moths", the speaker records how she is "perishing" as she perceives her "child's shadow longer than [her] own" (*Collected*, 221). This similarly occurs in other poems from this volume such as "The Water-Clock", "A Sparrow Hawk in the Suburbs", "Legends", and "Story" (pp. 219-224, 229, 236-237). The beginning of "The Water-Clock", for instance, shows Boland's increased interest in recording linear time. The title itself summarises her main concern: to transform her poems into clocks, instruments for measuring the passage of time:

> Thinking of ageing on a summer day
>   of rain and more rain
> I took a book down from a shelf
>   and stopped to read (*Collected*, 219)

As is typical of her mature work, the poem begins with a present participle that situates the woman speaker in the middle of an action.[33] The disruption of lay-out and the rainy landscape enhance what is going to be the speaker's desire: to record the passing of time and the perishing of things. The speaker is drawn to take down a book from the shelf, and read about "the absurd creation of the water-clock", a clepsydra used by the ancient world in order to measure time by the passing of water from one container to another one. Fascinated by this rare invention, the speaker wonders how they could have

Taken an element, that is.
Which swallowed faces, stars, irises, Narcissus.
And posed as frost, ice, snow. (*Collected*, 220)

As in poems such as "Lava Cameo" where Boland questioned her own ability to record "the flux of hell" in a firm and compact poetic representation, here the speaker questions the ancient ability to place in a specific position something that is constantly flowing rather than solid. Water is a very recurrent metaphor in Boland's poetry. As she has recently asserted, it has strong family associations for her, because her grandfather was a sea-captain and he drowned on the Bay of Biscay (interview with Villar Argáiz). But this image is more than a simple anecdote in Boland's life. As we will see, rivers, seas, lakes, streams, and raining are constantly present in her work, in order to suggest the fluidity of a life that cannot adequately be grasped by the artist. Thus, the irony of the very creation of the water-clock: an instrument that can measure time by 'freezing' as frost, ice or snow an element that is constantly eroding the earth. Like the speaker who is inevitably "ageing on a summer day", the landscape that Boland describes in this poem is inevitably dissolved by a constant drizzle. In contrast to the water-clock that cannot record the change of weather, Boland's poem becomes a more suitable instrument to measure linear time. Recording how rain suddenly stops, the poem ends by presenting a completely different landscape, as the sun comes out and the afternoon clears. In this sense, the poem becomes a suitable site that can bear witness to the constant change that affects both the speaker and her surroundings.

This emphasis on linear time is more explicitly manifested in "Anna Liffey", "Time and Violence", and "A Woman Painted on a Leaf" (*Collected*, 230-239, 241-242). In these three poems, Boland follows what Fulford (2002a: 215-216) has explained as her characteristic way of setting a poem. Firstly, Boland criticises monumental representations of Irish women in art; secondly, she "re-imagines [...] alternative and more authentic female experience[s] which risk[...] misrepresentation"; and finally, "with only misrepresentation available, she takes her female figure[s] into death or 'nothingness'". Indeed, this process from construction to destruction of identity is a feature of most of Boland's poems in her mature work. In this sense, I disagree with Hagen and Zelman (2004: 20), who argue that "Boland's poetic 'repossession' is [...] a fluid process of de- and re-construction". Boland constantly reveals that even her own poetic representations run the risk of been misrepresentative, and therefore, her movement is always from reconstruction to deconstruction, and not vice versa.

In contrast to the preference that Boland has shown in previous volumes for quartets and tercets, "Anna Liffey" is exemplary of Boland's increasing concern for more open poetic forms. In this poem, the woman poet invokes the traditional association between river and woman in man-made myth and slightly changes Joyce's celebration in *Finnegans Wake* of Dublin's river Liffey "as the feminine principle eternal in its cycles" (Gelpi 1999: 225).[34] The speaker begins by narrating the mythological story of Life, the daughter of Cannan, who, after arriving at Kildare, is so amazed by the beauty of "the flat-lands and the ditches" that she "asked that it be named for her" (*Collected*, 230). Boland is drawn to this figure for its national importance. Anna Livia has become so popular that it has even become a symbol of Dublin city (Hurtley et al. 1996: 8).[35] Proof of this is the sculpture, popularly known as "The Floozie in the Jacuzzi", that, until very recently, was erected in O'Connell Street, in the very heart of the city. It was a fountain depicting the figure of a woman with sheets of water pouring over it. Originally conceived as a tribute to the goddess of the river, this sculpture has been highly controversial; Irish feminist critics such as Gray Martin (2000: 275) view it as an instance of "the sexual exploitation of women's bodies".[36] Even though this woman is lying on her back with water running from head to toe, she is, as all those women in artistic representations, frozen in monumental time. In this sense, Boland finds the need to reconstruct this image. She shows how the mythological association river-land and land-woman turns active and bodily women into passive, bodiless, and desexualised beings. Myth and art, in their attempt to define and mould their emblems, destroy the complexity and totality of lived experiences, which, as a consequence, can only be perceived fragmentarily as

> One body. One spirit.
> One place. One name. (*Collected*, 231)

Boland shows how the body is not connected to the spirit, and how place is totally detached from Life's name, in spite of the myth's attempt to stress the connection between land and womanhood. In this sense, her identity is fragmented into different pieces. As typical in her mature poems, Boland identifies with this mythological creature. By "[b]ecoming a figure in a poem" and "[u]surping a name and a theme", the speaker herself turns out to be a new Life who is now described as

> A woman in the doorway of a house.
> A river in the city of her birth. (*Collected*, 230)

Standing in the "doorway" of her house is in itself an interstitial location, 'in-between' the public version of the myth, and the rather private account of a housewife and mother. It is significant to note how "doorway" is repeated five times in this poem, together with other words such as "edge", "threshold", and "boundary". Locating herself in a line of intersection is, as hinted earlier, extremely important for Boland. Once again, she describes herself within a place that stands outside definite contours, a landscape in which "[d]usk is coming" and "[r]ain is moving east from the hills" (p. 230). As we have seen in "The Water-Clock", Boland's landscapes are typically softened by the rain. Fulford (2002a: 217) has noted how rain stands in Boland's poetry as "a national characteristic which is appropriately fluid", suggesting "little foundational sense of 'Irishness'". The poet's persistent reference to raining suggests this is the best (and perhaps the only) feature that properly defines 'Irishness', the Irish nation. The "hard rock" (1995a) she mentions in *Object Lessons* might be understood as a metaphor of national identity, an identity founded on myths and legends such as Life's. By focusing on the power of the rain to change the 'hard rock' of the Irish landscape, Boland attempts to dissolve consolidated national emblems such as Anna Livia. This is further exemplified in the following lines, where the speaker praises the "gifts of the river", for

> Its shiftless and glittering
> Re-telling of a city,
> Its clarity as it flows (*Collected*, 231)

In this sense, Boland finds bodies of water such as seas, lakes, or rivers necessary to acquire more than one perspective of national identity: as it is fluid, it escapes definite and restrictive ideologies and impositions. In this sense, although she subverts the Joycean link between the river Liffey and an immortal female goddess, she is drawn to this equation of woman and water, as she makes explicit in the following passage:

> A river is not a woman.
>   Although the names it finds,
>   The history it makes
> And suffers –
>   The Viking blades beside it,
>   The muskets of the Redcoats,
>   The flames of the Four Courts
> Blazing into it
>   Are a sign.
>   Any more than
> A woman is a river,
>   Although the course it takes,
>   Through swans courting and distraught willows,
> Its patience
>   Which is also its powerlessness,
>   From Callary to Islandbridge,
>   And from source to mouth,
> Is another one. (*Collected*, 232-233)

Boland finds water an appropriate medium through which to describe the suffering, patience, and powerlessness that has characterised womanhood throughout centuries. But she is also drawn to this image of Anna Livia because, as a river, it is constantly running freely. Therefore, Boland conceptualises womanhood, as Cixous and Irigaray have done, in terms of liquefaction and diffusion. As she has recently argued, water is "the great feminine element" (interview with Villar Argáiz). It is my contention that Boland is drawn to this rather traditional image because, in her view, womanhood cannot be objectified, and like water, it is a fluid and unstable category. As in "The Water-Clock", the disruption of the lay-out of this passage suggests the versatility of her poetic images. In contrast to the initial stanzas, the lines increasingly become longer, unfolding down the page. Unlike those figures represented in engravings and paintings, Boland attempts to write verse which is as unstable as the new Anna Livia she portrays. By doing so, Boland forces us to see the falsifications involved in all sorts of national representations.

But national representations are not only dismantled by turning to the fluidity of water. Boland also uses her own example of fragmentation and dispossession in order to suggest how notions such as 'being at home' are relative, rather than absolute and pure. Rather than founding her 'sense of place' on a "nation" that, as she says, "elude[s]" her, Boland connects 'home' with her role as a mother:

> My country took hold of me.
> My children were born.
>
> I walked out in a summer dusk
> To call them in.
>
> One name. Then the other one.
> The beautiful vowels sounding out home. (*Collected*, 232)

As the verbal parallelism of these lines indicate, "my country" is equated with "my children" and "the beautiful vowels" of their names with "home". Boland's sense of 'Irishness' is only rooted in her role as a mother looking after her children. But even this notion of stable identity is going to be deconstructed as the poem proceeds. Once her children are away from her, she loses all sense of being 'at home':

> I feel it change.
> My children are
> Growing up, getting older.
> My country holds on
> To its own pain.
>
> I turn off
> The harsh yellow
> Porch light and
> Stand in the hall.
> Where is home now? (*Collected*, 235)

In this sense, Boland's female identity is perceived in terms of loss. As a young child in London, she felt a tremendous sense of uneasiness. In one of her diasporic poems, "In Which the Ancient History I Learn Is Not My Own", Boland suddenly wondered "where exactly/ was my old house?" (*Collected*, 224). The question that troubled this exiled child still disturbs the speaker who, even though she is now located inside her house, wonders "Where is home now?". In this sense, the grown-up mother, now back in her home-country, feels a similar estrangement and dispossession. In spite of this, the poet realises that having "neither/ Children nor country" is a disguised blessing. By not being grounded in a particular place, the speaker is "free"

> To imagine a spirit
> In the blues and greens,
> The hills and fogs
> Of a small city. (*Collected*, 234)

'Place', as the very word suggests, denotes a space of definite boundaries, boundaries that become even more enclosing in "a small city". Thus, at the end of the poem, Boland advocates exile as the best place to construct her poetic self:

> Follow the rain
> Out to the Dublin hills.
> Let it become the river.
> Let the spirit of place be
> A lost soul again. (*Collected*, 235)

The subject, constantly in exile as "a lost soul", is able to surpass and cross established boundary lines, and as postcolonial theorists such as Bhabha (1995: 278) and Said (1994: 385) advocate, can subvert those authoritarian ideologies that confer identity in terms of nation, class, gender, and/or race. Like Anna Livia, the poet envisages herself as a "[s]pirit of water" who can escape national stories, whether historical or mythological. The end of "Anna Liffey" emphasises precisely how marginality, the lack of a firm identity, is positive rather than negative:

> In the end
> It will not matter
> That I was a woman. I am sure of it.
> The body is a source. Nothing more.
> There is time for it. There is a certainty
> About the way it seeks its own dissolution.
> Consider rivers,
> They are always en route to
> Their own nothingness. From the first moment
> They are going home. (*Collected*, 235)

As "Anna Liffey" shows, Boland's representation of identity is neither fixed nor rooted in a particular place. Like the identity of the river, Boland feels that her identity is "en route to its own nothingness". As she claims in the last lines of the poem,

In the end
Everything that burdened and distinguished me
Will be lost in this:
I was a voice. (Ibid)

Having a fixed sense of place, a stable identity is nothing but a "burden" for the woman poet. In this sense, as Fulford (2002a: 217) argues, Boland "deterritorialis[es]" rather than "reterritorialis[es]" identity. The "real subject" of "Anna Liffey" is, in Boland's own words, "that progress from individuality to dissolution which happens with age" (interview with Villar Argáiz). As Boland grows old, she realises that, whereas her body will eventually perish, the only thing that manages to survive is the "voice". Cixous (1994: xviii) states that "[p]ure I, identical to I-self, does not exist. I is always in difference. I is the open set of the trances of an I by definition changing, mobile, because of living-speaking-thinking-dreaming". The deconstruction of identity that Cixous advocates is also emphasised by the speaker in "Anna Liffey". Because of "speaking-thinking-dreaming" and mostly because of "living" and, therefore, ageing, Boland cannot represent the self in solid and stable grounds. As the speaker puts it in "The Singers", her main concern becomes, therefore, to "find a voice where [she] found a vision" (*Collected*, 203). It is this very "voice" that succeeds over the body at the end of "Anna Liffey". In this sense, Boland bases her identity not on biology as in *In Her Own Image*, but on her very ability to transcend the limits imposed on gender, as in Virginia Woolf's (1974: 139) androgynous vision. The end of "Anna Liffey" connects sexlessness and dissolution with artistic freedom. As Boland has recently expressed, "[t]here is something very liberating in the idea that art can release you from the restrictions of the identity you already have or have inherited" (interview with Villar Argáiz). By dissolving the image of the apparently solid statue of Anna Liffey, Boland moves towards a representation of the self that surpasses the binary 'self'/'Other' and reconfigures those singular identities that nationalism and feminism reinforce. As Fulford (2002a: 213) states, Boland's versatile identity manages to abandon "the pathos of authenticity that has informed first-generation nationalist and feminist projects alike" (p. 213). Her disintegrated self opens up a place of future potential where new identities, not founded this time on ideas of authenticity, can emerge.

In this sense, Boland's act of speaking always leads to absence and death, as in another poem from this collection "Time and Violence" (*Collected*, 237-239). Here, Boland follows a similar movement to the one we have just observed: from reconstruction to deconstruction of traditional female images, from cyclical and monumental time into linear time. The poem begins by describing a general setting that reminds one of "The Photograph on My Father's Desk": "The evening was the same as any other" (p. 237). The main difference is that the image now, rather than fixed in the timelessness of a photograph, represents a vulnerable subject who is overwhelmed by "the melancholy/ of growing older". The speaker describes a landscape of rapid change where she is threatened with dissolution. This fluidity, as in "Suburban Woman: A Detail", becomes the starting point from which different mythological voices and presences magically announce themselves to her. Suddenly, the boundaries of Boland's suburban landscape begin to extend in order to incorporate a "world of vision" (Boland 1995a: 192) inhabited by a pastoral shepherdess, a legendary mermaid, and Cassiopeia, trapped in the night sky constellations. The shepherdess represents the land, the mermaid the sea, and Cassiopeia the sky. All these mythological figures have been frozen and silenced into icons in all possible planes of existence. In contrast to the speaker, they cannot experience the consequences of linear time upon their bodies, condemned as they are to inhabit a cyclical and monumental time of youthfulness and beauty. If Boland is to choose between the conditions of the stars (in their eternity) and the human condition, she explicitly announces her choice of the second one (Foster 1999: 11). As the title "Time and Violence" suggests, linear time is not as pleasant as monumental and cyclical time: instead of eternity, it only brings a painful 'violence' over the speaker's body. But it is precisely this pleading for humanity that these mythological figures make at the end of this poem:

> We cannot sweat here. Our skin is icy.
> We cannot breed here. Our wombs are empty.
> Help us to escape youth and beauty.
>
> Write us out of the poem. Make us human
> in cadences of change and mortal pain
> and words we can grow old and die in. (*Collected*, 239)

The vulnerable speaker becomes a desired model for these women entrapped in myth, who want to experience motherhood and humanity in all its rawness. In order to cease being eternal and lifeless emblems, they invoke a poetic space where they "can grow old and die in". In this sense, deletion and therefore death is the only way these images can be "written out" of legend.

In fact, Boland's poetry constantly engages with death, as in her poem "A Woman Painted on a Leaf",[37] where the poetic voice claims: "I want a poem/ I can grow old in. I want a poem I can die in" (*Collected*, 242). In particular, this poem focuses on a woman's profile inscribed on a leaf, and how the poet makes explicit her task to return this image "to its element [...] of ending". Giving bodily form to the leaf, Boland allows her subject not only to be human and grow old, but even to die:

> I want to take
> This dried-out face
> [...]
>
> so that [it]
>
> will be from now on,
> a crisp tinder underfoot. Cheekbones. Eyes. Will be
> a mouth crying out. Let me.
>
> Let me die. (*Collected*, 242)

The very short sentences and clipped language of the final lines parallel the gradual dissolution of the poetic voice. As Boland argues in "Story": "I am writing/// a woman out of legend. I am thinking/ how new it is – this story. How hard it will be to tell" (*Collected*, 237). Despite this difficulty, Boland manages to liberate the woman at the end of this poem by bringing her to death. The fragmented body described becomes in this way, "a crisp tinder", an easily combustible material ready to be set on fire. Boland draws on fire as a mechanism to destroy women's fossilisation in art. These burning images can bear witness to the destiny that awaits us all: death and erasure. On the other hand, by dissolving this image into "[c]heekbones", "[e]yes", and "a mouth", the speaker suggests, as in "Anna Liffey", that the body is but "a source" and nothing else. The woman's "voice" is the only thing that will pervade at the end. As is common in Boland's poetry, the poem finishes with a profusion of the modal 'will' indicating certainty. This is a confident speaker that knows that articulation allows agency, that by allowing these 'mute' images to speak, positive changes can be brought about in Irish poetry.

4.3.4. Conclusion

Boland's subjectivity is constructed more in terms of fluidity and else-whereness, rather than in terms of domination and subordination. Her poetry should be read as a series of boundary crossings, beyond fixed geographical, national, and cultural borders. As the preceding sections have shown, Boland asserts agency, to use Boyce's (1994: 37) words, as she "crosses, journeys, migrates, and so re-claims as it re-asserts". The positive effects of conceiving 'agency' in such a way have been well theorised by Foley et al. (1995: 10), who argue when discussing contemporary women's poetry:

> Relations between the construction of 'gender' and 'colonialism' are seen to throw into crisis the identity-thinking which characterises the ideologies of patriarchy, imperialism and bourgeois nationalism, the apprehension of

> these relations may be at least potentially productive of a more fluid and politically versatile sense of identity, one which can be used more effectively as an agent of resistance.

Boland's act of resistance lies precisely in showing that all forms of identity politics are authoritarian and restrictive. Her poetry constantly shows how any act of representation already involves a simplification and misrepresentation. By suggesting that any process of rendering an image is itself erroneous, Boland dismantles imperialist, nationalist, and feminist representations. As she has argued, real artistic decolonisation lies in the poet's ability to carry out an "anti-authoritarian exploration of identities of place and margin as against the set texts of canon and nation" (Boland 1996a: 139). It is here where the woman poet finds a productive place to exert her agency, without imposing her own artistic images as more 'real' and 'truthful' representations.

4.4. An 'authentic' Irish past which cannot be grasped

4.4.1. Introduction

As Fanon (1990: 180) puts it, the final stage of writing in the decolonisation process goes "against the current of history", for the writer decides to embody history in his/her own person, a history formerly defined both by imperialists and nationalists alike. Similarly, Boland at this stage denounces the absence of women from official historical records (whether English or Irish). National literature is, according to her, an accomplice in this enterprise, not only because it has simplified women as emblems, but also because it has deprived women of a real past, "women whose silence [Irish poets] should have broken" (Boland 1995a: 153). In this sense, Boland feels bound to rewrite a true version of Ireland's past, to right the "violation" that both history and art have exerted on Irish women.

In order to understand Boland's approach to this issue, it is essential to consider the distinction that she makes between history and the past:

In my own case, when I was young, one of the real shaping influences was my gradual discovery of the difference between the past and history. In Ireland, there's a wide and instructive distance between those two. I believe history is an official version of events – it is itself a constructed narrative. But the past, at least as I came to see it, is a place of silences and losses and disappearances. That gap, that distance between those two narratives – and my own gradual understanding of it – has been a powerful motive for me to make certain arguments and to challenge certain concepts. (Interview with Villar Argáiz)

In this sense, Boland views history as an imposed narrative constructed at the expense of the sufferings and silences of those neglected voices that existed in the past. One of her main objectives is to attack narrow versions of history and re-tell those historical events which have previously obliterated women's lives and experiences, in order to include them. That is why women's involvement in Irish historical events such as emigration and the Great Famine becomes almost an obsession in her work.[38]

Before focusing on how Boland's work attempts to bring womanhood from the margins to the centre of history, some explanation is needed about the ways in which women's real past has been obliterated from official historical and literary records, in order to gain some insight into the reasons which prompt this woman poet to rewrite their history. The private lives of women have generally seemed to be irrelevant to historians. Women have been absent in historical accounts, because theses accounts were almost exclusively concerned with events whose protagonists were admired male heroes, influential politicians, rebellious peasants, and revolutionary workers, among others. Well-known women writers (such as Jane Austen, Charlotte Brontë, George Eliot, and Virginia Woolf) have self-consciously explored the ways in which history as a 'master' narrative has only indirectly affected women because it has been mainly concerned with external issues "never experienced at first hand in the privatised lives of women" (Gilbert & Gubar: 2000: 132-133). As they have been denied a place in history, they tend to see this hegemonic masculine history "from the disillusion and disaffected perspective of the outsider" (p. 134).

As outsiders in history, women writers find the need to search for their own stories, so that they make their own contribution to official accounts. Mohanty (1991a: 34) has argued that a central concern of postcolonial literature by women is "to rewrite and remember history". This process is significant not only for correcting the empty spaces and misrepresentations of a male-dominated history, but also "because the very practice or remembering and rewriting leads to the formation of politicised consciousness and self-identity" (ibid). In this sense, women's potential to rewrite and invent their past responds to a desire to define their reality as women. The quest for history is, therefore, a quest for self-definition, for self-assertion: knowing their origins is essential for explaining their identity. As Cixous (1981: 252) states, "in woman, personal history blends together with the history of all women, as well as national and world history". In this sense, women writers, mostly at their final stage of artistic decolonisation, have been compelled "to rediscover the past anew" (Showalter 1999: 11-12). On their journey towards self-definition as women, they begin a process of remembering the lost mothers, their silences, sufferings, and struggles to survive. Woolf's imaginary story about Shakespeare's sister, Judith Shakespeare, in *A Room of One's Own* (1974: 70-73) and Walker's essay "In Search of Our Mothers' Gardens" (1983) are two significant examples of this trend.

4.4.2. The dangers of presenting oneself as a spokesperson

With the painful realisation that women have been absent from the pages of history, Boland's poetry moves towards the possibility of speaking on behalf of a lost and unrecorded Irish community, mostly female. When approaching this aspect of Boland's work, we should consider the risks involved in her becoming a representative of a women's community. One of the central problems that has emerged from postcolonial and feminist debates is that of representation. The difficulty for women writers to speak 'on behalf' of their oppressed 'sisters' has been addressed by Boyce (1994: 36), who argues the following when discussing Black women's writing:

Scholarship and theoretical writing by Black women, because they exist in an academic context, have become distant and removed from the day-to-day lives of most people. But it is not only the fact of the critic distantly removed from the people which is the issue, but the ways in which Black women as writers, academics, teachers, who live lives of multiple oppression, still end up paradoxically unintelligible to those who are unschooled in critical discourses and also to those who are.

Because of the dangers of misrepresentation that such an act entail, Boland's poetic ventriloquism has been highly contested. As McCallum (2004: 41) has argued, questions of authenticity in the criticism of Boland's verse result from the risk that critics run nowadays in laying claim to Irishness and Ireland:

[A]ll poets who address their nation's history and culture – even Seamus Heaney, whose Irishness has not been called into question in the same manner – face charges of being voyeuristic or opportunistic in their choice of subject and must confront the technical difficulty and ethical question of how, as an individual, one can speak convincingly to history and for a people.

Several critics have questioned Boland's right to be the speaking witness of Irish women's past. Fulford (2002a: 215) has acknowledged the danger of misrepresentation involved in Boland's project. As this critic asserts, using Bhabha's terminology, "[s]peaking for marginal voices or the subaltern carries with it the difficulty of how to make this a malleable or performative articulation, rather than just another pedagogical formation of identity and temporality" (ibid). Meaney (1993: 139) and Longley (1994: 188) have also criticised Boland on the grounds that, by acting as a spokesperson, the woman poet repeats the political nationalist discourse. According to Meaney (1993: 139), "the relationship between poet and community" characteristic of the nationalist tradition recurs in Boland's poetry, for she constantly tries to bear witness, to speak on behalf of a lost community of women. Meaney's (1993: 140) main argument is that, by acting as a spokesperson, Boland undermines difference, because "nationality, gender, or indeed womanhood" do not have "the same meaning" for all women.[39]

Being aware of accusations such as this, Boland has recently defended herself by arguing that she is not interested in being representative (interview with Villar Argáiz). Nevertheless, her poetry comes worryingly close to surrogating that nationalist discourse attempting to speak on behalf of a nation. Although, as we will see, Boland will show the difficulty involved in any act of recovering the past, her work is moulded according to an "ethical" imperative that demands the poet to chronicle accurately, without simplifying. For Boland (1995a: 127), every poet must make an "ethical choice": "what he or she nominates as a proper theme for poetry, what selves poets discover and confirm through [their] subject matter".[40] Furthermore, Boland believes that "[a]ll good poetry depends on an ethical relation between imagination and image. Images are not ornaments; they are truths [...]. [If] the image is distorted, the truth is demeaned" (p. 152). Therefore, Boland's objective is "to formalise the truth", that is to say, to recover the silences of Irish women in the past (Boland 1995a: xv). By relying on the 'truthfulness' of images, Boland seems to suggest that the poet has the ability to grasp the 'real', a project akin to the one she carried out in *In Her Own Image*. Because of Boland's statement that poetry has the ethical function to transmit 'truth', Haberstroh (1996: 88-89) has remarked that "for all the emphasis on Boland as a new and different voice, she is in many ways a very traditional poet, a judgement that I do not think she would object to" (Quoted in Hagen & Zelman 2004: 91).

Boland's belief in the existence of a 'truth' that the female poet must be able to bring to the surface of her work is observed in "Envoi", a poem included in *The Journey and Other Poems*. This poem seems to justify Meaney's (1993: 139) critique that Boland perpetuates the nationalist rhetoric in her reliance on the conventional relation between the poet and his/her community. As regards linguistic techniques and poetic content, this poem stands as an exception in Boland's mature phase. First of all, in contrast to the unfolding language and melancholic loose movement between stanzas of most of the poems in *The Journey*, "Envoi" is composed of very short sentences (such as those found in *In*

Her Own Image) which make the speaker's message clear and straightforward. Secondly, it is perhaps the only mature poem where Boland regards the male sex as what Woolf (1974: 139) would call "the opposing faction". Even though her mature work ultimately rejects the negative consequences of adopting a separatist stance, in this poem Boland emphasises the dichotomy between male poetry and her own work:

> My muse must be better than those of men
> who made theirs in the image of their myth. [...]
>
> She must come to me. Let her come
> to be among the donnée, the given.
> I need her to remain with me until
> the day is over and the song is proven.
>
> Surely she comes, surely she comes to me –
> no lizard skin, no paps, no podded womb
> about her but a brightening and
> the consequences of an April tomb.
>
> What I have done I have done alone.
> What I have seen is unverified.
> I have the truth and I need the faith.
> It is time I put my hand in her side.
>
> If she will not bless the ordinary,
> if she will not sanctify the common,
> then here I am and here I stay and then am I
> the most miserable of women. (*Collected*, 150-151)

In this poem, Boland grants herself permission to bear witness to women's ordinary lives in poetry. This is an authoritative speaker casting herself as a messenger who apparently distinguishes herself as a bard: she is a "donnée", a "given". Like those figures in "Solitary" and "Exhibitionist", the narrator is alone in her task: she and only she knows the "truth". Notions such as the 'real' are no longer scrutinised and poetry does not stand as an ambiguous and contradictory terrain. In contrast to poems such as "The Women", the speaker seems to have united the words 'woman' and 'poet' without difficulty. The use of imperatives, the repetition of adverbs such as "surely" and first person pronouns, typical linguistic features of *In Her Own Image*, both place emphasis on what the speaker is saying, and highlight her assurance and confidence. The only difference from those feminist voices in Boland's second phase is that the speaker now clearly rejects praising the sensuality of the female body. She refuses to see her muse in bodily terms, discarding the "lizard skin", her "paps", and "podded womb". Although by doing so, she moves away from a poetry conceived in strictly biological terms, Boland nonetheless adopts the radical feminist stance that she generally rejects in her mature work. The speaker of "Envoi" advocates the superiority of her female muse, and therefore perpetuates the difference between sexes that patriarchal tradition has maintained. In this sense, while Boland's tendency is to reject notions of superiority and inferiority, poems such as this one instinctively praise women's extraordinary qualities of seeing what is "unverified". This self-adulation and superiority may be needed in a country where women have traditionally been on the margins of both history and literature. By blessing the ordinary and sanctifying the common, Boland stands as a spokesperson of those realities omitted in official accounts, those "wretched of the earth" as Fanon (1990) would put it. Boland's "ethical choice" (1995a: 127) is nonetheless risky. In the Irish poetic tradition, the trope of Mother Ireland has become an essential figure in a political discourse where the poet is a spokesperson for the community. Boland reiterates the process by suggesting that she is the only one who can speak on behalf of a lost and undervalued female community.

Despite the radicalism of poems such as "Envoi", it is important to note that Boland has acknowledged, both in her prose work and in her poetry, her limitations when acting as a spokesperson, something that critics such as Longley (1994: 188) and Meaney (1993: 140) have ignored. As Hagen and Zelman (2004: 6), have argued, Boland's "poems are not merely about the past, but about the investigator and the limits of investigation as well". In order to study this aspect of her work, I will turn to Spivak and her controversial assertions in "Can the Subaltern Speak?" as regards the impossibility of recovering the "native voice" (1994).[41] As we will see, this postcolonial critic implies that there is ultimately no possibility for the poorest and most marginalised community to make themselves known to anyone and themselves. Young (1992: 164) argues that this is Spivak's "most far-reaching argument of all"; indeed, this is not an exaggeration, for the theoretical implications of her formulations are extremely important.

Spivak's central concern in the essay is if the "lowest strata", the subaltern, can know and speak their conditions (Spivak 1994: 78). As Said (1988: v) explains, the word 'subaltern' is first coined by Gramsci in the *Prison Notebooks* (1947) in order to define the oppressed, the minority groups, in particular the proletariat and rural labour. Therefore, the term has political and intellectual connotations, and its implied opposite is 'dominant' or 'elite', that is, the groups in power. The (Indian) *Subaltern Studies* group has also employed the term to refer to non-elite sectors of Indian society (Young 1992: 160). The idea behind the *Subaltern Studies'* work is that orthodox and authoritatively national and institutional versions of history tend to consolidate highly disputable versions of the past into official identities, obliterating the reality of many men and women belonging to the lowest strata (Guha 1997: ix-xxii).

In invoking the subaltern, Spivak is influenced by Gramsci and the *Subaltern Studies* group. She uses the term to signify "the margins, […] men and women among the illiterate peasantry, the tribals, the lowest strata of the urban subproletariat" (Spivak 1994: 78). The subaltern is composed by those social groups at the bottom of the social scale, almost invisible to colonial and Third World national-bourgeois historiography alike.

"Can the Subaltern Speak?" starts from the premise that the subaltern, be it male or female, cannot know and speak their conditions, for they cannot criticise what they inhabit intimately (1994: 78). As Hall (1990: 222) explains, recent theories of enunciation suggest [...] that, though we speak, so to say 'in our own name', of ourselves and from our experience, nevertheless who speaks, and the subject who is spoken of, are never identical, never exactly in the same place.

Spivak is one of those theorists who stress the difficulties and contradictions in constructing a 'speaking position' for the subaltern. When Spivak claims that the subaltern "cannot speak", she means that, once they raise their voices, they would move from the margins to the centre, and thus, they would no longer occupy a subaltern status:

> If the subaltern were able to make herself heard [...] – as has happened when particular subalterns have emerged, in Antonio Gramsci's terms, as organic intellectuals and spokespeople for their communities – her status as a subaltern would be changed utterly; she would cease to be a subaltern. (Spivak 1994: 78)

In this sense, Spivak moves away from Foucault and Deleuze, who argue that the oppressed can act self-resistantly, can have full self-awareness and can speak for him/herself (p. 71). Spivak accuses them of having "an essentialist, utopian politics" (ibid).

Furthermore, Spivak argues that the subaltern as such cannot be heard by the privileged of either the First or Third World, on the grounds a culture can never be understood whose own references are so different (Spivak 1994: 84). One of her main arguments is that we cannot represent a culture whose historical past and origins have been damaged by the colonial encounter, and the possibility of dialogue or communication no longer exists (p. 80). Therefore, she is very critical of Ranajit Guha's *Subaltern Studies* project, which is based on the assumption that there is a 'pure' and 'essential' form of subaltern consciousness that can be recovered:

> The[ir] task of research [...] is to "investigate, identify and measure the *specific* nature and degree of the *deviation* of [the] elements [...] from the

ideal and situate it historically". "Investigate, identify, and measure the specific": a program could hardly be more essentialist and specific. (Spivak 1994: 80)

In this sense, Spivak suggests that the recovery of a subaltern voice is a kind of essentialist "fiction". Her main view is that one cannot construct an 'essentialist' category of the 'subaltern' without ignoring its inevitable heterogeneity (ibid). She believes that it is better to preserve the subaltern experience as an "inaccessible blankness", as an empty space, than to objectify it as the "Other" (p. 89). Therefore, a subaltern collective consciousness is impossible to grasp, and there is no determinate position from which they could speak.

Spivak's analysis focuses particularly on the figure of the female subaltern, who is described as doubly colonised both by economic marginalisation and by gender subordination (p. 82). The "sexed" female subaltern has been remoulded both as the object of imperialism and patriarchy (ibid). Everyone speaks for her and writes about her, and consequently, she is described as "even more deeply in shadow" (p. 83). For Spivak, the most marginalised people of all are those rural Indian women subject to sati, the widow's ritualistic self-sacrifice on her husband's funeral (p. 93). Even when "benevolent" Western outsiders attempt to speak on behalf of them, their project fails (p. 84). Spivak subjects this ostensible benevolence to rigorous critical scrutiny, as when she attacks First World feminism for ignoring the reality of Third World women (interview with Threadgold & Bartkowski 1990: 118). Furthermore, she argues that there is a danger in becoming what she calls "a native informant" (Spivak 1999: ix) and is very suspicious of the possibly benign identification with the subaltern, because subalternity is not a condition to be desired. As Papastergiadis (1997: 276-277) asserts, "[t]he subaltern condition cannot even bear the privilege of its own 'organic intellectuals'[…], as [Spivak] reminds us, to be in position to speak for the subaltern is both impossible and unenviable". Furthermore, Spivak ponders on the danger of acting as a spokesperson for the Third World, admitting that as an

Asian woman educated in India and in the US, she is usually considered as a suitable representative of the "Third World Woman" (interview with Gunew 1990: 63). "Clinging to marginality", she argues, runs the risk of homogenising and misrepresenting the reality of subaltern communities (Spivak 1993: 9).

"Can the Subaltern Speak?" has been highly controversial among postcolonial critics. Very few defend Spivak's formulations, for most postcolonial voices tend to stress the contradictions, as well as the imminent pessimism implicit in its formulations. Rey Chow (2003: 326-333) stands out as one of the few postcolonial voices who defends Spivak's argument. In "Where Have all Natives Gone?", Chow (2003: 326-329) complicates the possibility of finding an authentic 'native' voice. Such recovery, she contends, can end up perpetuating the construction of the native as an 'alien' category outside the 'standard' and 'normal' subject of Western modernity (p. 329). According to this critic, anti-imperialist texts which try to replace bad/inauthentic images with good/authentic images of the native will not solve this problem (p. 333). In this sense, Chow agrees with Spivak that it is impossible and undesirable to recover and/or discover the true native.

Nevertheless, the general tendency among postcolonial critics is to question and/or reject Spivak's formulations altogether. The fiercest critiques made of Spivak have been as regards her formulations on the subaltern agency. In fact, to assert that the subaltern cannot speak can dangerously be conceived as denying any possible resistant and self-liberating agency on the part of the most marginalised people. Moore-Gilbert (2000: 107) accuses Spivak of legitimising "political apathy" and of ignoring the numerous effective instances of subaltern's mobilisation, in particular subaltern women's emancipation. Parry (1987: 34) has similarly criticised the work of Gayatri Spivak (although her attack includes also Homi Bhabha and Abdul Jan Mohamed's theories), on the basis that "the protocols of their dissimilar methods act to constrain the development of anti-imperialist critique".[42] Furthermore, this postcolonial critic accuses Spivak of assigning absolute power to the imperialist discourse, and argues that the native woman can actually speak through multiple voices (p. 35). Similarly, Tiffin and Lawson (1994: 10) argue against those theories that state that the subaltern cannot speak, on the grounds that they ignore the extent to which the subalterns "*are speaking*" in much postcolonial literature. These critics locate subaltern agency in the hands of postcolonial writers who open up new liberating spaces by "engaging with canonical texts [and] rewriting not just the tradition but the episteme which underpins it" (ibid).

Realising the problems that her theoretical premises posit for any sort of subaltern active resistance, Spivak (1988a: 205) defends, contradicting some of her statements, what she calls an occasional "strategic" use of essentialism. Her notion of "strategic essentialism" has its antecedent in Fanon's defence of 'negritude' in *Black Skin, White Masks* (1991: 133-138) and in *The Wretched of the Earth* (1990: 179). Like Fanon, Spivak asserts that the construction of essentialist forms of 'native' identity is a legitimate and necessary stage in the process of decolonisation. Although she criticises the *Subaltern Studies* program, she nevertheless admits to being sympathetic to their project:

> To investigate, discover, and establish a subaltern or peasant consciousness seems at first to be a positivistic project – a project which assumes that, if properly prosecuted, it will lead to firm ground, to some *thing* that can be disclosed. (Spivak 1988b: 10)

Spivak suggests that the idea of a 'pure' and accessible subaltern history, although it is ultimately impossible, is a "necessary theoretical fiction", for it enables the critique of dominant colonial and national-bourgeois historical models (ibid). Thus, in contradiction to her view that essentialism is a trap, she reads the group's project as "a *strategic* use of a positivist essentialism in a scrupulously visible political interest" (Spivak 1988a: 205).

Boland's separatist stance in "Envoi" (*Collected*, 150-151) is certainly the result of adopting that "strategic essentialism" Spivak defends. Her attempt to recover the past of Irish women, those stories neglected by imperialist and nationalist historical accounts, resembles the work of the *Subaltern Studies* scholars. Like them, Boland becomes "a subversive historian" (Boland 1997b: 26). Said (1988: vi) had established an interesting analogy between the *Subaltern Studies* work and women's work, asserting that

> [a]s an alternative discourse then, the work of the Subaltern scholars can be seen as an analogue of all those recent attempts in the West and throughout the rest of the world to articulate the hidden or suppressed accounts of numerous groups – women, minorities, disadvantaged or dispossessed groups, refugees, exiles, etc.

For Boland, who as an Irish woman poet attempts to recover women's contribution in history, this strategic use of essentialism has tremendous implications, because it opens up the possibility of fighting back, even if this means perpetuating, as she does in "Envoi", the binary logic male vs. female muse.

Nevertheless, Boland's poetry emphasises more the poet's powerlessness to recover the "subaltern" than her ability to do so. Like Spivak (1994: 83), who describes the gendered colonial subject as "deeply in shadow", Boland frequently characterises women from the Irish past as "shadows". Boland should be considered, according to this critic, as "a native informant" who is irremediably distant from the colonial past (Spivak 1999: ix). It is this distance between her present reality (as a woman poet) and an Irish (male and female) past that her mature work constantly highlights.

Boland consistently emphasises in prose accounts and interviews the limitations involved in presenting herself as a spokesperson. First of all, she feels that the recovery of women's past is inadequate, for it is impossible to recover what has already disappeared. We have observed in the previous section how Boland (1995a: 33-34) questioned her ability to record a life in a poem without simplifying or holding it fixed "in the cold rock". Nevertheless, it is not only simplification at stake. She also feels limited by the fact that she cannot make a statement about something which has been destroyed, "something which was already a statement of random and unsparing destruction" (ibid). That is why she always refers to Ireland's past as an "unreachable" and an ungraspable terrain (interview with Villar Argáiz). Secondly, Boland believes that "[n]o artist can really represent their past. They can only represent their own view of it" (interview with Villar Argáiz). The poet's view, as her poetry constantly exemplifies, is always partial and incomplete, for no one can ultimately offer a final and viable version of what really happened. As Boland has recently argued, "[w]hat you construct from your past is usually a process of selection rather than a construction; there is no actual model on which to build a past or a present" (interview with Villar Argáiz). In this sense, Boland's historical sense is selective, and as such, it requires the acceptance of some stories as valid, and the discrimination of others as invalid. Thirdly, Boland has acknowledged that, by recovering women's reality, she runs the risk of objectifying and simplifying it, as national literature has done in Ireland. For Boland (1995a: 178), there is a "real danger" in taking a private emblem (i.e. any woman of the past), because it "immediately takes on communal reference against a background of communal suffering". This is a way of aestheticising violence and defeat, as the nationalist tradition in Ireland has done, which Boland sharply criticises in her attack on the Irish political poem. In this sense, Boland faces the following problem: in taking any "subaltern" woman as an emblem of an Irish past, she runs the risk of turning her into "a communal reference", what would irremediably erase her distinctiveness and individuality. As she wonders in *Object Lessons*, how can we prevent "the difficult 'I' of perception [from becoming] the easier 'we' of a subtle claim"? (Boland 1995a: 178).

The answer to this question lies in Boland's ability to become a powerless poetic voice rather than a powerful and authoritarian one. Boland discards the idea of the Irish poet as a subject gifted with an inherited power of expression, an idea that goes back to that bardic belief that "poetry and privilege [are] inflexibly associated" (Boland 1995a: 191). Boland does not seek her authority as a poet from a privileged or historical stance. Much the contrary, her poetic subjects always stand out for their limitability of access, for their inability to bridge that gap between past and present. Instead of writing "from the centre, with the whole weight of authority and bardic force behind", Boland decides to "displace that centre" and write from the "margin" (interview with Villar Argáiz). In this sense, Boland puts into practice Spivak's belief that "[i]n seeking to learn to speak to (rather than listen to or speak for) the historically muted subject of the subaltern woman, the postcolonial intellectual *systematically* 'unlearns' female privilege" (Spivak 1994: 91). This lack of privilege and powerlessness is in itself a subversive strategy. In fact, Boland's vulnerable, marginalised, and fragile poetic self allows her to change those foundational parameters on which Irish poetry has been based. The woman poet dismantles that nationalist discourse which encouraged the subject to be representative and the object to be ornamental. Bhabha (1995: 148) believes that being "historically displaced", suffering from a "social ellipsis", is positive rather than negative, for it allows the colonial and/or gendered subject to occupy a marginal position from which to contest fixed forms of national narratives. Boland is one of these marginal voices for whom historical exclusion becomes a source of resistance. As she states, "I have never felt I owned Irish history; I have never felt entitled to the Irish experience. There have been Irish poets who have written the political poem with exactly this sense of ownership and entitlement" (Boland 1995b: 487). Boland's marginalisation from historical accounts allows her to subvert the traditional Irish political poem that inspired the poet to act as an "envoy [...] of dispossession" (ibid). It is her position of powerlessness, of 'subalternity' as an Irish woman, which enables her to write a more truthful political poem.

In order to observe how Boland's poetry reflects a powerless poetic speaker, who, in Spivak's (1994: 91) words, "unlearns [her] privilege" when attempting to recover a subaltern history, I will discuss some significant poems from *Outside History* (1990). This volume of poetry is notable for its emphasis on the speaker's disconnection with, her physical and spiritual distance from, the

Irish past. A significant feature of *Outside History* is its obsessive repetition of words such as "shadow(s)" and "distance(s)": for Boland past figures only appear as shadows and she is irremediably distant from them. Although these references had already appeared in *The Journey* and they continue in later volumes of poetry, their use are not as reiterative as in *Outside History*. In fact, Boland has recorded that her project of "writing about the lost, the voiceless, the silent" and "exploring [her] relation to them" started in *Outside History*, whereas the previous volumes were mainly concerned with "artistic experimentation" (interview with Allen-Randoplh 1993b: 129).

One of the poems in which Boland highlights her difficulty of access to the Irish past is "Our Origins Are in the Sea" (*Collected*, 192-193). This poem centres around the speaker's grandfather, who drowned in the Bay of Biscay. This figure stands as a metonymy of an Irish past unrecorded within historical accounts. The poem begins by focusing on the distance between the speaker and this subaltern reality:

> I live near the coast. On these summer nights
> the dog-star rises somewhere near the hunter,
> near the sun. I stand at the edge of our grass.
>
> I do not connect them: once they were connected –
> the fixity of stars and unruly salt water –
> by sailors with an avarice for landfall. (*Collected*, 192)

In contrast to what Boland has accustomed her readers to expect, she is not depicted in movement and she uses the present tense in order to suggest motionlessness and a well-established location. The dog-star is the turning point for reflecting on a past life, the life of those sailors who were able to read the constellations in the sky. Boland attempts to recover the lived experience of this subaltern reality. Spivak (1993: 228) has argued that attempts such as this are bound to fail, because the metropolitan lifestyle that postcolonial literature records is different from the subaltern experience in the colony. In fact, "Our Origins Are in the Sea" records a contemporary subaltern woman who, although she lives "near the coast", has not experienced sailing the "unruly salt water". From where she stands, as the speaker later argues, "the sea is just a rumour" and the only stars she can see are those "put out by our streetlamp" (ibid). Whereas sailors were able to connect "the fixity of stars and unruly salt water", the speaker can "not connect them". As a suburban woman, she is grounded in a certain place, a place where light and seawater are well separated. Unable to share this ability, the speaker is not only excluded from the Irish past, but she also stands as an inappropriate spokesperson for her grandfather's story:

> And how little
>
> survives of the sea-captain in his granddaughter
> is everywhere apparent. Such things get lost. (*Collected*, 192)

Distant from a past that directly affects her, Boland is unable to go back to her roots, to recover what is "lost". The very title dismantles those myths of 'origin' on which all sorts of identities are based. There is no origin as such: and only water is what the speaker finds on her journey towards her own past, her own roots. But Boland is also suggesting something else. For her, the past is as difficult to grasp as the water of the ocean her grandfather navigated: it is fluid and constantly dissolving just as the speaker tries to recover it. Here, once again, the possibility of recovering a subaltern subject is lost and overdetermined.

Boland's use of constellations recurs in recording an Irish past which, although visible to the speaker, remains largely unnoticed by historians. In "Outside History", Boland is drawn, as the title indicates, to those marginal voices that are occluded from national accounts:

> There are outsiders, always. These stars –
> these iron inklings of an Irish January,
> whose light happened

thousands of years before
our pain did: they are, they have always been
outside history. (*Collected*, 188)

The stars that the speaker sees in the night constellations, an allegory of the dying victims of the Great Famine, are remote and distant from her own reality. They suggest the separation between present and past. Time and space separate the speaker from these stars, whose light was radiated "thousands of years before", and which are located at a great distance for her. In this sense, the speaker continues to be far away from this reality, as she makes explicit in the final lines of the poem:

How slowly they die
as we kneel beside them, whisper in their ear.
And we are too late. We are always too late. (Ibid)

The existence of final short sentences or clauses, sometimes beginning in motion with the conjuction 'And', is a very characteristic feature of Boland's mature style.[43] Like in "The Achill Woman" (*Collected*, 177), Boland is able to hear those "songs crying out their ironies", in this case, a soft voice coming from the past. Nevertheless, these are only whispers, and even worse, she ultimately fails to establish any sort of communicative exchange. Boland is "always too late" to answer back, to solve those injustices committed by constrained versions of history.

The final line of "Outside History" becomes the title of another poem in *Outside History*. In "We Are Always Too Late", Boland recounts a scene of a woman weeping at a New England coffee shop. Her way to go back to this remembrance is a dual process of returning and reconstructing:

Memory
is in two parts.

First, the re-visiting:

the way even now I can see
those lovers at the café table. She is weeping. (*Collected*, 186)

On her journey towards this local memory, Boland describes the background setting as well: a winter landscape of white pines in which the snow gradually loses its balance on the branches and falls down. Deciding to enter the scene, Boland walks away from her own table and approaches the woman.

Then

the re-enactment. Always that –
I am getting up, pushing away
coffee. Always, I am going towards her.

The flush and scald is
to her a forehead now, and back down to her neck. (Ibid)

By entering the scene, Boland focuses on the woman more closely. Her emotional excitement is perceived physically on her forehead and neck. Whereas in her first re-visiting she described the scene more superficially, by going back a second time she is able to see the woman almost in her totality. It is as if the speaker can understand the woman's sorrow. Having eventually arrived at the scene, the narrator, now close to the woman, addresses her with the intention to relieve her grief:

I raise one hand. I am pointing to
those trees, I am showing her our need for these
beautiful upstagings of
what we suffer by
what survives. And she never even sees me. (Ibid)

Boland attempts to tell her that her suffering, although private and personal, is insignificant. Like that snow that is falling and constantly changing the outside landscape, this woman's grief is only temporal, and what will "survive" will be rather more important things. As Foster (1999: 10) explains, Boland "offers the possibility of renewal, an awareness that our own plight is not the universe". Nevertheless, her proximity to this woman is only an illusion. The fact that the woman does not even look at the speaker, indicates that she cannot eventually help and instruct her. The poem finishes with Boland's characteristic "tag-line", an afterthought that reformulates the previous meaning (Foster 1999: 10). Although the speaker has knowledge, she cannot communicate it to her intended addressee, and so, Boland's poetic authority is undermined. The speaker is, once again, "too late" to carry out any significant change, to retrieve that scene and address the woman again. As Spivak (1988a: 253-254) has argued, "whatever the advisability of attempting to "identify" (with) the other as subject in order to know her, knowledge is made possible and is sustained by irreducible difference, not identity". Any attempt to grasp this difference would inevitably perpetuate the homogenising views of identity defended by imperialism and nationalism, and would therefore hinder the process of decolonisation. It is this "irreducible difference" that separates Boland from this woman in the New England café. The poem finishes with the speaker's failure to communicate with the woman, but this failure is in itself Boland's own recognition that, despite our knowledge and wisdom, one cannot totally advise the 'Other' in our own terms. This woman's grief is too private for anyone to claim that he or she has the right and eventual solution, the remedy to relieve her pain.

As poems such as "We Are Always Too Late" exemplify, Boland favours the movement from an apparent ability to connect with the (Irish) past to an ultimate impossibility to do so. In fact, Boland's inability to act as a spokesperson is constantly emphasised in the poems from *Outside History*. In "Midnight Flowers", lilacs and fuchsias stand as "subtexts" of a "subaltern" and unrecorded past: they are located at "the margins of light" and "they have no roots" (*Collected*, 193). In an attempt to record them within her poem, Boland walks towards them, but she cannot ultimately establish a connection: "I reach out a hand; they are gone" (ibid). The very title of poems such as "Distances" and "What We Lost" draw us into those gaps that Boland encounters between past and present, recovery and representation (*Collected*, 187, 199). Phrases like "what we lost", "get lost", "such a loss for now", "nothing more", "nothing to look forward", and "elegy", recur throughout *Outside History* (pp. 187, 168, 192). Rather than bridging those gaps by "the possible corruptions of invention" (Boland 2001c: 14), Boland decides to leave the past ungraspable. In poems such as "On the Gift of 'The Birds of America' by John James Audubon" and "A Different Light", she specifies that her view is particular, and that others might have another different opinion, by using constructions such as "from this angle anyway" or "it seemed" (*Collected*, 168, 195). Undermining the traditional power of the poet's (male) gaze to immortalise his images in visual representation, Boland never states with assurance, she only suggests, without imposing her assertions as transcendental truisms. As has been hinted at earlier on, Boland conceives poetry as a terrain where she can express her own ambiguities and contradictions, not as a place to exert her own authority. That is why her poems are loaded with questions indicating uncertainty and sentences that indicate that the speaker lacks access to knowledge. Foucault and the French poststructuralist model on the relationship between discourse, knowledge, and power are significant in this respect. Foucault (1980: 196) has explained the link between power and discourse as follows:

> The apparatus is [...] always inscribed in a play of power, but it is also always linked to certain coordinates of knowledge which issue from it but, to an equal degree, condition it. This is what the apparatus consists in: strategies of relations of forces supporting, and supported by, types of knowledge.

Foucault shows that the establishment of knowledge and academic disciplines is never innocent, because knowledge always engenders power, not only by determining specific inclusions but also by reinforcing overt and covert exclusions (Lewis & Mills 2003: 1). Boland's poems, mostly in *Outside History*, constantly show a poetic speaker who lacks sufficient knowledge of what she is talking about. By doing so, Boland avoids entering what Foucault would call "the apparatus", and adopts an anti-authoritarian poetic stance which does not lead to exclusion or seclusion. In this sense, whereas an adverb such as "perhaps" is recurrent in poems such as "White Hawthorn in the West of Ireland", "In Exile", and "Doorstep Kisses" (*Collected*, 180, 185, 194), other poems display more explicitly how the speaker is not in command of the experience she is talking about: "no way now to know what happened then" ("The Black Lace Fan my Mother Gave me", *Collected*, 165) or "I never knew" ("In Exile", *Collected*, 185). It is also significant how the word "truth" does not appear a single time in *Outside History*, in contrast to the profusion of this word in previous volumes such as *The Journey*. It seems that, as Boland's mature work progresses, the woman poet is gradually "unlearn[ing her] privilege", as Spivak (1994: 91) would argue, in her attempt to speak on behalf of Ireland's history and its women.

This volume's emphasis on a defeated and powerless poet who is unable to retrieve Ireland's past is in itself a subversive strategy. Boland (1995a: 129) has argued that, by creating "archive[s] of defeat", her poems try to dismantle the belief the Irish poem must record action, resistance and "a diagram of victory". As she has argued, the problem with much Irish poetry is that it transformed the losses into victories, and rephrased the humiliations as triumphs. This betrays Ireland's history, for

[a]t a far deeper level – and here the Achill woman returns – [the Irish experience] was about defeat. The coffin ships, the soup queues, those desperate villagers in the shoreline – these things had actually happened. The songs, persuasive, hypnotic, could wish them away. Poetry could not. (Boland 1995a: 130)

Boland's vulnerable and defeated poetic selves stand in direct opposition to those authoritarian nationalist voices which claim to speak on behalf of the "imagined community" Anderson (1983) talks about. Unlike Daniel Corkery in *The Hidden Ireland* (1924), Boland is not a spokesperson for "a pure, untouched and somehow golden land of saints and scholars" (interview with Villar Argáiz). Hers is not a "pure Ireland", but rather an Ireland which cannot be grasped, an Ireland whose heterogeneous reality and "fragmentations" stand beyond the poet's artistic representation (ibid). By showing her inability to recover an Irish "subaltern" reality, Boland avoids simplifying it. Furthermore, only by recording her powerlessness and failure when attempting to go back, can her poems offer "a more accurate inscription", as she says in "The Making of an Irish Goddess" (*Collected*, 179), of an Irish history of defeat and agony.

Therefore, Boland's inability to recover a native voice, rather than a failure (as most contesters to Spivak's theories would argue) is an achievement. Speaking for "a lost consciousness that cannot be recovered" (Young 1992: 164), allows Boland to avoid simplification, to subvert the traditional assumptions on which canonical poetry has been based, and also, funnily enough, to draw us into a past of defeat that parallels the speaker's failure. In her recent introduction to an anthology of German women poets who reflect the devastation of World War II in their poetry, Boland (2004: 5) expresses her belief that "[i]t is the very powerlessness of these [women] which becomes, with hindsight, both a retrieval system and a searing critique of power". In the following section, I will continue demonstrating with the critical example of Boland's poetry, how the powerlessness that Spivak ascribes to the postcolonial writer is, rather than politically ineffective, highly subversive. By recording that only 'silences' is what she encounters on her journey towards the past, Boland is able to dismantle those 'authoritarian' (imperialist and nationalist) languages that claim to be able to "speak of and for something" (interview with Villar Argáiz).

4.4.3. Silence as a politically effective strategy

4.4.3.1. In search of a new language

Boehmer (1995: 234) has argued that postcolonial writers at times introduce to their work an "*un*translatable strangeness". According to this critic, this obscurity of the postcolonial text is due to the mingling of traditional indigenous and

European forms which makes it strange both to Western and Eastern eyes. But this "*un*translatable strangeness" can also refer to the fact that postcolonial writers face a troubling limitation when attempting to express themselves within the imperial language. Ashcroft, Griffiths and Tiffin (2002: 82-83) refer to this aspect when explaining how, due to this "linguistic displacement", the postcolonial writer struggles with language in order to overcome the inarticulacy and the silence imposed on him/her by the imperial centre. Even though postcolonial writers have "the literal freedom to speak", they can find themselves "languageless" and constrained by the imposition of the English language.

It is precisely this point that Deane emphasises in "Dumbness and Eloquence: A Note on English as We Write it in Ireland". In this essay, Deane (2003: 114) argues that "Irish writing in the English language" has been, and still is, "obsessed with the problems involved in the idea of representation", how to record in a creditable way an Irish community or communities that are supposed to have always been misrepresented. The English language seems to be "ultimately insufficient for the purpose[s] of representation": whereas it provides a "[m]etropolitan sophistication and eloquence", there is also a native aspect, an "index of authentic feeling", which is left inarticulate (ibid). Using psychoanalytic terminology, Deane (2003: 117-118) argues that the automatic "acquisition of language" that all human beings experience differs from the process of learning "a new language". For the colonised Irish, the acquisition of the English language leaves a vacuum that is impossible to verbalise: what he calls "the language of the unconscious" (p. 117).[44]

This endeavour to speak "the language of the unconscious", to express "an index of authentic feeling" as an Irish woman poet, is observed in Boland's work, because she is constantly attempting to find a proper language by means of which to articulate Ireland's past and her own contemporary and ordinary reality. For the woman poet, having a language of one's own is extremely important, for, as she argues, language is "home truth", that is, it gives her an identity, and illusion of belonging somewhere (Boland 1995a: 45). Nevertheless, Boland has always faced the loss of language, and this is the reason why she constantly "struggles with the Trojan horse of language", as Hagen and Zelman (2004: 53) put it. Boland (1995a: 55-56) has recorded how, when returning to Ireland after a long exile at the age of fourteen, she was tormented by a feeling of inadequacy as regards language and ownership:

> Language. At first this was what I lacked. Not just the historic speech of the country. I lacked that too, but so did others. This was a deeper loss; I returned to find that my vocabulary of belonging was missing. The street names, the meeting names – it was not just that I did not know them. It was something more. I had never known them. I had lost not only a place but the past that goes with it, the clues from which to construct a present self.

As we observe in this quotation, Boland describes herself as a young child profoundly marked by a sense of what is called "linguistic displacement" or "deterritorialisation", concepts that, as Ashcroft, Griffiths and Tiffin (2002: 10) and Lloyd (1993: 16) explain, involve the postcolonial writer's disjunction between place and language. As a more mature poet, Boland feels a similar linguistic dislocation. One of the problems she identifies within Irish poetry is "the odd and abrasive disjunctions between the Irish reality and the Irish poem" (Boland 1995a: 136). This disjunction between language and reality, between the sayable (poetic) and the unsayable (unpoetic), is well explained in an interview with Consalvo (1992: 96):

> In Ireland we've always had this terrible gap between rhetoric and reality. In the void between those two things some of the worst parts of our history have happened. The reality is that people have been wounded, murdered, degraded in this so-called freedom struggle. But the rhetoric grinds on relentlessly. It says that we are one nation, one territory. That we need to get the British out and resume the purity of Irish nationhood.

Boland's attempt to get to "the void between those two things", language and reality, is, as we will see, not an easy project. Deane (2003: 118) has argued that in Ireland, "the language of the real" is the Irish language, but that this language, especially for Irish writers with no knowledge of Gaelic, only "emerges as silence", "dumbness", and "aphasia". The English language is, for these writers, the only "language of the possible", but, as it stands in opposition to 'the real' (the reality conveyed in the native language), the English language is an "index of hypocrisy [and] moral vacuity" (pp. 118, 114). According to Deane (2003: 119), the "silence" of the Irish language "haunts" Irish literature.[45] Boland's inability to express herself within poetic language can be interpreted from this postcolonial perspective. Boland's silences, like her colleagues', can certainly respond to her own wish to express herself in the Irish language, her native tongue. In her prose account, Boland (1995a: 73) has insisted on how she had to do the General Certificate of the British System, because she had no knowledge of Gaelic. Nevertheless, Boland's situation as an Irish woman poet is more complex than that of male writers'. As an Irish woman, Boland has been doubly silenced: whatever the language used, Gaelic or English, there is a further vacuum, a silence inscribed within the very nature of poetic language itself. As Boland (1995a: 153) asserts, national literature has not only simplified women as emblems but it has deprived them of a past, and therefore, it has "silence[d]" them. In this sense, Boland's project is to break women's silences, to search for a poetic language that records women's reality in a more truthful way. Her concern is, as she asserts, to recover what the Irish poem has not grasped, that which has always been excluded (Boland 1996a: 146). For Boland, the "visible place", the final draft of the poem (what is heard, published, known) owes its existence to "the invisible one" (ibid). In order to study how Boland's poetry always attempts to make the "invisible" (or unsayable) "visible" (and therefore poetic), I will draw on Kristeva's "Revolution in Poetic Language" (1986a).

4.4.3.2. Recording the 'unpoetic': Boland's silences and dissonances

Boland's objective to articulate what has usually been unrecorded in Irish poetry is linked to Julia Kristeva's insistence on inserting the "semiotic" within the "symbolic" realm of the poem.[46] As Moi (1986: vi) has pointed out, Kristeva's project has been from the outset "[t]o think the unthinkable". In "Revolution in Poetic Language", Kristeva (1986a: 89-136) discusses (mostly following Freud's and Lacan's theories) how poetic discourse constantly crosses the "thetic" border between the symbolic linguistic realm and a semiotic unarticulated realm.[47] For Kristeva, the semiotic is the "feminine" and "enigmatic", that realm indifferent to language and "irreducible to its intelligible verbal translation" (p. 97). In contrast to the symbolic, the semiotic is prior to language (sign and syntax), and therefore, is not cognitive (ibid). It is a phase dominated by the space of the mother's body, what is called the *chora* (p. 93). The *chora* (a term borrowed from Plato's *Timaeus*) is defined by everything that precedes the symbolic: bodily eroticism, melodies, and maternal rhythms. Although Kristeva equates the semiotic and pre-Oedipal with femininity, she does not identify the 'feminine' with a biological woman or the 'masculine' with a biological man. The pre-Oedipal mother actually encompasses both 'masculinity and 'femininity'. In her emphasis on marginality, Kristeva defines the 'feminine' more in terms of "positionality" (occupying a position of marginality) than in terms of "essences" (Moi 1997: 112). On the other hand, the symbolic is used by Kristeva to refer to the paternal zone, an Oedipalised system regulated by the Law of the Father and "established through the objective constraints of biological (including sexual) differences and concrete, historical family structures" (Kristeva 1986a: 97). The symbolic is an order superimposed on the semiotic; in other words, it controls the various semiotic processes (p. 98). Whereas the semiotic maternal realm is unrepresentable, the symbolic phallic realm is always articulated (pp. 99-100).

Kristeva's main thesis is that, in poetry, the semiotic surpasses its boundaries and disrupts the symbolic realm: "In 'artistic' practices the semiotic – the precondition of the symbolic – is revealed as that which also destroys the symbolic" (Kristeva 1986a: 103). By transgressing the boundaries of the symbolic order, the poet is able to articulate what is usually unspoken. It is here where Kristeva locates resistance to the conventional (and symbolic) patriarchal culture through which we experience the world (p. 113).[48] The return of the semiotic is manifested, for example, in the 'marginal' discourse of avant-garde literature. Kristeva (1986a: 89) applies her theory to the texts of two early modernist poets: Mallarmé and Lautréamont. Their work provides, according to Kristeva, a more direct manifestation of the semiotic than is usually possible in more conventional symbolic representations. In their close involvement with the unconscious and the semiotic, these poets challenge the traditional gender divisions that are at the core of the symbolic. According to this critic, these marginal and repressed aspects of language surface in poetry by means of several techniques, techniques that happen to appear in Boland's poetry.

One of the ways by which the semiotic can surface within the symbolic is by means of negation, which involves the existence of a "death drive" (Kristeva 1986a: 120). The poet introduces a "death drive" that threatens to reduce the subject to non-existence, something that the symbolic order suppresses. As Kristeva (1986a: 120) argues,

> 'art' takes on murder and moves through it. It assumes murder in so far as artistic practice considers death the inner boundary of the signifying process. Crossing that boundary is precisely what constitutes 'art'. In other words, it is as if death becomes interiorised by the subject of such a practice; in order to function, he must make himself the bearer of death [...]. Through themes, ideologies, and social meanings, the artist introduces into the symbolic order an asocial drive.

The existence of this semiotic "death-drive" that would ultimately dissolve the identity of the subject is clearly observed in Boland's poetry. As we have seen in poems such as "Anna Liffey", "Time and Violence", and "A Woman Painted in a Leaf" (*Collected*, 230-239, 241-242), Boland's act of speaking always leads to death and absence. In this sense, Boland's 'self' in these poems (her 'Irishness' and 'womanhood') is always represented in terms of erasure.

Another way by which the *chora* is perceived within the symbolic realm of language is, according to Kristeva (1986a: 89) by "subversion", which implies the presence of an unfixed, volatile, and subversive writing subject, which she calls "the subject in process". This writer subverts the symbolic by means of "contradictions, meaninglessness, disruption, silences, and absences" (Moi 1986: 13).

This unfixed, volatile, and subversive writing subject, these silences, contradictions, and absences that Kristeva mentions, surface in Boland's poetry. One way to escape the symbolic is by means of adopting a subversive attitude towards the rationality of language. By means of silences and dissonant gaps, Boland creates what Fulford (2002a: 214) calls "a differential space" to counteract the authoritarian languages of nationalism and imperialism (which have in their own ways simplified and distorted women's reality). Boland's poetry constantly alludes to an "absence that cannot be written" with the effect of questioning the "authenticity" of imperialist and nationalist representations alike (ibid).

It is significant how Irigaray (1991: 176), like Kristeva, also conceives the 'feminine' as a category outside the symbolic, and therefore connected to silence: "in the most extreme moments of sensation, which still lie in the future, each self-discovery takes place in that area which cannot be spoken of, but that forms the fluid basis of life and language". As women remain outside "the father's discourse", their moment of articulation also occurs outside the very margins of language and, as such, it can only be grasped as "that strange word of silence" (p. 175). According to Irigaray, it is because of their fluid female sex that women turn out to be not only mysterious to the male, but also silent in the very moment when they attempt to express their inner selves/sensations.[49] Nevertheless, the main difference between both feminist critics is that whereas Irigaray refers to women more explicitly, Kristeva does not locate the "feminine" in terms of sex but, as we have seen, in terms of occupying a position of marginality. Rather than to her fluid sexuality, as Irigaray would say, Boland's silences and disruptions in language respond to the marginal position Kristeva refers to. The two constitutive aspects of Boland's identity, her 'Irishness' and her 'womanhood', have always been marginalised and oppressed, just like the semiotic realm, both in imperialist and nationalist accounts.

If one looks closely both at her prose accounts and her poetry, whenever Boland talks about 'Irishness' (in particular the Irish past) and 'womanhood' (women's experiences), they only stand as powerful metaphors for types of humiliation and types of silences. In this sense, Boland views these two categories more in terms of marginality, like Kristeva, and not in terms of essences. Throughout *Object Lessons*, Boland defines 'Irishness' and 'womanhood' by means of words such as "silence", "dispossession", and "suffering". She narrates how, when she set herself to write a poem, she came to the table with "an Irishness which was not bardic or historic but full of silences" (Boland 1995a: 114). For Boland, "silence" is what defines Irishness. The colonial attempts to define 'Irishness' are not adequate for Boland, for they are loaded with racist and distorted accounts that do not bear witness to the reality of the Irish. But these silences that Boland finds in 'Irishness' also recall women's silences, their omission from national and historical accounts. Later, Boland (1995a: 135) asserts that what unites Irishness and womanhood are their common features of dispossession and suffering: "The wrath and grief of Irish history seemed to me, as it did to many, one of our true possessions. Women were part of that wrath, had endured that grief". In an interview with Wilson (1990b: 84), Boland makes even clearer the explicit association between both terms: "Womanhood and Irishness are metaphors for one another. There are resonances of humiliations, oppression, and silence in both of them and I think you can understand one better by experiencing the other". Here, Boland seems to be uniting in the same description both sorts of colonialisms, the imperialistic and the patriarchal. Fulford (2002a: 205) is indeed right when she sharply criticises Boland for "eliding the differences between patriarchal victimisation and colonial exploitation". Nevertheless, Boland here is not only linking both forms of colonial oppression, she is also questioning the very nature of identity-making itself. Boland exposes the ways in which language has worked as a vehicle of oppression. Colonial and imperialist attempts to define the Irish as an inferior race have oppressed and silenced their reality. Similarly, nationalist attempts to heal the damage caused by imperialism in their construction of Irishness have fallen into the same trap. In a country that has suffered the colonial presence, the construction of a national identity has run the risk of reiterating the similar structures of oppression found in colonial and racist representations, by simplifying images of women in its literature. Boland's own way of defining womanhood and nationhood as 'silences' clearly shows how she tries to move away from authoritarian defining procedures, which could lead to further simplification and misrepresentation. By focusing on her inability to express herself within language, Boland avoids using her own poem as another form of oppression.

As early as *Night Feed* (1982), we start to perceive in poems such as "The Muse Mother", Boland's need to find another language which can express more truthfully women's ordinary world. The 'symbolic' language seems to be insufficient for the poet's purpose of describing, in this case, mother and daughter relationships. As Irigaray (1991: 39-40) has argued, the exclusively masculine symbolic world avoids the representation of "the relationship with the placenta", of that "first bodily encounter with the mother". Boland's desire is, therefore, to create a new language that gives voice to the relationship with the primitive mother, just as feminists such as Irigaray (1991: 160) advocate. In this poem, the speaker is standing, as is typical in Boland's poetry, inside her own house, watching from her window. Suddenly, she glimpses an ordinary scene: "a woman hunkering/ her busy hand/ worrying a child's face" (*Collected*, 102). The narrator is suddenly captured by the mother's gesture of wiping her child's face and taking him to her lap. Drawn to this 'vision', Boland attempts to create a poetic place that can shelter this scene:

> If I could only decline her –
> lost noun
> out of context,
> stray figure of speech –

from this rainy street

again to her roots,
she might teach me
a new language:

to be a sibyl
able to sing the past
in pure syllables,
limning hymns sung
to belly wheat or a woman –

able to speak at last
my mother tongue. (*Collected*, 103)

Whereas the poem starts with no enjambments between stanzas, at the end there are very strong enjambments and long unfolding sentences that parallel the speaker's melancholic tone. The poet's main purpose is to return to a "mother tongue", to a primitive language that gives voice to mother and child relationships. As Hagen and Zelman (2004: 54) explain, this language would express the routinised act of a mother cleaning her child's face; "it would connect past and present", by the common and ordinary rituals of motherhood. In this sense, this language is also connected with a subaltern world, an Irish "past", the speaker's "roots". Nevertheless, Boland faces the impossibility of her project. This new language stands out of her reach: it is a "lost noun/ out of context", a "stray figure of speech". In this sense, the language Boland aspires to belongs more to a semiotic realm than to a symbolic one, a pre-Oedipal space where, as Kristeva (1986a: 97) notes, mother and child are not separated. As Boland can only express herself within the symbolic language, she can only imagine what it would look like to be "able to speak at last/ my mother tongue". The presence of the conditional 'if' as well as modals such as 'could' and 'might' in the passage quoted above indicates that, for the speaker, recovery becomes a matter of conjecture. Boland can only, as she says in "Listen. This is the Noise of Myth", create a "sequence of evicted possibilities" (*Collected*, 154). She has no access to a more 'authentic' idiom, a language of "pure syllables". Her "roots" become as unstable and volatile as that rain that is constantly described in her poems. In this sense, she stands, once again, for an inappropriate spokesperson, an unsuitable "sibyl" of the women's past. In her rejection of an authoritative stance, she is at least, as a powerless poet, able to draw us into a language of 'silences' that expresses the vestiges of past lives.

Boland's interest in creating a woman's language of 'gestures', a past idiom of 'silences', is continued more strongly and consistently in poems such as "Fever" (*Collected*, 133-134). As in "Our Origins Are in the Sea", the woman poet attempts in this poem to come to terms not only with the Irish past but also with her family heritage. In particular, "Fever" focuses on Boland's grandmother, who died in a fever ward "leaving five orphan daughters behind" (Haberstroh 1996: 78). Haberstroh (1996: 215) notes that the new generation of women poets in Ireland is usually concerned with "the sacrifices that mothering demands". This trend among Irish women writers responds to a desire to counteract the conventional ideas of motherhood of the Irish national tradition, by presenting the hardships of women in raising their children alone and creating "a home without a man" (ibid). In fact, Boland's grandmother is an emblem which stands for all those women who struggled with great adversity in their lives. Her forgotten death represents the lost history of women's lives, ignored by the legacy of the Irish past. Both in her prose work and in poems such as "What We Lost", "Lava Cameo", and "How the Earth and All the Planets Were Created" (*Collected*, 187-188, 227-228, 303-304), Boland finds the need to remember her grandmother's life, for she realises that "the story of Irish history is not her story. [...] Inasmuch as her adult life had a landscape, it was made of the water her husband sailed on and not the fractured, much-claimed piece of earth she was born to" (1995a: 32). In this sense, as the *Subaltern Studies*' project, Boland's main objective in "Fever" is to recover those traces of a life that remain on the margins of imperialist and nationalist accounts. The first stanza significantly starts with the omission of the grammatical subject:

is what remained or what they thought
remained after the ague and the sweats
were over and the shock of wild flowers
at the bedside had been taken away (*Collected*, 133)

The absence of the noun phrase in the initial position is telling. On the one hand, the title "Fever" may be understood as the subject of the sentence: the contagious disease, the fever of the speaker's grandmother, is the only thing that was left after her death; her perishing only brought more infection and illness. On the other hand, the woman poet is deliberately omitting the subject in order to suggest that nothing has remained after her terrible death. In other words, there is no official evidence of her sufferings, her painful febrile condition. Even the "wild flowers" at her bedside, which could have been the only possible indication that someone cared for her, "had been taken away". From the very first stanza, the woman speaker makes explicit that the fever which killed her grandmother stands for a misplaced story, unrecorded by official accounts. The repetition of subjectless clause structures in subsequent stanzas indicates that Boland is constantly entering the past, in her obsession to bring back this local story.

Nevertheless, the poet's task is not only difficult but impossible as well, because, as Boland (1995a: 5) explains in *Object Lessons*, she tries to give evidence to "a woman I never knew and cannot now recover". As she later argues, "whenever I tried to find the quick meanings of my day in the deeper ones of the past, she interposed a fierce presence in case the transaction should be too comfortable, too lyric" (p. 171). The main problem Boland faces is that she finds no appropriate language to reconstruct her grandmother's past. As she argues in "Lava Cameo", this woman's story only stands as "a rumour or a folk memory,/ something thrown out once in a random conversation,/ a hint merely" (*Collected*, 227). Similarly, in "Fever", her grandmother's past only makes itself explicit to the speaker in spectral and phantasmagorical terms: "Names, shadows, visitations, hints/ and a half-sense of half-lives remain./ And nothing else, nothing more" (p.

134). Since Boland lacks the necessary facts to give an accurate description of her grandmother's experiences, she decides to reinvent her life:

> I re-construct the soaked-through midnights;
> Vigils, the histories I never learned
> to predict the lyric of; and re-construct
> risk; as if silence could become rage,
>
> as if what we lost is a contagion
> that breaks out in what cannot be
> shaken out from words or beaten out
> from meaning and survives to weaken
>
> what is given, what is certain
> and burns away everything that this
> exact moment of delirium when
> someone cries out someone's name. (*Collected*, 134)

Haberstroh (1996: 78) believes that these stanzas "probably" contain "Boland's most direct statement of intent". Indeed, these lines exemplify the poet's purpose to represent her grandmother and all the women from the past as more than simple "names, shadows, visitations". Her attempt to "re-construct the soaked-through midnights/ Vigils, the histories" of Irish women within the poem is connected to Kristeva's project of recording the semiotic within the symbolic. Her project is difficult, because, like the semiotic realm, women's past has not been recorded through language. Boland searches for a reality that lies outside the symbolic, a reality that "cannot be/ shaken out from words or beaten out/ from meaning". There is no information whatsoever on which to rely, and mixing facts, memories, rumour, and imagination are the only possible means Boland has to bring women's past into the present context of the poem: "And the way I build that legend now is the way I heard it: out of rumour, fossil fact, half memories […]. I must become a fictional interventionist" (Boland 1995a: 10). Rumours and half memories stand in contrast to the authoritarian language of British imperialism, Irish nationalism, and the Roman Catholic Church, 'languages' which, in their various forms, have simplified and distorted women's reality with images such as Hibernia, Mother Ireland, and the Virgin Mary. The fragmented pieces of information that Boland recovers seem to belong to a semiotic realm more than to a symbolic one. They recall the existence of an oral tradition which is connected to women's lives, and which, in Nuala Ní Dhomhnaill's (1992: 29) words, is more "in touch with the irrational" than with the rational aspect of language. Nevertheless, in spite of having access to these fragments of oral tradition, Boland cannot recover her grandmother's reality. She can only create a world of possibilities, "a pastiche of what is/ real and what is/ not", as the speaker in "Lava Cameo" argues (*Collected*, 227). Hagen and Zelman (2004: 5) explain that the kind of art Boland favours is "that which offers an air of conditionality and possibilities". In fact, as we have seen, conditional clauses are typical in Boland's evocation of the Irish past.[50] The reiterative presence of the hesitant 'as if' in "Fever" indicates the speaker's limitations in her act of re-enactment. Fiction and imagination do not guarantee recovery, and Boland's attempt "to cry out someone's name" in "Fever" inevitably leads to "silence" and "to what we lost". Nevertheless, and as Kristeva (1986a: 89) has pointed out, silence in artistic representation is one manifestation of the semiotic, and as such, it can subvert the symbolic. Furthermore, as Sarup (1993: 124) has explained, Kristeva also believes that "madness" together with poetry, is another "privileged moment" when the semiotic surpasses its boundaries and disrupts the symbolic. "Fever" not only ends with silence, but also with a woman's unreasonable and incoherent cry. The new language Boland speaks is uttered in a state of fever; it is full of anxiety and hallucinations. The lack of punctuation of the whole poem reinforces the state of uncontrolled excitement and emotion in which the speaker is immersed. By recording her grandmother's "silence" and "delirium", Boland's project is as subversive as Kristeva's, for she manages to "weaken/ what is given, what is certain", to counteract the 'certainty' and 'truthfulness' of colonial and nationalist narratives. The feminist postcolonial critic Chow (2003: 333) has suggested that silence, rather than a failure, is the best evidence of the existence of a subaltern female figure which has suffered imperialist and nationalist oppression:

> The native's victimisation consists in the fact that the active evidence – the original witness – of her victimisation may no longer exist in any intelligible, coherent shape. Rather than [...] restoring her to her 'authentic' context, we should argue that it is the native's silence which is the most important clue to her displacement.

By focusing on the 'silences' that she encounters on her journey towards the past, Boland is able to bring to the fore women's displacement in history. This is one of the benefits Boland encounters in her impossibility to retrieve the past: although unable to recover the life of her grandmother, she manages to show the deficiency of historical accounts. It is significant how the poem favours the movement from a personal to an impersonal voice, something typical in Boland's poetry as observed in "Lace" (*Collected*, 136-137). The repetition of "someone" at the end of "Fever" indicates not only Boland's difficulty to give a name, to consign an identity to the person who is crying out, but also her reluctance to define her poetic images. Poetic definition, as we have seen, runs the risk of being misrepresentative. On the other hand, silence can suggest the existence of another life, rather than categorise it.

Therefore, and with Kristeva in mind, Boland's poems focus on a female subjectivity and an Irish past which cannot be articulated in language. The very title of poems such as "The Unlived Life", "We Are Always Too Late", "What We Lost", and "Outside History" (*Collected*, 135-136, 186-188), indicate the inadequacy the female artist finds to represent reality by means of poetic language. This aspect of Boland's work has been unexplored within Irish criticism, with the exception of Meaney (1993) and Fulford (2002b). Meaney (1993: 150) has argued that gaps and silences occupy the centre of Boland's poems, as if there is something "which cannot be troped", put into language. Similarly, Fulford (2002b: 147) notes that Boland attempts to record a woman's time/space that is by implication ungraspable, and that in her poems "[d]isruptions in the syntax, usually in the form of a hyphen, offer the sense of a silent space being alluded to in the language [...] at moments when it is as if the poet swallows her own tongue" (ibid). In fact, the reiterative use of hyphens in Boland's poetry indicates an elusive meaning, the fact that Ireland's past cannot adequately be told within the symbolic.

As was hinted at in "Fever", Boland attempts to reconstruct an appropriate women's history by relying on the oral tradition. The importance of the oral tradition is acknowledged by other Irish women poets such as Nuala Ní Dhomhnaill (1992: 29), who praises it as follows:

> I love this aspect of our culture. It is one of the main things that drew me back to live here, after seven years on the shaughrawn. It is infinitely more exciting and much more a human challenge to live in a country which is even just intermittently in touch with the irrational than in one which has set its face resolutely against it.

Although both Ní Dhomhnaill (1992: 29) and Boland (1997/1998: 155) have acknowledged the inherent danger of the Irish oral tradition in denying the incorporation of the lives of women as being fit subject matter, they both believe that women's oral tradition stands as an appropriate medium to counteract the narratives of the Irish nationalist tradition. In "The Oral Tradition" (*Collected*, 131-133), Boland focuses on a local story she hears by chance in order to offer an alternative to traditional heroic tales. This poem starts by recalling the moment when, "at the end of a reading/ or a workshop or whatever", the speaker starts to reflect on the contrast between the poems she has just heard and the fragility of less sophisticated forms of oral expression:

> only half-wondering
> what becomes of words,
> the brisk herbs of language,
> the fragrances we think we sing,
> if anything. (*Collected*, 131)

For Boland, the oral tradition is far removed from the language of poetry. Whereas the written word is immortalised in poetry, the spoken word seems to disappear in the air. Not recorded within symbolic representation, the remnants of an oral tradition stand as cultural remains that can only be perceived, "if anything", as "fragrances", or as the speaker later says, "in the suggestion of a texture/ like the low flax gleam/ that comes off polished leather" (ibid). It is typical of Boland to record women's language in terms of texture. In "The Unlived Life", the speaker describes herself in the middle of a conversation about sewing with her neighbour. Their interaction revolves around "the texture of synthetics as compared/ with the touch of strong cloth/ and how they both washed" (*Collected*, 135). In "The Oral Tradition", Boland tries to capture a similar moment. The speaker, "only half-listening", suddenly overhears two women in conversation:

> Two women
> were standing in shadow,
> one with her back turned.
> Their talk was a gesture,
> an outstretched hand.
>
> They talked to each other
> and words like "summer"
> "birth" "great-grandmother"
> kept pleading with me,
> urging me to follow. (*Collected*, 131)

Women's oral tradition is described in terms of gestures ("an outstretched hand") rather than in symbolic terms. The speaker is magnetically attracted to the story of a woman giving birth to her son in an open field, because she feels that this story contains something which connects her with an Irish female past. Nevertheless, the fact that one of the speakers has her back turned to Boland advances the poet's exclusion from this conversation and her later impossibility to reconstruct this tale. Boland can only hear scraps and fragments of their talk: "summer", "birth",

and "great-grandmother". Nevertheless, in the following stanzas, these separated
words seem to be put finally in their context:

> "She could feel it coming" –
> one of them was saying –
> "all the way there,
> across the fields at evening
> and no one there, God help her,
>
> "and she had on a skirt
> of cross-woven linen
> and the little one
> kept pulling at it.
> It was nearly night ..."
>
> (Wood hissed and split
> in the open grate,
> broke apart in sparks,
> a windfall of light
> in the room's darkness)
>
> "...when she lay down
> and gave birth to him
> in an open meadow.
> What a child that was
> to be born without a blemish!" (*Collected*, 132)

Boland incorporates in the poem an important fragment of the women's
actual conversation. Nevertheless, the interruptive use of hyphens in the first
stanza and the flickering parenthesis in the story emphasise, as Johnston (1997:
199) explains, the vulnerability of her retelling. While the speaker tries to narrate
this story in her own words, she feels that something is lost in the process. Indeed,
as the woman from the past lifts her son from the ground, both figures are
suddenly inscribed in

> the archive
> they would shelter in:

> the oral song
> avid as superstition,
> layered like an amber in
> the wreck of language
> and the remnants of a nation. (*Collected*, 133)

The sheltering "archive" becomes "the oral song", a residuum that lies hidden under the rhetoric of the nation. Because of the relegation of women's lives to poetic obscurity, ordinary stories such as this are of no importance. Dispatched by what is symbolically relevant, they enter a semiotic terrain on the margins of official languages. This local story about a girl giving birth is like an unpolished fossil resin, "an amber", that lies hidden under a rather polished and sophisticated poetic tradition, a tradition merely concerned with singing the heroic glories of nationhood. As the speaker at the end of the poem leaves the workshop and returns home, she encounters a landscape that contrasts sharply with the story's summer setting of "lilac[s]" and "laburnum[s]": "It was bitter outside,/ a real winter's night". By describing the place where she is located as "real", Boland seems to imply that the landscape of the oral tradition is 'non-real'. Like those poems she was listening to in the reading, this oral tale seems to be a mere rhetoric construction with its own conventions, an artificial mingling of fiction and folklore. She realises that the story she hears is more a legend than a 'truthful' account. Nevertheless, as she heads home by train, she suddenly feels that the scattered fragments of this oral conversation contain an authentic vestige of the Irish past:

> I had distances
> ahead of me: iron miles
> in trains, iron rails
> repeating instances
> and reasons; the wheels
>
> singing innuendoes, hints,
> outlines underneath
> the surface, a sense

suddenly of truth,
its resonance. (*Collected*, 133)

At the end of this poem, Boland feels that this oral story is authentic, that it can bear witness to what really happened in the past, without distorting or simplifying reality. The reiterative and prolonged sound of the wheels of the train offer a "musical sub-text" from which an unrecorded 'subaltern' past comes back to life (p. 132).[51] These echoing and semiotic sounds, although "underneath/ the surface" of those national and historical accounts, open a whole new visionary world where Boland can locate her 'origin' as a suburban ordinary woman, where she can establish a link with those women from the past. But this sound is only perceived "suddenly". As in "Fever", where the speaker's cry was abruptly addressed in a "moment of delirium" (p. 134), this moment of semiotic revelation is for the speaker temporal and fragile. The sound will quickly fade away, just as the poet attempts to grasp it within the poem. Boland, once again, stands out as an unsuitable "sibyl": she cannot sing the past in "pure syllables" (p. 103). Her enlightenment is only momentary, and as such her authority to act as a spokesperson is undermined. Nevertheless, in recounting her difficulty in giving voice to what lies "underneath/ the surface", in a semiotic realm which is inarticulate and full of 'silences', Boland is able to be subversive. As a form of representation of those who have stood on the margins of power, the oral tradition is in fact what Bhabha (1995: 147) would call a "performative" representation, a counter-narrative of more heterogeneous stories. By inserting within the symbolic realm of her poem this local and ordinary story, Boland calls into question the authority not only of imperialist accounts of Ireland's history, but also of "pedagogical" nationalist discourses, by exposing their gaps and incongruities (ibid).

The importance of women's oral tradition becomes also the topic of a poem included in *Outside History*, "What We Lost" (*Collected*, 187-188). The poem introduces us into the richness of a female domestic world, by focusing on a private setting of cambric bodices, lavender sachets, love letters, bed linen, and "scented closets". All these images suggest women's rich lived experiences, an Irish female collective memory of quotidian stories. In this particular setting, Boland focuses on an ordinary woman who is sewing in the kitchen:

> Dusk. And the candles brought in then.
> One by one. And the quiet sweat of wax.
>
> There is a child at her side.
> The tea is poured, the stitching put down.
> The child grows still, sensing something of importance.
> The woman settles and begins her story. (*Collected*, 187)

As Hagen and Zelman (2004: 54) note, these verse lines are constructed like "stage directions for a play". The curtains have opened, and the candle light gradually brings both actors, mother and child, to the foreground of the stage. The woman is about to start addressing her child, as we, the readers and audience, also wait for "something of importance" to happen. But unlike "The Oral Tradition", no conversation or dramatic soliloquy is documented within the poem. Instead, the speaker takes us directly into the end of the play:

> The woman finishes. The story ends.
> The child, who is my mother, gets up, moves away.
>
> In the winter air, unheard, unshared,
> the moment happens, hangs fire, leads nowhere.
> The light will fail and the room darken,
> the child fall asleep and the story be forgotten.
>
> The fields are dark already.
> The frail connections have been made and are broken.
> The dumb-show of legend has become language,
> is becoming silence (*Collected*, 187)

The moment has happened so fast that the woman's story is left unrecorded within the poem. The dialogue between mother and child is already lost, as a "dumb-show of legend" which is "unheard, unshared", and "forgotten". Boland yearns to speak, once again, a 'mother tongue', a lexicon of women, but as we learn, her attempt fails and she can only speak a language of "silence[s]". The inheritance that the poet's mother could have passed on to her is fractured and is no longer recoverable. As Boland declared in a poetry reading on June 19th 2004, in the National Concert Hall, Dublin, her mother "never referred to her history and she never discussed it with me. No matter how I tried, and no matter how much I would be interested, she would turn it aside".[52] In fact, Boland's poems always stress the disconnection between mother and daughters, as we have seen in "The Making of an Irish Goddess". That is why Meaney (1993: 150) has expressed her belief that Boland usually exposes in her poems an inadequacy "to represent the maternal", the unity between mother and child. But Boland is not only emphasising the separation between mother and child. She is also focusing on her detachment from women's oral tradition, from a more viable and suitable representation of 'subaltern' consciousness. Boland's attempt to get to "the void between […] rhetoric and reality" (interview with Consalvo 1992: 96) is not an easy project. As "What We Lost" indicates, language and reality cannot be reunited.

In any case, the very absence of the actual conversation between mother and child is in itself the best evidence that "something of importance" actually happened, for the speaker recalls: "Believe me, what is lost is here in this room/ on this veiled evening" (*Collected*, 187). Once again, Kristeva's semiotic realm emerges and disrupts the symbolic domain. The "silence" that Boland records is not ineffective, for it forces us to focus on the gap between the nationalist rhetoric and a subaltern unrecorded past. Speechlessness is the best evidence that national narrations are incomplete in their exclusion of women's stories. On the other hand, the richness of women's lived experiences is not left inarticulate in the poem. Boland manages to give voice to women's language by an inventory of ordinary items, palpable pieces of evidence of her grandmother's life:

who will know that once

words were possibilities and disappointments,
were scented closets filled with love-letters
and memories and lavender hemmed into muslin,
stored in sachets, aired in bed-linen;

and travelled silks and the tones of cotton
tautened into bodices, subtly shaped by breathing;
were the rooms of childhood with their griefless peace,
their hands and whispers, their candles weeping brightly? (*Collected*, 188)

The presence of this rhetorical question indicating uncertainty undermines Boland's authority to give voice to her grandmother's story. As in the previous poems, the mood here is distinctly elegiac. The change from present tense into past tense, so typical of Boland's poetry, is used to indicate melancholy. On the other hand, sentences become longer at the end of the poem, as if the speaker deliberately stretches language to suggest what apparently escapes linguistic representation. As in "The Oral Tradition", women's language is recorded by means of textures (what can be touched) and fragrances (what can be smelled) rather than by means of spoken utterances (what can be heard). Her grandmother's "words", although silent now, can be perceived by the richness of her fabric and textures (i.e. linen, silks, and cotton), and also by the fragrances of her "scented closet" filled with lavender and the smell of candle wax. As Hagen and Zelman (2004: 56, 58) notice, Boland is drawn to express a woman's world by "a non-verbal 'grammar'", by "a language neither oral nor written, but rather a shadowy rhetoric of relics, gestures, silences". This "non-verbal 'grammar'" is in fact a semiotic terrain: having no appropriate words to talk about women and their ordinary tales, Boland can only record them by other means, which suggest (but not state) the existence of another life. That is why Boland also describes her grandmother's conversation by means of "whispers", and not as a high declamatory language. Unlike the nationalist rhetoric, Boland avoids exerting poetic authority and writing what can be understood as another dominant discourse. Whispers are in fact constantly present in Boland's work, in poems such as "Outside History", "Contingencies", "The Dolls Museum in Dublin" and "Beautiful Speech" (*Collected*, 188, 191, 208-209, 211-212). Like in these poems, the "whispers" that we hear in "What We Lost" recall a lived existence which is unrecorded, and therefore belongs more to a semiotic realm than to a symbolic one.

This powerlessness of language, these gaps and silences Boland encounters in her process of reconstructing women's past, is constantly present in her mature poetry. In "The Journey" (*Collected*, 147-150), we similarly come across the feeling that there is something that cannot be recovered. This poem alludes, as its epigraph shows, to Book VI of Virgil's *Aeneid*, where Aeneas descends into the Underworld, the world of the dead, across the banks of the Stynx. The context is based on the genre of the medieval "dream vision" (Gelpi 1999: 221). The speaker, a mother who is watching over her children at night, falls asleep and dreams of the weeping children described in the *Aeneid*. Unlike Virgil's, in Boland's poem, the woman is going to share the grief of the terrified mothers who must deal with their children's death.

Most postcolonial theorists point out that one of the dominant motives of many postcolonial works is their forms of cross-cultural contact and interaction. As Bhabha (1995: 185) and Said (1994: 261) have argued, the postcolonial text is always a complex and hybridised formation, because it records a clear combination of forms derived from pre-colonial, nationalist, and European (imperialist) literary traditions. It is significant how Caribbean poets such as Derek Walcott and Irish writers such as James Joyce have rewritten Greek epic poems such as Homer's *Odyssey*. In Book VII (Chapter 58) of his *Omeros*, Walcott's poetic speaker similarly travels into the Underworld of the dead (Walcott 1990: 289-294). Like Boland in "The Journey", Walcott's use of this classical epic is subversive, for he attempts to construct a counter-epic with non-heroic figures such as Achille. Joyce's *Ulysses*, as Lloyd (1993: 104-109) explains, is similarly subversive. This work mingles stylistic elements, pastiches of different modes (biblical/liturgical, medieval, epic, legal, scientific, and journalistic) in order to parody biblical invocations as well as Ireland's nationalist conservatism. Like Walcott and Joyce, Boland rewrites the classical epic tale with a subversive project in mind. She uses Virgil's story in order to refer to an Irish event, in particular the Great Famine, and to women's involvement in it. Although Boland is influenced by the national literary tradition, classical literature has a remarkable impact on her work (remember her use of the Ceres and Persephone myth in poems such as "The Making of an Irish Goddess" or "The Pomegranate"). Greek and Latin traditions are constantly intermingled in her poems with Irish myths, exemplifying the hybridity that Bhabha and Said identify in postcolonial literary works. In contrast to the nationalist emphasis on creating a singular and homogeneous voice, Boland is able to dismantle this voice by recurring to different literary traditions.

Whereas in Virgil's *Aeneid* the male pilgrim is led to the Underworld by a male guide, in "The Journey", the woman speaker follows Sappho, "her female literary mentor" (Haberstroh 1996: 75).[53] In this sense, Boland appropriates the male heroic journey motif (using elite conventions of poetry) from a female perspective. Falling asleep, the speaker dreams of Sappho suddenly appearing to her:

> she came and stood beside me
>
> and I would have known her anywhere
> and I would have gone with her anywhere
> and she came wordlessly
> and without a word I went with her (*Collected*, 148)

Obediently, the woman in the poem follows Sappho without hesitation. Punctuation marks disappear, to indicate that the speaker is in a sort of trance, a cataleptic state, in the face of her powerful muse. In fact, Boland frequently imagines her journey into the past in a ghostly way, as the following stanzas indicate in their portrayal of the poet's descent into the Underworld:

down down down without so much as
ever touching down but always, always
with a sense of mulch beneath us
the way of stairs winding down to a river. (Ibid)

The repetition of lexical items and the presence of present participles indicate that the woman is in a period of transition, moving from the earthly world to the world of the dead. This is the journey the title records, from consciousness into unconsciousness, from her ordinary life to the obliterated world of the past. Boland' descent into the Underworld can be identified with what Said (1994: 261) has called the "voyage in", one of the most important features of postcolonial literature. Said's notion of the "voyage in" refers to those postcolonial writers who strive to "enter into the discourse of Europe and the West, to mix with it, transform it, to make it acknowledge marginalised or suppressed or forgotten histories".[54] In fact, by entering a male story, Boland transforms it, and gives it a new dimension. Her descent into Aeneas's Underworld preludes a world of revelation. There, Sappho shows a vision of unhappy mothers sucking and cradling their children, who were killed by multiple infectious diseases:

"Cholera, typhus, croup, diphtheria"
she said, "in those days they racketed
in every backstreet and alley of old Europe.
Behold the children of the plague". (*Collected*, 148)

Although Shappho describes a terrible and horrid scene, the "terrible pietas" awaken in the poet "the grace of love"; the mystery that, even in the world of the dead, mother and child are united. The female guide teaches Boland that human bonds do not perish with death. Nevertheless, the union between the past and the present the poet seems to establish eventually fails. She realises that the Styx, the "melancholy river", inevitably separates the world of the dead from the world of the living. Boland encounters a reality that has not been recorded previously, a reality that she feels the need to insert within artistic representation.

When realising this, the woman poet implores: "let me be/ let me at least be their witness", but Sappho immediately tells her that what she has seen is "beyond speech,/ beyond song" (p. 149). As Meaney (1993: 148) states, "[w]hatever it is that Boland wants to record and pass on, it is always 'beyond speech'", and, consequently, there is always a sense of loss in her continuous quest for "the real thing". Returning to the world of the living, as they "emerged under the stars of heaven", Sappho proclaims the woman speaker as her special sibyl, with these prophetic words:

> I have brought you here so you will know forever
> the silences in which are our beginnings
> in which we have an origin like water (*Collected*, 150)

In this sense, Boland creates a tension between her act of witnessing and her impossibility to give testimony. Whereas Sappho consecrates her "as my own daughter", Boland still stands as an inappropriate spokesperson: one who finds no words to communicate what she has seen. "[A]n origin like water" is an important metaphor for Boland. In fact, she has used this passage for the title of the American edition of her *Collected Poems* (Boland 1996b), and also, as we have seen, she has employed a similar metaphor in "Our Origins Are in the Sea" (*Collected*, 192-193). The source of inspiration for Boland is the lost past of Irish women. Her origins are as essential for her as water is for animals, plants, and human beings. But this metaphor suggests something else. Ireland's past is as diffusive, fluid, and difficult to retain as the water in the ocean. Gelpi (1999: 221) explains this metaphor as follows: "The well-spring of her words of remembrance is the worldless of the lost: mother and child, generation after generation 'beyond speech,/ beyond song'". In contrast to much historical writing, Boland discards clearly defined origins and linear narratives. It is significant how in poems such as "The Proof that Plato Was Wrong", Boland also records water as the origin of life, by arguing that the "roots and sinews [of these trees]/ are only – after all –/ rain" (*Collected*, 272). In this sense, for Boland, identities cannot be grounded in any essence or myth of origin because there is no origin as such. That is why, whenever Boland attempts to go back to a source, her project ultimately fails. In "What Love Intended", Boland tries to visualise the place where she was born, "the beds where it all began", but this seems to be impossible (p. 197). This poem ends with the voice of a confused speaker whose origin is diffused and darkened. Similarly, in "The Source", Boland describes the adults' disappointment when failing to find the source of the river. The only thing the poet, as well as the characters in this poem, can do is to imagine where the origin can be: "Maybe. Nearly. It could almost be" (p. 229).

In this sense, Boland aligns herself with postmodernist and poststructuralist visions of history. As Sarup (1993: 58) has explained, postmodernists such as Jean-François Lyotard and poststructuralists like Michel Foucault are adamantly against traditional forms of historical analysis, such as the Hegelian model which views history dialectically, as an evolutionist narrative. Lyotard understands that "grand narratives" such as history have "totalising ambitions", and as such they are reductionist and simplistic (pp. 146-147). Under the influence of Nietzsche, Foucault conceives of history more in terms of "genealogy" (p. 58). For Foucault, there is a gap and discontinuity between past and present. Furthermore, he views "historical beginnings as lowly, complex, and contingent" (p. 59). As poems such as "Outside History" and "Our Origins Are in the Sea" exemplify, Boland constantly stresses the discontinuities between past and present, the disruptions of history. On the other hand, in poems such as "The Journey" and "The Source", Boland rejects the pursuit of the origin in favour of a "contingent" past, a past that is liable to have occurred but not with certainty. Nevertheless, and as Russell (2002: 116) has claimed, in contrast to the tenets of postmodernism, Boland does not claim "that history or meaning do not exist", because as we have seen, she is a traditional poet who believes that there is something 'truthful' she must be able to decipher. What her poetry implies, though, is that the retrieval of 'real' history is fraught with difficulty. By expressing her doubts in reconstructing Ireland's past, Boland reveals the fragility of historical accounts: there are no essences and constants behind official historical narratives. The project the poet sets for herself in "The Journey" is a difficult task, perhaps impossible, because in her voyage into the past she encounters a troubling "silence", an "origin like water". As she has asserted, "[t]he way to the past is never smooth. For a woman poet it can especially be tortuous. Every step towards an origin is also an advance towards a silence" (Boland 1995a: 23-24). In the Underworld scene Boland witnesses in "The Journey", the power of language disappears; the figures Boland encounters there cannot speak, they are silent, and much worse, Boland cannot record their voices either. But this silence, this impossibility to recover 'subaltern consciousness' is, once again, another manifestation of the semiotic, and therefore, it can act subversively. As Boland (1995a: 167) has noted, the "world of vision" her poetry opens is "never so powerful as when it is suffered in silence".

This passage from the *Aeneid* has always caught Boland's attention, as she makes explicit in *Object Lessons*:

> For that moment I could make a single experience out of the fractures of language, country, and womanhood that had brought me here. The old place of power and heroism – the stairs and bricks of an alien building, the sting of exile – were gathered into a hell with old inscriptions and immediate force. […] In the face of the underworld, and by the force of poetry itself, language had been shown to be fallible. The heroes had spoken, and their voices had not carried. Memory was a whisper, a sound that died in your throat. Amidst the triumphs of language and civilisation it was a moment of sheer powerlessness. It was something I would look back to when I became a poet. (1995a: 86-87)

Here, Boland is not only linking her own imposed exile as a child with this Underworld, as she has done in poems such as "The Pomegranate" (*Collected*, 215-216). She is also using this image, as "The Journey" indicates, as an emblem of other lost and unrecorded Irish stories. Agha-Jaffar (2002: 115) understands the Underworld to be "a metaphor for the personal and collective unconscious". It is a place that shelters the images, patterns, instincts, and feelings that we share in common with all humanity. In this sense, the Underworld is also a place that transcends both time and space, a place of liminality where the past and those hidden 'truths' are harboured. Taking the above into consideration, it is therefore unsurprising that Boland exploits this metaphor in her poetry in order to talk about a subaltern past. In "The Bottle Garden" (*Collected*, 137-138), Boland narrates the moment when she decided to keep different plants in a container: feather mosses, begonias, ferns, etc. As in "The Botanic Gardens", this wide variety of plants co-existing in the same place act as a metaphor for the different communities (whether Anglo-Irish, Irish, Catholic, or Protestant) that co-habit Ireland. Boland uses the garden bottle as an ideal emblem where warring factions can live together in peace. In her "sweet, greenish, inlaid underwater" (a clear metonymy of Ireland), the relationship between the "rock spleenwort, creeping fig/ and English ivy" is one of concord and harmony (p. 137). But, unlike "The Botanic Gardens", Boland does not use these plants only as a reference to the Troubles, but also in order to talk about Ireland's past. The speaker suddenly records herself, as

> a gangling schoolgirl
> in the convent library, the April evening outside,
> reading the *Aeneid* as the room darkens
> to the underworld of the Sixth book –
>
> the Stynx, the damned, the pity and
> the improvised poetic of imprisoned meanings. (p. 138)

The wide variety of plants that Boland keeps in the bottle garden also suggest an Irish past that is composed of heterogeneous experiences. The past is composed by so many diverse and multiform realities that any attempt to grasp it will inevitably simplify it. If Boland is to act as a communal voice, she will create a uniform and therefore incorrect version of what happened. In this sense, she locates her poetry not on the side of the privileged (those who are allowed to act 'on behalf'), but on the other side of the river "Stynx", in the place where "the damned" and "the pity" live. By situating her own work in the Underworld, she is

314

able to experience the same powerlessness. The hollow voices of Aeneas's rivals not only represent the silence of the Irish past, but also the poet's inability to find words to record this reality. Boland's is a poetry of "imprisoned meanings", an art in which the content (what the poet wishes to convey) and rhetoric (what the poet is able to express) are irremediably disconnected.

The great influence that Virgil's story exerts on Boland even as a school girl is also reflected in "The Latin Lesson" (*Collected*, 172-173). In this poem, Boland depicts herself as a young girl at school, reading the Sixth Book in the original version. As she gradually deciphers those "strange" and "beautiful" words on the page, she slowly walks along the pathway to hell. There, the poet is able to witness once again dead "shadows in their shadowy bodies", "signalling their hunger". Boland feels compelled to act as their spokesperson, to relieve their pain at least by giving voice to their anguish. Nevertheless, the end of the poem focuses on her limitations:

> And how
> before the bell
>
> will I hail the black keel and flatter the dark
> boatman and cross the river and still
>   keep a civil tongue
>   in my head? (*Collected*, 173)

By finishing the poem with a question indicating uncertainty, Boland shows her own powerlessness to act as a communal voice. As she returns to the world of the living, she is as muted as that mob she saw in the Underworld. In one of her numerous essays, Boland (2003a: 26) has explained how she was drawn as a child to the Latin language:

> I would never forget those evenings. I would never forget that I had been alone and enchanted in a space mastered by language, deluded by verbs, kept at bay by the compressions of gerundives and ablatives. [...] That I

had felt my local, frail contemporary moment dissolve in the power of a syntax made somewhere else, and thousands of years later.

What Boland feels strongly attracted to is the power of the Latin language to survive after so many centuries, its magic and strength to open up a whole new world of difference, the world of the past and the Underworld. But Boland lacks this "civil tongue", that powerful language that would entitle her to speak about the past with such force and authority. Once again, she encounters a troubling inadequacy to express 'reality' in language.

In other poems such as "A False Spring" and "Love" (*Collected*, 177-178, 213-214), Boland continues focusing on the powerlessness of language that she encounters in the Underworld, and by extension, her own failure to give voice to Ireland's past. In "Love", Boland expresses her own limitations as a poet in an interesting manner. This poem is addressed to her husband in the present tense, and focuses on those years when the couple were living in Iowa, and their daughter almost died of meningitis (Gelpi 1999: 225). This event becomes the turning point from which Boland establishes a link with those who had lost their lives in Virgil's Underworld. Unlike them, the speaker's child was "spared" (*Collected*, 214). Nevertheless, in her recollection of the event, Boland becomes also a voiceless shadow. When she asks her husband "[w]ill we ever live so intensively again?", she realises that her "words are mere shadows and you cannot hear me./ You walk away and I cannot follow" (ibid). As the communication between the speaker and her husband fails, even their shared married life seems to be lost. As is typical, her poem ends with desolation. Boland's questions are always left hanging, with "[n]o answer in the air", as she says in "The Scar" (*Collected*, 250), not so much because they are not heard, but because she fails when addressing them. Like Aeneas's comrades in hell, her mouth has opened, but her voice has been ineffective.

The inadequacy of language to record the 'real' is constantly present in Boland's poetry. "The River" evokes that moment when the speaker was taken by her husband to a "mouth of a river/ in mid-October" (*Collected*, 171). She describes a beautiful landscape full of maples and swamps. Remembering that moment, the speaker declares

> how strange it felt –
> not having any
> names for the red oak
> and the rail
> and the slantways plunge
> of the osprey.
>
> What we said was less
> than what we saw. (Ibid)

As is typical in Boland's poetry, the disruption of the lay-out suggests fluidity and volatility. Reading Boland's poetry is to enter a text of multiple signifiers, of images that suggest in limitless numbers of ways the reality that Boland wishes to convey. In this sense, the poem becomes an unwinding path that leads to those 'subtexts' underneath the Irish landscape. But Boland's reading of nature is apparently insufficient, for she lacks the necessary words to describe what it really suggests. What she actually sees (which is in fact a remembrance of an Irish subaltern past) cannot be put into language, and therefore, there is a feeling that something is left out of reach.

Thus, if Boland is to be faithful to her own limitations as a poet in her access to the 'real', her poetic images must similarly express her own failure and powerlessness. In "The Glass King" (*Collected*, 161-162), Boland subverts nationalist icons such as Mother Ireland or Cathleen ní Houlihan, by electing as an emblem a figure which cannot be objectified and made passive by the poet. In particular, she focuses on King Charles VI. Charles VI, also called "the Foolish", was King of France between 1380 and 1422. He was defeated by Henry V of England at the Battle of Agincourt in 1415. His inefficacy as a king was due to the fact that, from 1392 onwards, he suffered from fits of madness (Lenman 2001:

158). In "The Glass King", Charles's madness turns him into a figure out of the speaker's control:

> My prince, demented
>
> in a crystal past, a lost France, I elect you emblem
> and ancestor of our lyric; it fits you like a glove –
> doesn't it? – the part; untouchable, outlandish,
> esoteric, inarticulate and out of reach (*Collected*, 162)

Like that Irish past that Boland attempts constantly to grasp in her poems, Charles stands beyond the poet's symbolic domain. Rather, he is located in a semiotic order, and as such, he is "untouchable, outlandish,/ esoteric, inarticulate and out of reach". This prince is occult and silenced under those prescriptive layers of nationhood and poetry. He has no place in official narrations, and he is another victim, stuck and "demented in a crystal past". Despised for his madness, he becomes a symbol of those marginalised figures that Boland is drawn to in her poetry. But even as she attempts to bring him out of his shadowy past, Boland lacks the means to do so: her poem is, like the traditional Irish "lyric", an inappropriate linguistic medium that inevitably transforms 'reality' into a false 'rhetoric'. By focusing on his irrational madness and the silences that surround him, Boland brings the semiotic into the (rational and loquacious) symbolic order of her poem, forcing her readers to understand those voices which are left unrecorded in official colonial and nationalist historical accounts. Within the Irish academic context, Smyth (2000: 52) has embraced 'silence' as a viable strategy of resistance. Attacking Bhabha on the grounds that he absorbs too easily concepts such as hybridity and rejects the usefulness of other coherent discourses of resistance, Smyth draws attention to silence as a more effective form of resistance to institutionalised power.[55] For Smyth (2000: 52), subaltern silence might represent "the subject's active withdrawal from the coloniser's discourse rather than a passive acceptance of the range of marginalised roles on offer". It is this voluntary retreat from dominant (imperialist and nationalist) discourses that

Boland shows in her mature poems. Silence acts as a viable form of resistance to essentialist ideologies that wish to delineate what it means to be 'Irish' and how 'womanhood' is to be described in artistic representations.

This uncrossable gap between reality and language is not only manifested in those poems where Boland attempts to recover an Irish past, but also whenever she tries to bear witness to women's ordinary life experiences. In "The Art of Grief" (*Collected*, 239-241), Boland attempts to record the moment when, as a child, she saw her mother crying. Nevertheless, she can only describe her mother's sorrow as outside the artistic realm, something that Fulford (2002a: 211) has also identified:

> I saw my mother weep once. It was under
> circumstances I can never, even now,
> weave into or reveal by these cadences.
> As I watched, and I was younger then,
> I could see that weeping itself has no cadence.
> It is unrhythmical, unpredictable and
> the intake of breath one sob needs to
> become another sob, so one tear can succeed
> another, is unmusical: whoever the muse is
> or was of weeping, she has put the sound of it
> beyond the reach of metric-makers, music-makers. (*Collected*, 239)

First of all, Boland shows her limitations when accessing the feeling of her mother. As she tries to describe this woman's grief, she realises that her cadences are imperfect, because, to start with, they cannot reveal what made her mother cry in the first place. As Boland later argues, "I could not ask her, she could not tell me/ why something had once made her weep" (p. 241). Like in "Love", the communication between the speaker and her companion fails. Moreover, Boland also feels limited by language in her attempt to represent the 'real'. She tries to say the unpoetic, that which lies "beyond the reach of metric-makers, music-makers", but this can only be done, as Fulford (2002a: 211-212) notes, within the poetic "limits of composure". Kristeva (1986a: 110) has explained that the semiotic can only be thinkable within the symbolic; in other words, in order to be understandable, the semiotic (however subversively) needs to be written within the symbolic order. Like Kristeva, Boland attempts to record grief through art, but this can only be done by means of dissonance: it is "unrhythmical", "unpredicatable", and "unmusical". In this sense, grief can only be defined as an absence, as that which is not 'rhythmical', 'predictable', and 'musical', in other words, as something outside poetry, and therefore, symbolic representations. Dissonance is, in fact, very important in Boland's mature work. As she has recently expressed, she is interested in breaking "auditory and linguistic expectations", and this involves creating at times "a subtle disorder of sound" (interview with Villar Argáiz). In "New Wave 2: Born in the 50s; Irish Poets of the Global Village", Boland (1996a: 141) has declared that, although there are "real thematic radicals" in contemporary Irish poetry, that is, innovations as regards arguments, she regrets the fact that there is no linguistic experiment: "[b]ut the technical colour, as it appears in poem after poem, is conservative. The short line is rarely used as a dissonance – more often it's an orphaned iamb". This dissonance is what Boland tries to capture in this poem. By doing so, she shows how we cannot record a woman's simple act of crying by using language. As the woman poet does not find words to record grief, she emphasises the inadequacy of language to represent reality, to get to the 'real thing'. We have seen how poems like "Anna Liffey" and "Time and Violence" (*Collected*, 230-239) highlighted the possibility of finding "a voice" that would succeed over the poet's death. In "The Art of Grief" we see that this voice is composed of what it cannot say, rather than what it actually says. Boland's is a language of silences and dissonances, a language that makes us think about the dangers involved in "speak[ing] of and for something" (interview with Villar Argáiz). At the end of the poem, the speaker invokes an interstitial space, a daylight composed of "black-/ and-white and menial in-betweens", an "hour between planets" (*Collected*, 241). This blurring of boundaries and the fluidity of sentences at the end of the poem is Boland's attempt to push language to the limit, to move away from essentialist definitions,

320

in this case of her grieving mother. It seems that dissolution and fluidity are the only possible means by which categories such as 'womanhood', with all its complexity, can be grasped.

As "The Art of Grief" shows, it is not only the Irish past that escapes linguistic representation, but also female lived experiences. Therefore, Boland stands out as an inappropriate representative not only for a 'subaltern' consciousness, but also for women's ordinary world. In "Woman in Kitchen", we come across a woman whose life seems to be frozen and solidified in her role as a housewife. The kitchen is portrayed as an enclosing and burying landscape. It is significant how the colour white invades the whole poem, as in the second stanza:

> White surfaces retract. White
> sideboards light the white of walls.
> Cups wink white in their saucers.
> The light of day bleaches as it falls
> on cups and sideboards. (*Collected*, 109)

The continuous references to this colour (not so much a colour but the combination of all of them) are significant. Gilbert and Gubar (2000: 613-621) explain that in the nineteenth century white was a distinctively female colour, frequently chosen as emblematic by, or of, women. Some of the examples which they give to illustrate this point are interesting. Gilbert and Gubar (2000: 613) explain that Emily Dickinson literally got dressed in white (for she took to wearing a white dress for almost all her mature life), and also wrote poems in which she figuratively covered herself in a white garment.[56] For Dickinson, whiteness figuratively and literally represented various things. Firstly, white was for this woman poet "the ultimate symbol of enigma, paradox, and irony" (p. 614). In her poetry, white frequently represents both the potential (the white heat) of Romantic creativity, and the isolation (the polar cold) Romantic creativity may demand (p. 615). In this sense, whiteness is both flame and snow, "the passion of the bride and the snow of the virgin" (ibid). Secondly, this colour also suggests, for Dickinson, "the pure potential of a *tabula rasa*, a blank page, an unlived life" (ibid). In order to understand Dickinson's symbology, we must understand the Victorian iconography of female whiteness. Gilbert and Gubar explain that the traditional ideal of feminine purity was usually represented as a woman in white (ibid). She was the white "angel in the house", the passive and submissive woman (note the prototype of Snow White in the fairy tale). Whiteness symbolised virginity and purity. As these critics explain, "[i]n its absence of colour, the childish white dress [of this angel in the house] is a blank page that asks to be written on just as her virginity asks to be 'taken', 'despoiled', 'deflowered'" (p. 616). Thus, whiteness implied an invitation for someone to finish with the woman's virginity. On the other hand, and paradoxically, the 'frigid' colour white also meant refusal and resistance. If we analyse the morphology of the word 'virginity', we may gain some significant insight on this point: "the word *virginity*, because its root associates with the word *vir*, mean[s] manliness or power" (ibid). Thus, whiteness is ambiguous: it suggests both virginal fragility and virginal power (p. 617). Furthermore, whiteness, according to the complex Victorian symbolism, was an emblem of death: a woman in white is "a dead *objet d'art*" (p. 616). White is the colour of the dead, of ghosts and shrouds, of the unknown. By recurring to the colour white, women writers were figuratively implying that they were buried alive in their own society. In short, and as Gilbert and Gubar (2000: 613-621) explain, whiteness could suggest, according to Victorian aesthetics, two paradoxical extremes. On the one hand, it implied virginity, feminine purity, and powerlessness, and also death and aesthetic isolation. On the other hand, white was the garment of the female imagination, of the unknown, worn by a mad woman who had the potential of writing on a *tabula rasa*.

It is clear that Boland exploits in "Woman in Kitchen" the complex and traditional symbology of this colour. She is here deliberately incarnating the paradox of the Victorian woman poet: there is both entrapment and liberation in the whiteness surrounding her. On the one hand, the woman feels surrounded by the white cups and sideboards, and, along with them, she is just another "dead *objet d'art*", a sort of ghost, or "angel in the house", enclosed in a living burial. The whiteness of the kitchen symbolises the powerlessness of this woman, imprisoned in her own society by the demands imposed on her gender. By fulfilling her role as a housewife, she is both excluded from public life, and also denied the opportunity to exploit her creative potential and her artistic skills as a poet. Once again, we encounter the troubling paradox that overwhelms Boland as a woman poet: whether to follow the routines of domesticity that womanhood demands, or whether to dedicate herself to her routines as a writer. On the other hand, the whiteness of her kitchen also shows that her environs have the pure potential of a *tabula rasa*. This woman's reality is perceived as enigmatic, something that waits to be written, as that blank page that Gilbert and Gubar mention. Boland needs to find a language, a 'mother tongue' that would give voice to this woman, without further simplifying her as an 'angel in the house'. Nevertheless, the last stanza of the poem shows the impossibility of her project:

> The wash done, the kettle boiled, the sheets
> spun and clean, the dryer stops dead.
> The silence is a death. It starts to bury
> the room in white spaces. She turns to spread
> a cloth on the board and iron sheets
> in a room white and quiet as a mortuary. (*Collected*, 109)

It is significant how the woman in the poem is granted no speaking voice. It seems that her essence is inarticulable. The poem finishes with "silence", which is also indicative of "death". Her white kitchen becomes, therefore, a funeral place: this woman is shrouded in her own society. The shortness of sentences, in contrast to the linguistic fluidity that characterises Boland's mature poems, enhances this woman's enclosure and impossibility of movement. It seems that death and silence are the only means that Boland finds to define 'womanhood'.

This impossibility to give voice to women's reality, to "speak of and for something" (interview with Villar Argáiz), is further emphasised in "Code"

(*Collected*, 290-291), a poem included in Boland's latest collection of poetry. As its epigraph explains, "Code" is an ode to Grace Murray Hopper, the American creator of the computer compiler and verifier of COBOL. Boland identifies with this woman, for she is also a language-maker:

> Poet to poet. I imagine you
>   at the edge of language, at the start of summer
>   in Wolfeboro, New Hampshire, writing code.
>   You have no sense of time. No sense of minutes even.
>   They cannot reach inside your world,
>   your gray workstation
>   with *when yet now never* and *once*. (*Collected*, 290)

Like Hopper, Boland also writes "at the edge of language", because, as we have seen, she conceptualises 'the real' as a semiotic domain on the margins of symbolic official languages. The disruption of the lay-out indicates the subversive nature of both discourses. While this woman compiles binaries and zeroes on the blue screen, Boland assembles silences and dissonances on the page. Both forms of 'languages' are 'codes', systems of signals that must be constantly deciphered. Nevertheless, Hopper's language stands outside time itself, it will always be valid, and therefore, "minutes" and temporal adverbs such as "*when yet now never* and *once*" lose all their significance. This woman's syntax, just as the Latin language, can survive, can remain alive and persist throughout different epochs. As Boland (2003a: 27) has put it, this "true architect of the computer" had been able to create a

> [h]igh-level language [...] that made an abstract of machine language, that issued declarations and control statements. [...] And compilers that took the source code made by a programme and turned it into a machine code; something that the machine could work with.

This abstract language has the capacity to release power, by its ability to offer "exemptions to the process of time" (pp. 27-28). Nevertheless, Boland does not

324

wish to locate her own 'code' outside a spatial and temporal continuum. As she argues in the poem, "I never made it timeless as you have" (*Collected*, 291). In this sense, "Code" sets an interesting contrast between the power of this computerised language and Boland's own powerless language. As the speaker says in "Anna Liffey", "[a]n ageing woman/ Finds no shelter in language" (p. 234). Boland wants to incorporate a new language that can bear witness to the passing of time and the loss of beauty. This is difficult to do in a poem, for once words are written, the female body is fixed both in time and space. That is why Boland becomes a powerless poet whose language carries, as she says here, only "shadows" on to the page. Whereas Hopper's computer language leads straight to power, her own language is frail and brings us directly to losses and disappearances.

4.4.4. Conclusion

Marginalised figures are constantly present in Boland's work. Her poetry focuses on those "subaltern" figures Spivak (1994) refers to, those (Irish) victims that have suffered most terribly the consequences of imperialism and nationalism alike. As Hagen and Zelman (2004: 1) put it, "[t]o read Boland [...] is to enter into a quiet world, one in which the poet aspires to amanuensis, bringing to the fore shadowy and mute subjects". While Boland attempts to become a suitable spokesperson for an oppressed community, she shows that she lacks the ultimate authority to grasp the past, to recover lost voices. It is not only that these lives have been lost, but also that Boland wishes to leave them as ungraspable. For the poet, every process of recovery itself involves an inevitable misrepresentation. Rather than becoming a loquacious representative of the Irish past, she becomes a powerless speaker that shares the wordlessness of figures like those in Virgil's Underworld.

That is why silences, dissonances, and dissolution abound in Boland's poetry whenever she attempts to reconstruct a more 'authentic' subaltern Irish past, and whenever she wants to incorporate 'real' female experiences. In this sense, her poems move towards that "inaccessible blankness" or "*un*translatable strangeness" Spivak (1994: 89) and Boehmer (1995: 234) identify in postcolonial texts. Boland tries to record those lives marginalised in powerful nationalist and imperialist discourses (Kristeva's semiotic realm) within the poem (the symbolic realm), but her project is ultimately impossible. As language is an insufficient medium of representation, 'reality' can only be suggested by other means, such as textures, gestures, hints, repetitions and echoes, irrational and incoherent cries, dissonances, and, above all, silences. Three years after the publication of *In a Time of Violence*, Boland (1997b: 24) declared that she "still need[ed] to find a language with which to approach that past". In this very same essay, she also said that "at the end of the day, what matters is language. Is the unspoken at the edge of the spoken" (p. 23). In this sense, Boland's new language is defined by what has always been unheard ("the unspoken"), rather than by what has been heard ("the spoken"). Unsurprisingly, Boland's new concerns nowadays continue to be to write about "the untold and the untellable" (interview with Villar Argáiz).[57] This apparent inability to find an appropriate medium of expression is indeed one of Boland's great achievements in her poetry. As Deane (2003: 121) states,

> The political requirement is not that we become eloquent in a language that is our own, whether that be Irish or English or both; it is to become eloquent in a language that we never had, but which is believed to exist, if only because of our dumbness in it. That is the language of freedom.

Boland's linguistic independence, her "language of freedom" as an Irish woman poet, lies in her attempt to speak the inarticulate, the unspeakable, that (semiotic) realm where Irish lives are more truthfully recorded. Boland's "dumbness" in expressing herself is itself a subversive strategy. First of all, her silences force us to perceive those gaps between what has happened and what official historical accounts tell us happened. Boland describes 'the real' (Ireland's past) in such a way that it always stands in a subversive relation with the (nationalist) sanctioned 'rhetoric'. Secondly, Boland manages to criticise the adequacy of language to grasp categories such as 'Irishness' and 'womanhood', and therefore shows the fallibility of those essentialist and singular identities defended by hegemonic discourses. As Fulford (2002a: 213) contends, Boland abandons "the pathos of authenticity" of imperialist, nationalist, and feminist projects by representing identity as unfixed and differential. In this sense, Boland carries out a deconstruction of identity similar to the one advocated by feminists such as Kristeva in "Women's Time" (1986c: 209) and by postcolonial critics such as Spivak (1993: 5).

4.5. A more assertive 'marginal' writer?

4.5.1. Introduction

Boland has now acquired both critical respect and a large readership not only in Ireland but also abroad, to the extent that she has become, as American critics such as Daniels (1999: 390) say, "one of the most celebrated poets writing today". In 1990, Mary Robinson quoted Boland's "The Singers" (*Collected*, 203) in her first presidential address (Hagen & Zelman 2004: 118). Since then, extracts of this poem can be read in the upholstery of Aer Lingus aircrafts. Seven years later, in 1997, her work became part of the Irish Leaving Certificate exam. Because of this, the new generation in Ireland is getting used to the fact that there are Irish women poets as well as Irish male poets. Boland's increasing popularity in her native country has, interestingly enough, coincided with her mature exile in the US, where she has been living ever since 1995.[58] It may be ironical that now that she has finally found her own place within the Irish literary panorama, she feels compelled to emigrate from Ireland. This section will study this aspect of Boland's work, which until now has been overlooked by critics. I will particularly consider Boland's established status as an Irish woman poet and her mature exile from Ireland as two interrelated factors that have influenced her latest volumes of poetry: *The Lost Land* (1998) and *Code* (2001).

4.5.2. Boland's mature exile in the US

Boland's life records a process of constant exile and emigration. As a child, she spent part of her childhood in London and New York. As an adult, she has been living in California since 1995, when she replaced Denise Levertov as a professor of English at Stanford University. In 1998, she took the directorship of the Stegner Poetry Workshop at this university's Creative Writing Program.[59] Although she keeps a house in Ireland, Boland lives most of the time in California, and only returns to her native country in summer.

Boland recently declared that her living between the two countries, the US and Ireland, has not affected the way she writes poetry on the grounds that by the time she moved to California her life was already set and her "sense of poetry was confirmed" (interview with Villar Argáiz). Nevertheless, the extent to which her latest work is shaped by her mature exile is significant.

If the postcolonial text is generally, as Bhabha (1995:185) and Said (1994: 261) explain, a hybrid text, then the texts by exiled postcolonial writers take this notion of hybridity to the limit. Postcolonial theorists such as Bhabha, Said, and Hall have acknowledged the empowering condition of hybridity for the migrant. Bhabha (1995: 209) argues that, by being in exile, any postcolonial writer or intellectual can more easily take advantage of "the productive capacities of [the] Third Space". This "Third Space" that the migrant occupies is described as "neither the One [...] nor the Other, [...] but something else besides which contests the terms and territories of both" (Bhabha 1995: 25). In this sense, the postcolonial subject, by constantly crossing boundaries and occupying a liminal position, is able to elude the politics of polarity and break down all imposed dualities (coloniser/colonised; self/other; West/East; even masculine/feminine). He or she inhabits "the rim of an 'in-between' reality", a liminal space, where an ideal relationship between cultures lies, and where individual freedom is ultimately found (p. 13). As Moore-Gilbert (2000: 143) explains:

For Bhabha, culture is located between levels. He suggests that only when this postcolonial perspective, revealed by the light of cultural hybridity, diaspora, and *differance*, is acknowledged, will liminality replace the unities of nationalism and the binaries of colonial discourse.

As Bhabha implies, hybridity enables active forms of resistance, by opening a space which enables other positions to emerge. That is why Bhabha defends in an interview hybridity as politically effective: it is this form of "Third Space" that brings political change, because "new sites are always being opened" (Rutherford 1990: 216).

Similarly, Said (1994: 284) believes that the exiled nature of most postcolonial writers allows them to experience the crossing of boundaries, "the charting of new territories in defiance of the classic canonic[al] enclosures". In *Culture and Imperialism*, Said advocates negotiation and expresses his disagreement with binary divisions such as East and West, North and South, and white and coloured:

> Gone are the binary oppositions dear to the nationalist and imperialist enterprise. Instead we begin to sense that old authority cannot simply be replaced by new authority, but that new alignments made across borders, types, nations, and essences are rapidly coming into view; and it is those new alignments that now provoke and challenge the fundamentally static notion of *identity* that has been the core of cultural thought during the era of imperialism. (Said 1994: xxviii)

By adopting the privileged 'liminal' and 'median' role of the artist or critic in exile, Said states, decolonisation is possible. This subversive figure, whose "philological home is the world" (p. 385), is neither inside nor outside. He or she benefits from a "double vision", from what he calls a "contrapuntal" mediation, that would enable a genuine dialogue between East and West (p. 78). Thus, like Bhabha, Said views hybridity as crucial in enabling a powerful and transnational perspective, escaping from the narrow and limited vision of both orientalism and nationalism.

Like Bhabha and Said, Hall (1996a: 447) states that writers that experience diaspora can easily adopt a "politics of positionality" that disturbs hegemonic discourses by a process of "recombination, hybridisation, and 'cut-and-mix'". As this postcolonial critic argues, the diaspora experience allows writers to recognise the "necessary heterogeneity and diversity" to contest existing social structures that rely on essentialist subjectivities. In this sense, for the three theorists mentioned above, artistic decolonisation implies the movement and integration of Third World thinkers into the metropolitan First World, enabling exiled intellectuals to "write back to the centre", in Rushdie's words (1992: 295).

As an exiled writer, Boland exploits the benefits that her physical distance from Ireland entails. Her living in the US allows her to maintain a psychological detachment from dominant nationalist discourses. Her poems in *The Lost Land*, published three years after her self imposed exile from Ireland, move towards the possibility of conceiving identity more in terms of fluidity and boundary crossing. Boland's earlier volumes of poetry show how she has also attempted to overcome hegemonic ideologies by recording a notion of identity that is unstable rather than fixed. But it is in *The Lost Land* that she crosses national boundaries even more deeply, challenging what Said (1994: 406) calls "[t]he authoritative, compelling image" of empire and of nationalism. In order to demonstrate this point, I will focus on two significant poems included in *The Lost Land*. One of these poems is "Home" (*Collected*, 258-259). Here, Boland recalls one morning in mid-October when she went with a friend to a eucalyptus grove in southern California. As in "The Botanic Gardens", Boland imagines that these trees were placed there by a foreign gardener:

> It looks as if
> someone once came here with a handful
>
> of shadows not seeds and planted them.
> And they turned into trees.
> But the leaves
> have a tell-tale blueness and deepness. (*Collected*, 258)

As is typical in Boland's poetry, nature hides historical messages the speaker feels the need to decipher. The shadowy eucalyptus' leaves are in fact a subtext of an unrecorded past; their blueness, like in other poems such as "A Sparrow Hawk in the Suburbs" (*Collected*, 221-222), is reminiscent of a subaltern world on the margins of historical accounts. But in contrast to all those poems in *Outside History*, Boland does not limit her task to recovering this past. Her attention focuses on an unexpected incident. Suddenly, "the monarch butterflies/ arrive from their westward migration" (*Collected*, 258). Thousands of insects place themselves on these leaves, changing "the trees to iron". The migratory butterflies do not only alter and transform this apparent unpolluted landscape (suggestive of an 'authentic' and untouched subaltern past), but also fill it with a tremendous and magnetic energy:

> Every inch and atom of daylight
> was filled with their beating and flitting,
> their rising and flying at the hour
> when dusk falls on a coastal city
>
> where I had my hands full of shadows.
> Once. And planted them.
> And they became
> a suburb and a house and a doorway
> entered by and open to an evening
> every room was lighted to offset. (*Collected*, 259)

The fluttering struggle of these new immigrants, intensified by the use of present participles, attracts the speaker's attention. They exemplify the menace and radical transformation that "a coastal city" and its native inhabitants experience by the arrival of new settlers. Boland feels captivated by this sight, because, as she recognises, she was also an immigrant arriving in a foreign land. The planter of the initial stanza becomes now the speaker herself: her "hands full of shadows" are suddenly transformed into "a suburb and a house and a doorway" in a distant and new territory. Boland shows the instability and relativity of apparently fixed identities such as 'coloniser' and 'colonised', by admitting that she has also been a colonist, setting her own house in an alien territory. In this sense, her arrival also meant a menace for all those native Americans, a threatening prospect that could annihilate and destroy a pure landscape filled with "a tell-tale blueness and deepness". Boland's use of the passive structure is significant. Her own room and house are "lighted" and "entered by" someone who is not clearly specified, a person who is not given any identity whatsoever. Boland uses her own mature experience of exile to engender it as common and universal. As Boland has recently argued, "we will always be 'exiles in our own country'" (interview with Villar Argáiz). In "Home", Boland rather implies that everyone is sooner or later an exile, entering a foreign territory and disrupting the dream and purity of others' nationhood.

García García (2002: 44-45) has established an interesting distinction between the Irish emigrant and the Irish exile. According to this critic, the emigrant experiences a sense of uprooting from his native country and looks for a sense of belonging in his new destination. In this sense, this figure is overwhelmed by a deep sense of "dislocation": he feels that he neither belongs to his native country nor to the place where he is living. On the other hand, the Irish exile never discards his own roots and his sense of belonging to the native country. He reflects an intense sense of "bilocation": living in a particular place and identifying with it, while still living in his imagination in his native country. In this sense, the exile shows an ability to live in two places at the same time. These concepts of "dislocation" and "bilocation", which do not exclude each other, also appear in Boland's poetry. In diasporic poems such as "An Irish Childhood in England: 1951" and "Fond Memory" (*Collected*, 155-156), Boland describes herself as a child who is overwhelmed by a deep feeling of 'dislocation', neither feeling Irish nor entirely English. In her mature poems, Boland also exposes a deep sense of 'bilocation' in her ability to live in two places at the same time. "Home" records precisely this feeling. This woman is living happily in US, and both her new house and her friends are there. Nevertheless, the end of the poem presents a speaker who nostalgically recalls her native country, her "home" and "the Irish night":

> If I could not say the word *home*.
> If I could not breathe the Irish night
> air and inference of rain coming from the east,
>
> I could at least be sure –
> far below them and unmoved by movement –
> of one house with its window, making
> an oblong of wheat out of light. (*Collected*, 259)

Clearly, this woman experiences 'bilocation', the ability to live physically in the US and imaginatively in Ireland. For Said (1994: 403), liberation is incarnated in the migrant "whose consciousness is that of the intellectual and artist in exile, the political figure between domains, between forms, between homes, and between languages". Similarly, the woman poet here is located within two homes. The rain coming from the east brings her native country back. It is here where her sense of "home" and roots are inscribed. Nevertheless, as we have seen, Boland always scrutinises all notions of origin. Her ultimate inability to ground herself in a certain place teaches her that, while place is fixed (as she says, the only thing she can "at least be sure" is that there is a "house" and a "doorway" where she once lived), the 'sense of place' is something relative and unstable. Love and knowledge of a place, Boland implies, neither convey ownership nor a grounded and fixed identity.

This necessity to belong somewhere, to ground her sense of identity in a certain place, becomes the main topic of the title poem of *The Lost Land*. Like in "Anna Liffey", Boland makes explicit how her identity is constructed upon categories such as 'motherhood' and 'Irishness':

> I have two daughters.
>
> They are all I ever wanted from the earth.

Or almost all.

I also wanted one piece of ground:

One city trapped by hills. One urban river.
An island in its element.

So I could say *mine. My own.*
And mean it. (*Collected*, 260)

Boland's identity, as she makes explicit here, is rooted in her role as a mother, and also in Dublin, a "city trapped by hills" with its own "urban river". Her 'sense of home' is therefore shaped by the two constituent categories of femininity and nationhood. These notions allow Boland to claim "one piece of ground" as her own, so that she can allege them to be "*mine. My own*". In any case, the shortness of the sentences and their incompletion indicate that the speaker's identity is not stable and fixed but rather fractioned and fractured. As we learn in the subsequent lines, all those foundations on which her self is based are shattered by the separation of her daughters and by her exile in the US:

Now they are grown up and far away

and memory itself
has become an emigrant,
wandering in a place
where love dissembles itself as landscape:

Where the hills
are the colours of a child's eyes,
where my children are distances, horizons:

At night,
on the edge of sleep,
I can see the shore of Dublin Bay,
its rocky sweep and its granite pier. (Ibid)

In contrast to the fragmented language of the initial stanzas, lines become longer, unfolding down the page. This linguistic technique parallels Boland's description of a more fluid identity. Separated from her daughters, Boland becomes, as a consequence, an emigrant soul "wandering in a place" of remembrance and memory. Landscape is perceived as a place where the poet tries to project a more stable sense of self. The hills are subtexts in which she imagines her children's eyes, staring at their mother. Nevertheless, they quickly disappear as "distances, horizons". As Boland's identity as a motherhood is undermined, so is her identity as an Irish citizen. Distanced from her beloved city of birth, and in a similar way to "Home", Boland nostalgically recalls "the shore of Dublin Bay,/ its rocky deep and its granite pier". Boland's 'bilocation' becomes here rather an intense dispossession and deterritorialisation. Because of her exile, Boland has perhaps an even more strongly emotional "bond" with Ireland, and that is why memories of Irish places and landscapes are constantly evoked in these diasporic poems. Nevertheless, as this poem shows, Boland can only conceive of 'home' and nation in terms of distance, "loss", and fluidity. The only way she can bring these notions back is by an act of imaginary recovery. The poet's intense dislocation enables her to embrace more heterogeneous experiences. She can now identify with those Irishmen and women who were forced to emigrate from Ireland, and also with those 'wretched of the earth', as Fanon (1990) calls them, of Virgil's Underworld:

> Is this, I say
> how they must have seen it,
> backing out on the mailboat at twilight,
>
> shadows falling
> on everything they had to leave?
> And would love forever?
> And then
>
> I imagine myself
> at the landward rail of that boat
> searching for the last light of a hand.
>
> I see myself
> on the underworld side of that water,
> the darkness coming in fast, saying

all the names I know for a lost land:

Ireland. Absence. Daughter. (*Collected*, 260-261)

Boland's use of fractured questions is typical of *The Lost Land*, as reflected in poems such as "The Blossom" (*Collected*, 262-263). They create an atmosphere of uncertainty and contingency in which the boundaries between past and present are suddenly blurred. Boland's displacement becomes the starting point from which to reflect on those Irish emigrants and later on those dead shadows enclosed in the Underworld. As Stuart Hall (1990: 230) has suggested, "the exiled writer is constantly *positioning* him/herself both geographically and ontologically". It is this constant "positioning" that "The Lost Land" exemplifies. First of all, Boland describes her own reality and imagines what it would be like to have her own "piece of ground" back. Secondly, she remembers all those Irish emigrants who, like her, were displaced from all they love on earth. Finally, Boland ends in the Virgilian Underworld, in a place where language has proved to be unsuccessful. In this sense, Boland undermines her own ability to act as a spokesperson, because she eventually shares the silences and powerlessness of the dead. The preponderance of present participles at the end of the poem enhances Boland's movement downwards. As she enters the Underworld, her identity becomes as dissolved as those shadowy figures she encounters. As she says in "Witness", the "old divisions" of Ireland's history "are deep" in her (*Collected*, 247). The only way to overcome these divisions the past inscribes in her body is to take her own self to dissolution and fluidity. In this sense, this poem, as is characteristic of Boland's mature work, moves from identity to self-erasure, from the possibility of becoming a spokesperson, to her own failure to do so. Unable to express herself by means of the symbolic realm of language, the final one-line stanza records a speaker who can only talk in terms of fractions and silences. Like in "Anna Liffey", the only thing that is left at the end of the poem is Boland's voice, "saying/ all those names" she knows "for a lost land:/// *Ireland. Absence. Daughter*". These lines function both as an invoking memory and as a subversive statement. The fractured language indicates the speaker's contradictions as she strives to write her own self within the poem. Absence, and therefore, silence surrounds the words "Ireland" and "Daughter" on the page. As an exiled mother who is separated from her daughters, Boland can only imagine her Irishness and her femininity in terms of effacement. As Fulford (2002b: 164) has argued, in Boland's poetry "[r]epresentation of the self is always made in the context of misrepresentation or erasure".

In Boland's subsequent volume of poetry, *Code*, her mature exile continues to be the starting point from which she reflects on one of the most painful experiences in Irish history: emigration to the US. Poems such as "Exile! Exile!" and "Emigrant Letters" deal with the dispossession that leaving one's native land entails (*Collected*, 294, 297-298). In this latter poem, Boland recounts how, when she was heading for the concourse at Detroit airport, she suddenly overhears "an Irish voice":

> Its owner must have been away for years:
> Vowels half-sounds and syllables
> from somewhere else had nearly smoothed out
> a way of speaking you could tell a region by,
>
> much less an origin. (*Collected*, 297)

As the speaker in "Daughters of Colony" and "The Mother Tongue", the language of the Irish emigrant cannot be a 'pure' speech, but rather a "broken" and "forked tongue" (*Collected*, 248, 257). The speaker's Irish accent has almost disappeared to the extent that it would be nearly impossible to determine his/her "origin" and regional background. Emigration, Boland implies, creates a hybrid language, a mixed and imperfect code that turns their owners into 'non-authentic' Irishmen and women. As Boland boards, she rises high up in the sky. Closing her eyes, she reflects on the influence that place exerts on the construction of one's language, and therefore, one's identity:

towns, farms, fields – all of them at that very moment
moulding the speech of whoever lived there:

An accent overwritten by a voice. A voice
by a place. (*Collected*, 297)

The woman speaker realises how accent, voice, and place are intrinsically related.
As she has recently expressed, "we are constructed by the construct" (interview
with Villar Argáiz). Boland shows in this poem how geography and language are
composite parts of this construct. For those emigrants, their dislocation from
Ireland and their distance from their native tongues transform them into new
selves, neither totally American nor completely Irish. The only point of reference
that tells them that they once belonged somewhere are those letters they receive
from their homeland:

How their readers stood in cold kitchens,
heads bent, until the time came to begin again
folding over those chambers of light:
ice and owl noise and the crystal freight on

branches and fences and added them
to the stitchwort of late spring, the mosquitoes,
the unheard of heat, the wild leaves, snow again –
the overnight disappearances of wood and stone (*Collected*, 298)

The fluid language and chains of modifiers at the end of the poem introduce us to
a world of remembrance and memory, and to the richness of these emigrant lives.
Displaced in a cold New England, the ghost figures in Boland's poems remember
a warmer landscape, a late Irish spring. For these emigrants, their letters were
valuable possessions, tangible evidence of their personal and public history.
Nevertheless, the fact that these are bound to "disappear[...]" and that their
readers can only imagine "the unheard of heat" implies that, for these displaced
Irishmen and women, Ireland can only be imagined in terms of silence and 'what
is lost'. Once again, Boland stresses how for those who are physically removed

from Ireland, pure 'Irishness' is nothing but a dream, an unreal fiction. The end of the poem stresses this feeling. As these characters carefully kept their letters in a cupboard drawer, this piece of furniture becomes an emblem that is

> [...] informed as it was
> by those distant seasons. And warped by its own. (Ibid)

What this object represents is its owners themselves. Removed from their native land, their identities are founded both on remembrance, and on all the fractures and deformations they experience by living somewhere else. While they feel the need to keep alive in their memories "those distant seasons", Irish emigrants also become corrupted and contaminated by their immersion in an alien and distant territory. As exiled Irishmen or women, they are hybrid selves who belong 'neither here nor there'.

In this sense, the fluid conception of identity Boland ascribes both to herself and to her characters, and the instability of notions such as nationhood and femininity in her poems are highly subversive strategies. They allow her to show the fallacy of ideologies such as imperialism, nationalism, and feminism, which defend a unitary and fixed self, an universal transcendental subject. Boland asserts herself as an exiled writer as she constantly crosses not only national frontiers, but also conventional boundaries. She adopts what Hall (1990: 447) calls a "politics of positioning", a subversive ideology which embraces heterogeneity and apparently irreconcilable differences. Her exile becomes the starting point from which to reflect on other heterogeneous and unrecorded realities. Boyce's characterisation of women's migration is significant here:

> My mother's journeys redefine space. Her annual migrations, between the Caribbean and the United States, are ones of persistent re-membering and re-connection. She lives in the Caribbean; she lives in the United States; she lives in America. She also lives in that in-between space that is neither here nor there, locating herself in the communities where her children, grandchildren, family, and friends reside. Hers is a deliberate and

fundamental migration that defies the sense of specific location that even her children would want to force on her. (Boyce 1994: 1)

Boland's mature exile is as subversive as Boyce explains here. Her physical removal from Ireland becomes the starting point from which the woman poet can "re-member" and "re-connect" with other divergent experiences, such as those stories of Irish, German, and Huguenot emigrants.[60] On the other hand, Boland's positioning "in an in-between space that is neither here nor there", permits her to undermine the politics of polarity. Boland shows how she is also a coloniser, by setting up her own house in an alien American territory. In this sense, her poetry teaches us that the boundaries between categories such as 'coloniser' and 'colonised' are not fixed. Although Boland is unable to establish herself in a certain place, although hers is but a *Lost Land*, her dispossession and deterritorialisation allow her to occupy a productive space where new decolonising identities can emerge.

4.5.3. A marriage that endures

In her latest volume of poetry, *Code*, Boland goes back to issues that have already appeared in her previous work: the importance of women's ordinary lives and her attempt to offer a more accurate version of Ireland's past. Nevertheless, in this new collection there are some innovations as regards content, changes that are partly due to Boland's physical removal from Ireland. The most interesting and perhaps defining feature of this new collection of poems is that Boland is more adamantly concerned with 'what endures' after a married life rather than with 'what is lost' from an Irish subaltern past. Of course, there are poems such as "Quarantine", "Making Money", "The Burdens of a History", "How the Earth and All the Planets Were Created", and "A Model Ship Made by Prisoners Long Ago" in which Boland focuses on those unrecorded stories which need to be brought out of a shadowy past into the pages of her poems: the life of her grandmother, the suffering of the famine victims, and the painful experiences of Irish prisoners

(*Collected*, 282, 292-293, 298-300, 303-305). Nevertheless, it is her thirty years of married life that Boland pays the most attention to, predominantly in those poems included in the first section of *Code*: "Marriage". It seems that after two decades of voluntary exile in the US, Boland comes back again to her own family roots, in order to focus on what she has, what she possesses, rather than on what she is dispossessed from. It is therefore unsurprising that the whole volume of poetry is dedicated to her husband Kevin Casey, and not like in *The Lost Land* to Mary Robinson, a more openly public and political figure.[61]

As I hinted in section 4.2., one of the key motives of this volume is to subvert the traditional idealisation of love in conventional poetry. The husband and wife in Boland's poems are no longer eternal, no longer perfect figures whose love is romanticised. Her main objective in *Code* is to depict a couple who are united by their very ordinariness, whose love is strengthened by their sharing everyday and apparently 'insignificant' events. In poems such as "Once" and "Thanked be Fortune", Boland defines marriage as an "ordinary, ageing human love", as a close union between two people who communicate themselves with their own "code": "*duty dailyness routine*" (*Collected*, 285-286). Boland implies that it is precisely this kind of non-idealised love which is able to survive despite the passing of time. This concern is the one which dominates poems such as "Embers", "Once", and above all, "Lines for a Thirtieth Wedding Anniversary" – one of the most powerful and suggestive poems in this volume (*Collected*, 283, 285, 288). Written in the form of one single long stanza, this poem describes Boland's own married life as follows:

> Somewhere up in the eaves it began:
> high in the roof – in a sort of vault
> between the slates and gutter – a small leak.
> Through it, rain which came from the east,
> in from the lights and foghorns of the coast –
> water with a ghost of ocean salt in it –
> spilled down on the path below.
> Over and over and over

years stone began to alter,
its grain searched out, worn in:
granite rounding down, giving way,
taking into its own inertia that
information water brought: of ships,
wings, fog and phosphor in the harbour.
It happened under our lives: the rain,
the stone. We hardly noticed. Now
this is the day to think of it, to wonder:
All those years, all those years together –
the stars in a frozen arc overhead,
the quick noise of a thaw in the air,
the blue stare of the hills – through it all
this constancy: what wears, what endures. (*Collected*, 288)

This poem depicts married life by means of two opposing metaphors: the union between husband and wife is allegorised both by the rigidity of architecture and the fluidity of water. First of all, Boland describes the house as the place where "the soul of a marriage" is kept ("First Year", *Collected*, 284). The roof, vault, slates, stone, grain, and granite provide a firm and solid ground where the speaker's identity as a married woman can be inscribed. Some psychoanalytic texts have stressed the proximity of home and self-identity. This is the case of Carl Jung (1969: 253), who develops a thesis that explicitly reads an individual's home as the "universal archetypical symbol of the self". Later feminist postcolonial critics such as Boyce (1994: 126) have identified how many postcolonial women writers metaphorically draw on their homes in order to represent self-definition: "[t]he house and its specific rooms become metaphors of self and loci of self-identification". Similarly, in this poem Boland equates self and home. Nevertheless, the stability that architecture would provide to her identity as a married woman is dismantled by her reliance on the eroding potential of water. Instead of tracing the origin of her wedlock in the floor of the house, she locates it in the roof. Through a gutter, rain begins to filter, slowly and gradually wearing away the solidity of those foundations on which her marriage is based. The erosion of the materials in which the house is constructed parallels the gradual decrease of that passion and fervour which characterised the first years of marriage. "[P]assion" as she argues in "Thankëd be Fortune" is gradually substituted by "*duty dailyness routine*" (*Collected*, 286). As years pass and both figures grow old, marriage loses that sense of "wonder" and "admiration" that Irigaray (1991: 171) envisaged in the "amorous exchange". Nevertheless, this progressive erosion of emotion and intensity does not imply detachment, but much the contrary. As stones, grains, and granites are altered and disfigured, both figures are more united than ever. There is something which remains changeless: a 'real' and 'true' love that survives the erosions of time: "what wears, what endures". The final image of "the stars in a frozen arc overhead" suggests eternity. On the other hand, "the quick noise of a thaw" and "the blue stare of the hills" implies dissolution and self-erasure. Firstly, water gradually melts down the solidity of their lives. Secondly, like that "blueness and deepness" Boland observed in the Californian coast ("Home", *Collected*, 258), blueness here stands for that subaltern reality which will eventually be omitted from official accounts. As Boland and her husband's lives expire, they are also threatened with becoming mere 'subtexts' in nature, subjects whose lives and experiences will be forgotten. By linking the eternity of the constellations with the fluidity and erasure of water, Boland implies that as herself and her husband gradually approach death, their love paradoxically enough becomes more enduring and everlasting than ever.

On the other hand, watery imagery is also used by the poet, as we have seen in poems such as "The Journey" and "Anna Liffey", as a metaphor of the impossibility of describing the 'real', the flowing of human lived experiences. First of all, Boland implies that the origin of everything is, after all, water. In "The Journey", she stated that we are all "an origin like water" (*Collected*, 150); here she argues that her marriage began in the "small leak", up in "the roof" of her house. Secondly, Boland suggests that her married life is like the fluidity of water, an intimate experience that cannot be grasped, fixed in terms of language. The long unfolding sentences of this single stanza enhance the fluidity of both the speaker's and her husband's identities. In contrast to those conventional love poems, Boland suggests that "what there is between a man and a woman", as she says in "Quarantine" (*Collected*, 282), cannot be solidified in any sort of artistic representation, for this would inevitably simplify the complex interweave of emotions and experiences that joins in complicity husband and wife. In this sense, whereas in poems such as "In Which Hester Bateman, Eighteenth-Century English Silversmith, Takes an Irish Commission", the artist (Hester Bateman) inscribes "in miniature a man and a woman" in a silver spoon, in "the seams of rock" (*Collected*, 279), Boland envisages a new medium, not solid this time, where these images are represented more truthfully. In "the smooth/ Mimicry of a lake" the spoon is making, Boland writes "[a] flowing script", where she can record "their names" and where she avoids immobilising the husband and the wife as silvery figures (ibid). It is, of course, impossible to write these figures in water, and in fact their names are not mentioned in the poem. In spite of this, Boland seems to imply that it is preferable to open a poetic place that avoids solidification, even if this inevitably leads to anonymity. As Spivak (1994: 89) believes, it is better to record lived experience as an "inaccessible blankness" rather than simplify it as official historical and cultural accounts have done. By describing marriage in such fluid terms, Boland shows in "Lines for a Thirtieth Wedding Anniversary", as in most of the poems in this collection, how "[a]rt and marriage: now make a match" (*Collected*, 279).

4.5.4. Boland's reconciliation with Irish poetry

One constituent feature of Boland's mature work is her revision and subversion of conventional images of womanhood in Irish poetry (i.e. the mythical, bodiless, and idealised figure of Mother Ireland, for instance). A striking change in *Code* is that now Boland seems to come to terms with the Irish literary tradition. This is clearly observed in "How We Made a New Art on Old Ground" and "Irish Poetry" (*Collected*, 296-297, 307), poems in which the woman poet offers a retrospective and reconciliatory view of national cultural conventions. In these two poems, Boland not only includes herself within the Irish literary community by the use of the first person pronoun in plural ('we'), but also reflects on the ways in which literary simplifications and idealisations of "images" as "ornaments" were necessarily used at a time of national convulsion and confusion (Boland 1995a: 152).

The first of these poems, "How We Made a New Art on Old Ground", specifically focuses on the Irish pastoral genre. As it has been explained when commenting on Boland's initial work, the tradition of nature poetry dates back to early Irish literature, with its genre of *dinnsheanchas*, manuscripts and poems which explain place-names by reference to myths and legendary stories (Welch 2000: 90-91). This Gaelic tradition was revived in the Irish Literary Renaissance period, with writers such as Yeats, Synge, and Lady Gregory. Up to *Code*, Boland's mature work has attempted to subvert the nature poem by means of two strategies. First of all, the Revival idealised and romantic view of the Irish landscape has been overturned in poems such as "The Making of an Irish Goddess" (*Collected*, 178-179), which, as we have seen, describes a rural landscape that is destroyed, burned, and wounded, rather than untouched by national violence. Secondly, and perhaps more importantly, her poems have not presented Ireland as a world of peasants, farms, and cattle, but as a suburban neighbourhood and a domestic environment inhabited by ordinary mothers and housewives. As Boland explains, her project is to subvert the traditional political nature poem by becoming an "indoor nature poet", a poet whose "lexicon was the kettle and the steam, and the machine in the corner and the kitchen, and the baby's bottle" (interview with Allen-Randoplh 1993b: 124).

For the first time in her mature work, Boland re-establishes in "How We Made a New Art on Old Ground" a close relationship with this important cultural legacy. This poem, constructed upon stanzas of four lines, begins by invoking that silent past which remains occluded under cultural idealisations of the Irish landscape:

A famous battle happened in this valley.

> You never understood the nature poem.
> Till now. Till this moment – if these statements
>   seem separate, unrelated, follow this
>
> silence to its edge and you will hear
>   the history of air: the crispness of a fern
> or the upward cut and turn around of
>   a fieldfare or thrush written on it.
>
> The other history is silent. The estuary
>   is over there. The issue was decided here:
> Two kings prepared to give no quarter.
>   Then one king and one dead tradition. (*Collected*, 296)

As she makes explicit here, nature poetry has not represented what really happened in the past. The Battle of the Boyne in 1690 between the Jacobite and the Williamite armies is one of the most important events in Irish history, for it confirmed the Protestant ascendancy in Ireland (Welch 2000: 38). Even though this is a heroic story, and, as such, would be easily inserted in Irish historical annals, Boland suggests that literature has avoided representing this event. The defeat of the Catholic army is not something to be proud of for those Irish Revivalists who attempted to stress an unbroken chain of Gaelic traditions, and who wished to hide their discontinuity towards their own 'authentic' roots. In their idealisation of nature, of ferns, fieldfares, and thrushes, nature poetry, in this sense, omits representing a defeated past. In this sense, the Battle of the Boyne becomes an unrecorded story, an event which is only "written on" the Irish landscape in terms of absence, as "silence" and "air". The speaker encourages us to follow "this silence" and enter a darker reality on the other side of the river, in order to see an 'Underworld' which is situated at the edge of language. As is typical in Boland's mature work, the woman poet implies that the past still needs to be brought to the surface of Irish poetry:

> Now the humid dusk, the old wounds
>   wait for language, for a different truth.
> When you see the silk of the willow

        and the wider edge of the river turn

    and grow dark and then darker, then
            you will know that the nature poem
    is not the action nor its end: it is
            this rust on the gate beside the trees, on

    the cattle grid underneath our feet,
            on the steering wheel shaft: it is
    an aftermath, an overlay and even in
            its own modest way, an art of peace (*Collected*, 296)

Once again, Boland implies that "the gap between rhetoric and reality" needs to be bridged, in order to incorporate "the worst parts of our history" (interview with Consalvo 1992: 96). Conventional language has gradually steered away from "the old wounds", from a subaltern past of ordeal and defeat. Nevertheless, this acknowledgement is counteracted by the speaker's realisation that the misrepresentation Irish poetry has exerted on 'the real' has been necessary. The "nature poem" has been "an art of peace" because it has slowly healed the wounds in the land, and occluded the marks of battle. By allowing rust to grow on the gates, this literary convention has not intended to arouse national resistance, to record "the action nor [the] end" of Irish rebellion, but to cover and "overlay" both hatred and defeat with an utopian vision of a pure and untouched Irish landscape. Introducing her own voice, the speaker shows her conspiracy with nature poetry's idealisation of the Irish landscape. As she tries "the word *distance*", her poem "fills with/ sycamores, a summer's worth of pollen" (*Collected*, 296). As she writes "*valley*", those "blood, oaths, armour" are left "unwritten" and unrecorded within artistic representation (ibid). In this sense, Boland does not wish to grasp the violence of the Battle of the Boyne; rather, she desires to maintain a literary convention that offers exemption from hostilities. At the end, Boland makes this point even more explicit, by arguing that her poem attempts to show

> [...] how this sweet corrosion
> 　　　begins to be complete: what we see
> is what the poem says:
> 　　　evening coming – cattle, cattle-shadows –
>
> and whin bushes and a change of weather
> 　　　about to change them all: what we see is how
> the place and the torment of place are
> 　　　for this moment free of one another. (*Collected*, 297)

As an art of peace, nature poetry is able to separate "the place" from "the torment of place", to forget injustices, Irish oppression and dispossession, and move forwards. Praga (1996: 35) has explained that there are almost no 'neutral' landscapes in Ireland, but highly sectorial ones, divided, most of them, by religious and historical boundaries. As landscape, in this sense, directly brings for the Irish writer mental associations of dispossession, violence, and suffering, a romantic idealisation of nature can help him/her to leave the past behind. In this sense, the landscape Boland portrays is no longer reminiscent of a history of oppression but a volatile place which, in its constant change of light and weather, erodes and 'unwrites' history. The disruption of the lay-out in this poem, as in "The Water-Clock", indicates this passing of time, the natural process of weathering, dissolution, abrasion, and corrosion of those historical remnants in the Irish landscape. Hers is, in this sense, another 'nature poem', a "sweet corruption" that maintains the distance between what it represents and what actually happened. The speaker now understands that, by omitting 'the real' one both forgets violence and oppression and moves away from the painful realisation that both her "king" and her "tradition", in other words, her 'authentic' and native roots, are dead and no longer recoverable. Instead of criticising the cultural and political implications of the Revivalist idealisation of nature, Boland now strongly shares their wish to erase all historical traces and to forget, at least momentarily, her desire to recuperate a subaltern past through memory and language. This is Boland's own way, as she says in the title, of making "a new" and liberating "art on old ground".

This new and more positive attitude towards her national literary tradition is further observed in "Irish Poetry", the poem that closes *Code*. It is significant that this poem is dedicated to Michael Hartnett. For the first time after *New Territory*, Boland praises an Irish male poet, which indicates that she has a more reconciliatory attitude to the Irish literary canon. Hartnett (1941-1999) was a poet who identified greatly with Gaelic Ireland. His poems in many ways follow the tradition of the *dánta grádha*, love poems and dramatic lyrics composed around the middle of the fourteenth to the seventieth century by men with bardic training (Welch 2000: 81). He dedicated most of his life to translating early Irish lyrics and poets who exclusively wrote or are writing in Irish (i.e. Daibhí Ó Bruadair and Nuala Ní Dhomhnaill) (p. 146). Hartnett's collection *A Farewell to English* (1975) marked his desire to write poetry exclusively in Gaelic, although he returned to English years later with *Inchicore Haiku* (1985) (ibid). "Irish Poetry" is not only dedicated to Hartnett, but also addressed to him. Like in the poem commented above, Boland uses the first person pronoun in plural ('we') in order to include herself within the Irish literary tradition. The poem recalls the speaker's encounter with this writer one evening, and their conversation about Irish poetry:

> We always knew there was no Orpheus in Ireland.
> No music stored at the doors of hell.
> No god to make it.
> No wild breasts to weep and lie down to it.
>
> But I remember an evening when the sky
> was underworld-dark at four,
> when ice had seized every part of the city
> and we sat talking –
> the air making a wreath for our cups of tea.
>
> And you began to speak of our own gods.
> Our heartbroken pantheon.
>
> No Attic light for them and no Herodotus. (*Collected*, 307)

Orpheus was a legendary Thracian poet and musician of Greek mythology. His soothing music had the power to tame the wild beasts, to calm down warriors and storms, and to move even inanimate objects and plants (Falcon Martínez et al. 1980: 477). In Hades's Underworld, he was also able to paralyse momentarily the torture of those condemned in hell (p. 478). Boland establishes an interestingly parallelism between the power and authority of Orpheus's music, and the powerlessness and desolation of Irish poets themselves. Poets in Ireland, the speaker implies, are not able to change the past, to soothe the pain of those dispossessed Irishmen and women who lie hidden under the layers of history and culture. Furthermore, there is no equal to Herodotus in Irish poetry, no historian who is able to create a narrative that can let the past speak through him/her. On the other hand, Irish poetry is itself a lost tradition with no "gods" to rely on. As a culture based on the few remnants that have survived throughout centuries, theirs is a "heartbroken pantheon" of ancient bards and singers that can only appear in ghostly terms. As Montague (1974: 21) has noted, the "true condition" of Irish poetry is that is has been affected by the "mutilation" of its original medium of expression. According to this Irish poet, even contemporary poets writing in Irish have to face the fact that their native tongue has been irrevocably damaged, and as such, it cannot compete on equal terms with the new literature written in the language of the conqueror. Nevertheless, and in contrast to "My Country in Darkness" (*Collected*, 245), where Boland presented Gaelic culture and language as irremediably lost, the speaker here is able to hear, with the aid of Hartnett, the music of Bardic lyric, "the sound/ of a bird's wing in a lost language":

You made the noise for me.
Made it again.
Until I could see the flight of it: suddenly

the silvery lithe rivers of the southwest
lay down in silence
and the savage acres no one could predict
were all at ease, soothed and quiet and

listening to you, as I was. As if to music, as if to peace. (*Collected*, 307)

The well-constructed language in the first stanza gradually gives way at the end to longer sentences, unfolding by the only enjambment that appears in the poem. This fluidity of language parallels the blurring of past and present. Hartnett's new language is "stored at the doors of hell", between the Underworld, the Gaelic unrecorded past, and the speaker's contemporary reality. In this sense, he becomes a new Orpheus in Ireland, who is able to bring change and whose voice suddenly paralyses rivers and subdues "savage acres". The moment is described as magical and hypnotic, both for the Irish landscape and the speaker herself. As in "How We Made a New Art on Old Ground", Boland views her cultural legacy no longer as restrictive and limiting, but as a rich literary tradition that can bring "peace" and relieve the pain of an oppressed past. In this sense, she praises the ability of her Irish male colleague to find a voice that can bring an end to Irish cultural and historical dispossession.

4.5.5. A more assertive woman poet

As we have seen in *Code*, Boland offers a more positive perspective on her reality as a contemporary woman poet in Ireland, by reflecting on 'what endures' after thirty years of being married, and on the liberating and decolonising qualities of the Irish literary tradition. The main reason why her poetry experiences such a change stems from the fact that her status as an Irish woman poet is no longer questioned in her native country. Now that Boland has her own place within the Irish literary tradition, she has gradually ceased to feel intense restrictions when writing. In an interview, she has recently recognised that, although when she began writing, "there was almost a magnetic distance between the word 'woman' and the word 'poet'", she admits that "I don't feel that now" (interview with Destiny 2003).

This newly acquired assurance is observed in "Is It Still the Same", a poem in which Boland recalls the initial years of her poetic career. Like in "Fever" (*Collected*, 133), the title becomes the sentence that opens the poem:

> young woman who climbs the stairs,
> who closes a child's door,
> who goes to her table
> in a room at the back of a house?
> The same unlighted corridor?
> The same night air
> over the wheelbarrows and rain-tanks?
> The same inky sky and pin-bright stars?
> You can see nothing of her, but her head
> bent over the page, her hand moving,
> moving again, and her hair.
> I wrote like that once.
> But this is different:
> This time, when she looks up, I will be there. (*Collected*, 305)

In this poem, Boland reflects on the distance between her own past and her contemporary reality. Like in poems such as "A False Spring", in which the speaker says: "I want to find her,/ the woman I once was" (*Collected*,177), Boland here feels compelled to retrieve her former (and presumably happier) years as she just moved to Dundrum and raised her two daughters there. Nevertheless, she is unable to do so, because she is not young and her children are not with her anymore. She "can see nothing of her" now, except imagining her movement and excitement while she was writing. In spite of her failure to go back to those years in full detail, she stands as a more assured and assertive poet. Whereas her former self was constantly assailed by the contrary pulls of womanhood and poetry, she "will be there" to solve these contradictions, as a more mature poet who seems to know how to handle the complexities involved in being a woman writer in Ireland. If we compare this poem with "A False Spring", published thirteen years before, we find a significant change. In both, Boland stands as a writer affected by linear time, as someone who cannot recover what she had been before.

Nevertheless, whereas in "A False Spring", Boland failed when addressing her younger self ("I want to tell her she can rest,/ she is embodied now./ But narcissi,/ opening too early,/ are all I find", *Collected*, 178), in this poem, this "is different", because "[t]his time, when she looks back", the speaker will be able to establish a fruitful communication.

Therefore, it seems that, for Boland, age has allowed her to have more security and confidence in her poetic enterprise. She has acquired assurance and wisdom, as a result of the learned experience that usually comes with growing older. Those doubts and hesitations that abounded in volumes such as *The Journey and Other Poems* and *Outside History* are no longer predominant in *Code*. It is significant how, in contrast to *The Lost Land*, for instance, there are not so many references to lexical items such as 'country' and 'nation'. Now Boland feels more assured in dealing with these concepts, as her place within the literary canon is well grounded. Therefore, she takes these notions for granted, and does not feel compelled to mention them so often or to call them into question. On the other hand, those structures that emphasised that the speaker lacked knowledge about her subject matter are substituted by other expressions that indicate Boland is now in command of her experience. In poems such as "The Pinhole Camera" and "Once", both of them addressed to her husband, Boland proclaims herself as someone who is able to transmit some desirable piece of information: "You know/ the reason for the red berries/ darkening, and the road outside/ darkening, but did you know/ that the wedding/ of light and gravity/ is forever?"; "Did you know our suburb was a forest?" (*Collected*, 281, 285). Similarly, in the first of these two poems, Boland asserts how, after thirty years of marriage, both she and her husband have spent enough time together "to know about power and nature", "to know which is which" (p. 282). Not only has marriage granted Boland more knowledge, but also, after forty years writing poetry, has acquainted her with the Irish literary tradition. As we have seen in "How We Made a New Art on Old Ground" and "Irish Poetry", she assertively claims that she "will know that the nature poem/ is not the action nor its end", and that she "always knew there was no Orpheus in Ireland" (pp. 296, 307).

4.5.6. A more assertive 'vulnerable' woman poet?

As we have seen in poems such as "Is It Still the Same", Boland stands out as an assertive writer, confident of her writing skills. Nevertheless, this is not a general tendency in *Code*. In poems such as "Quarantine" and "Suburban Woman: Another Detail" (*Collected*, 282, 306), Boland continues writing with that powerless and non-authoritarian stance that characterises her previous volumes of poetry. One of the reasons why Boland wishes to continue writing from a marginal and displaced position is because, by being at the edges, she can subvert how Irish poets have traditionally written at the centre, "in courts, at the seat of power" (interview with Destiny 2003). Only by exerting her voice from the margins, can she more powerfully bring the past back and recover those silences that have characterised Irish experience.

This powerless stance is observed in "Quarantine", a poem about the Great Famine. As she has recently described in a poetry reading on June 19th 2004, in the National Concert Hall, Dublin, this poem is based on a local incident that happened in Ireland in the nineteenth century, a story recorded by a man sixty years later.[62] A man and a woman left a workhouse in Carrigstyra, West Cork, at the time of the 1847 famine. They walked north, back to their cabin:

> In the worst hour of the worst season
>   of the worst year of a whole people
> a man set out from the workhouse with his wife.
> He was walking – they were both walking – north.
>
> She was sick with famine fever and could not keep up.
>   He lifted her and put her on his back.
> He walked like that west and west and north.
> Until at nightfall under freezing stars they arrived.
>
> In the morning they were both found dead.

> Of cold. Of hunger. Of the toxins of a whole history.
> But her feet were held against his breastbone.
> The last heat of his flesh was his last gift to her. (*Collected*, 282)

Like the poems in *The Lost Land*, "Quarantine" avoids the rhetorical complexity that characterised *The Journey and Other Poems* and *Outside History* for instance, in favour of a plainer style with repetitions and simpler sentences, some of them incomplete. This stripping method is Boland's own way of moving away from a "false rhetoric", from a style loaded with unnecessary ornaments that would distance her from 'the real' (Boland 1997d: xii). 'The real' here is this local story, omitted from official historical accounts. As Boland argues, their death was caused not only by the "cold" and "hunger" of the winter famine, but also by "the toxins of a whole history", a history that did not wish to include this story in its annals. As the very same title "Quarantine" indicates, both are 'subaltern' figures who inhabit an enforced isolation and restriction from national and cultural narrations. Boland, therefore, feels the need to reinsert this local story, uncovering and revealing love in one of the most tragic events in Irish history. As both figures are found dead in the morning, she explains how the woman's feet were against the man's chest, because he had tried to warm them. For Boland, this is "a dark love story, an exemplary one",[63] because it shows how the emotional attachment of husband and wife becomes stronger as they face death. According to Boland, conventional love poetry has failed to record stories such as this, because it has mainly been concerned with portraying an idealised couple. That is why the speaker claims at the end of the poem that she prefers to create a de-romaticised story:

> Let no love poem ever come to this threshold.
> There is no place here for the inexact
> praise of the easy graces and sensuality of the body.
> There is only time for this merciless inventory:
>
> Their death together in the winter of 1847.
> Also what they suffered. How they lived.

And what there is between a man and a woman.
And in which darkness it can be best proved. (*Collected*, 282)

If Boland is to choose between praising the female body and creating a "merciless inventory", she obviously opts for the second possibility. The detailed facts of their lives at the end of the poem are more accurate inscriptions of their suffering and painful experience. Any attempt to idealise their love would inevitably strip away all the dispossession and oppression of both figures. It is interesting to note how Boland, as her popularity increases, continues to be concerned with the oppression and dispossession that has influenced Irish experience so dramatically. It is as if she feels more entitled now to talk about these issues. Nevertheless, she still tries to avoid acting as a communal voice, speaking 'on behalf' of the past. As "Quarantine" shows, love poetry and elegy go together. Boland refuses to bring relief to both characters, and she argues that "darkness" is her best way of explaining "what there is between a man and a woman". Instead of writing as an authoritative poet who might create a more compassionate version of the past, she decides to leave it as it was: a "merciless inventory", a defeated story of death, hunger, and suffering, but also full of intense love. On the other hand, her poem is written not from the centre of the Irish canon, but from a "threshold" between what is and what has never been recorded. As Keen (2000: 27) has noticed:

> Boland now possesses considerable influence within the Irish literary community as a result of her achievements, but any opportunity that this may create to retreat to the relative safety of an authoritarian voice is undermined by her insistence that the political authority of any poem "grows the more the speaker is weakened and made vulnerable by the tensions he or she creates".

The vulnerability and fragility of both figures in "Quarantine" stands in opposition to those idealised and romantic stories recorded in conventional love poetry. It is precisely this "tension" that makes "Quarantine" a poem filled with "political authority". For Boland, as she says in the poem, it would be all too "easy" to sing the "graces and sensuality of the body". Instead, she decides to share the powerlessness of both figures. Ashcroft (1994: 34) has argued that postcolonial literature often relies on "a strategic insistence upon the *marginality* of [...] experience". This position, instead of perpetuating the binary logic of centre and margin, is able to dismantle it. It is this "excess" of "marginality" that we constantly perceive in Boland's mature work. By embracing marginality as a source of resistance, she not only creates a more "accurate inscription" of what happened ("The Making of an Irish Goddess", *Collected*, 179), but also dismantles the belief that the Irish poet must seek his/her authority by creating an idealised past.

In this sense, in spite of the assurance that we have identified in *Code*, it is significant how Boland continues describing herself as a vulnerable and non-authoritarian subject. In a similar way to "Is It Still the Same", in "Suburban Woman: Another Detail" the speaker attempts to recover in full detail her earlier years as a housewife and mother in Dundrum. Writing at her desk in a twilight setting, she starts to imagine "an uncurtained/ front room where"

> another woman is living my life.
> Another woman is lifting my child.
>
> Is setting her down.
> Is cutting oily rind from a lemon.
> Is crushing that smell against the skin of her fingers.
>
> She goes to my door and closes it.
> Goes to my window and pulls the curtains slowly. (*Collected*, 306)

As in "Quarantine", Boland avoids the verbal excess that appeared in previous collections. Furthermore, sentences are not unfolding down the page, but rather are fractured. Nevertheless, the preponderance of present progressives, together with the verbal parallelism of these lines, create a feeling that the woman described is in constant movement. Boland's poem records a volatile landscape of constant change. The woman cannot be solidified by the speaker, and therefore, she cannot fix and recover the woman she once was, above all because she is not that person anymore:

> The kitchen,
> the child she lifts again and holds
> are all mine:
>   and all the time
> the bitter, citric fragrance stays against her skin.
>
> She stares at the road
> in the featureless November twilight.
>
> Stares for a moment at
> the moon which has drained it.
>
> Then pulls the curtains shut.
> And puts herself and my children beyond it. (Ibid)

Although both the kitchen and the child are identified by the woman as "mine", the inevitable erosions of the passing of time create an uncrossable distance between younger and mature selves. The disruption of the lay-out in these lines enhances the fluidity of this poetic image, and the absence that Boland finds when uttering this assertion. In contrast to previous poems, the diffused and "featureless" light of twilight does not blur the boundaries between past and present, as both her younger self and her children stand "beyond" the poet's grasp. In "Hide this place from Angels", the speaker advances that "soon the weight/ of the lives we lived would become inert/ house and tree shadows" (*Collected*, 302). This painful realisation is manifested in this poem, in which the scene she tries to retrieve can only be imagined in terms of darkness: "the neighbourhood/ is the colour of shadow" (p. 306). In both poems, shadows no longer refer to an Irish subaltern past, but to Boland's own journey to death. The end of the poem focuses on the desolation and powerlessness of the speaker when realising this: "I can see nothing now./ I write at my desk alone" (*Against Love Poetry* 2001: 47).[64] After mentioning her kitchen, her window, her children, the only thing that the speaker truly possesses at the end of the poem is "my desk", a room of one's own where she can at least write about what she has lost. Once again, Boland describes her identity as based on her role as a mother and her life in Dundrum. But, as an exiled mother living in the US, those foundations on which Boland's identity as a woman poet is based are damaged. Her nationhood is "faraway" and her motherhood can only be imagined in terms of "elegy" (ibid). In this sense, Boland's "root[s]", her 'authentic' origins, can only be perceived in terms of absences rather than presences. She is an adult woman who, separated from her children and living somewhere else, faces both her life and poetic enterprise "alone".

This melancholic stance is continued in "Once in Dublin" and "Limits 2", poems in which Boland reflects on her impossibility to go back, as a woman affected by linear time (*Collected*, 295, 302-303). As Boland says in "Once in Dublin", "[s]mall things/ make the past./ Make the present seem out of place" (p. 295). Boland's main dislocation as a woman writer in this volume does not stem so much from her own dispossession in terms of history and nationhood, but from the fact that she now feels her experiences of ageing and erasure more powerfully than ever. As a result, she describes herself as a "woman cracking and twisting", perishing like those "[b]lack atoms falling down/ on green leaves" (ibid). Instead of describing herself as a stable and immortal writing subject, Boland imagines herself, once again, as a woman subject to death and erasure.

4.5.7. Conclusion

It is interesting to note how Boland, in spite of her achieved 'authority' within the American and Irish literary panoramas, continues to adopt in *Code* a strongly marginal position when writing. Boland's movement is, therefore, symptomatic of that feminist advocacy to "unlearn[...] female privilege" (Spivak 1994: 91) or to "become minor" (Kaplan 1990: 357). A general overview of Boland's poetic production from 1972 to 2001 shows that as she becomes more widely read, she appears more dispossessed in her poems. Boland's literal movement from the margins to the centre of her national literary canon is, significantly enough, reflected in reversed terms. Although she wrote volumes such as *New Territory* as a woman poet disenfranchised from the national tradition, she wrote as an authoritarian poetic voice, imitating that Irish traditional poetry which encourages the subject to write with a "bardic force behind him" (interview with Villar Argáiz). As Boland gradually becomes a prominent voice within the Irish literary panorama, her poetic voice experiences an increasing powerlessness and marginalisation. The reason she does this is because of the subversive possibilities that a marginal position grants her. As Boland has argued, even though "the history of poetry shows that [...] the centre dictates the margin [...], in the end the margin always defines the centre" (interview with Villar Argáiz). For Boland, adopting a powerless position as a writer affords many subversive possibilities. First of all, she consciously relegates herself to being an Irish woman poet who inherits an oppressive past in order to bring to the fore in her poems those 'silences' and painful experiences that have characterised Ireland's history. Secondly, self-marginalisation allows her to avoid adopting that authoritarian and communal stance that has been at the centre of Irish poetry. Finally, by describing herself as an unstable and vulnerable subject who experiences displacement and deterritorialisation, Boland shows the fallacy of those hegemonic beliefs in the subject's right to possess and to claim a place as his/her own. When Boland was asked recently if she has eventually come to terms with those painful childhood memories of exile and displacement in *Code*, she answered that she still feels an intense estrangement from her own country (interview with Villar Argáiz). Indeed, one of her most recent unpublished poems, "In Our Own Country", ends by arguing that "we will always be 'exiles in our own country'" (ibid).

360

Notes to chapter 4

[1] In her introduction to the 1999 edition of *A Literature of Their Own*, Showalter (1999: xix) defends herself from attacks such as this by arguing that when she finished this book in 1974, she had not even heard of Cixous, Irigaray, and Kristeva, as their work was not introduced to American scholars until 1980, in a translation by Elaine Marks and Isabelle de Courtivron.

[2] Note the similitude between Fanon's project and Kristeva's feminist advocacy for an "analysis of the potentialities of *victim/executer* which characterises each identity, each subject, each sex" (Kristeva 1986c: 210). Both Fanon and Kristeva defend moving beyond the dichotomy 'One' vs. the 'Other' which is intrinsic to the process of identity-making, by identifying 'the Other' in oneself.

[3] "From the Irish of Pangur Ban", "Elegy for a Youth Changed to a Swan", "O Fons Bandusiae", "Conversation with an Inspector of Taxes", and "The Atlantic Ocean" are, broadly speaking, still firmly in the formal conservatism of Boland's first phase (*Collected*, 53-60). It is interesting to note how in the 1980 Arlen Edition, Boland arranges these poems so that they appear in the middle of the volume. The fact that they are surrounded by more innovative poems, both in their theme and their poetic language ("The Other Woman", "The Famine Road", "The Greek Experience", "Suburban Woman", and "Ode to Suburbia", for instance) indicates that Boland deliberately wishes to set a contrast, a tension between literary convention and subversion. This contrast parallels Boland's confusion in those years: whether to stick to formal parameters, or to open new avenues of experimentation.

[4] Because of this lack of consistency in her subversion of the Irish poetic tradition, *The War Horse* has received some negative reviews. See in particular Dodsworth (1986: 96).

[5] In "The Hanging Judge", war is presented as a battle between fathers and sons (*Collected*, 67-68). The poetic speaker becomes at the end the son who is been hanged, killed by his own father. In "The Family Tree", Boland also represents her cousins as "wag[ing] their sterile fight, their arid battle/ Pleasuring to poison enemy cattle,/ Innocent children now" (p. 51). These poems, together with "Sisters", where two sisters are presented as in enmity for a long time (pp. 47-49), help to show war as something closer to the domestic environment, as a battle that takes place between members of the same family.

[6] Cixous (1994: 135) argues that it is only because of women's assigned position within the socio-symbolic system that they are potentially closer to a "feminine economy".

[7] One of the reasons why sexual difference and therefore "amorous exchanges" have not flourished in Western culture, according to Irigaray (1991: 172-173), is because the binary thought, or split dichotomies, have not allowed the alliance between the sexes. Dichotomies such as "body and soul, sexuality and spirituality, [...] inside and outside", have been hierarchically distributed among the two sexes, to the extent that everything has been "constructed in such a way as to keep these realities apart, if not opposed to one another" (ibid).

[8] As in the case of "Ready for Flight", "The Botanic Gardens" is composed of five sestets which follow a pattern of half-rhyme. This is Boland's transition from a purely formalised poetic style, to a poetry in which syntax is more flexible. As we will see, open forms will dominate her mature poetry.

[9] In this sort of stream of consciousness, one is inevitably reminded of Virginia Woolf's short story "Kew Gardens" (1967) [1919], where the speaker, while wandering through a botanic garden,

gives free rein to her thoughts, finding mixed sensations in the colours and shapes of the plants and flowers, and in the noises of the garden. In fact, Boland makes explicit her own admiration for Virginia Woolf in her prose work *Object Lessons* (1995a: 132-133), where she quotes some passages from *A Room of One's Own*.

[10] The metaphor of the moon and constellations to express positive influence between people has been common in Boland's poetry. As early as *Eavan Boland Poetry*, poems such as "On Giving a Cyclamen 1961" employ the metaphor of the moon to express the positive influence that her mother exerts on her: "you sped my way with more than moonlight/ You have circled all my heritage/ With brightness" (*Boland Poetry*, 6). In another poem in *The War Horse*, "Sisters", this metaphor is used to indicate a relationship of equality, in which one sister learns from the other: "since you hauled my one eye blind,/ Round like the morning globe to meet/ Light" (*Collected*, 48). In Boland's more mature work, constellations will acquire a different significance, as we will see.

[11] Note the similarity of approach that Kristeva (2004) adopts. In the recent study that she has published on the work of three twentieth-century women (Arendt, Klein, and Collete), Kristeva (2004: 12) argues that she can only approach them by admitting that they expose in their writings an "irreducible subjectivity". My reading of Kristeva's paper delivered in May 2004 at the Royal Irish Academy, Dublin, is indebted to Dr. Ríóna Ní Fhrighil, who attended her presentation and very generously provided me with a copy of it.

[12] At the age of five, in 1950, Boland had to leave Ireland for England (Boland 1995a: 35-37). Her father, the diplomat Frederick H. Boland, was commissioned to London, to work as the Irish Ambassador to the Court of St. James. Both in her prose work and in her poetry, Boland has focused on the six years she lived in London, and she describes this time as an unhappy and discontented one. Later, she spent a few years in New York, where her father served as President of the UN General Assembly.

[13] This refusal to adopt an explicit political attitude has been the source of much controversy. Sarup (1993: 186) has criticised postmodernist theories such as Lyotard's as leading to "moral and political nihilism". Critics such as Ahmad (1992: 69) and Parry (1987: 29) have also accused Said, Bhabha, and Spivak of ignoring the political struggle of the Third World. According to them, their methodological affiliation to deconstructivist theory constrains the development of anti-imperialist critique and leaves no room for active resistance outside the discursive level.

[14] Whereas Bhabha and Hall focus on the diasporic and Caribbean communities respectively, Boyce draws her theoretical premises from her study of black women's literary texts. What is interesting to note is that these three theorists coincide in asserting that the colonised subject is constituted by multiple identities that do not always make for harmony.

[15] This splitting of identity is reflected in those poems where Boland reflects on her young exile from Ireland. Diasporic poems such as "An Irish Childhood in England: 1951" and "Fond Memory" (*Collected*, 155-156) record the confusions and contradictions of a girl who does not know where she belongs. Neither feeling entirely English nor 'authentically' Irish, Boland advocates an exiled place, 'in-between' identity claims.

[16] See Green et al. (1996: xvi) who focuses on Francophone postcolonial women writers. Other postcolonial feminist critics, such as Rajan (1993) and Smith and Watson (1992), have similarly embraced hybridity in their discussion of postcolonial literature written by Third World women.

[17] Bakhtin's double notion of hybridity has been applied by postcolonial critics such as Young (1995: 21-25) and Werbner (1997: 4-5).

[18] Young (1995: 24-25) also applies Bakhtin's doubled notion of hybridity when focusing on Hall's discussion of black cultural politics in "New Ethnicities" (1996a).

[19] This fluid sense of identity is also observed in other Irish women writers, such as Medbh McGuckian, whose poetry records "the tension between the evolving selves and identities of a [...] woman in a troubled land" (Haberstroh 2001: 9).

[20] Cixous was born in Oran, Algeria, in 1937, of a Spanish/French/Jewish father and a German/Jewish mother (Sellers 1994: xxvi). As she explains: "I was born at/from the intersection of migrations and memories from the Occident and Orient, from the North and South. I was born a foreigner in 'France' in a said-to-be 'French' Algeria. I was born in not-France calling itself France" (Cixous 1994: xv).

[21] As Cixous (1994: xvii) argues:
> A subject is at least a thousand people. This is why I never ask myself "who am I?" (*qui suis-je?*). I ask myself "who are I?" (*qui sont-je?*) – an untranslatable phrase. Who can say who I are, how many I are, which I is the most I of my I's? Of course we each have a solid social identity, all the more solid and stable as all our other phases of identity are unstable, surprising. [...]. We: are (untranslatable).

[22] "Volume without Contours" is the title of one of Irigaray's essays (1991: 53-67).

[23] For an interesting comparison between "From the Painting *Back from Market* by Chardin" and "Self-Portrait on a Summer Evening", see Martin (1993) and McGuckian (1993).

[24] This feminist postcolonial critic particularly mentions Gloria Anzaldúa's *Borderlands/ La Frontera* (1987) as one of the best examples of "borderland consciousness". The New Mestiza Anzaldúa talks about, Boyce (1994: 15-16) asserts, inhabits more than one place at the same time. Gloria Anzaldúa's theorisation of border and border lines has exerted a tremendous influence on feminist writing. See, for instance, Brah (2003: 625).

[25] Another example in which Boland describes herself in the middle of the staircase, in a moment of transition, is in "Monotony" (*Collected*, 101-102).

[26] The colour blue is a characteristic metaphor of Boland's poetry to talk about the Irish past, those men and women who are unrecorded by historical and nationalist accounts. A possible explanation for this is that the colour blue is generally related to the sky, a place where women's past lives may be more truthfully recorded. In fact, Boland uses constellations to signify women's cultural and historical displacement (see, for instance, her poem "Monotony", *Collected*, 101-102). Like the stars in the sky, women have always been there, their presence is unquestionable, but they have generally been unnoticeable to the contemporary world. The colour blue will become significant in volumes such as *In a Time of Violence* (see, for instance, "A Sparrow Hawk in the Suburbs", *Collected*, 221-222), and in particular poems such as "Home" (pp. 258-259).

[27] Fulford (2002b: 144-147) has carried out a similar reading of Boland's poetry from the perspective of Kristeva's theories.

[28] Feminist critics such as Irigaray (1991: 217) have also envisaged a possible female imaginary with its own time-space modality, according to which women conceive the concepts of time and

space as "interminable", as "[d]imensions that go beyond the sideral, [...] beyond the imaginary of any consciousness". Irigaray would be what Kristeva labels a radical feminist, for her desire to remain outside the linearity of historical time.

[29] In poems such as "The Pomegranate" and "Daughter" (*Collected*, 215-216, 263-264), for instance, Boland finds in the Ceres and Persephone legend an appropriate representation of the complexity of mother and daughter relationships.

[30] The trip with which Boland starts the poem is, as Thurston (1999: 240) explains, a trip Ceres does not undertake in classical sources.

[31] For a similar approach to the woman's body, see "The Famine Road" (*Collected*, 42-43).

[32] Note that a similar disruption of history occurs in "Daphne Heard with Horror the Addresses of the God" (*Collected*, 181). The mythical story of Daphne is intermingled with a local story Boland hears about a woman and her bridegroom, a merchant from Agyll. These two stories are, in turn, associated with the speaker, a woman located in the garden of her house. In this sense, these two poems establish a connection between mythical women and past Irish women. Both figures equally stand outside linear history: the first because she inhabits myth, and the second because her life story is unrecorded in official historical accounts. For a similar intermingling of local and historical stories, see "A Model Ship Made by Prisoners Long Ago" (*Collected*, 304-305), where Boland juxtaposes the story of her grandfather, a "Master of the Union", with those oppressed Irish prisoners forced to make a model ship.

[33] Note the beginnings of poems such as "Contingencies" ("Waiting in the kitchen for power-cuts") or "A Different Light" ("Talking just like this") (*Collected*, 191, 194).

[34] For an interesting comparison between Joyce's and Boland's treatment of gender and language in their work, see Pérez Valverde (2001).

[35] In poems such as "Canaletto in the National Gallery of Ireland" and "The Scar" (*Collected*, 157, 249-250), Boland also uses the river Liffey as an emblem of Dublin and nationhood.

[36] Ailbhe Smyth's "The Floozie in the Jacuzzi" is another interesting example of the Irish feminist controversy around this female figure (1989).

[37] For an interesting comparison of Boland's "A Woman Painted on a Leaf" and Yeats's "Sailing to Byzantium", see Hagen and Zelman (2004: 103-104).

[38] Poems like "The Emigrant Irish", "Distances", "In a Bad Light", "The Lost Land", and "Exile! Exile!" show Boland's concern with the historical event of emigration (*Collected*, 158, 199, 207-208, 260-261, 294). On the other hand, the famine is recorded in "The Famine Road", "The Journey", "The Achill Woman", "The Making of an Irish Goddess", "That the Science of Cartography is Limited", and "Quarantine" (*Collected*, 42-43, 147-150, 176-179, 204-205, 282).

[39] As Griffiths (1994: 70) has argued, "[t]here are real dangers in recent representations of indigenous peoples in popular discourse, especially in the media, which stress claims to an 'authentic' voice. For these claims may be a form of overwriting the complex actuality of difference".

---

[40] According to Boland (1995a: 127), poetic ethics are always present in a country that has suffered the consequences of colonial displacement. As she argues, they "are evident and urgent in any culture where tensions between a poet and his or her birthplace are inherited and established".

[41] Although I am here using the essay included in an anthology of postcolonial criticism published in 1994, "Can the Subaltern Speak?" dates back to 1988. Spivak has later revised this essay in *A Critique of Postcolonial Reason* (1999).

[42] To this critique, Spivak answers as follows: "When Benita Parry takes us to task for not being able to listen to the natives, or to let the natives speak, she forgets that the three of us, postcolonials, are 'natives' too" (Spivak 1990b: 227). In fact, it is not so much that Spivak does not let the natives speak, but that, according to her, the colonial system does not provide them with the choice to speak.

[43] See, for instance, the endings of "Fond Memory", "The Shadow Doll", "An Old Steel Engraving", "We Are Always Too Late", "Beautiful Speech" and "The Huguenot Graveyard at the Heart of the City" (*Collected*, 156, 170, 184, 186, 212, 225). Foster (1999: 10) calls them "tag-line[s]", and argues that Boland uses them in order to insert an afterthought, which reinterprets or turns over the meaning of the preceding passage.

[44] Deane (2003: 118) observes this condition of inarticulacy in Joyce's *Portrait of the Artist as a Young Man* and Synge's *The Playboy of the Western World*. The languages that Stephen Dedalus and Christy Mahon have inherited are "authoritarian in structure": they stand for the tenets of British imperialism, Irish nationalism, and the Roman Catholic Church. For both figures, achieving linguistic decolonisation involves an act of "imagining or forging" a new language (ibid).

[45] Deane (2003: 119-120) justifies his argument by asserting that in Beckett's *All That Fall*, the Irish language functions as "the language for that which is unsayable in English, or simply unsayable as such"; and that Brian Friel's *Translations* similarly deals with the issue of the "language loss".

[46] The most obvious similarity between Boland and Kristeva is that both reject radical feminism. Kristeva's uneasy relationship with feminism stems from her fear that any sort of political discourse "will necessarily reveal itself as another master-discourse" (Moi 1986: 10). Kristeva moves away from feminist attempts to homogenise 'Woman' under what she calls the "totalising use" of the plural "we" (Kristeva 1986c: 199), and adopts a sceptical attitude to any notion of a universal sexual identity. Likewise, Boland (1995a: 234) has declared her fear that feminism threatens her project as a poet. As we have already seen in those poems where Boland focuses on the simplification involved in any sort of artistic representation, her work constantly exemplifies the fallibility involved in recuperating a woman's essence. Boland's mature work is located outside the realm of essentialist ideologies such as feminism and nationalism, for they construct identity on differences and opposition. As a result of this, both Kristeva and Boland, adopt a politics of marginality.

[47] By means of these two orders, semiotic and symbolic, Kristeva transforms Lacan's distinction between the imaginary and the symbolic. Whereas Lacan insists on a definite separation between the imaginary and the symbolic, Kristeva stresses a continuation between these two orders (Sarup 1993: 123).

[48] Bhabha's definition of minority discourse is helpful here: the "in-between of image and sign, the accumulative and the adjunct, presence and proxy" (1995: 307). Like Kristeva, to whom Bhabha is

greatly indebted, Bhabha understands the subversive as located outside the limits of conventional language. By referring to what is "in-between image and sign", Bhabha refers to an unidentifiable and inarticulate void, which lies in what Kristeva has called the semiotic.

[49] French feminist Gauthier (1981a: 164) has also identified women's language with silences and wordlessness:

> And then, blank pages, gaps, borders, spaces, and silence, holes in discourse: these women emphasise the aspect of feminine writing which is the most difficult to verbalise. [...] If the reader feels a bit disoriented in this new space, one which is obscure and silent, it proves perhaps that it is women's place.

[50] It is significant how, when Spivak (1994: 103) narrates in "Can the Subaltern Speak?" the local story of an Indian girl who committed suicide, her discourse is constructed upon words such as "perhaps" and "possible".

[51] The sound of the wheels of a train also stand as a "musical sub-text" for a subaltern past in "The Unlived Life", where the train stands as an "iron omen/ of another life passing, passing" (*Collected*, 135), and "Happiness", where the speaker hears "the wheels/ saying [...] *never again, never again*" (p. 270).

[52] This reading was recorded with the permission of Eavan Boland.

[53] The emblematic figure of Sappho has also been the source of inspiration for contemporary male poets in Ireland, such as Theo Dorgan, who in *Sappho's Daughter* (2001) establishes an imaginary dialogue between Sappho and her lover.

[54] Said (1994: 261) notes this tendency in Rushdie's *The Satanic Verses* and Aimé Césaire's *Une Tempête*. In these "voyages in", Said (1994: 295) states, "the separations and exclusions of 'divide and rule' are erased and surprising new configurations spring up".

[55] Although this Irish critic ends up embracing the ability of employing hybridity for transgressing the borders between supposedly established and essentially different categories, Smyth (2000: 46, 51) asserts that Bhabha's employment of hybridity is a "merely critical rationale [...] for the new phase of global capitalism into which we have moved rather than an explanation of the non-West's mode of resistance and survival".

[56] Gilbert and Gubar (2000: 262, 328) also mention Emily Brontë's *Wuthering Heights* and Charlotte Brontë's *The Professor*. For Emily Brontë, the snowy landscapes symbolise the female, an angry goddess who manifests its potential by shaking locks of ice. Her sister also recurs to the image of the wintry forest in order to suggest, instead of female potential, female desolation and lovelessness.

[57] The new collection of poems she was working on at the time I was writing this book contains a section entitled "Domestic Violence", based on the memory of the suburban violence that was going on in the 70s and 80s in Ireland (interview with Villar Argáiz).

[58] Boland's work has also had a tremendous reception in the United States: American publishing companies have opened their doors to her poetry and her photograph was even featured noticeably in the newspaper *Los Angeles Times* (Faggen 2003: 231). Among her honours and awards, she has received a Lannan Foundation Award in Poetry and an American Ireland Fund Literary Award. Thanks to the New York City Transit Authority, excerpts of "Ceres Looks at the Morning" (from

In a Time of Violence) were read on New York buses and subways in 2001 (Hagen & Zelman 2004: 118).

[59] For further information on Boland's professional activities in Stanford University, see Boland (1999a).

[60] In poems such as "In Exile" and "The Huguenot Graveyard at the Heart of the City" (*Collected*, 185, 225), Boland has remembered the exile of German and Huguenot communities in Ireland.

[61] It is important to note that Boland does not merely dedicate *Code* to her husband: he also becomes the speaker's addressee in poems such as "The Pinhole Camera", "Embers", "First Year", "Once", "Thankëd be Fortune", "Lines for a Thirtieth Wedding Anniversary", and "A Marriage for the Millennium" (*Collected*, 280-288).

[62] This reading was recorded with the permission of Eavan Boland.

[63] Poetry reading, June 19th 2004, in the National Concert Hall, Dublin. Recorded with the permission of Eavan Boland.

[64] These verse lines are taken from the American version of "Suburban Woman: Another Detail", which includes a final stanza that does not appear in the English version of the poem.

5

Conclusion

> Give her another hundred years, I concluded, [...] give her a
> room of her own and five hundred a year, let her speak her
> mind and leave out half that she now puts in, and she will
> write a better book one of these days. She will be a poet, I
> said, putting *Life's Adventure*, by Mary Carmichael, at the
> end of the shelf, in another hundred years' time. (Woolf
> 1974: 142)

Virginia Woolf wrote *A Room of One's Own* in 1929, seven decades before

Boland established herself as one of the most important contemporary women

poets in Ireland and abroad. In fact, Boland has become a 'poet' by having a room

of her own, both in a literal and in a figurative sense. Boland's change of life as

she moved from the (exclusively male) academic life in Dublin to the suburbs

triggered her reaction to the dominant aesthetics of the literary tradition. Her

marriage to the novelist Kevin Casey, based on mutual understanding and liberal

ideals, the raising of her two children, and the creation of a homely atmosphere

where she could both combine her roles as wife, mother and housewife, and her

role as literary creator made it possible for her to own that room Woolf talks

about, a room where she could write freely, where she could "let [...] her mind"

speak (p. 142). From the 1980s onwards, women poets in Ireland have won more

recognition and more possibilities of publication in a country where literature has been conceived as a masculine terrain. Boland has achieved a room, not only in her house, but also in the literary panorama of Ireland.

This study has aimed to show Boland's evolution in her writing career. Her 'Feminine'/'Assimilationist' and 'Feminist'/'Cultural Nationalist' phases, though of short duration, have been necessary for the quest of the woman poet's artistic decolonisation, for her finding of a *new territory* in Irish poetry, a more authentic one, where her reality as an Irish woman can be more truthfully recorded. As de Beauvoir (1997: 295) says, "[o]ne is not born, but rather becomes a woman". What these two earlier stages show is that Boland has found difficulty in becoming, in her poems, that *kind* of Irish woman she wants to be: not the female muse, object of desire, and nationalist emblem of male literary texts, but a woman who becomes the speaking voice, the creative author of poems. Furthermore, these stages have been necessary for her forging of a new form of being 'Irish', for her transformation of a category which has been defended as 'pure' and 'distinctive', and her subsequent vindication of an enriching hybrid and cross-cultural form of 'Irishness' that surpasses national boundaries.

As has been hypothesised by Showalter (1999: 13), Fanon (1990: 178), and Memmi (1990: 168), members of the minority culture (i.e. women, the colonised) are initially forced to master the dominant/hegemonic culture, in order to make themselves heard as agentive subjects. In her early years as a writer, Boland experiences this process of assimilation of the conventional parameters on which Irish poetry has been founded. In volumes such as *Eavan Boland Poetry/ Prose Joseph O'Malley* and *New Territory*, she becomes an "honorary male poet", a speaking voice which writes with that weight of bardic authority nationalist literature demanded from Irish writers (interview with Allen-Randolph 1993b: 118). Womanhood is not a prerogative for Boland at this stage in her literary career. She rather focuses her energy on recording 'Irishness' with the highest degree of accuracy possible. This concept is described as a coherent notion: to be an Irish poet means to be a communal voice speaking on behalf of Irish oppression under British rule; to commemorate those dead heroes that have fought for Ireland's independence; to express love and admiration for a beautiful landscape, an Edenic rural place where Gaelic traditions and native authenticity are preserved. To be 'Irish', in short, is to be 'different' and to be able to express this 'difference' by creating a distinctive national culture, just as Revivalists like Yeats advocated.

In *In Her Own Image*, Boland writes new poems, adventures along radical and different paths. In contrast to the uncritical attitude of Boland's initial poems towards the objectification of women in art, Boland starts to be fully conscious of the implications traditional literary images have for her as a woman writer. Now, the woman poet finds the Irish poetic tradition oppressive and disaffecting. She embraces feminism at the aesthetic level, a stance which she would later refuse as "separatist" (Boland 1995a: 234). Like 'Cultural Nationalism', this ideology is based on prescriptive demands, because it encourages the woman poet to defend her own reality as distinctive, unique, and different from the (masculine and imperialist) 'Other'. Boland maintains a critical attitude towards cultural feminine representations by presenting a counter-image: a woman who is fully active and who is in command of her own experience. The commonplace 'knowledge is power' becomes at this stage almost a political manifesto behind her feminist poems. Whereas in her mature work Boland subjects all knowledge to scrutiny, the speaking voices in *In Her Own Image* make explicit that they know the source of their oppression and that they are able to express with accuracy their own reality. What they know, above all, is their female body, and it is through this knowledge that they attempt to dominate and control their own existence. By placing the body as a source of resistance, as the site where women's reality can be truthfully sheltered, Boland, like Irigaray (1991: 24) and Cixous (1994: 38), returns to biology in order to counteract patriarchal discourse. In this sense, gender becomes a priory essence for Boland to reassert her own identity as a woman. As Showalter (1999: 13), Memmi (1990: 7), Fanon (1991: 11), and other feminist and postcolonial critics have explained (Minh-ha 1989: 38; Christian 1990: 45; Donaldson 1992: 11; Spivak 1993: 17), this action is bound to fail.

Notions such as 'womanhood' and 'negritude' should not be defended in essentialist terms, for this ultimately leads to an oppositional affirmation that falls back into a hegemonic discourse, and reiterates the patterns of dominance and authority of ideologies such as imperialism and nationalism.

It is not until her 'Female'/'Liberationist' phase that Boland's poetry deals simultaneously with both categories, 'Irishness' and 'womanhood'. Nevertheless, in contrast to her previous volumes of poetry, nationalism and feminism (and their corresponding views on identity), are not perceived anymore as enabling ideologies. Boland constructs a complex Irish and female identity, an identity which is not based this time on notions such as 'purity', 'authenticity', 'race', and 'biology'. In this sense, her poetry stretches beyond the boundaries of gender and nationality in which the notion of selfhood has been fostered.

First of all, Boland subjects concepts like national and cultural identity, concepts which have played an important role in the formation of anti-colonial resistance, to a process of unravelling. Like postcolonial theorists such as Bhabha (1995: 167), Said (1994: 276), and Hall (1990: 223-224), she condemns nationalism as an essentialist ideological formation, and defends the legitimacy of her own fragmented experience as an Irish citizen. The process by which she does so is dual. On the one hand, by legitimising as literary what has traditionally been considered unliterary, Boland defends a more inclusive national identity, an idea of nationalism in which women's realities and experiences are not obliterated anymore. The realities of her own life (as a suburban married woman, a housewife, and a mother) become themes for her writing, and her personal experience acts as an antidote to mythical patriarchal constructs of women, and in particular, to nationalist icons such as Mother Ireland. Boland's women are neither saintly 'angels in the house' nor malevolent witches, as the patriarchal tradition has described them. Furthermore, her mothers do not correspond to the model of mother and wife as advocated by the Church, the State, and Irish society in general: these figures are highly humanised, they experience complex feelings (e.g. unconditional love and distressing melancholy), and they are affected by the passing of time and the loss of beauty. On the other hand, the idea of 'Ireland' Boland envisages is not a community composed by a "People [as] One" (Bhabha 1995: 141), an imagined cohesive 'whole'. Rather, her nation is characterised by fragmentary experiences, hybrid emigrant subjects whose interstitial location allow them to marry oppositions. As a consequence, Boland defends a more fluid notion of national identity. For Boland, Ireland is a map without frontiers, a free space of exploration and peregrination where the subject, constantly in exile, is able to inhabit different spaces: domestic and suburban settings of houses, urban settings inhabited by ordinary citizens, rotten and destroyed rural settings peopled by famine victims, and underworlds of emigrant Irishmen and women. Boland's definition of Ireland is in this sense accomplished by her interest in traditional 'insignificant', 'unheroic', and 'unpleasant' issues. In all these things, the poet finds the source of her poetic creativity, as well as the strength to subvert the nationalist dream of a (pre-colonial) 'Irishness' which is pure and authentic.

Secondly, the idea of 'womanhood' is not taken for granted either. Although Boland's mature work focuses on women's experiences as wives, housewives, and mothers, her poetry is not grounded in an oppositional politics. On the one hand, the woman poet avoids universalising women's experiences, by focusing on a wide variety of women: for example, upper class rich women, laundresses, seamstresses, prostitutes, poor farmers, and apparently privileged Anglo-Irish women. On the other hand, whereas in *In Her Own Image* Boland seems to suggest that only by defining woman in essentialist terms (as a grounded and stable self) female emancipation can be achieved, in her mature poetry it is her lack of specification and ambiguity when describing her female characters that leads to a more real and accurate representation. In contrast to her second phase, where Boland mostly focused on "sexual difference" (or the distance between the male and the female worlds), the woman poet is now concerned with another kind of distance: the significant gap between reality and artistic images. In her poetry, there is always a void between artistic representations and 'the real': art fixes and defines (female) images in its pursuit for artistic beauty; in the process, the complexity of lived experience is omitted and/or simplified. Therefore, one of the most important techniques Boland employs in her poetry to record her 'womanhood' without yielding to the temptations of feminism and its attempt to capture "womanness", as Rooney (1993: 2) would put it, is to create a landscape of 'in-betweeness'. It is in this landscape where her poetic figures are described, with the result that they avoid artistic solidification, and therefore simplification. The technique is as follows: Boland usually presents a female figure which is victimised or defeated, both by history (Ireland's oppression under colonial rule) and by poetry (women's simplification under nationalist allegories). The second step in this process is usually to establish an identification with this subject, either by ventriloquism (becoming the voice of this 'object'), or simply by sharing her grief and dispossession. When this identification occurs, a landscape of fluidity, constant change, and diffused lights invades the poem, with the consequence that the figure of the woman and/or the poet become (equally) dissolved. In this sense, the usual movement in Boland's mature work is from expression and denunciation of women's dual colonisation to disintegration, and with this, paradoxically, to liberation. Only by moving away from restrictive boundaries and fixed images, Boland seems to suggest, can the gendered colonial subject be liberated.

In this sense, by describing her 'Irishness' and 'womanhood' as fluid and unstable categories, Boland's poetry both exposes the constructedness of identity itself and allows the speaker to find a place freed from authoritative ideologies. Nevertheless, if Boland apparently manages to find artistic decolonisation so easily, one might wonder why in her latest productions (*The Lost Land* and *Code*), she continues refusing to describe herself as a subject liberated from the colonial and patriarchal legacy. Some postcolonial critics have argued that the ultimate liberation for the colonised subject can only be viewed as a process and not as an achievable goal. Rajan (1993: 8) summarises this view as follows: "We are forced to concede that a 'non-colonialist' (and therefore non-contaminated) space remains a wish-fulfilment within postcolonial knowledge production". According to Ashcroft, Griffiths and Tiffin (2002a: 195), this is due to the fact that we can never entirely discard the legacy of the past, and although we can "appropriate and transform it in infinite ways", history is always there, as a ghostly presence. The Irish woman historian Beddoe (1998: 3) has put it as follows: "Without a knowledge of our past, we are always having to begin again" (quoted in Hill 2003: 1). This is precisely what Boland experiences. Distant from a past that, she feels, directly affects her as an Irish women poet, she constantly finds the need to recover a subaltern marginal and oppressed reality, obliterated from official national and historical narratives. She establishes a comradeship with those shadowy figures of Ireland's past, and therefore, she continues presenting herself as a marginal and colonised entity. Nevertheless, this (obsessive) emphasis on her dual oppression as an Irish woman is itself a subversive strategy. Marginality is not only an index of suffering, but it can also be per se positive. Locating herself at the edges of the (powerful and authoritarian) Irish literary tradition gives Boland a vantage point from which to subvert all those assumptions upon which canonical poetry has been constructed. First of all, marginality allows Boland to subvert the dichotomy established between a powerful male author and a submissive female object, which is at the heart of lyric poetry. As an author, Boland becomes a powerless, non-authoritarian, and vulnerable speaker, someone who shares that displacement and 'deterritorialisation' Irish women have experienced by simplified cultural and nationalist images. By so doing, she dismantles the power and authority of official cultural discourses in which women have neither had a place from which to speak, nor a place where to be included as an active agent. Secondly, Boland's self-marginalisation allows her to dismantle that nationalist rhetoric which encouraged the poet to act as a representative and communal figure, speaking on behalf of Ireland's oppression. In approaching the Irish past, Boland interrogates the terms of representation. The woman poet avoids acting as an appropriate spokesperson, as someone who is able to offer more 'truthful' accounts of Ireland's past. Like Spivak (1994: 80), she believes that such an act runs the risk of being misrepresentative, of undermining difference and simplifying a subaltern reality which is heterogeneous. In this sense, she shows the fallacy involved in believing in the authority and the 'accurate' representation of official cultural and historical accounts (whether imperialist or nationalist). Boland's poetry teaches us that no one can truly speak on behalf of his/her own country, that one can never entirely be an 'envoy' of his/her own community. Thirdly, by highlighting her marginalisation, Boland is, funnily enough, able to retrieve this 'inaccessible' Irish past. Her language of silences, doubts, and hesitations not only counteracts colonial, nationalist, and patriarchal discourses, but also offers a more accurate representation of the subaltern, by bringing to the fore of her poems Irish women's muteness, dumbness, and painful experiences in the past. In this sense, Boland's mature representation of herself as a marginal (and still colonised) entity is in fact a technique with allows her to achieve artistic decolonisation.

I end this conclusion by stressing the two contradictory pulls which underlie Boland's poetry, mostly her mature production. On the one hand, Boland stresses a postmodernist celebration of diversity and plurality, and a recognition of the multiple and fragmentary identities that constitute categories such as 'Irishness' and 'womanhood'. Faithful to poststructuralism, Boland demonstrates the artificiality of identity claims such as those defended by imperialism, nationalism, and feminism. Her mature poetry constantly overcomes binary oppositions (such as coloniser/ colonised and masculine/ feminine) by means of hybridity and fluidity. This postmodernist anti-essentialism observed in her work is simultaneously counteracted by her desire to maintain a sense of cultural identity. Her work is moulded according to an imperative to create an imagined female community, a social bond with all Irish women from the past. Boland constantly attempts to establish a dialogue with the idea of the nation, and to search for a different relationship with the past and to Irish identity.

In this sense, Boland occupies an ideological position which is paradoxical, as a woman poet who yearns simultaneously for an anti-essentialist depiction of the 'self' and an essentialist connection with national identity. Terry Eagleton (1997: 11-12) has expressed his belief that the richness of Irish cultural studies is that it has to analyse a category which is both pure and impure, in the sense that it is both strictly traditional, but at the same time, radically hybrid:

> [...] the ideological category of Irishness signifies on the one hand roots, belonging, tradition, Gemeinschaft, and on the other hand, again with marvellous convenience, exile, difussion, globality, diaspora. [...] With wonderful economy, it signifies a communitarism nostalgically seductive in a disorientatingly cosmopolitan world, while offering itself at the same time as a very icon of that world in its resonance of political defeat, hybridity, marginality, fragmentation.

In the plenary panel "The Politics of Irish Studies" organised by the Academy for Irish Cultural Heritages at the University of Ulster, on February 7th 2004, Eagleton expanded this argument by asserting that Ireland is "the most desirable nation to study nowadays".[1] The reason for this, according to Eagleton, is that Ireland combines the "two most contradictory factors present in any society": there is an "intense 'sense of place' and local identity, rootedness and a belief of historical uniqueness"; while at the same time, it is a society shaped by the postmodernist themes of "migrancy, displacement, and diaspora". The dream of a spiritual homeland is a consoling alternative for those Irish writers who wish to counteract their "grooving reality" as exiled and rootless subjects, as individuals who know they belong nowhere.

Similarly, I believe that Boland's poetry is also one of "the most desirable" literary productions "to study nowadays". The two contradictory tendencies Eagleton identifies in Irish literature are also manifested in her poetry. The evolution Boland's poetic career experiences from 1972 onwards illustrates in an exemplary way the tensions Irish women writers experience as gendered postcolonial subjects. Boland desires to find a stable 'sense of place'; she yearns for a spiritual rootedness as an Irish citizen and also as a woman writer. In the process, she is constantly assailed by a profound experience of historical and cultural displacement. In this sense, Boland is divided between two identities, her Irish national identity (which demands her identification with the nation, in order to be an agent and participant of its discourse), and her hybrid identity as a migrant subject (which allows her to move freely between those ideologies which confer identity in terms of categories such as nation and gender). Out of this tension, Boland manages to present a background where new decolonising identities can emerge. In other words, it is here where she finds her way out as *an outsider within an outsider's culture.*

Notes to chapter 5

---

[1] Recorded with the permission of Terry Eagleton.

Appendix
An Interview with Eavan Boland[1]

Dublin,
18th June, 2004

PVA: In your introduction to Carol Shloss's session, you have mentioned that "biography is an ethic" for yourself.[2] I found that very interesting, because in fact reading your poetry is entering constant biographies about the past. One of the questions I wanted to ask you is related to this comment of yours. How is identity constructed in your poetry, by recording these biographies, these silences of the past?

EB: It's an interesting question. I think all human identity is fictional in some way. What you construct from your past is usually a process of selection rather than construction: there's no actual model on which to build a past or a present. Inevitably, you select what serves the construction. In my own case, when I was young, one of the real shaping influences was my gradual discovery of the difference between the past and history. In Ireland, there's a wide and instructive distance between those two. I believe history is an official version of events – it is itself a constructed narrative. But the past, at least as I came to see it, is a place of silences and losses and disappearances. That gap, that distance between those two narratives –and my own gradual understanding of it –has been a powerful motive for me to make certain arguments and to challenge certain concepts. I also came to believe that if I, as a poet, didn't explore that difference I ran the risk of being captured by a pre-ordained version of my life. I didn't want that.

PVA: I find very interesting what you are saying, the fact that the past is full of silences and whispers, as one may observe when reading your poetry. By defining the past in such a way, can real subaltern consciousness, the native voice, be grasped? Can an artist represent in an authentic way the past?

EB: No artist can really represent a past. They can only represent their own view of it. If you want to accept the historical version of events, then you'll deduce the past by what is not said, rather than what is. Ireland is a small country. It struggled with the whole reality of oppression, colony and liberation. But when it came to construct the version of its history which would address those realities what emerged, perhaps inevitably, was a relentless narrative of heroes. Constructing that narrative was a reflex that goes to the heart of Irish history. In 1848 there was collection of songs and ballads, published by Gavan Duffy and Thomas Davis, called The Spirit of the Nation. It's a stirring, musical book – it has ballads, refrains, stanzas about Irish resistance. But it was published in a year when the Irish were still dying in their thousands or perishing on coffin ships. Yet not a word in that book refers to the crisis of the famine. That's a fairly representative example of the exclusions that come with a story of heroes. When you look closely at something like that you realise that not only is there a difference between the past and history, but in certain circumstances a version of history can actually suppress what is really happening. In reality, Irish history is a hard and relentless account of suffering. It is about failure, defeat, and the harshness of the most brutal kinds of survival. It is not about heroism. The fact that Irish history chose to be about heroism opened a fault line for me. It made me question what the real Irish story was, and where I fitted into it as an Irish poet. Inevitably, all this served to gender my sense of Irishness. The history and the heroism seemed male: the past, with all its silences, seemed female. But that's a gendering by effect, not cause. In the Famine Museum in Strokestown, there's a letter from a woman, written in 1848. She is trying to get her children out of the workhouse. She may have left them there. She's writing to the middleman on an estate to try to find them. Almost certainly they were dead by then. It's a letter from the deepest regions of the underworld. I don't want a history that – by its emphasis on victory – overwrites the profound human defeat expressed in that letter.

PVA: When talking about this history of dispossession and humiliation, there is a passage in Object Lessons *where you recount how you went to the table with "an Irishness which was not bardic or historic", but an Irishness "full of silences". I was drawn to this definition of Irishness. How do you view Irishness, Irish identity? Like an easy identifiable self, or like a polyglot culture with different traditions, different selves?*

EB: Ireland's history was defined – at least when I was young – by its story of resistance. It was a small country which had bested a large one, and an empire to boot. It became an emblem of succeeding against the odds. I was never comfortable with just that and only that. I think I realised there were two possible views of Irishness. In the first, you could follow writers like Daniel Corkery –he makes a powerful case in his book *The Hidden Ireland* – who argues that below the surface of colony, below all the humiliations, there is a pure, untouched and somehow golden land of saints and scholars. A pure Ireland. It's a surprisingly dangerous notion. Or you can believe, as I came to, that the island and all the people on it are deeply marked by the humiliation and pain of what happened. That we ourselves are the text of it. That we are, in other words, constructed by the construct of colony itself: we are the sum total of the fragmentations, compromises, sufferings that occurred. And the more real, the more substantial for being so. If you don't have that sense, you may fall into the nostalgia for an Ireland which never really existed, and reject the present for an unreachable past. There are real, living dangers in that attitude: we had 25 years of violence in this

382

country because some people thought that they were more Irish than others. We should have learned that whatever we stood for, whatever we were, it perished the moment somebody died for being perceived as less Irish than someone else. The real achievement of Irish literature is itself a recognition of colony: we took the language of the conqueror and made it tell our story. By doing that, we made a language, in which every suppression of who we were occurred, serve as the vehicle of our self-expression. I think that's central.

PVA: So in this sense, do you feel comfortable when writing in English?

EB: Yes. It's both my language and a recognition of what happened. I've nothing but respect and admiration for those who write in the Irish language. But in a practical way, I was never going to write in Irish because I was educated outside of Ireland. Like many other Irish writers, I wrote in English because it was the language I was left with, both personally and historically. That being said, there also seems to me something wonderfully subversive about being an Irish writer in the English language. The very injustices which made it inevitable that an Irish writer would write in English can be addressed in that writing. It can also be addressed in reality. I think Irish writing in the twentieth century proves that losing a language – which is always a tragedy – doesn't mean that you lose an identity. In fact identity is often a composite of all those fragmentations which caused the language to be lost in the first place.

PVA: In your essay "Daughters of Colony", you mention when talking about Ireland as a postcolonial country that it is very difficult to measure the colonial effects because they vary not only from one culture to another one, but also among those people belonging to the same community. According to this point, would you agree with using those theoretical paradigms proposed by postcolonial theorists such as Homi Bhabha, Edward Said, or Gayatri Spivak to talk about Ireland, or to talk about Irish literature, and in particular your poetry?

EB: I agree with some of it. Some of it doesn't seem relevant. There can be problems with a global post-colonial template, including the fact – ironically – that it can be both oppressive and exclusive. When the *Field Day Anthology of Irish Writing* – an openly postcolonial Irish anthology – was published in 1992 it excluded many women. My work was represented in it; many others were left out. It was a striking anomaly: a statement about colonial behaviour which perpetuated it. But those contradictions can happen.

PVA: I would like to focus now on your own evolution as a poet, something that I am greatly interested in. There is a clear evolution from New Territory *onwards which I think it is perceived not only as regards poetic concerns but also as regards language. I think that this evolution deserves further research. You have stated at one point that a truly important poet changes the interior of the poem together with the external perceptions of identity of the poet. Your poetry has opened the way for new concerns never talked about in Irish poetry, such as the private and domestic world of women. How do you think that these new images of femininity and nationality are reflected in your poetic language, your writing techniques?*

EB: I certainly didn't know how to reflect them in *New Territory*. By the time I finished *The War Horse* I was beginning to struggle with a different subject matter, but still uncertain. It wasn't till the very end of that book, in a poem called "Suburban Woman" that I touched on those themes, and then only briefly. It's hard to change the way you write. It's hard to unlearn the way you've learned to be a poet. Both were involved with the poems I was trying to write in *In Her Own Image*, *Night Feed* and *The Journey*. There's a lot of different ways of talking about changing a style. For me, I felt the interior of the poem could only be changed by changing where the poet stood in the poem. I felt that the Irish poem had traditionally been written with the poet standing in one place and throwing their voice from that location only. It's an inexact way of putting it, but it's what I felt. The Irish poet had traditionally written from the centre, with the whole weight of authority and bardic force behind him. I wondered what would happen if you shifted to the margin, if you displaced that centre. A poem like "Mise Eire" was an attempt at that.

Maybe I can expand that inexact language in this way: where a poet stands in a poem – to continue with that image – isn't just arbitrary. The poet's stance is a cipher for so much more. That stance can imply privilege and an inherited, ordained poetic authority – the right to speak of and for something. I was troubled by the idea of a ready-made authority in the Irish poem: who had it, and who didn't. By those definitions I, as a woman, certainly didn't. So I had to be the source of my own authority – not easy when you're a young poet in a powerful literary tradition. By the early eighties I was thinking I could try to shift things, rearrange that interior space. "Mise Eire" is one of the poems that came out of that. I was trying to find my own place in things.

PVA: Taking into account your idea that poets should write not at the centre, but on the margins, at the edges, so to speak, is marginality then at the very moment of writing positive rather than negative?

EB: That's hard to answer. I'll try to be particular about it. Years ago, I wrote a poem called "The Wild Spray". It's in *The Journey*. The poem is about flowers my mother brought me – how they looked inside the house, what they suggested about what was outside, beyond the house. That poem was central for me personally, at least at that time. But as far as the tradition of Irish poetry went then – with all its assumptions of what an Irish poem was – it could only be marginal. Too domestic, too private, too unsanctioned in terms of its subject matter. The marginality in the tradition certainly affects the centrality of the writing. There are different ways of talking about that. I was aware that some of my themes, my interests were right at the edges of Irish poetry, at the very margins. That became an additional spur for me. And of course, I was discouraged at times by being at the margins. But I also knew that the history of poetry shows that if the centre dictates the margin – at the beginning, that is – in the end the margin always defines the centre. It was easier to believe that intellectually than to feel it when I was young. The climate for a young woman poet in Ireland was relatively bleak when I began. At worst, there was a sort of intimidatory disrespect. At best, there was an unspoken assumption that a woman poet could never change the inherited Irish poem in the way a man could. That she could never own it or write it in such a way as to shift the tradition. For me, that was a subtle and painful exclusion. But it was also a motive to think more carefully about what I was doing – more carefully than I might have done if conditions hadn't been so inhospitable. The more I thought about it – I'm not sure I had this worked out clearly then – the more it seemed that if history and the past were as divided as I thought they were, then the tension between the centre and the margin in Irish poetry was even more important. It also seemed vital to me that some two-tiered system of poetry didn't develop – with Irish poetry in one place and women's poetry in another, so that women's poetry would be isolated from having real importance. The resistances and pressures were subtle. Some of them came from the fact that the Irish poetic tradition was bardic. There was a backdrop of heroic speech in the Irish poem. So it wasn't easy to introduce a different subject matter. I've said before that it was much easier back then to have a political murder in an Irish poem than a washing machine. There was a feeling that the first was poetic and the second wasn't.

PVA: You have described yourself as feminist and not a feminist poet. Similarly, you have argued that the nation is a very important image in your poetry, but that you don't consider yourself a nationalist poet. In this sense, I think that your poetry is located between critical extremes, authoritarian ideologies such as nationalism or feminism. Is it possible not to be the result or the expression of any of these ideologies when writing?

EB: Involvement or knowledge of a particular ideology or belief doesn't require that you're constructed by it; but it does require you have a dialogue with it. That was true in my case. To be sceptical about Irishness and have no dialogue with it would have made no sense. Irish nationalism, the physical intensity of its songs, images, traditions, is not something an Irish poet could easily walk away from. There's no way to simply and intellectually disown where you come from, because it would mean disowning who you are. The dialogue with your origins is always dialogue with yourself. Joyce's statement "non serviam" seemed to me to express something central about resisting the orthodoxies of Irishness. I certainly didn't feel bound to serve in any way. I suspect most writers don't. Nationalism, of course, doesn't seem to me as enabling an orthodoxy as feminism. Feminism is a powerful, ethical ideology. As such it's been extremely important to me as a woman. But even the most enabling ethical ideologies are anti-imaginative, painful as it may be to admit it. To prescribe a poem by my feminism would be like saying to a nature poet in today's world "from now on, when you write nature poetry, you must indicate that you are an environmentalist". If I did that, I would be asking them to limit their imaginative reach. However compelling environmentalism is, it can't and shouldn't prescribe the ambiguities, darknesses and fears of the good nature poet. Poetry begins where certainties ends. That's why I'm a feminist but not a feminist poet.

PVA: Much of your poetry reveals that all acts of representation are inevitably partial. In fact, there is a passage in Object Lessons *where you reflect on the difficulties involved in the process of "inscribing a profile in the hard rock". I understood that passage as the difficulties involved in describing the fluidity of a life, the changes that constantly affect women, for instance, in a poem without freezing the moment, without simplifying these images any further. Is it possible to create a place in poetry that avoids misrepresentation? How can poetry emulate or bear witness to the passing of time, to the loss of beauty? In other words, how to represent in an authentic way what sometimes runs the risk of misrepresentation?*

EB: Representation is an elusive term. Who is misrepresenting or representing? And for what purpose? And who decides the rules of it anyway?

Women writers – myself among them – have often been accused of misrepresentation. But all too often accused by a critique which has little to do with the work or its real identity. At the heart of this is the fact that women's poetry pre-existed the critique for it. Many women poets wrote fine poems. Few of them wrote any critique of what they were doing. There are outstanding exceptions – such as Adrienne Rich, whose critiques provided an essential access, not just to her own work but to wider issues about poetic authority. Women who wrote no critique ran the risk of having their work judged by a set of assumptions which had little relation to it. I wrote *Object Lessons* because I wanted to make that critique. There's a special risk factor for women poets if they don't make that critique. I'm fascinated, for instance, by those women poets of the 19th century who became labelled as "poetesses" – Rossetti and Browning in England and even Dickinson in the United States. It was a destructive context to be put in. And they had no defence against it. No intellectual, argumentative defence, that is, such as a critique would be. Without a critique of their own, they were helpless in the face of the critique – Victorian, Imperial, Anglo-heroic – which put them in a demeaning category. But the fact is that the very idea of the poetess was a corrupt construction of a society which preserved itself through that and other fictions. When I was young in Ireland I felt those fictions in a very real way. They were all around: one manifestation of them is that they represented Irish poetry as heroic and bardic. They offered no place for a poet like myself who wanted to take a different path. The only solution was to make my own statement, my own critique. If I hadn't I could see a two-tiered critique developing where there was women's poetry and there was Irish poetry. I didn't want that for myself. I was a woman poet *and* I was an Irish poet. I felt both identities could interpret and re-interpret each other in some rich, demanding ways. I also felt I had the right to re-interpret the past of the Irish poem as well as the present. That brings me back to your question and the start of this answer – it isn't how women represent themselves that concerns me. It's how they are represented before they even begin to write – that's the area of conflict.

PVA: I would like to focus now on your latest volume of poetry, which I think is amazing, something for me completely unexpected.

EB: It was helpful for me to write it...

PVA: Why this change of title, from the American Against Love Poetry *[2001] to the English* Code *[2001]?*

EB: My working title was *Code*. That was the name of one of the poems. But the title was meant to flag more than one poem. The codes, protocols, arrangements of living itself are part of the book. Then more of the poems were written and my American publisher liked the title *Against Love Poetry* as did I at that stage. By then the English title was set. I prefer the American title now – but I don't in the least mind having two separate titles in two different places.

PVA: In this volume, you sound more assertive as regards notions such as Ireland, if we compare it to The Lost Land. *It is my impression that you find less difficulty in achieving a sense of belonging in Ireland. Have you eventually found a balance with the idea of Ireland? I mean, have you come to terms with those pained memories of exile or dislocation?*

EB: It's always there – it's always a presence to me. I've been writing some new poems. One of them – it's actually a sequence of three poems – is called "In Our Own Country". It's partly about the changes in Dublin – in fact in all of Ireland. It ends by saying that we will always be "exiles in our own country". I believe that. Of course, some of that sense comes from my childhood. But it's also general, less personal. For a lot of people as they grow older, given the estrangements of modern life, the true and most poignant exile is in their own country and not beyond it.

PVA: Does your living between two countries, Ireland and the United States, have an effect in the way you write poetry?

EB: By the time I went to Stanford my life was set – my children were grown and my sense of poetry was confirmed. You may locate yourself in two places, but you only live in one. At least I do. All the same, I think going there has made me aware of place in a different way. I think that's gone into the poetry in some new way. This year I'm publishing a book of translations called *After Every War*. These are poems by German-speaking women poets – from Germany, Poland, Czernowitz. They're not necessarily poets who lived in Germany. But they're all poets who wrote in German. All the poems are inflected, in some way, by the Second World War which devastated their homelands. Many of them are hardly at all represented in English translations, like Elizabeth Langgässer – and some are celebrated in Germany, like Else Lasker-Schüler, but not enough known in English. For me, the book closed an important circle. After the war, my mother and father brought German girls to our house in Dublin. They were two teenage sisters, and in one way or another, the girls from that family remained in our house for more than twenty years. I never learned to speak German, but I listened to it – sometimes unconsciously – for a good part of my childhood. What drew me especially to these poems, apart from childhood memory, is that they are poems about war seen from an intensely private perspective. I'm thinking particularly of a splendid poem by Else Lasker-Schüler called "My Blue Piano". It comes from her last book, published in 1945, which has the same name. It canvasses a whole world of destruction in the guise of a broken musical instrument, which once belonged in a home. It's such a beautiful, persuasive rendering of the link between the public event and the private loss – which is the reason that no European poem means more to me. And it was also the displacement – the sheer placelessness in fact – of some of these poets which drew me in. There's a beautiful poem by Rose Auslander whose last line is "I do not reside. I live".

PVA: Did you translate these poems or edit them?

EB: I translated them. Towards the end of the process, when the poems were already translated, I had the help of a wonderful Stanford graduate in

German studies, Alys George. She corrected mistakes, suggested amendments, but also had a unique feel for the poems as they were written in their time. Talking about those poems with her was an especially happy part of making the book.

PVA: Talking about placelessness, do you think that the Irish artist, or any artist in general, has to be exiled at a certain point in order to have a more critical view of things?

EB: Writers can be exiled in different ways. Some leave their country. Some don't. There can be an interior exile as well, which is more subtle than the physical statement of leaving. I think I felt something like that when I lived in a suburb and was writing a poem which didn't seem to be sanctioned by the Irish tradition. It produced a sense of estrangement in me – I think many writers experience something like that at some stage of their writing lives.

PVA: Sometimes in your poetry, Iowa, St. Louis, California and New England stand as background settings in your work. Your actual exile from Ireland serves at times to establish a link with one of the most terrible stories of displacement in Irish history, emigration to the United States. Some critics argue when analysing this aspect of your poetry that it runs the risk of being nationalist, in the sense of perpetuating the poet's function as a spokesperson in order to talk on behalf of the community. Let me tell you that I don't particularly agree with this criticism because, when reading your poetry, I can see that you highlight precisely the discontinuities between the past and the present, and the fact that a poet cannot experience the same experiences, and therefore, cannot easily talk on behalf of the past. I would like to know your own view as regards those criticisms...

EB: I'm not an ideological poet. I have no interest in representation. That's for another kind of writer. I'm interested in the individual – in the self as it encounters the event or the experience. There's a rich enough field there to keep me occupied. But although I'm interested in the private self, I'm not interested in conveying that through a private language. So in a way, I'm aware that I visibly transgress on the settled ideas of the public and private poem. That's part of the reason I think that there have been challenges and criticisms to my poetry. It was plain to me at a certain point that I was writing about things which were unacceptable to received notions of Irish poetry. I seemed to be elevating the life of motherhood, the life in a suburban house, the life of domesticity to be a subject matter that had a claim on the Irish poem. That wasn't acceptable to critics of a certain kind, those who felt they had already defined the Irish poetic canon – at least not when I was publishing in the early eighties. In fact, it was that disrespect for the domestic world which forced me towards my own critique. Why were these subjects so menacing to the status quo in Irish poetry? Why were they so unsuitable? Those questions sparked my interest more and more. It was still a long way from becoming a proper debate, but I found the questions compelling. I still do. Recently I've been writing some poems and prose with the working title "Domestic Violence". It's about that time of the seventies and eighties, when Irish writing was defined in a certain way, when the Irish world was being brutally re-defined by its own violence.

PVA: What inspired you to write "Domestic Violence"? The violence happening in Ireland?

EB: Yes, the memory of the 70s and the 80s, when violence was commonplace. But more than that. There were such contradictions in my life at that time. In a private sense, those were happy times for me. I lived in the suburbs, raised my children, was happy with my husband. And yet for all that, the country, the nature, the culture beyond our four walls was poisoned. The question must be therefore – surely the life within the four walls was poisoned too? Surely no one could escape? So this is a way of looking back. In one of the poems in this sequence there is a reference to the myth of Philomel – the legendary figure, raped by her brother-in law, her tongue cut out so she couldn't tell her story. She decides to weave a tapestry to tell what really happened. That's what happened in Ireland too: a succession of brutal silencings and re-stating of the story. The new poems are experimental – and for me this is also a new way of revisiting the domestic poem.

PVA: And talking about the untold as well, right?

EB: Yes, the untold and the untellable. My generation in Ireland lived through a time of change, of challenge, of the upset of received ideas. It was a time of confusion. Now I look back I can see my own ideas being changed, but I couldn't feel that so clearly at the time. There were always poems for me which touched on this and then left it again – "The War Horse" was one. That was a poem I wrote in the early seventies. Much later there was *In a Time of Violence*. The truth is there is a subtle, mysterious and sometimes corrupt way in which people survive a time of violence – by thinking it can't touch their lives.

PVA: What is going to be the name of the new book?

EB: It's still so much in process I can't be sure. Perhaps *In Our Own Country*. Perhaps *Domestic Violence*.

PVA: Considering the feedback that your work has received as regards the number of sales, the audience that go to your poetry readings, or the academic journals on your work, would you consider that there is a difference between the American audience and the Irish audience?

EB: Yes I think so. Different audiences to start with. One audience, the Irish one, originated where I did, which was both liberating and confining. The other has a far more tenuous sense of whether the poem is Irish or not. I think the Irish audience has changed, at least critically. In 1992 when the *Field Day Anthology of Irish Writing* was published, I gave a talk at a summer conference. I made the point then, which of course I still would, that a literature without the voice and vision of women can't really be a national literature. It is centrally wanting, essentially incomplete. That point, of course, was a glimpse of what was obvious. As time has gone on, there has been a definite shift in Ireland. The work of women is on the Leaving Certificate, is well represented in anthologies. It's a different climate. But back then there were strange contradictions in attitude. The belief that you could have a distinguished postcolonial argument about Ireland – with all the exclusions and suppressions colony implies – and then end up excluding the work of women, as the *Field Day Anthology* did, makes no sense at all. I think that point was taken.

PVA: So, now with the new Field Day Anthology of Women's Writing and Traditions *[2001], do you think that the landscape is changing in Ireland? Isn't it more welcoming for women poets?*

EB: Yes I do. I'm glad the anthology is out. It puts in the public domain some wonderful texts – although, of course, they should have been there earlier.

PVA: Do you think that your message has been truthfully interpreted, or do you think that your poetry has been misunderstood in a particular or certain way?

EB: To begin with, I wouldn't think of it as a message. And then, the whole question of misunderstanding is a thorny one. Certainly – especially in the beginning – my work was read in ways which made me think some critics had fixed points and fixed views. There was an arc of association that followed me round for a while. It went something like this: because I was a woman, because my life was presumed to be not epic, not bardic, not centrally Irish – these were all unstated assumptions – I must write a lesser poem, a poem that held a smaller mirror to the Irish reality. By definition, that was the domestic poem. But I didn't see it that way at all. I didn't understand the concept of the domestic poem as an opposition to the political poem; the domestic poem *is* the political poem. I thought of that old image of a train approaching, and how the water in the glass on the windowsill shivers and announces it. That was the kind of poem I wanted to write.

PVA: Regarding metaphor, water is a recurrent image in you poetry, the rain, the ocean, the river. There is a very suggestive metaphor in "White Hawthorn in the West of Ireland" where you mention how water is able to "redefine land". In Code, *in the poem "Lines for a Thirtieth Wedding Anniversary", you also talk about water and how it erodes the rock over the years. It seems to me that whenever you talk about water, as in "an origin like water" for instance, you suggest that the origin of life, or the past, is as difficult to grasp as the water of the ocean. Is water a deliberate metaphor in your poetry? I mean, does it stand for something in particular?*

EB: Water certainly has strong associations for me. My grandfather was a sea-captain. He drowned in the Bay of Biscay. So I heard about that all through my childhood. Then again, I was born in a coastal city. And a city very much defined by its river – I've always loved rivers, and especially the Liffey. And of course, water is the great feminine element.

PVA: In the poem "Anna Liffey", you talk about the river, and how it is connected to the image of the woman, and also the fact that both of them are equally dissolved by the end of the poem. You were just saying that water is a feminine element. It seems to me that by the end of "Anna Liffey" you are talking more in terms of sexlessness than in terms of a feminine element?

EB: That comes at the end of "Anna Liffey" which is a poem about the river, but also a poem about my life when I was writing it. The poem is named after the river which really defines Dublin. In fact, the Liffey is one of the only feminine rivers in the world. I think it and the Amazon are the two main ones. And yes, the poem's real subject is that progress from individuality to dissolution which happens with age. Rivers are such a symbol of that. And it's something which interests me still – the idea of everything else being lost, being dissolved, and yet the voice remaining. That's how the poem ends.

PVA: Is this how artistic decolonisation is found? By moving beyond the restrictions imposed on the self by gender, by nationality?

EB: That's difficult. I would like to say yes. There is something very liberating in the idea that art can release you from the restrictions of the identity you already have or have inherited. I'm just not sure it's true. The problem is, art itself is a form of restriction. And a powerful one. In a poem called "Degas's Laundresses" in *Night Feed* I tried to get at that. The poem is about the painter watching the toil of these two laundresses. And how much control – almost predatory control – is needed to turn these living, shiftless, struggling women into fixed images. There's another poem I wrote called "We Are Human History. We Are not Natural History". It's just about my children finding a nest of wild bees in the garden when they were young. But it's also about something else – about the fixing of the moment. It's an odd paradox of art that it can only work by fixing the moment – whether it's painting or poetry or fiction – and yet once the moment gets fixed, everything in expression restricts it and limits it. It's one of the most interesting aspects of writing a poem. It also divides poets. There are modernists like Eliot who made part of their theme, their subject, out of the limitations of the poem. For me, the limits are the strengths. I've always found freedom in those limits.

PVA: You mentioned in another interview that poetry is a more limited form of expression as compared to photographs and theatre.

EB: I believe that. The fact is – though this certainly isn't taught in the classroom – that poetry is a relatively deprived method of expression. Photography, painting, music certainly excel as methods of expression. Not poetry. It's arcane and rule-bound. It doesn't leap to the moment the way a photograph can. Where poetry excels is as a method of experience, not expression. It has a unique capacity to render an experience in a fresh, unsettling way. I don't write a poem to express an experience, but to experience it again. In a truly good poem the experience is alive, unfinished, set there by sound and meaning. What's so thrilling about that is that the reader can finish it out of their own experience. That's the real power of poetry.

PVA: This reminds me of one of my favourite poems, "The Art of Grief"...
EB: I'm so glad you like that...

PVA: I love that poem. It seems to me that in this poem, now that you are talking about writing poetry to experience the experience, the experience of grief is represented as beyond artistic expression. You describe it as "unrhythmical", "unpredictable", "something beyond the reach of metric-makers, music-makers".
EB: The statue in that poem actually exists. I saw it as a child in Iveagh House, which was then the Department of Foreign Affairs on Stephen's Green, where my father worked. I was probably four or five then. But I remembered it. It's an old statue, maybe Italian, certainly from the 19th century. It's of a veiled woman and carved in marble. I know when I thought about it later I wondered how did the sculptor put the veil on the face. Were they carved together? How did that work? And that became part of the poem's subject.

PVA: Is it still there, the statue?
EB: I think so – I gave a reading there in Iveagh House a few years ago and it was there.

PVA: How would you describe your own evolution as a poet, from New Territory *to your very latest volume?*
EB: That's an almost impossible question. A critic sees an arc, a line of development. A poet goes from poem to poem. For me, the thing that really brings you forward is the poem that fails. When I look back at *New Territory* there are

still a few poems I connect to. One of them is "Athene's Song" – that idea that a private voice can be recruited to a public event. But by the time I came to *The War Horse* I thought "that just doesn't work for me". I began to explore the private voice in opposition to the public world, as a register of it. All of this, of course, is instinctive. A poet does have an ethical journey – I believe that – but a lot of that journey is found in working with one individual poem and not in any conscious plan. *New Territory* was my first book. It was finished when I was 22 years of age. I was in love with the power of language, and the exemption that being a poet provides – from what I wasn't sure, but I sensed some exemption. Later I felt there was an infinite danger in having any kind of exemption, especially for a woman poet. The traditional role of a poet, as it was constructed, with its historical prestige and importance, could easily exempt a woman from the far more powerless and less valued world of womanhood itself. But all of that came later. And what I learned, I learned from failed poems.

PVA: Prior to the publication of New Territory, *there was a particular volume I discovered while doing research in University College Dublin; a volume that you published together with Joseph O'Malley. It said in the cover there were only 300 hundred copies.*

EB: There were three of those books. More chapbooks, really. The first was called *Twenty Three Poems* and was published when I was seventeen. The second was published with a friend, Joseph O'Malley and was prose and poetry. The third was called *Autumn Essay*. They are completely unavailable, for which I'm very grateful. They're just apprentice work.

PVA: There is a poem in one of these volumes called "February 1963" that I was particularly drawn to. I think it's completely different from all the poems included in New Territory. *It's such a mature poem. You talk about standing on Stephen's Green. I think the poem finishes by saying "my head upon the breast of eighteen years". You talk in this poem about your "need to be found". I think it is an amazing poem, how you say all the ambiguities of your childhood there...*

EB: It's hard to get back to those poems in my mind. I haven't opened any of them in twenty or thirty years. I was a teenager, and an immature one at that. I think real feeling went into them, but no craft. But writing and publishing those books helped me at the time.

PVA: So, what's your favourite poem written by yourself? Something that still makes you feel alive when you read it?

EB: "Favourite" is not a word I connect to my own poems. There are some poems that stay with you, where you feel they accurately caught that moment, or were more complete than other poems. One of those is "The Pomegranate". Another is a more recent poem "Quarantine". There are poems like "The Glass King", "The Blossom" and "The Journey" which are important to me in one way or another and for different reasons. But I hold by what I said earlier – the real forcing house of good poems is the poems that fail, the ones that never appear. Those are your real teachers.

PVA: In your introduction to The Christmas Show *by Harriet Levin, you praise this woman poet on the grounds that she writes with no ornaments, and therefore she doesn't write a false rhetoric. And I find this movement, this stripping of any kind of ornament in* The Lost Land *and* Code. *There is a change as regards how you write the line, your style is plainer.*

EB: That's always a difficult question. As a poet I have a love for rhetoric, ornament, language that is sinuous. In *The Lost Land* that didn't seem appropriate. In *Code* the same. A poem like "Quarantine", which is really the centre of the book, couldn't have been written without stripping away the ornament. The same with the Colony sequence in "The Lost land".

PVA: I admire the different versions of colony that you offer there. You move away from that sort of anti-colonial writing that merely attacks the imperialist source as the unique form of oppression...

EB: The idea of colony always holds me, always fascinates me. I'm interested in the conflicts, the arguments about it which are at the heart of the Irish canon, and the way that contested views of our identity weave in and out of the whole idea of writing a national literature. Writers like Daniel Corkery – he wrote a beautiful, partisan book called *The Hidden Ireland* – believed that twentieth century Irish literature was flawed from the start, because it was a national literature, but not an indigenous one. Those are his words. He believed in a pure Ireland, a place we could get back to if we tried. I don't. I believe the strength of Irish literature is that it's built on those fragmentations which most injured us. That's the reality. Yeats and Joyce recognised that. We are constructed by the construct. We can't deny all those compromises and revisions which colony entails. The power of Irish writing, it seems to me, is precisely that we didn't deny it. The major Irish writers used the language in which all the humiliations happened, and used it explore the identity that language had once oppressed. That also leaves a very interesting, powerful space for Irish women writers. They are part of the narrative of oppression in interesting, subtle ways. They have a complicated story to tell about colony. You can see that in some wonderful earlier writing by Irish women. Mary Lavin's story "The Will", for instance, is a superb exploration of a conflict between single identity and inherited custom. There are others. So I think the various narratives of colony really enrich Irish writing.

PVA: What aspect of your poetry do you think deserves further research? Something that readers or critical studies tend to have ignored?

EB: The movement from the margin to the centre. And what it entails. To be assigned a place on the margins of literature seems to imply that your writing destiny is decided for you before you can even write. I didn't accept that. What's more it made me suspicious of how these things work their way from prejudices to assumptions. That in turn made me want to make my own critique, rather than live by anyone else's. It's always an interesting study in any literature, especially a national one – just where the centre is, and how the margin is defined.

PVA: Now that your position as a woman poet is so firmly established in Ireland, and your popularity is increasingly growing not only in the United States, but in countries like Spain, do you consider yourself a poet writing on the margins of mainstream literature?

EB: When I was a young poet I was on the margins. I felt the isolation of that, for good and ill. I felt isolated by the resistances and prejudices that seemed part of the very literature I was trying to write myself into – the unspoken assumption that a woman couldn't write an essential Irish poem. I was bewildered and angered by that. It also made my youth as a poet more thorny than it need have been. When you are young you want to be at the centre of a literature, at the centre of a society. It's only natural. It took me time to realise that being on the margins gives you a unique vantage point. I was able to make a critique of the tradition and its resistances that helped me, and I hope might help other writers. But that sense of isolation disenfranchised me in certain ways as well. And what stays with me now is how wasteful certain prejudices are. There could have been interesting conversations about poetry which just never happened. Instead of talking with other poets in a civil dialogue about the future of Irish poetry, I was always advocating and arguing. Because that was what was needed – at least I felt it was. There were poetry anthologies coming out which excluded women – like Thomas Kinsella's *Oxford Anthology* in 1988 and *The Field Day* in 1992 – and it was important to contest those exclusions. And I certainly did that. But the waste of a generous discourse on Irish poetry shouldn't be overlooked or condoned.

PVA: One of the interesting aspects of your poetry is that you represent your women always in a constant movement. The time of day is usually dusk, a moment of instabilities when things are constantly changing. By the end of poems such as "Doorstep Kisses", "Suburban Woman: A Detail", or "Self-Portrait on a Summer Evening", your women are suddenly threatened with dissolution. And I think this is also observed in how the verse is constructed. It starts with very short sentences, and gradually they become longer, like unfolding by the end of the poem. Is this a conscious attempt to represent your poetic images in such a way that they avoid being simplistic, that the artistic definition of these images is not reductive in a certain way?

EB: There's a wonderful comment made by the American painter Edward Hopper. It's something about painting from a moving perspective. I think he said that when he was in a train and it flashed past an office window at night, his memory was of stillness and not movement. In fact he has a painting of an office window, with that kind of eerie non-movement. Perhaps he got that from the speed at which he himself passed the image. I'm interested in that. The mobility of images in a poem often has to do with the poet's movement, not that of the images. But it's hard to see. Poetry offers technical opportunities to change and dissolve time and space. Sometimes the best way of doing it is just to disrupt auditory or linguistic expectations. Just for an example, if you rhyme three lines, and one ends with "wore" and the other with "more" but the third ends with "star", you create a subtle disorder of sound which opens an interesting space. That said, each poem is a different eco-system and you have to mix the elements of expectation or dissonance differently every time.

PVA: A final question, out of curiosity. Have you ever thought about writing fiction?

EB: I've never had any interest in writing fiction. The elements by which time is restructured in a poem are radically different from fiction. I've never tried it for a moment.

PVA: Thank you very much. It has been really helpful for me…

EB: I'm glad it has been…

Notes to appendix

[1] Portions of this interview first appeared in *New Hibernia Review*, volume 10, number 2 (Summer 2006), a publication of the University of St Thomas in Minnesota.

[2] My conversation with Eavan Boland came after Carol Shloss's reading from her biography *Lucia Joyce: To Dance in the Wake*, on June 18, 2004, during the Bloomsday 100 International James Joyce Symposium at the Docklands campus of the National College of Ireland.

Bibliography

Abrams, M.H. et al. *The Norton Anthology of English Literature*, vol. 1. New York, London: W.W. Norton & Company, 1962, 1993a.

————. *The Norton Anthology of English Literature*, vol. 2. New York, London: W.W. Norton & Company, 1962, 1993b.

Adcock, Betty. "Permanent Enchantments". *Southern Review* 30.4 (1994): 792-808.

Agha-Jaffar, Tamara. *Demeter and Persephone: Lessons from a Myth*. North Carolina, London: McFarland & Company, 2002.

Ahmad, Aijaz. *In Theory: Classes, Nations, Literatures*. London, New York: Verso, 1992.

Allen-Randolph, Jody. "Écriture Feminine and the Authorship of Self in Eavan Boland's *In Her Own Image*". *Colby Library Quarterly* 27.1 (1991): 48-59.

————. "Private Worlds, Public Realities: Eavan Boland's Poetry, 1967-1990". *Irish University Review* 23.1 (1993a): 5-22.

————. "An Interview with Eavan Boland". *Irish University Review* 23.1 (1993b): 117-130.

————. "The New Critics: Adrienne Rich and Eavan Boland". *PN Review* 22.2 (1995): 15-17.

————. "Introduction". *Colby Quarterly*, 35.4 (1999a): 205-209.

————. "A Backward Look: An Interview with Eavan Boland". *Colby Quarterly* 35.4 (1999b): 292-304.

Amuta, Chidi. "Fanon, Cabral and Ngugi on National Liberation". *The Postcolonial Studies Reader*. Eds. Bill Ashcroft, Gareth Griffiths & Helen Tiffin. London, New York: Routledge, 1995, 2002. 158-163.

Andermatt Conly, Verena. *Hélène Cixous: Writing the Feminine*. Lincoln, London: University of Nebraska Press, 1984.

Anderson, Benedict. *Imagined Communities: Reflections on the Origin and Spread of Nationalism*. London: Verso & New Left Books, 1983.

Anzaldúa, Gloria. *Borderlands/ La Frontera*. San Francisco, California: Spinsters Aunt Lute, 1987.

Armengol, Josep M. "Gendering the Irish Land: Seamus Heaney's 'Act of Union' (1975)". *Atlantis* 23.1 (2001): 7-26.

404

Ashcroft, Bill. "Excess: Post-Colonialism and the Verandahs of Meaning". *Describing Empire: Post-Colonialism and Textuality*. Eds. Chris Tiffin & Alan Lawson. London, New York: Routledge, 1994. 33-44.

Ashcroft, Bill, Gareth Griffiths & Helen Tiffin. *The Empire Writes Back*. London, New York: Routledge, 1989, 2002.

Atfield, Rose. "Postcolonialism in the Poetry and Essays of Eavan Boland". *Women: A Cultural Review* 8.2 (1997):168-182.

Bakhtin, Mikhail. *The Dialogic Imagination: Four Essays*. (Trans by Caryl Emerson & Michael Holquist). Austin: University Of Texas Press, 1981.

Bartlett, Thomas. "'What Ish My Nation?': Themes in Irish History, 1550-1850". *Irish Studies: A General Introduction*. Eds. Thomas Bartlett et al. Dublin: Gill & Macmillan, 1988. 44-49.

Battersby, Eileen. "'The Beauty of Ordinary Things': An Interview with Eavan Boland". *The Irish Times*, 1998: 1-5.

Beauvoir, Simone de. "An interview by Alice Schwarzer in *Marie Claire* (Oct 1976)", (trans. by Elaine Marks). Eds. Elaine Marks & Isabelle de Courtivon. *New French Feminisms, An Anthology*. New York, London: Harvester & Wheatsheaf, 1976, 1981. 151-153.

———. *The Second Sex*. (Trans. by M.H. Parshley). London: Vintage, 1949, 1997.

Beddoe, Deirdre. *Discovering Women's History: A Practical Guide to Researching the Lives of Women's since 1800*. Harlow: Essex, 1998.

Bell, Vikki. "Reading Macey, Reflecting on Fanon". *New Formations: After Fanon (A Journal of Culture/ Theory/ Politics)* 47 (2002): 16-20.

Berresford Ellis, Peter. *Celtic Women: Women in Celtic Society and Literature*. London: Constable, 1995.

Bery Ashok & Patricia Murray (eds). "Introduction". *Comparing Postcolonial Literatures: Dislocations*. London: Macmillan Press, 2000. 1-17.

Bewes, Timothy. "'At the Level of Individuals, Violence is a Cleansing Force': Fanon, Internationalism and Terror". *New Formations: After Fanon (A Journal of Culture/ Theory/ Politics)* 47 (2002): 21-24.

Bhabha, Homi K. *The Location of Culture*. London, New York: Routledge, 1994, 1995.

———. (ed.). "Dissemination: Time, Narrative, and the Margins of the Modern Nation". *Nation and Narration*. London, New York: Routledge, 1990, 1994. 291-322.

Bhatnagar, Rashmi, Lola Chatterjee & Rajeshwari Sunder Rajan. "The Post-colonial Critic". *The Postcolonial Critic: Interviews, Strategies, Dialogues*. Ed. Sarah Harasym.New York, London: Routledge, 1990. 67-74.

Boehmer, Elleke. *Colonial and Postcolonial Literature: Migrant Metaphors*. Oxford, New York: Oxford University Press, 1995.

Boland, Eavan. *Twenty-three Poems*. Dublin: Gallagher, 1962.

———. *Autumn Essay*. Dublin: Gallagher; 1963a.

———. *Eavan Boland Poetry/Prose Joseph O'Malley*. Dublin: Gallagher, 1963b.

————. *New Territory*. Dublin: Allen Figgis & Company Limited, 1967.

————. "The Weasel's Tooth". *Irish Times*, 7 June 1974: 56-57.

————. *The War Horse*. Dublin: Arlen House, 1975, 1980a.

————. *In Her Own Image*. Dublin: Arlen House, 1980b.

————. *Introducing Eavan Boland*. New Jersey: The Notario Review Press (Collection of poems from *New Territory*, *The War Horse*, and *In Her Own Image*), 1981.

————. *Night Feed*. Manchester: Carcanet Press, 1982, 1994.

————. *The Journey and Other Poems*. Dublin: Carcanet Press, 1986, 1987.

————. *Selected Poems*. Dublin: Carcanet Press, 1989a.

————. *A Kind of Scar, The Woman Poet and the National Tradition*. Dublin: Attic Press, 1989b.

————. *Outside History*. Manchester: Carcanet Press, 1990.

————. *Outside History – Selected Poems 1980-1990*. London, New York: W.W. Norton & Company, 1991a.

————. "The Art of Grief", in *House: Aileen MacKeogh*. Dublin: Project Press, 1991b. 10-17.

————. *In a Time of Violence/ En un Tiempo de Violencia*. Bilingual edition. (Trans. by Pilar Salamanca). Madrid: Ediciones Hiparión, 1994.

————. *Object Lessons: The Life of the Woman and the poet in Our Time*. Manchester: Carcanet Press, 1995a.

————. "Writing the Political Poem in Ireland". *Southern Review* 31.3 (1995b): 485-498.

————. "New Wave 2: Born in the 50s; Irish Poets of the Global Village". *Irish Poetry Since Kavanagh*. Ed. Theo Dorgan. Dublin: Four Courts Press, 1996a. 136-146.

————. *An Origin like Water: Collected Poems 1967-1987*. New York: W.W. Norton & Company, 1996b.

————. "Daughters of Colony: A Personal Interpretation of the Place of Gender Issues in the Postcolonial Interpretation of Irish Literature". *Eire/Ireland: A Journal of Irish Studies* 32.2/3 (1997a): 9-20.

————. "Letter to a Young Woman Poet". *American Poetry Review* 26.3 (1997b): 23-26.

————. "Imagining Ireland". *Arguing at the Crossroads: Essays on Changing Ireland*. Eds. Paul Brennan & Catherine de Saint Phalle. Dublin: New Island Books, 1997c. 13-23.

————. "Introduction", *The Christmas Show* by Harriet Levin. Massachusetts, Beacon Press, 1997d. xi-xiv.

————. "The Erotics of History". *American Poetry Review* 26.3 (1997e): 26-27.

————. "A Visionary Element". *Renascence: Essays on Values in Literature* 50.1/2 (1997/1998): 153-158.

————. *The Lost Land*. Manchester: Carcanet Press, 1998a.

————. "A Lyric Voice at Bay". *PN Review* 24.5 (1998b): 18-20.

406

————. "A Stegner Anthology", *PN Review* 25.5 (1999a): 28.
————. "Ted Hughes: A Reconciliation", *PN Review* 25.5 (1999b): 5-6.
————. "A Question". *Literary Review: An International Journal of Contemporary Writing* 44.1 (2000a): 23-26.
————. "Poetic Form: A Personal Encounter". *The Making of a Poem: A Norton Anthology of Poetic Forms*. Eds. Mark Strand & Eavan Boland. New York & London: W.W. Norton & Company, 2000b. xxv-xxix.
————. *Against Love Poetry*. New York & London: W.W. Norton & Company, 2001a.
————. *Code*. Manchester: Carcanet Press, 2001b.
————. "Two Worlds". *PN Review* (2001c): 11-15.
————. "The Irish Woman Poet: Her Place in Irish Literature". *My Self, My Muse: Irish Women Poets Reflect on Life and Art*. Ed. Patricia Boyle Haberstroh. New York: Syracuse University Press, 2001d. 92-107.
————. "Virtual Syntax, Actual Dreams", *PN Review* 29.4 (2003a): 25-28.
————. (ed.). "Introduction", *Three Women Poets: An Anthology of Paula Meeham, Mary O'Malley and Eavan Boland*. Manchester: Carcanet Press, 2003b. ix-xviii.
————. (ed.). "Introduction", *After Every War: Twentieth-Century Women Poets*. Oxford: Princeton University Press, 2004. 1-14.
————. *New Collected Poems*. Manchester: Carcanet Press, 2005.
Boland, Eavan & Micheál Mac Liammóir. *W.B. Yeats*. London: Thames & Hudson Press, 1971.
Boyce Davies, Carole. *Black Women, Writing and Identity: Migrations of the Subject*. London, New York: Routledge, 1994.
Boyce, George D. *Nationalism in Ireland*. London, New York: Routledge, 1982, 1991.
Brah, Avtar. "Diaspora, Border and Transnational Identities". *Feminist Postcolonial Theory: A Reader*. Eds. Reina Lewis & Sara Mills. New York: Routledge, 1996, 2003. 613-634.
Brathwaite, Edward. *The Development of Creole Society in Jamaica 1770-1820*. Oxford: Clarendon Press, 1971.
Brennan, Timothy. "The National Longing for Form". *Nation and Narration*. Ed. Homi K. Bhabha. London, New York: Routledge, 1990, 1994. 44-70.
Brown, Terence. "Heart Mysteries There: *The War Horse*". *Irish University Review* 23.1 (1993): 34-39.
Butler Cullingford, Elizabeth. *Ireland's Others: Gender and Ethnicity in Irish Literature and Popular Culture*. Cork: Cork University Press & Field Day, 2001.
Calle-Gruber, Mireille. "Afterword". *The Hélène Cixous Reader*. Ed. Susan Sellers. New York: Routledge, 1994. 207-220.
Canny, Nicholas. "Early Modern Ireland: 1500-1700". *The Oxford History of Ireland*. Ed. Roy Foster. Oxford, New York: Oxford University Press, 1989. 88-133.

Carroll, Clare. "Introduction: The Nation and Postcolonial Theory". *Ireland and Postcolonial Theory*. Eds. Clare Carroll & Patricia King. Cork: Cork University Press, 2003a. 1-15.

——. "Barbarous Slaves and Civil Cannibals: Translating Civility in Early Modern Ireland". *Ireland and Postcolonial Theory*. Eds. Clare Carroll & Patricia King. Cork: Cork University Press, 2003b. 63-80.

Chawaf, Chantal. "La Chair Linguistique", (trans. by Yvonne Rochette-Ozzello). *New French Feminisms, An Anthology*. Eds. Elaine Marks & Isabelle de Courtivon. New York, London: Harvester & Wheatsheaf, 1976, 1981. 177-178.

Chow, Rey. "Where Have all the Natives Gone?". *Feminist Postcolonial Theory: A Reader*. Eds. Reina Lewis & Sara Mills. New York: Routledge, 1994, 2003. 324-249.

Christian, Barbara. "The Race for Theory". *The Nature and Context of Minority Discourse*. Eds. JanMohamed Abdul R. & David Lloyd. Oxford, New York: Oxford University Press, 1990. 37-49.

Cixous, Hélène. "The Laugh of the Medusa", (trans. by Keith Cohen & Paula Cohen). *New French Feminisms, An Anthology*. Eds. Elaine Marks & Isabelle de Courtivon. New York, London: Harvester & Wheatsheaf, 1976, 1981. 245-264.

——. *The Hélène Cixous Reader*. Ed. Susan Sellers. New York: Routledge, 1994.

Cleary, Joe. "'Misplaced Ideas'?: Colonialism, Location, and Dislocation in Irish Studies". *Ireland and Postcolonial Theory*. Eds. Clare Carroll & Patricia King. Cork: Cork University Press, 2003. 16-45.

Clutterbuck, Catriona. "Irish Critical Responses to Self-Representation in Eavan Boland 1987-1995". *Colby Quarterly* 25.4 (1999): 275-287.

Collins, Lucy. "'My Mother's Tongue': The Poetry of Eavan Boland". *Making it New: Essays on the Revised Leaving Certificate English Syllabus*. Ed. Margaret Kelleher. Dublin: The Lilliput Press, 2000. 29-44.

Comerford, Richard Vincent. "Political Myths in Ireland". *Irishness in a Changing Society*. Ed. Princess Grace Irish Library. Gerrards Cross: Colin Smythe, 1988. 1-17.

Condren, Mary. *The Serpent and the Goddess: Women, Religion, and Power in Celtic Ireland*. New York: Harper & Row, 1989.

Consalvo, Deborah McWilliams. "An Interview with Eavan Boland". *Studies: An Irish Quarterly Review* 81.321 (1992): 89-100.

Corkery, Daniel. *The Hidden Ireland: A Study of Gaelic Munster in the Eighteenth Century*. Dublin: MH Gill & Son, 1924, 1970.

Daniels, Kate. "Ireland's Best". *Southern Review* 35.2 (1999): 387-402.

Davis, Angela. "Racism, Birth Control and Reproductive Rights". *Feminist Postcolonial Theory: A Reader*. Eds. Reina Lewis & Sara Mills. New York: Routledge, 1982, 2003. 353-367.

Deane, Seamus. *A Short History of Irish Literature*. Indiana: Notre Dame University Press, 1986, 1994.

———. "Dumbness and Eloquence: A Note on English as We Write it in Ireland". *Ireland and Postcolonial Theory*. Eds. Clare Carroll & Patricia King. Cork: Cork University Press, 2003. 109-121.

Derrida, Jacques. *Positions*. (Trans. by Alan Bass). Chicago: University of Chicago Press, 1981.

Destiny, Caffeine. "An Interview on Eavan Boland". http://www.caffeinedestiny. com/boland.html, 2003

Dienst, Richard et al. "Negotiating the Structures of Violence". *The Postcolonial Critic: Interviews, Strategies, Dialogues*. Ed. Sarah Harasym. New York, London: Routledge, 1990. 138-151.

Dodsworth, Martin. "Under Duress: A Review of *The War Horse*". *Contemporary Literary Criticism: Excerpts from Criticism of the Works of Today's Novelists, Poets, Playwrights, Short Story Writers, Scriptwriters and Other Creative Writers*. Ed. Daniel G. Maroski. Detroit: Gale Research Co., 1986. 96.

Donaldson, Laura E.. *Decolonizing Feminisms: Race, Gender and Empire-Building*. London: Routledge, 1992.

Donoghue, Denis. "The Delirium of the Brave". *The New York Review of Books* 41.10 (1994): 26.

Dorgan, The. *Sappho's Daughter/ La Hija de Safo*. (Trans. by Francisco Castaño, José Manuel Martín Morillas, Jesús Munárriz & Manuel Villar Raso). Madrid: Ediciones Hiperión, 1998, 2001.

Dubey, Madhu. "The 'True Lie' of the Nation: Fanon and Feminism". *differences* 10.2 (1998): 1-29.

Eagleton, Terry. *Heathcliff and the Great Hunger: Studies in Irish Culture*. London, New York: Verso Press, 1995.

———. "The Ideology of Irish Studies". *Bullán: An Irish Studies Journal* 3.1 (1997): 5-14.

Faggen, Robert. "Irish Poets and the World". *The Cambridge Companion to Contemporary Irish Poetry*. Ed. Matthew Campbell. Cambridge: Cambridge University Press, 2003. 229-249.

Falcon Martínez, Constantino et al. *Diccionario de la Mitología Clásica*. Madrid: Alianza Editorial, 1980.

Fanon, Frantz. *Black Skin, White Masks*. (Trans. by Charles Lam Markmann). London: Pluto Press, 1952, 1991.

———. "Algeria Unveiled". *Studies in a Dying Colonialism*. (Trans. by Haakon Chevalier). New York: Grove Press, 1959, 1965. 35-67.

———. *The Wretched of the Earth*. London, New York: Penguin Books, 1961, 1990.

Fitzpatrick, David. "Ireland since 1870". *The Oxford History of Ireland*. Ed. Roy Foster. Oxford, New York: Oxford University Press, 1989. 174-229.

Fogarty, Anne. "'A Noise of Myth': Speaking (as) Woman in the poetry of Eavan Boland and Medbh McGuckian". *Paragraph* 15.1 (1994): 92-102.

————. "Fault Lines". *Graph* 2.1 (1995): 7-14.

————. "'The Influence of Absences': Eavan Boland and the Silenced History of Irish Women's Poetry". *Colby Quarterly* 35.4 (1999): 256-274.

Foley, J. Anthony & Stephen Lalor (eds). *Annotated Constitution of Ireland 1937-1994*. Dublin: Gill & Macmillan, 1995.

Foley, Timothy et al. (eds). "Introduction". *Gender and Colonialism*. Galway: Galway University Press, 1995. 8-11.

Foster, Roy. *Modern Ireland 1600-1972*. London: Penguin, 1988, 1989.

Foster, Thomas C. "In from the Margin: Eavan Boland's "Outside History" Sequence". *Contemporary Irish Women Poets: Some Male Perspectives*. Ed. Alexander G. González. Westport, Connecticut, London: Greenwood Press, 1999. 1-12.

Foucault, Michel. "The confession of the flesh". *Power/Knowledge: Selected Interviews and other Writings 1972- 1977*. Ed. Colin Gordon. Brighton: The Harvester Press, 1972, 1980. 194-228.

Fulford, Sarah. "Eavan Boland: Forging a Postcolonial Herstory". *Irish and Postcolonial Writing: History, Theory, Practice*. Eds. Glenn Hooper & Colin Graham. London: Palgrave Macmillan, 2002a. 202-221.

————. *Gendered Spaces in Contemporary Irish Poetry*. Oxford, New York: Peter Lang, 2002b.

Gamble, Sarah (ed.). *The Routledge Companion to Feminism and Postfeminism*. London, New York: Routledge, 2001.

García García, Ana Rosa. *'The Sense of Place' en la Poesía de Eavan Boland*. Burgos: University of Burgos, 2002. (Unpublished Thesis).

Gauthier, Xavière. "Existe-t-il une écriture de femme?", (trans. by Marilyn A. August). *New French Feminisms, An Anthology*. Eds. Elaine Marks & Isabelle de Courtivon. New York, London: Harvester & Wheatsheaf, 1974, 1981a. 161-164.

————. "Pourquoi Sorcières?", (trans. by Erica M. Eisinger). *New French Feminisms, An Anthology*. Eds. Elaine Marks & Isabelle de Courtivon. New York, London: Harvester & Wheatsheaf, 1976, 1981b. 199-203.

Gelpi, Albert. "'Hazard and Death': The Poetry of Eavan Boland". *Colby Quarterly* 35.4 (1999): 210-228.

Gibbons, Luke. *Transformations in Irish Culture*. Cork: Cork University Press, 1996.

Gilbert, Sandra M. & Susan Gubar. *The Madwoman in the Attic: the Woman Writer and the Nineteenth-Century Literary Imagination*. New Haven, London: Yale University Press, 1979, 2000.

González Arias, Luz Mar. "Nacionalismo y Feminismo: La Conceptualización del Cuerpo Femenino en la Literatura Irlandesa Contemporánea". *Exilios Femeninos*. Ed. Pilar Cuder Domínguez. Huelva: Servicio de Publicaciones de la Universidad de Huelva, 2000a. 35-43.

──────. *Otra Irlanda: La Estética Postnacionalista de Poetas y Artistas Irlandesas Contemporáneas*. Oviedo: Servicio de Publicaciones de la Universidad de Oviedo, 2000b.

Gopal, Priyamvada. "Frantz Fanon, Feminism and the Question of Relativism", *New Formations: After Fanon (A Journal of Culture/ Theory/ Politics)* 47 (2002): 38-43.

Graham, Colin. "Post-Nationalism/Post-Colonialism: Reading Irish Culture". *Irish Studies Review* 8 (1994a): 35-37.

──────. "'Defining Borders': Liminal Spaces, Post-Colonial Theories and Irish Culture". *The Irish Review* 16 (1994b): 29-43.

──────. "Rejoinder: the Irish "Post-"? A Reply to Gerry Smyth". *Irish Studies Review* 13 (1995/6): 33-36.

──────. "History, Gender and the Colonial Moment: Castle Rackrent". *Gender Perspectives in 19ᵗʰ Century Ireland: Public and Private Spheres*. Eds. Margaret Kelleher & James H. Murphy. Dublin: Irish Academic Press, 1997. 93-104.

──────. "'...maybe that's just Blarney': Irish Culture and the Persistence of Authenticity". *Ireland and Cultural Theory*. Eds. Colin Graham & Richard Kirkland. Basingstoke: Macmillan Press, 1999. 7-28.

──────. *Deconstructing Ireland: Identity, Theory and Culture*. Edinburgh: Edinburgh University Press, 2001.

Gramsci, Antonio. *The Prison Notebooks*. Trans. and Ed. Joseph A. Buttigieg. New York: Columbia University Press, 1947, 1996.

Gray Martin, Katherine. "The Attic LIPs: Feminist Pamphleteering for the New Ireland". Ed. Kathryn Kirkpatrick. *Border Crossings: Irish Women Writers and National Identities*. Dublin: Wolfhound Press, 2000. 269-298.

Green, Mary Jean et al. (eds). "Introduction: Women Writing Beyond the Hexagon". *Postcolonial Subjects: Francophone Women Writers*. Minneapolis, London: University of Minnesota Press, 1996. ix-xxii.

Green, Miranda J. *Exploring the World of the Druids*. London: Thames & Hudson, 1997.

Griffiths, Gareth. "The Myth of Authenticity: Representation, Discourse and Social Practice". *De-scribing Empire: Post-Colonialism and Textuality*. Eds. Chris Tiffin & Alan Lawson. London: Routledge, 1994. 70-85.

Grosz, Elizabeth. "Criticism, Feminism, and the Institution". *The Postcolonial Critic: Interviews, Strategies, Dialogues*. Ed. Sarah Harasym. New York, London: Routledge, 1990. 1-16.

Guha, Ranajit (ed.). "Introduction", *A Subaltern Studies Reader, 1986-1995*. Minneapolis, London: University of Minnesota Press, 1997. ix-xxii.

Gunew, Sneja. "Questions of Multi-Culturalism". *The Postcolonial Critic: Interviews, Strategies, Dialogues*. Ed. Sarah Harasym. New York, London: Routledge, 1990. 59-66.

Haberstroh, Patricia Boyle. "Woman, Artist and Image in *Night Feed*". *Irish University Review* 23.1 (1993): 67-74.

———. "Eavan Boland". *Poetry Ireland Review: The Sacred and the Secular* 47 (1995): 20-23.

———. *Women Creating Women: Contemporary Irish Women Poets.* New York: Syracuse University Press, 1996.

———. (ed.). "Introduction", *My Self, My Muse: Irish Women Poets Reflect on Life and Art.* New York: Syracuse University Press, 2001. 3-15.

Hagen, Patricia L. & Thomas W. Zelman. "'We Were Never on the Scene of the Crime': Eavan Boland's Repossession of History". *Twentieth Century Literature* 37.4 (1991): 442-453.

———. *Eavan Boland and the History of the Ordinary.* Dublin: Maunsel & Company, 2004.

Hall, Stuart. "Cultural Identity and Diaspora". *Identity: Community, Culture, Difference.* Ed. Jonathan Rutherford. London: Lawrence & Wishart, 1990. 222-237.

———. "New Ethnicities". *Critical Dialogues in Cultural Studies.* Eds. David Morley & Kuan-Hsing Chen. London, New York: Routledge, 1988, 1996a. 441-449.

———. "When was 'the Post-Colonial'? Thinking at the Limit". *The Postcolonial Question: Common Skies, Divided Horizons.* Eds. Ian Chambers & Lidia Curti. London, New York: Routledge, 1996b. 242-260.

———. "Old and New Identities, Old and New Ethnicities". *Culture, Globalization and the World-System: Contemporary Conditions for the Representations of Identity.* Ed. Anthony D. King. Minneapolis: University of Minnesota Press, 1991, 1997. 41-68.

Harte, Liam & Lance Pettit. "States of Dislocation: William Trevor's *Felicia's Journey* and Maurice Leitch's *Gilchrist. Comparing Postcolonial Literatures: Dislocations.* Eds. Ashok Bery & Patricia Murray. London: Macmillan Press, 2000. 70-80.

Hartnett, Michael. *A Farewell to English.* Dublin: Gallery Press, 1975.

———. *Inchicore Haiku.* Dublin: Raven Arts Press, 1985.

Heaney, Seamus. *Death of a Naturalist.* London: Faber & Faber, 1966.

———. "The Sense of Place". *Preoccupations: Selected Prose 1968-1978.* London, Boston: Faber & Faber, 1980, 1984a. 131-149.

———. "The God in the Tree: Early Irish Nature Poetry". *Preoccupations: Selected Prose 1968-1978.* London, Boston: Faber & Faber, 1980, 1984b. 181-189.

Henderson, Diana E. "Female Power and the Devaluation of Renaissance Love Lyrics". *Dwelling in Possibility: Women Poets and Critics on Poetry.* Eds. Yopie Prins & Maeera Shreiber. New York: Cornell University Press, 1997. 38-59.

Hidalgo Tenorio, Encarnación. "El Particular Exilio de la Mujer Irlandesa, ¿Heroínas Domésticas?". *Exilios Femeninos.* Ed. Pilar Cuder Domínguez. Huelva: Servicio Publicaciones de la Universidad de Huelva, 2000. 387-395.

412

Hill, Myrtle. *Women in Ireland: A Century of Change.* Belfast: The Blackstaff Press, 2003.

Hollander, John (ed.). *Committed to Memory: 100 Best Poems to Memorize.* New York: Riverhead Books, 1996.

Hooper, Glenn & Colin Graham (eds). *Irish and Postcolonial Writing: History, Theory, Practice.* London: Palgrave Macmillan, 2002.

Howe, Stephen. *Ireland and Empire: Colonial Legacies in Irish History and Culture.* Oxford: Oxford University Press, 2000, 2002.

Hurtley, Jacqueline et al. *Diccionario Cultural e Histórico de Irlanda.* Barcelona: Ariel, 1996.

Hywel, Elin Ap. "Elise and the Great Queens of Ireland: "Femininity" as Constructed by Sinn Féin and the Abbey Theatre, 1901-1907". *Gender in Irish Writing.* Eds. Toni O'Brien Johnson & David Cairns. Philadelphia: Open University Press & Milton Keynes, 1991. 23-39.

Innes, Catherine L. "Postcolonial Studies in Ireland". *Comparing Postcolonial Literatures: Dislocations.* Eds. Ashok Bery & Patricia Murray. London: Macmillan Press, 2000. 21-30.

Irigaray, Luce. *This Sex Which is not One.* Ithaca, NY: Cornell University Press, 1977, 1985.

————. *The Irigaray Reader.* Ed. Margaret Whitford. Oxford: Basil Blackwell, 1991.

JanMohamed, Abdul. *Manichean Aesthetics: The Politics of Literature in Colonial Africa.* Massachusetts: The University of Massachusetts Press, 1983.

Johnston, Dillon. "'Our Bodies' Eyes and Writing Hands': Secrecy and Sensuality in Ní Chuilleanáin's Baroque Art". *Gender and Sexuality in Modern Ireland.* Eds. Anthony Bradley & Maryann Gialanella Valiulis. Massachusetts, Amherst: University of Massachusetts Press, 1997. 187-211.

Jung, Carl. *Memories, Dreams and Reflections.* London: Collins, 1969.

Kaplan, Caren. "Deterritorializations: The Rewriting of Home and Exile in Western Feminist Discourse". *The Nature and Context of Minority Discourse.* Eds. JanMohamed Abdul R. & David Lloyd. Oxford, New York: Oxford University Press, 1990. 357-368.

Kavanagh, Patrick. *Collected Prose.* London: MacGibbon & Kee, 1967.

Kearney, Richard. "Myth and Motherland". *Ireland's Field Day.* Ed. Seamus Deane. Derry: Field Day Theatre Company, 1985. 61-88.

Keen, Paul. "The Double Edge: Identity and Alterity in the Poetry of Eavan Boland and Nuala Ní Dhomhnaill". *Mosaic: A Journal for the Interdisciplinary Study of Literature* 33.3 (2000): 19-34.

Kelly, A.A. (ed.). *Pillars of the House: An Anthology of Verse by Irish Women from 1690 to the Present.* Dublin: Wolfhound, 1987, 1997.

Kelly, Sylvia. "The Silent cage and Female Creativity in *In Her Own Image*". *Irish University Review* 23.1 (1993): 45-56.

Kennedy, Liam (ed.). "Modern Ireland: Post-Colonial Society or Post-Colonial Pretensions". *Colonialism, Religion and Nationalism in Ireland*. Belfast: Queen's University Institute of Irish Studies, 1996. 167-181.

Kennelly, Brendan (ed.). *The Penguin Book of Irish Verse*. London: Penguin Books, 1970.

Kiberd, Declan. *Inventing Ireland: The Literature of the Modern Nation*. London: Vintage, 1995, 1996.

Kirkland, Richard. "Questioning the Frame: Hybridity, Ireland and the Institution". *Ireland and Cultural Theory*. Eds. Colin Graham & Richard Kirkland. Basingstoke: Macmillan Press, 1999. 210-227.

Kristeva, Julia. "Oscillation du 'pouvoir' au 'refus'", (trans. by Marilyn A. August). *New French Feminisms, An Anthology*. Eds. Elaine Marks & Isabelle de Courtivon. New York, London: Harvester & Wheatsheaf, 1974, 1981. 165-167.

———. "Revolution in Poetic Language". *The Kristeva Reader*. Ed. Toril Moi. Oxford: Blackwell, 1974, 1986a. 89-136.

———. "Stabat Mater". *The Kristeva Reader*. Ed. Toril Moi. Oxford: Blackwell, 1977, 1986b. 160-186.

———. "Women's Time". *The Kristeva Reader*. Ed. Toril Moi. Oxford: Blackwell, 1979, 1986c. 187-213.

———. "A New Type of Intellectual: The Dissident". *The Kristeva Reader*. Ed. Toril Moi. Oxford: Blackwell, 1977, 1986d. 292-300.

———. "Kristeva on Europe: Female Genius, Freedom and Culture". Dublin: Royal Irish Academy, 2004. 1-26.

Kupillas, Peter. "Bringing It All Back Home: Unity and Meaning in Eavan Boland's "Domestic Interior" Sequence". *Contemporary Irish Women poets: Some Male Perspectives*. Ed. Alexander G. González. Westport, Connecticut, London: Greenwood Press, 1999. 13-32.

Kwadwo Osei-Nyame, Jnr. "On Revolutionary Humanism: The Existentialist Legacy of Frantz Fanon". *New Formations: After Fanon (A Journal of Culture/ Theory/ Politics)* 47 (2002): 29-33.

Leech, G.N. *A Linguistic Guide to English Poetry*. London: Longman Press, 1969.

Lenman, Bruce P. (ed.). *Dictionary of World History*. New York: Chambers, 1993, 2001.

Lewis, Reina & Sara Mills (eds). "Introduction". *Feminist Postcolonial Theory: A Reader*. New York: Routledge, 2003. 1-21.

Lloyd, David. *Nationalism and Minor Literature: James Clarence Mangan and the Emergence of Irish Cultural Nationalism*. Berkeley, CA: University of California Press, 1987.

———. *Anomalous States: Irish Writing and the Post-colonial Moment*. Dublin: Lilliput Press, 1993.

———. Lloyd, David (2003). "After History: Historicism and Irish Postcolonial Studies". *Ireland and Postcolonial Theory*. Eds. Clare Carroll & Patricia King. Cork: Cork University Press, 2003. 46-62.

414

Logan, William. "Animal Instincts and Natural Powers". *New York Times Book Review*, 1991: 22.

Longley, Edna. *The Living Stream: Literature and Revisionism in Ireland*. Newcastle: Bloodaxe, 1994.

Luftig, Victor. "'Something Will Happen to you Who Read': Adrienne Rich, Eavan Boland". *Irish University Review* 23.1 (1993): 57-66.

Mahon, Derek. "Young Boland and Early Boland". *Irish University Review* 23.1 (1993): 23-28.

Maguire, Sarah. "Dilemmas and Developments: Eavan Boland Re-examined". *Feminist Review* 62 (Summer 1999): 58-66.

Maley, Willy. "Varieties of Nationalism: Post-Revisionist Irish Studies". *Irish Studies Review* 15 (1996): 34-37.

————. "Crossing the Hyphen of History: the Scottish Borders of Anglo-Irishness". *Comparing Postcolonial Literatures: Dislocations*. Eds. Ashok Bery & Patricia Murray. London: Macmillan Press, 2000. 31-42.

Marcey, David. *Frantz Fanon: A Life*. London: Granta, 2000.

Marks, Elaine. & Isabelle de Courtivron (eds). *New French Feminisms, An Anthology*. New York, London: Harvester & Wheatsheaf, 1981.

Martin, Augustine. "Quest and Vision: *The Journey*". *Irish University Review* 23.1 (1993): 75-85.

McCallum, Shara. "Eavan Boland's Gift: Sex, History, and Myth". *The Antioch Review* 62.1 (2004): 37-43.

McGuckian, Medbh. "Birds and their Masters". *Irish University Review* 23.1 (1993): 29-33.

Meaney, Gerardine. "Myth, History and the Politics of Subjectivity: Eavan Boland and Irish Women's Writing". *Women: A Cultural Review* 4.2 (1993): 136-153.

Memmi, Albert. *The Colonizer and the Colonized*. (Trans. by Howard Greenfeld). London: Earthscan Publications, 1957, 1990.

Miller, Jane. *Seductions: Studies in Reading and Culture*. London: Virago, 1990.

Mills Harper, Margaret. "First Principles and Last Things: Death and Poetry of Eavan Boland and Audre Lorde". *Representing Ireland: Gender, Class, Nationality*. Ed. Susan Shaw Sailer. Florida: Florida University Press, 1997. 181-193.

Minh-ha, Trinh T. *Woman, Native, Other: Writing Postcoloniality and Feminism*. Bloomington, Indianapolis: Indiana University Press, 1989.

Mohanty, Chandra Talpade. "Introduction: Cartographies of Struggle". *Third World Women and the Politics of Feminism*. Eds. Chandra Talpade Mohanty et al. Bloomington, Indianapolis: Indiana University Press, 1991a. 1-47.

————. "Under Western Eyes: Feminist Scholarship and Colonial Discourses". *Third World Women and the Politics of Feminism*. Eds. Chandra Talpade Mohanty et al. Bloomington, Indianapolis: Indiana University Press, 1991b. 51-80.

Moi, Toril (ed.). "Introduction". *The Kristeva Reader*. Oxford: Blackwell, 1986. 1-22.

——. *Sexual/Textual Politics: Feminist Literary Theory*. London, New York: Routledge, 1985, 1991.

——. "Feminist, Female, Feminine". *The Feminist Reader*. Eds. Catherine Belsey & Jane Moore. London: Macmillan Press, 1989, 1997. 104-116.

Montague, John (ed.). "In the Irish Grain". *The Book of Irish Verse: An Anthology of Irish Poetry from the Sixth Century to the Present*. New York: MacMillan, 1974. 21-39.

Moore-Gilbert, Bart. J. *Postcolonial Theory: Contexts, Practices, Politics*. London: Verso, 1997, 2000.

Murphy, Bruce F. "A Review of *Against Love Poetry*". *Poetry* 181.5 (2003): 347-349.

Murphy, Maureen. "The Fionnuala Factor: Irish Sibling Emigration at the Turn of the Century". *Gender and Sexuality in Modern Ireland*. Eds. Anthony Bradley & Maryann Gialanella Valiulis. Massachusetts, Amherst: Massachusetts University Press, 1997. 85-101.

Ní Dhomhnaill, Nuala. "What Foremothers?". *Poetry Ireland Review* 36 (1992). 18-31.

O'Donnell, Katherine. *Eavan Boland: Reworking the Irish Poetic Tradition*. Cork: University College Cork, 1995. (Unpublished Thesis)

O'Donnell, Mary. "*In Her Own Image*: An Assertion that Myths are made by Men, by the Poet in Transition". *Irish University Review* 23.1 (1993): 40-44.

O'Dowd, Liam. "New Introduction". *The Colonizer and the Colonized* by Albert Memmi. London: Earthscan Publications, 1990. 29-66.

O'Malley, Mary. "Poetry, Womanhood, and 'I amn't'". *Colby Quarterly* 35.4 (1999): 252-255.

Ó Ríodáin, Seán. *Tar Éis Mo Bháis*. Dublin: Sáirséal & Dill, 1978, 1986.

Ostriker Suskin, Alicia. *Stealing the Language: the Emergence of Women's Poetry in America*. London: The Women's Press, 1986.

Papastergiadis, Nikos. "Tracing Hybridity in Theory". *Debating Cultural Hybridity*. Eds. Pnina Werbner & Tariq Modood. London, New Jersey: Zed Books, 1997. 257-281.

Parry, Benita. "Problems in Current Theories of Colonial Discourse". *Oxford Literary Review* 1/2.9 (1987): 27-57.

Pérez Valverde, Cristina. "'A Woman is not a river': Joyce, Boland and McGuckian", *Estudios de Filología Inglesa* 2 (2001): 150-169.

Praga Terente, Inés. *Una Belleza Terrible: La Poesía Irlandesa Contemporánea (1940-1995)*. Barcelona: PPU, 1996.

Quereda Rodríguez-Navarro, Luis. *A Morphosyntactic Study of the English Verb Phrase*. Granada: Servicio de Publicaciones de la Universidad de Granada, 1993, 1997.

Quinn, Antoinette. "Cathleen ni Houlihan Writes Back: Maud Gonne and Irish National Theater". *Gender and Sexuality in Modern Ireland*. Eds. Anthony Bradley & Maryann Gialanella Valiulis. Massachusetts, Amherst: Massachusetts University Press, 1997. 39-59.

Rajan, Rajeswari Sunder. *Real and Imagined Women: Gender, Culture and Postcolonialism*. London, New York: Routledge, 1993.

Reeves, James. *Understanding Poetry*. London: Heinemann Press, 1965.

Reizbaum, Marilyn. "An Interview with Eavan Boland". *Contemporary Literature* 30.4 (1989): 471-479.

Rich, Adrienne. *Diving into the Wreck: Poems 1971-1972*. New York: W. W. Norton & Company, 1973.

———. *The Dream of a Common Language: Poems 1974-1977*. New York: W. W. Norton & Company, 1978.

———. (ed.). "When We Dead Awaken: Writing as Re-Vision". *On Lies, Secrets and Silence: Selected Prose 1966-1978*. New York: W.W. Norton & Company, 1971, 1979. 33-49.

Riley, Jeannette E. "'Becoming an Agent of Change': Eavan Boland's *Outside History* and *In a Time of Violence*". *Irish Studies Review* 20 (1997): 23-29.

Roche, Anthony. "Introduction to Eavan Boland". *Irish University Review* 23.1 (1993): 1-5.

Rolleston, Thomas. *Myths and Legends of the Celts*. Middlesex: Senate Press, 1998.

Rooney, Ellen. "In a Word: *Interview*". *Outside in the Teaching Machine*. Ed. Gayatri C. Spivak. New York, London: Routledge, 1993. 1-23.

Rushdie, Salman. *Imaginary Homelands: Essays and Criticism 1981-1991*. London: Granta, 1992.

Russell, Richard. "Boland's Lava Cameo". *Explicator* 60.2 (2002): 114-117.

Rutherford, Jonathan (ed.). "The Third Space: Interview with Homi Bhabha", *Identity: Community, Culture, Difference*. Lawrence & Wishart: London, 1990. 207-221.

Said, Edward. "Foreword". *Selected Subaltern Studies*. Eds. Ranajit Guha & Gayatri C. Spivak. New York, Oxford: Oxford University Press, 1988. v-x.

———. *Culture and Imperialism*. London: Vintage, 1993, 1994.

———. *Orientalism: Western Conceptions of the Orient*. London, New York: Penguin Books, 1978, 1995.

Sammells, Neil. "An Underground Poet: Eavan Boland talks to Neil Sammells". *Irish Studies Review* 4 (1993): 12-13.

Sartre, Jean Paul. "Orphée Noir, Preface". *Anthologie de la Nouvelle Poésie Nègre et Malgache*. Paris: Presses Universtaries de France, 1948.

———. "Preface". *The Wretched of the Earth* by Frantz Fanon. (Trans. by Constance Farrington). London, New York: Penguin Books, 1961, 1990. 7-26.

Sarup, Mada. *An Introductory Guide to Post-structuralism and Postmodernism*. London: Longman, 1988, 1993.

417

Schmidt, Elizabeth. "Where Poetry Begins: An Interview with Eavan Boland", http://www. poets.org/poems/Prose.ctm?prmID=2088, 2001.

Sellers, Susan (ed.). "Introduction". *The Hélène Cixous Reader*. New York: Routledge, 1994. xxvi-xxxi.

Sewell, Frank. "Between Two Languages: Poetry in Irish, English, and Irish English". *The Cambridge Companion to Contemporary Irish Poetry*. Ed. in Matthew Campbell. Cambridge: Cambridge University Press, 2003. 149-168.

Shannon, Catherine B.. "The Changing Face of Cahtleen ni Houlihan: Women and Politics in Ireland, 1960-1966". *Gender and Sexuality in Modern Ireland*. Eds. Anthony Bradley & Maryann Gialanella Valiulis. Massachusetts, Amherst: Massachusetts University Press, 1997. 257-274.

Showalter, Elaine. *A Literature of Their Own: British Women Novelists from Brontë to Lessing*. London: Virago Press, 1977, 1999.

Smith, Rod T. "Altered Light: *Outside History*". *Irish University Review* 23.1 (1993): 86-99.

———. "A Review of *In a Time of Violence*". *Southern Humanities Review* (1996): 304-307.

Smith, Sidonie & Julia Watson (eds). "Preface". *De/Colonizing the Subject: The Politics of Gender in Women's Autobiography*. Minneapolis: University of Minnesota Press, 1992. i-xxi.

Smyth, Ailbhe. "The Floozie in the Jacuzzi". *The Irish University Review* 6 (1989): 7-24.

Smyth, Gerry. "The Past, the Post, and the Utterly Changed: Intellectual Responsibility and Irish Cultural Criticism". *Irish Studies Review* 10 (1995): 25-29.

———. *Decolonisation and Criticism: The Construction of Irish Literature*. London: Pluto Press, 1998.

———. "Decolonisation and Criticism: Towards a Theory of Irish Critical Discourse". *Ireland and Cultural Theory*. Eds. Colin Graham & Richard Kirkland. Basingstoke: Macmillan Press, 1999. 29-49.

———. "The Politics of Hybridity: Some Problems with Crossing the Border". *Comparing Postcolonial Literatures: Dislocations*. Eds. Ashok Bery & Patricia Murray. London: Macmillan Press, 2000. 43-55.

Spivak, Gayatri Chakravorty. *In Other Worlds: Essays in Cultural Politics*. New York, London: Routledge, 1987, 1988a.

———. "Subaltern Studies: Deconstructing Historiography". *Selected Subaltern Studies*. Eds. Ranajit Guha & Gayatri C. Spivak. New York, Oxford: Oxford University Press, 1988b. 3-32.

———. "Poststructuralism, Marginality, Postcoloniality and Value". *Literary Theory Today*. Eds. Peter Collier & Helga Geyer-Ryan. Cambridge, Polity, 1990a. 219-244.

———. *The Postcolonial Critic: Interviews, Strategies, Dialogues*. Ed. Sarah Harasym. London, New York: Routledge, 1990b.

418

―――. "Woman in Difference: Mahasweta Devi's 'Doulati the Bountiful'". *Cultural Critique* 14 (1990c): 105-128.

―――. *Outside in the Teaching Machine*. New York, London: Routledge, 1993.

―――. "Can the Subaltern Speak?". *Colonial Discourse and Post-Colonial Theory: a Reader*. Eds. Patrick Williams & Laura Chrisman. New York, London: Harvester Wheatsheaf, 1988, 1994. 66-111.

―――. *A Critique of Postcolonial Reason: Toward a History of the Vanishing Present*. Cambridge, Massachusetts, London: Harvard University Press, 1999.

Strand Mark & Eavan Boland. *The Making of a Poem: A Norton Anthology of Poetic Forms*. New York: W.W. Norton & Company, 2000.

Threadgold, Terry & Frances Bartkowski. "The *Intervention* Interview". *The Postcolonial Critic: Interviews, Strategies, Dialogues*. Ed. Sarah Harasym. New York, London: Routledge, 1990. 113-132.

Thurston, Michael. "'A Deliberate Collection of Cross Purposes' Eavan Boland's Poetic Sequences". *Colby Quarterly* 35.4 (1999): 229-251.

Tiffin, Chris & Alan Lawson (eds). "Introduction: The Textuality of Empire". *Describing Empire: Post-Colonialism and Textuality*. London, New York: Routledge, 1994. 1-11.

Villar Argáiz, Pilar. "Eavan Boland' Rewriting of Mother Ireland: 'I won't go back to it-/ My nation displaced into old dactyls". *The Representation of Ireland/s: Images from Outside and from Within*. Ed. Rosa González. Barcelona: PPU, 2003a. 277-290.

―――. "The Perception of Landscape in Eavan Boland's Poetry: From a 'Romantic' Pilgrimage to a World of Constellations and Suburbs". *Irish Landscapes*. Eds. José Francisco Fernández Sánchez & Mª Elena Jaime de Pablos. Almería: Servicio de Publicaciones de la Universidad de Almería, 2003b. 265-275.

―――. "'The Text of It': A Conversation with Eavan Boland". *New Hibernia Review/ Irish Éireannach Nua: A Quarterly Record of Irish Studies* 10.2 (2005): 52-67.

Walcott, Derek. *Omeros*. London, Boston: Faber & Faber, 1988, 1990.

Walder, Dennis. *Post-Colonial Literatures in English: History, Language, Theory*. Massachusetts: Blackwell, 1998.

Walker, Alice. "In Search of Our Mothers' Gardens", *In Search of Our Mothers' Gardens: Womanist Prose*. London: The Women's Press, 1983, 1984. 231-243.

Webb, Timothy (ed.). "Introduction". *W.B. Yeats: Selected Poetry*. London: Penguin Books, 1991. xiv-xliii.

Welch, Robert. *Oxford Concise Companion to Irish Literature*. New York: Oxford University Press, 1996, 2000.

Werbner, Pnina. "Introduction: The Dialects of Cultural Hybridity". *Debating Cultural Hybridity*. Eds. Pnina Werbner & Tariq Modood. London, New Jersey: Zed Books, 1997. 1-26.

Whelan, Kevin. "Between Filiation and Affiliation: The Politics of Postcolonial Memory". *Ireland and Postcolonial Theory*. Eds. Clare Carroll & Patricia King. Cork: Cork University Press, 2003. 92-108.

Whitford, Margaret (ed.). "Introduction". *The Irigaray Reader*. Oxford: Basil Blackwell, 1991. 1-15.

Whitman, Walt. *Leaves of Grass/ Hojas de Hierba: Antología Bilingüe*. (Trans. by Manuel Villar Raso). Madrid: Alianza Editorial, 1995.

Wilson, Rebecca E. "Introduction". *Sleeping with Monsters: Conversations with Scottish and Irish Women Poets*. Eds. Gillean Somerville-Arjat & Rebecca E. Wilson. Edinburgh: Polygon, 1990a. xi-xv.

―――. "Eavan Boland". *Sleeping with Monsters: Conversations with Scottish and Irish Women Poets*. Eds. Gillean Somerville-Arjat & Rebecca E. Wilson. Edinburgh: Polygon, 1990b. 79-90.

Woolf, Virginia. "Kew Gardens". *The Penguin Book of English Short Stories*. Ed. Christopher Dolley. London, New York: Penguin Books, 1919, 1967. 201-207.

―――. *A Room of One's Own*. London: The Hogarth Press, 1929, 1974.

Yeats, William B. "A General Introduction for My Work". *Yeats on Yeats: The Last Introductions and the 'Dublin' Edition*. Ed. Edward Callan. Mountrath: Dolmen Press, 1924, 1981. 59-63.

―――. *W.B. Yeats: Selected Poetry*. Ed. Timothy Webb. London: Penguin Books, 1991.

―――. *W.B. Yeats: Collected Poems*. Ed. Augustine Martin. London: Vintage Press, 1992.

Young, Robert. *White Mythologies: Writing History and the West*. London, New York: Routledge, 1990, 1992.

―――. *Colonial Desire: Hybridity in Theory, Culture and Race*. London, New York: Routledge, 1995.

Index

422

424